Communicating

Commu

nicating

Anita Taylor

Teresa Rosegrant

Arthur Meyer

B. Thomas Samples

Prentice-Hall, Inc., Englewood Cliffs, New Jersey 07632

Library of Congress Cataloging in Publication Data
Main entry under title:

COMMUNICATING.

    (The Prentice-Hall series in speech communication)
    Includes bibliographies and index.
    1. Communication. I. Taylor, Anita, (date)
P90.C624   001.5   76-45752
ISBN 0-13-153106-9

THE PRENTICE-HALL SERIES IN SPEECH COMMUNICATION
Larry L. Barker and Robert J. Kibler
Consulting Editors

COMMUNICATING
Anita Taylor, Teresa Rosegrant, Arthur Meyer, and
B. Thomas Samples

Printed in the United States of America
10 9 8 7 6 5 4 3 2

PRENTICE-HALL INTERNATIONAL, INC., *London*
PRENTICE-HALL OF AUSTRALIA PTY. LIMITED, *Sydney*
PRENTICE-HALL OF CANADA, LTD., *Toronto*
PRENTICE-HALL OF INDIA PRIVATE LIMITED, *New Delhi*
PRENTICE-HALL OF JAPAN, INC., *Tokyo*
PRENTICE-HALL OF SOUTHEAST ASIA PTE. LTD., *Singapore*
WHITEHALL BOOKS LIMITED, *Wellington, New Zealand*

Contents

To The User

These comments are for the students who will use this book and their teachers. This book was written with you in mind. It has one basic purpose — to help people learn to use communication more effectively in their daily lives. To accomplish that purpose, it includes explanations of certain basic communication principles, and suggestions for applying those ideas to the situations people commonly experience.

Together, the four of us who wrote this book have been college teachers for more than thirty-five years. As we have been teachers, we have been students, for never have we left a classroom without having learned from those we met there. One of the greatest lessons we have learned from our students is that knowledge without application seems useless to most people, while application without knowledge results too often in shallow, ineffective, or even destructive communication.

Thus, we have tried in this book to provide knowledge by introducing the principles of communication and to show how the principles can be applied in everyday living. If any single word describes this book, it is "practical." We have tried always to keep in mind the question, *How can this information be used?*

In answering that question, we have kept constantly in mind those thousands of students we've had. They have included students still in high school and retirees back to college to broaden their horizons; 18-year-olds who never worked outside their homes in their lives and people already working full-time at their chosen professions. We've shared our classroom experiences with employed and unemployed housewives, autoworkers, engineers, police officers, fire fighters, truck drivers, plumbers, nurses, secretaries, managers, and many others — the list could extend for pages. We've learned from our students that effective communication is needed in all aspects of life, whether we are at home, church, work, or play; in small groups or large; with friends or strangers; in conversation, giving or listening to speeches, and even while watching television. For people in all these situations, we wrote this book.

Throughout this book are three learning aids, each based on a basic belief we have about teaching. First, we believe *people learn best from experience.* Only with experience do we really internalize our understandings. Thus, for important concepts, we've included exercises or suggested experiences. Some of these exercises are for students to do by themselves; others are to be shared with classmates; some guided by the instructor; some completed independently. All are intended to help students experience the ideas discussed, and thus to understand how to use the concepts more effectively.

More experiences are suggested than any one person or class could use. The choices will enable students and instructors to concentrate on their own interests and needs. Part of these exercises are included in an *Activity Guide.* This *Guide* provides forms and directions for many experiences, so that students have assistance in completing some of the exercises.

The Activity Guide has two parts. The second half is designed to allow the option of self-paced learning and almost total individualizing of the study of speech communication to students and teachers who want that option. By combining use of the Activity Guide and text, students can self-design their own course, setting their own goals and timetables. Combined with a contract approach, instructors and students have great flexibility within a well-structured sequence of studies. We have had students who followed these guides and finished the course in three weeks, others who took two full semesters to get done. This approach, fully explained in the *Instructor's Manual* and *Activity Guide,* allows great independence as learners to those students who choose to use it.

A second belief upon which the book is based is that *some ideas are best understood when an illustration of the concept is shared with others.* So we've included readings that illustrate a few of the concepts. Following these readings are questions to provoke thinking about the communication principles. We hope students and teachers will discuss these questions with each other. We're convinced doing so will improve understanding of communication.

Our third basic belief is that *people learn best when they know what they're trying to learn.* Thus, for each chapter we've identified a goal and listed the objectives students should be able to accomplish by reading the material and doing the exercises. If, after doing that, students don't think they can do the stated objectives, they can use the page numbers accompanying each objective to find the related materials for review. Each exercise also has an objective so that students will know why they are doing it.

To conclude this introduction, we wish we could share with you the names of all those to whom credit is due for this book. We can't— too many people helped us. We owe much to sensitive, perceptive editors — Brian Walker, Janet Palazzo-Craig, and Mary Miles Allen.

We owe thanks also to Sam Tracy and Lee Cohen for their work on the text design, as well as Irene Springer for her help on the selection of photo illustrations. We owe much to critical and thoughtful reviewers, to friends and colleagues, to several proofreaders, and to a tireless and devoted secretary—Eileen Hughes. We owe much to our best friends, our families, who shared with us the ordeals of writing, re-writing, editing, re-editing and authors' disagreements with each other. But perhaps we owe most of all to people *really* too numerous to mention, those thousands of students who taught us how to teach. To all of them we are in debt. To all of them, this book is dedicated.

CREDITS

We would like to thank the following publishers and authors for permission to reprint material used as displayed quotations.

CHAPTER 1   RAY BIRDWHISTELL quoted in *Schizophrenia: An Integrated Approach,* ed. Alfred Auerbach. Copyright © 1959 The Ronald Press Company, New York.
STEPHEN CRANE, *War Is Kind,* IV.

CHAPTER 2   FRANCIS BACON, *Essays* quoting Aesop.
WILLIAM HEDGEPETH, "New Language," *Look,* January 13, 1970.
WILLIAM MOULTON, *Linguistics in School Programs,* 69th Yearbook of the *Society,* 1970.
From *Listen to the Warm* by ROD McKUEN. Copyright © 1967 by Rod McKuen. Reprinted by permission of Random House, Inc. Quotes from poems 25 and 36.
BENJAMIN WHORF, *Language, Thought, and Reality.*

CHAPTER 3   BERTRAND RUSSELL, *Human Knowledge: Its Scope and Limits,* © 1948. By permission of Simon & Schuster, Inc. and Allen & Unwin.
WINSTON CHURCHILL, speech to the House of Commons, 1943.
RALPH WALDO EMERSON, *Social Aims.*
SHAKESPEARE, *Macbeth,* Act I, Sc. 4; and *Romeo and Juliet,* Act II, Sc. 2.
ALEXANDER POPE, *Epistle to Dr. Arbuthnot.*
WILLIAM PALEY, *Moral Philosophy.*
SIDNEY SMITH in reference to Macaulay, cited in *Pocket Book of Quotations,* p. 341.
EMILY DICKINSON, "I Like a Look of Agony," *Poems,* Vol. IV.

CHAPTER 4   LEWIS CARROLL, "Advice from a Caterpillar," *Alice's Adventures in Wonderland:* New York: Grosset & Dunlap, 1972.
SHAKESPEARE, *As You Like It,* Act II, Sc. 7.
T. S. ELIOT, "The Love Song of J. Alfred Prufrock," *Collected Poems 1909–1962.* New York: Harcourt, Brace & Jovanovich.
RALPH WALDO EMERSON, *Society and Solitude.*
SENECA, *Epistulae ad Lucilium.*
WENDELL JOHNSON, "The Fateful Process of Mr. A Talking to Mr. B.," *Harvard Business Review* (1953), XXXI, 49–56. Reprinted with permission of *Harvard Business Review.*

CHAPTER 5   From *Notes to Myself* by HUGH PRATHER. © 1970 Real People Press.
JOHN STEWART, ed., *Bridges Not Walls.* Reading, Mass.: Addison-Wesley, 1973.
R. D. LAING, H. PHILLIPSON, and A. R. LEE, "Interaction and Interexperience in Dyads," in *Interpersonal Perception.* New York: Springer, 1966.
ALBERT EINSTEIN, address at the Sorbonne.
PAUL TOURNIER, *The Meaning of Persons,* trans. Edwin Hudson, New York: Harper & Row, 1957.

CHAPTER 6   THOMAS SCHEIDEL, *Speech Communication and Human Interaction.* Glenview, Ill.: Scott, Foresman, 1972, p. 89.
MARK TWAIN, *Pudd'nhead Wilson's New Calendar.*
SAMUEL BUTLER quoted in *The Pocket Book of Quotations,* ed. Henry Davidoff. New York: Pocket Books, 1952.
WILLIAM BLAKE, *A Poison Tree.*

SAMUEL BUTLER, *Remains.*

PAUL TOURNIER, *The Meaning of Persons,* trans. Edwin Hudson. New York: Harper & Row, 1957.

ERICH FROMM, *The Art of Loving.* New York: Harper & Row, 1956.

CHAPTER 7   CARL ROGERS, "Communication: Its Blocking and Its Facilitation." Reprinted from *ETC.* IX, No. 2 by permission of the International Society for General Semantics: and "The Interpersonal Relationship: The Core of Guidance," *Harvard Educational Review,* XXXII (Fall 1962), 416–29.

MARTIN BUBER, "Elements of the Interhuman," in *The Knowledge of Man,* trans. Maurice Friedman and Ronald G. Smith. New York: Harper & Row, 1965.

JESS LAIR, *I Ain't Much, Baby—But I'm All I've Got.* New York: Doubleday, 1972, pp. 20, 114.

Excerpts from *Why Am I Afraid to Tell You Who I Am?* by JOHN POWELL, S. J. Copyright © Argus Communications, 1969. Reprinted with permission.

CHAPTER 8   Executive of a manufacturing firm quoted in RALPH G. NICHOLS and LEONARD A. STEVENS, "Listening to People," *Harvard Business Review* XXXV (1957).

RALPH G. NICHOLS, "Do We Know How to Listen?" *The Speech Teacher,* X (1961), 118–24.

CARL ROGERS, "Communication: Its Blocking and Its Facilitation." Reprinted from *ETC.,* IX, No. 2 by permission of the International Society for General Semantics.

CHAPTER 9   LAURENCE PETER, *The Peter Prescription.* New York: Morrow, 1972, p. 137.

ERIC BERNE, "The Structure and Dynamics of Organizations and Groups." Reprinted by permission of Grove Press, Inc. Copyright © 1963 by J. P. Lippincott Co.

SHAKESPEARE, *As You Like It,* Act II, Sc. 7.

THEODORE NEWCOMB, "An Approach to the Study of Communicative Acts," *Psychological Review,* Vol. 60 (1953), published by the American Psychological Association.

CHARLES WILKINSON, *U. S. Catholic Magazine* (August 1972).

CHAPTER 10   WALTER LIPPMANN, BERTRAND RUSSELL, and H. L. MENCKEN quoted in Laurence Peter, *The Peter Prescription.* New York: Morrow, 1972.

Lao-tzu quoted in ROBERT TOWNSEND, *Up the Organization.* Greenwich, Conn.: Fawcett Publications, 1970.

A. PAUL HARE, EDGAR F. BORGATTA, and ROBERT F. BALES, eds., "Small Groups Studies" in *Social Interaction.* New York: Knopf, 1965, pp. 196, 357.

CHAPTER 11   SHAKESPEARE, *Sonnet 87.*

TERENCE, *Adelphi.*

RALPH WALDO EMERSON, *Society and Solitude.*

Goethe quoted in LAURENCE PETER, *The Peter Prescription.* New York: Morrow, 1972, p. 33.

From *The Transparent Self* by SIDNEY JOURARD. © 1971 by Litton Educational Publishing, Inc. Reprinted by permission of D. Van Nostrand Company.

EMILY BRONTE, *A Little While.*

CHAPTER 12   ROBERT S. GOYER, W. CHARLES REDDING, and JOHN T. RICKEY, *Interviewing Principles and Techniques: A Project Text.* Dubuque, Iowa: William C. Brown, 1968, p. 6.

L. ULRICH and D. TRUMBO, "The Selection Interview from 1949," *Psychological Bulletin,* XLIV (1965), 100.

Reuel Howe quoted in KATHLEEN GALVIN and CASSANDRA BOOK, *Person to Person: An Introduction to Speech Communication.* Skokie, Ill.: National Textbook Company, 1974, p. 120.

From WILLIAM V. HANEY, *Communication and Organizational Behavior,* 3rd ed. Homewood, Ill.: Richard D. Irwin, Inc., 1973, p. 11.

Eleanor Roosevelt quoted in LAURENCE PETER, *The Peter Prescription.* New York: Morrow, 1972, p. 107.

CHAPTER 13   DANIEL WEBSTER and HUGH BLAIR cited in Robert C. Jeffrey and Owen Peterson, *Speech: Text with Adapted Readings,* 2nd ed. New York: Harper & Row, 1975.

CHAPTER 14   GEORGE BRAZILLER, Inc., from *A Rhetoric of Motives* by Kenneth Burke. Reprinted with the permission of the publisher.

DALE CARNEGIE, *How to Win Friends and Influence People.* New York: Simon & Schuster, 1936, p. 29.

SAMUEL BUTLER, *Hudibras, III.*

Mark Twain quoted in LAURENCE PETER, *The Peter Prescription.* New York: Morrow, 1972, p. 101.

CHAPTER 15   EDMUND CARPENTER quoted in *Explorations in Communication,* eds. Edmund Carpenter and Marshall McLuhan. Boston: Beacon Press, 1960.

MELVIN DeFLEUR, *Theories of Mass Communication.* New York: McKay, 1966, p. 156.

PLATO, *The Republic.*

BERNARD BERELSON, "Communications and Public Opinion," in *Mass Communication,* ed. Wilbur Schramm. Urbana, Ill.: University of Illinois Press, 1960, p. 531.

From *Understanding Media* by MARSHALL McLUHAN. © 1964 by Marshall McLuhan. Used with permission of McGraw-Hill Book Company.

The Processes of Communication

In Part One of this book you will find an overview of the processes of speech communication. Our premise is that if you understand communication processes, you can learn to better predict and control your own communication behaviors, and thus cope more effectively with the situations in which you find yourself.

So at first we pay close attention to the elements and processes. Study of these four chapters should provide a better understanding of how you and the communication processes interrelate. In later parts of the book we will discuss the resources and strategies available to you for coping more effectively in interpersonal, group, and public communication situations.

Relating to Your World

the communication process

goal:

To understand how communication happens.

probes:

The material in this chapter should help you to

1. Design a personal answer to the question, Why should I study speech communication? pp. 2–5
2. Explain the function of the communication elements:

Source	Interpretations
Stimuli	Noise
Receiver	Feedback
Sensations	Situation

   pp. 5–10
3. Explain why speech communication is referred to as a process rather than an act. pp. 12–22
4. Explain how speech communication is a process of processes. pp. 20–23
5. Distinguish between the basic levels of speech communication:
   Intrapersonal
   Interpersonal
   Public
   pp. 10–12
6. Design a model of communication and explain how it represents the process. pp. 3–24

WHY STUDY COMMUNICATION?

Most of us believe we communicate effectively. And on one level, most of us do. When we ask the druggist for aspirin, we get aspirin, not vitamin C. But do we always communicate as effectively as we want? Consider the following situations.

Scene: Two office workers on coffee break.

Chris: Boy, this city is certainly going to the dogs.
Pat: Then why don't you move somewhere else?
Chris: Why should I?
Pat: Didn't you just say you were fed up with this place?
Chris: No, I said that it was going to the dogs!
Pat: As far as I'm concerned, it means that you don't like it here. It sure doesn't mean that you're happy here, does it?
Chris: Listen, you, why don't you mind your own damn business!
Pat: Now hold on there, I didn't start this conversation—you did. If you didn't want my opinion, you should have just kept your mouth shut.

Scene: Parent and teenager at dinner.

Teen: Hey, can I use the car tonight?
Parent: Well, I don't know; it's a school night.
Teen: Aw, come on. It's early. The whole gang is going to the drive-in tonight.
Parent: I don't know. Don't you have homework?
Teen: Naw, got it all done.
Parent: Are you sure? Your grades haven't been too good lately. I don't think you're concentrating enough on school these days. That crowd you've been hanging around with isn't a very good influence on you.
Teen: You're always bitching, running me down. Why don't you get off my back? My grades are *my* business. Anyway, I can't remember the last time I saw *you* read a book!

3

What do these situations have in common? Communication breakdowns. In each case, someone is talking and someone is listening, but the listeners receive messages that are different from the ones the senders intend. For these communicators, the differences are major causes of communication breakdown.

Breakdowns of this sort are common. You could supply many examples from your own experience. Yet few of us can afford communication breakdowns. We depend on communication to take care of our physical needs, to exercise our minds, and to sustain our spirits. Communication is the most important human survival skill, but most of us take it for granted, and do not communicate as effectively as we could.

We wrote this book because so many people take communication for granted, and thus do not communicate as well as they might. The principles and points of view presented here can help you communicate better. We have tried to present ideas in a way that is as clear and easy to understand as possible. Some of the information is difficult, much is easily digestible; but all of it is useful. If you understand the information and apply the principles in your daily life, you will be able to communicate more effectively.

You should understand, though, that this isn't a cookbook. You'll find no simple recipes here, no formulas that will suddenly turn you into a superstar. You will find no simple answer to the question, How can I communicate more effectively? But principles do exist, and if you learn to apply them, you will improve your skill at communicating.

We don't offer pat answers, only tools. If you learn to use these tools, you will communicate better than you do now. Reading the information in this book, discussing the suggested questions with your colleagues in class, and experimenting with the exercises will help you learn how communication works, and how you can make communication work better for you.

What Role Does Communication Play in Your Life?

This question doesn't ask whether you need to make speeches at work or at school. Or if you need to listen more effectively to directions given by your supervisor. Or even if you need to express ideas more clearly to your friends and family. This is a more fundamental question.

Communication is the most important human survival skill because you need it to maintain contact with the world. Indeed, it is probably your only contact with the world. We believe a physical world exists regardless of our awareness of it, and would exist even if we weren't here. But what contact have we with that world? Communication is our only way of contacting the world "outside" our skins. When we receive stimuli from that world, and interpret the stimuli through our central nervous system, that is communication. That is how we know the world. That is why communication is the most important human survival skill.

WHAT ARE THE PROCESSES OF COMMUNICATION?

A man said to the universe: "Sir, I exist!"
"However," replied the universe,
"The fact has not created in me
A sense of obligation."
STEPHEN CRANE

Without communication, we can know little. The sensory mechanisms that receive and transmit sensations to the brain (sight, hearing, taste, smell, and touch) and the brain's interpretations let us relate to the world.[1] Because these communication processes have such a central role in our lives, an understanding of them is important. In this section, we introduce you to the processes of communication. But before we even begin, let's recognize that you may feel we make it awfully complicated. If so, good. You've gotten the idea. Communication is not a simple process. That's the first awareness you need to have to study it usefully. So with that said, let's turn first to the elements that make up the processes.

Elements of Communication

Eight elements can be identified as part of the communication processes. These are: (1) a source, (2) stimuli received from that source, (3) a receiver, (4) sensory receptors, (5) the receiver's interpretations of and responses to the sensations, (6) noise, (7) feedback, and (8) a situation or context.[2] To illustrate these elements, let's look at one example of communication: your reading of this text.

---

[1] To be accurate, we should point out that human beings actually have many more senses, but for our purposes, the obviously recognizable senses are all we need to keep in mind.

[2] For your convenience, there is a list of key words and phrases at the end of each major section of this book. For Part One this glossary can be found on pages 125–27. Words and phrases defined in the glossary appear in color throughout the text.

Source: David S. Strickler—Monkmeyer.

The book is the *source*. The images (words) on the page are the *stimuli* it sends. You are the *receiver*. The nerves and muscles of your eyes receive (see) the images and transmit them to your brain.

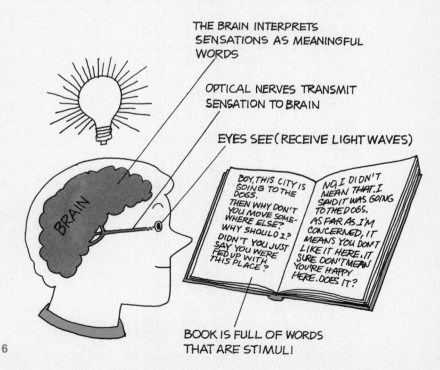

THE BRAIN INTERPRETS SENSATIONS AS MEANINGFUL WORDS

OPTICAL NERVES TRANSMIT SENSATION TO BRAIN

EYES SEE (RECEIVE LIGHT WAVES)

BOOK IS FULL OF WORDS THAT ARE STIMULI

You thus receive stimuli that cause *sensations.* Your brain perceives the images as words. They are words you recognize, and with which you associate a meaning. This association involves *interpretation,* which enables you to find the sentences meaningful. Interpretation is very important because it is how we convert sensations into communication messages (meanings). We will devote all of Chapter 2 to analysis of the interpretive processes.

Noise represents factors that interfere with receiving or interpreting sensations. Noise can be external or internal. *External noise is something that interferes with receiving.* If the lights in the room flicker while you are reading so that you can't read or see the pages any longer, that is external noise. If two people are talking and a radio blares so that they can't hear, or a passing plane or truck drowns out the words, external noise has occurred. *Internal noise is something that interferes with the interpretation processes.* If you are thinking about something else, or have a pounding headache, you have internal noise. Likewise, emotions or distorting attitudes represent internal noise.

Not all stimuli actually lead to communication. The marks on this page, for instance, are just marks until someone sees them. Only when you look at them (receive them) will they become stimuli for you and create visual images (sensations), and even then, no meaningful communication will result until the sensations are interpreted. Similarly, sound waves are merely disturbances of air until ears receive (hear) them and a brain perceives (interprets) them as words. If the air waves aren't picked up by a sensory mechanism, the waves exist, but communicate nothing. A sound tape playing in an automated radio station can cause sound waves to be transmitted into the air, but if no one has a radio tuned in to the frequency, no communication occurs. Distinguishing between transmitted and received messages is important because a common cause of communication breakdown is the difference between actual and received stimuli.

The sensations, the means by which we receive communication messages, parallel the human senses. People communicate through the senses of sight, sound, touch, taste, and smell.[3] In speech communication, the most used senses are sight and sound, although touch and smell are also common. When you recall how much meaning can be added to words by a pat on the back or a punch in the nose, you'll realize that touch is an important communicator. Widespread use of perfumes, colognes, aftershave lotions, and deodorants shows that smell often communicates. Taste is also used to communicate, though less commonly than the other senses.

---

[3] We recognize that extrasensory perception does occur. However, not enough evidence of how it works exists for us to discuss it as a means of communication.

Each person *receives* sight, smell (if either or both are wearing cologne), touch, and sound messages of which the other is the *source*.
Source: Sybil Shelton—Monkmeyer.

Your *responses* to sensations received include recognition and interpretation. Awareness is one level of response, and, returning to the example of your reading this text, your only responses as you read may be recognition and association of meaning. Or perhaps you found a sentence that is particularly difficult. You may have thought, or even said aloud, "Wait a minute, that doesn't make sense." You may have thought, "What does that word mean?" Perhaps you reread some sentences aloud. If so, your responses were more than awareness and understanding; they included observable behavior.

For *communication to occur, both a source and receiver are needed;* and for the communication to be *human* communication, either the source or the receiver must be a person. Often the source of communication messages is not another person, but rather an object. In the example cited, the source was a book, and the receiver a person. Usually, though, communication situations involve two or more persons, and they all become sources of stimuli that are messages. During communication, each participant (as well as the environment and objects in the situation) both sends and receives messages.

That all human participants in a communication situation are both source and receiver is due to the element of communication called *feedback*. Feedback is the link that connects source and receiver. *We define feedback as a receiver's response to communication messages as perceived by the source of the messages.* That is an important definition because it points out that *responses to communication and feedback aren't the same thing.* Whenever you perceive messages, you respond, but *not all responses are feedback.* Suppose three people are conversing—Tom, Dick, and Judy. Tom is speaking. Dick interrupts to ask, "Did you just say you *would* or you *wouldn't* go?" Dick's question is feedback to Tom, and Tom's answer is feedback to Dick. During the exchange, suppose that Judy, upon hearing Tom's answer, leans back with a disgusted look on her face and turns her eyes toward the ceiling. (These are unspoken or *nonverbal* messages.) However, although she's responding to Tom's answer, if he doesn't see her, her response isn't feedback to him.

It's also possible that *a response to a communication may not be observable.* For example, one possible response to communication is to change an attitude. But such a response may not be observable. Indeed, in the absence of an overt (observable) response by you, the source of the message may conclude that your attitude is unchanged. The feedback is *whatever the source of the original message perceives, and may not be the same as your response.*

As we saw above, *feedback can be both verbal and nonverbal.* If a friend asks, "How are you feeling today?" and you say nothing, but frown and shake your head, this is as meaningful as words. Perhaps more so. *Feedback also is both external and internal.* When you respond to the greeting of a friend by smiling and saying, "Hi," you are providing external feedback—that is, as long as your friend sees and hears you. But during this exchange, you probably also hear and feel yourself respond. That is internal feedback. Internal feedback is your internal check on your own communication. Internal feedback occurs because you are both source and receiver of your own messages.

To be totally accurate, we should identify all parties in communication as source/receiver, because no communicator is ever exclusively one or the other. When you talk, others aren't the only ones who hear you. You also hear yourself. You are both source and receiver of your own messages. And while you talk *to* someone else, you receive nonverbal messages *from* the other person. Look, for example, at two friends, Joe and Donna. While Joe talks, he hears his own words, and also receives feedback from Donna. He sees the expressions on her face, her eye contact or lack of it, movements indicating she is interested or bored, comfortable or nervous, passive or involved. He can use nonverbal cues to tell how she feels about their relationship or his messages. Does she sit close to him? Does she lean toward him or away from him? Does she look at him or avoid his eyes? All these behaviors send messages. At the same time, Donna receives both verbal and nonverbal messages *from* Joe and is source of feedback messages *to* him. Joe too is both source and receiver. He sends verbal messages and receives feedback both from Donna and his own verbal messages.

Feedback is vital in communication. When source and receiver have direct contact with each other, feedback will significantly and immediately influence the interactions. Feedback can influence goals, how messages are phrased and interpreted, and source and receiver behaviors. A person who is sensitive to feedback can use it to determine whether or not messages are perceived as intended. If they are not, adaptations can be made. The adaptations, called the *corrective* function of feedback, may be its most important function. In later chapters, we devote much attention to the processes of sending and interpreting feedback, because using this link between people is very important in becoming effective as communicators.

The final communication element we listed was *situation.* We use this word to refer to the total environment in which communication occurs. Situation includes the occasion, surroundings, people, and the interrelationships among these factors. All of these can affect the communication. Situation can determine which sensations sources receive and which they perceive. A noisy room can prevent your hearing what someone says; listening to a song on the radio while your mother talks to you can interfere with your receiving her message. Situations also influence interpretations and responses. Your mother, for instance, could be so angered by your attention to the radio that she concludes you're being insolent. On the other hand, if you are listening to an announcement of attempted presidential assassination, she probably won't be insulted by your inattention.

types of communication

Differences in communication are caused by the situations in which it takes place. Communication can be described as intrapersonal, interpersonal, or public, depending upon the situation. By *intrapersonal communication* we refer to communication with yourself. Hearing yourself speak, feeling yourself move, thinking or otherwise processing internal sensory messages are examples of intrapersonal communication. Consciously or unconsciously, intrapersonal communication continues as long as you are alive.

Intrapersonal communication.
Source: Mimi Forsyth—Monkmeyer.

Interpersonal communication occurs when you communicate directly with other people in a one-to-one situation or in small groups. The derivation of the word parts "inter" and "personal" suggests that *interpersonal* means any communication between persons. But that includes *all* human communication. We think it's more useful to define interpersonal communication as interactions in which participants have a one-to-one relationship. Practically speaking, these situations usually involve two to eight persons, but the number of people is not the factor that identifies interpersonal communication: direct interaction on a one-to-one basis is the essential feature.

Public communication takes place in situations where many people receive messages largely from one source. A movie, television show, sermon, political speech, advertiser's message, professor's lecture, and committee report are all examples of public communication. Some are examples of mass communication, a particular public communication situation. *Mass communication* is public communication transmitted electronically or mechanically. Televi-

Interpersonal communication.
Source: Hugh Rogers—Monkmeyer

sion, radio, movies, newspapers, books, and magazines are all examples of mass communication.

In public communication, most participants are receivers of verbal messages from only one or a few others. Speeches are the best known examples of public communication. Participants in public communication do not interact in direct one-to-one relationships. Interaction occurs, but in a different way than in interpersonal situations. In public communication feedback is sent and responded to, usually without receivers verbally responding. The professor who changes his lecture style because students fall asleep or look bored, and the politician who becomes angry when his proposal to raise the drinking age to 25 is booed are both interacting with receivers and responding to feedback.

All three types of communication can be illustrated by a single situation. Suppose you are watching TV with a friend. You haven't eaten for several hours, and an advertisement shows people at a dining table. You realize you are hungry, and you start to think about how good popcorn would taste. You say to your friend, "I'm hungry—are you? Want some popcorn?" Your thoughts about popcorn are intrapersonal communication. The question and your friend's answer are interpersonal communication. The TV program itself is an example of public communication.

The Communication Processes

> Individuals do not communicate; they engage in or become part of communication.
>
> R. BIRDWHISTELL

Now that you know what the elements of communication are, and understand better the different types of communication, let's explore the idea that communication is a process. Communication requires more than the elements we've just described. In communication the elements interact to produce an outcome. This outcome may be information shared, behavior, or feelings. We describe such interactions as *processes.*

what is a process?

When we use the word "process," we refer to events that interact to create something new. For example, film is processed into pictures; wheat into flour. Applications are processed; manufacturing cars is a process. In each process events interact, creating something new from the raw materials used. In each, materials are transformed, but nothing is eliminated or destroyed.

As pictures are developed, film is changed, not destroyed. As flour is made, wheat is changed but not eliminated. Information on applications may be transferred to a magnetic tape in a computer, and the application form burned, but the information isn't lost and the paper becomes carbon and gases in the process. In manufacturing cars, ore is changed from rock to iron, to steel, to car frames and bodies, creating by-products in the process, but nothing is totally eliminated. Events in a process don't happen and then end. Each element, or event, interacts with others to create something that interacts with still others, creating something else that will also interact with others, and so on in a never-ending cycle. This is what we mean by process.

What are the implications of referring to communication as a process? Processes are dynamic, creating something new by transforming raw materials. Each interaction in a process affects other interactions. Everything is interrelated. Everything affects everything else.

These implications are illustrated by Ray Bradbury's "Sound of Thunder." After reading the story, you may want to discuss the questions that follow it with your classmates.

Public communication. *Source: (left)* Cron—Monkmeyer; *(center)* Mimi Forsyth—Monkmeyer; *(right)* Hugh Rogers—Monkmeyer.

A SOUND OF THUNDER

Ray Bradbury

The sign on the wall seemed to quaver under a film of sliding warm water. Eckels felt his eyelids blink over his stare, and the sign burned in this momentary darkness:

TIME SAFARI, INC.
SAFARIS TO ANY YEAR IN THE PAST.
YOU NAME THE ANIMAL.
WE TAKE YOU THERE.
YOU SHOOT IT.

A warm phlegm gathered in Eckels' throat; he swallowed and pushed it down. The muscles around his mouth formed a smile as he put his hand slowly out upon the air, and in that hand waved a check for ten thousand dollars to the man behind the desk.

"Does this safari guarantee I come back alive?"

"We guarantee nothing," said the official, "except the dinosaurs." He turned. "This is Mr. Travis, your Safari Guide in the Past. He'll tell you what and where to shoot. If he says no shooting, no shooting. If you disobey instructions, there's a stiff penalty of another ten thousand dollars, plus possible government action, on your return."

Eckels glanced across the vast office at a mass and tangle, a snaking and humming of wires and steel boxes, at an aurora that flickered now orange, now silver, now blue. There was a sound like a gigantic bonfire burning all of Time, all the years and all the parchment calendars, all the hours piled high and set aflame.

A touch of the hand and this burning would, on the instant, beautifully reverse itself. Eckels remembered the wording in the advertisements to the letter. Out of chars and ashes, out of dust and coals, like golden salamanders, the old years, the green years, might leap; roses sweeten the air, white hair turn Irish-black, wrinkles vanish; all, everything fly back to seed, flee death, rush down to their beginnings, suns rise in western skies and set in glorious easts, moons eat themselves opposite to the custom, all and everything cupping one in another like Chinese boxes, rabbits into hats, all and everything returning to the fresh death, the seed death, the green death, to the time before the beginning. A touch of a hand might do it, the merest touch of a hand.

"Unbelievable." Eckels breathed, the light of the Machine on his thin face. "A real Time Machine." He shook his head. "Makes you think. If the election had gone badly yesterday, I might be here now running away from the results. Thank God Keith won. He'll make a fine President of the United States."

"Yes," said the man behind the desk. "We're lucky. If Deutscher had gotten in, we'd have the worst kind of dictatorship. There's an anti-everything man for you, a militarist, anti-Christ, anti-human, anti-intellectual. People called us up, you know, joking but not joking. Said if Deutscher became President they wanted to go live in 1492. Of course it's not our business to conduct Escapes, but to form Safaris. Anyway, Keith's President now. All you got to worry about is—"

"Shooting my dinosaur," Eckels finished it for him.

"A Tyrannosaurus rex. The Tyrant Lizard, the most incredible monster in history. Sign this release. Anything happens to you, we're not responsible. Those dinosaurs are hungry."

Eckels flushed angrily. "Trying to scare me!"

"Frankly, yes. We don't want anyone going who'll panic at the first shot. Six Safari leaders were killed last year, and a dozen hunters. We're here to give you the severest thrill a real hunter ever asked for. Traveling you back sixty million years to bag the biggest game in all of Time. Your personal check's still there. Tear it up."

Mr. Eckels looked at the check. His fingers twitched.

"Good luck," said the man behind the desk. "Mr. Travis, he's all yours."

They moved silently across the room, taking their guns with them, toward the Machine, toward the silver metal and the roaring light.

First a day and then a night and then a day and then a night, then it was day-night-day-night. A week, a month, a year, a decade! A.D. 2055. A.D. 2019. 1999! 1957! Gone! The Machine roared.

They put on their oxygen helmets and tested the intercoms.

Eckels swayed on the padded seat, his face pale, his jaw stiff. He felt the trembling in his arms and he looked down and found his hands tight on the new rifle. There were four other men in the Machine. Travis, the Safari Leader, his assistant, Lesperance, and two other hunters, Billings and Kramer. They sat looking at each other, and the years blazed around them.

"Can these guns get a dinosaur cold?" Eckels felt his mouth saying.

"If you hit them right," said Travis on the helmet radio. "Some dinosaurs have two brains, one in the head, another far down the spinal column. We stay away from those. That's stretching luck. Put your first two shots into the eyes, if you can, blind them, and go back into the brain."

The Machine howled. Time was a film run backward. Suns fled and ten million moons fled after them. "Think," said Eckels. "Every hunter that ever lived would envy us today. This makes Africa seem like Illinois."

The Machine slowed; its scream fell to a murmur. The Machine stopped.

The sun stopped in the sky.

The fog that had enveloped the Machine blew away and they were in an old time, a very old time indeed, three hunters and two Safari Heads with their blue metal guns across their knees.

"Christ isn't born yet," said Travis. "Moses has not gone to the mountains to talk with God. The Pyramids are still in the earth, waiting to be cut out and put up. Remember that. Alexander, Caesar, Napoleon, Hitler—none of them exists."

The man nodded.

"That"—Mr. Travis pointed—"is the jungle of sixty million two thousand and fifty-five years before President Keith."

He indicated a metal path that struck off into green wilderness, over streaming swamp, among giant ferns and palms.

"And that," he said, "is the Path, laid by Time Safari for your use. It floats six inches above the earth. Doesn't touch so much as one grass blade, flower, or tree. It's an anti-gravity metal. Its purpose is to keep you from touching this world of the past in any way. Stay on the Path. Don't go off it. I repeat. Don't go off. For any reason! If you fall off, there's a penalty. And don't shoot any animal we don't okay."

"Why?" asked Eckels.

They sat in the ancient wilderness. Far birds' cries blew on a wind, and the smell of tar and an old salt sea, moist grasses, and flowers the color of blood.

"We don't want to change the Future. We don't belong here in the Past. The government doesn't like us here. We have to pay big graft to keep our franchise. A Time Machine is finicky business. Not knowing it, we might kill an important animal, a small bird, a roach, a flower even, thus destroying an important link in a growing species."

"That's not clear," said Eckels.

"All right," Travis continued, "say we accidentally kill one mouse here. That means all the future families of this one particular mouse are destroyed, right?"

"Right."

"And all the families of the families of the families of that one mouse! With a stamp of your foot, you annihilate first one, then a dozen, then a thousand, a million, a billion possible mice!"

"So they're dead," said Eckels. "So what?"

"So what?" Travis snorted quietly. "Well, what about the foxes that'll need those mice to survive? For want of ten mice, a fox dies. For want of ten foxes a lion starves. For want of a lion, all manner of insects, vultures, infinite billions of life forms are thrown into chaos and destruction. Eventually it all boils down to this: fifty-nine million years later, a caveman, one of a dozen on the entire world, goes hunting wild boar or saber-toothed tiger for food. But you, friend, have stepped on all the tigers in that region. By stepping on one single mouse. So the caveman starves. And the caveman, please note, is not just any expendable man, no! He is an entire future nation. From his loins would have sprung ten sons. From their loins one hundred sons, and thus onward to a civilization. Destroy this one man, and you destroy a race, a people, an entire history of life. It is comparable to slaying some of Adam's grandchildren. The stomp of your foot, on one mouse, could start an earthquake, the effects of which could shake our earth and destinies down through Time, to their very foundations. With the death of that one caveman, a billion others yet unborn are throttled in the womb. Perhaps Rome never rises on its seven hills. Perhaps Europe is forever a dark forest, and only Asia waxes healthy and teeming. Step on a mouse and you crush the Pyramids. Step on a mouse and you leave your print, like a Grand Canyon, across Eternity. Queen Elizabeth might never be born, Washington might not cross the Delaware, there might never be a United States at all. So be careful. Stay on the Path. Never step off!"

"I see," said Eckels. "Then it wouldn't pay for us even to touch the grass?"

"Correct. Crushing certain plants could add up infinitesimally. A little error here would multiply in sixty million years, all out of proportion. Of course maybe our theory is wrong. Maybe Time can't be changed by us. Or maybe it can be changed only in little subtle ways. A dead mouse here makes an insect imbalance there, a population disproportion later, a bad harvest further on, a depression, mass starvation, and finally, a change in social temperament in far-flung countries. Something much more subtle, like that. Perhaps only a soft breath, a whisper, a hair, pollen on the air, such a slight, slight change that unless you looked close you wouldn't see it. Who knows? Who really can say he knows? We don't know. We're guessing. But until we do know for certain whether our messing around in Time can make a big roar or a little rustle in history, we're being careful. This Machine, this Path, your clothing and bodies, were sterilized, as you know, before the journey. We wear these oxygen helmets so we can't introduce our bacteria into an ancient atmosphere."

"How do we know which animals to shoot?"

"They're marked with red paint," said Travis. "Today, before our journey, we sent Lesperance here back with the Machine. He came to this particular era and followed certain animals."

"Studying them?"

"Right," said Lesperance. "I track them through their entire existence, noting which of them lives longest. Very few. How many times they mate. Not often. Life's short. When I find one that's going to die when a tree falls on him, or one that drowns in a tar pit, I note the exact hour, minute, and second. I shoot a paint bomb. It leaves a red patch on his side. We can't

miss it. Then I correlate our arrival in the Past so that we meet the Monster not more than two minutes before he would have died anyway. This way, we kill only animals with no future, that are never going to mate again. You see how careful we are?"

"But if you come back this morning in Time," said Eckels eagerly, "you must've bumped into us, our Safari! How did it turn out? Was it successful? Did all of us get through—alive?"

Travis and Lesperance gave each other a look.

"That'd be a paradox," said the latter. "Time doesn't permit that sort of mess—a man meeting himself. When such occasions threaten, Time steps aside. Like an airplane hitting an air pocket. You felt the Machine jump just before we stopped? That was us passing ourselves on the way back to the Future. We saw nothing. There's no way of telling if this expedition was a success, if we got our monster, or whether all of us—meaning you, Mr. Eckels—got out alive."

Eckels smiled palely.

"Cut that," said Travis sharply. "Everyone on his feet!"

They were ready to leave the Machine.

The jungle was high and the jungle was broad and the jungle was the entire world forever and forever. Sounds like music and sounds like flying tents filled the sky, and those were pterodactyls soaring with cavernous gray wings, gigantic bats of delirium and night fever. Eckels, balanced on the narrow Path, aimed his rifle playfully.

"Stop that!" said Travis. "Don't even aim for fun, blast you! If your guns should go off—"

Eckels flushed. "Where's our Tyrannosaurus?"

Lesperance checked his wristwatch. "Up ahead. We'll bisect his trail in sixty seconds. Look for the red paint! Don't shoot till we give the word. Stay on the Path. Stay on the Path!"

They moved forward in the wind of morning.

"Strange," murmured Eckels, "Up ahead, sixty million years, Election Day over, Keith made President. Everyone celebrating. And here we are, a million years lost, and they don't exist. The things we worried about for months, a lifetime, not even born or thought of yet."

"Safety catches off, everyone!" ordered Travis. "You, first shot, Eckels. Second, Billings, Third, Kramer."

"I've hunted tiger, wild boar, buffalo, elephant, but now, this is it," said Eckels. "I'm shaking like a kid."

"Ah," said Travis.

Everyone stopped.

Travis raised his hand. "Ahead," he whispered. "In the mist. There he is. There's His Royal Majesty now."

The jungle was wide and full of twitterings, rustlings, murmurs, and sighs.

Suddenly it all ceased, as if someone had shut a door.

Silence.

A sound of thunder.

Out of the mist, one hundred yards away, came Tyrannosaurus rex.

"It," whispered Eckels. "It. . . ."

"Sh!"

It came on great oiled, resilient, striding legs. It towered thirty feet above half of the trees, a great evil god, folding its delicate watchmaker's claws close to its oily reptilian chest. Each lower leg was a piston, a thousand pounds of white bone, sunk in thick ropes of muscle, sheathed over in a gleam of pebbled skin like the mail of a terrible warrior. Each thigh was a ton of meat, ivory, and steel mesh. And from the great breathing cage of the upper body those two delicate arms dangled out front, arms with hands which might pick up and examine men like toys, while the snake neck coiled. And the head itself, a ton of sculptured stone, lifted easily upon the sky. Its mouth gaped, exposing a fence of teeth like daggers. Its eyes rolled, ostrich eggs, empty of all expression save hunger. It closed its mouth in a death grin. It ran, its pelvic bones crushing aside trees and bushes, its taloned feet clawing damp earth, leaving prints six inches deep wherever it settled its weight. It ran with a gliding ballet step, far too poised and balanced for its ten tons. It moved into a sunlit area warily, its beautifully reptilian hands feeling the air.

"Why, why," Eckels twitched his mouth. "It could reach up and grab the moon."

"Sh!" Travis jerked angrily. "He hasn't seen us yet."

"It can't be killed," Eckels pronounced this verdict quietly, as if there could be no argument. He had weighed the evidence and this was his considered opinion. The rifle in his hands seemed a cap gun. "We were fools to come. This is impossible."

"Shut up!" hissed Travis.

"Nightmare."

"Turn around," commanded Travis. "Walk quietly to the Machine. We'll remit half your fee."

"I didn't realize it would be this big," said Eckels. "I miscalculated, that's all. And now I want out."

"It sees us!"

"There's the red paint on its chest!"

The Tyrant Lizard raised itself. Its armored flesh glittered like a thousand green coins. The coins, crusted with slime, steamed. In the slime, tiny insects wriggled, so that the entire body seemed to twitch and undulate, even while the monster itself did not move. It exhaled. The stink of raw flesh blew down the wilderness.

"Get me out of here," said Eckels. "It was never like this before. I was always sure I'd come through alive. I had good guides, good safaris, and safety. This time, I figured wrong. I've met my match and admit it. This is too much for me to get hold of."

"Don't run," said Lesperance. "Turn around. Hide in the Machine."

"Yes." Eckels seemed to be numb. He looked at his feet as if trying to make them move. He gave a grunt of helplessness.

"Eckels!"

He took a few steps, blinking, shuffling.

"Not that way!"

The Monster, at the first motion, lunged forward with a terrible scream. It covered one hundred yards in six seconds. The rifles jerked up and blazed fire. A windstorm from the beast's mouth engulfed them in the stench of slime and old blood. The Monster roared, teeth glittering with sun.

The rifles cracked again. Their sound was lost in shriek and lizard thunder. The great level of the reptile's tail swung up, lashed sideways. Trees exploded in clouds of leaf and branch. The Monster twitched its jeweler's hands down to fondle at the men, to twist them in half, to crush them like berries, to cram them into its teeth and its screaming throat. Its boulderstone eyes leveled with the men. They saw themselves mirrored. They fired at the metallic eyelids and the blazing black Iris.

Like a stone idol, like a mountain avalanche, Tyrannosaurus fell. Thundering, it clutched trees, pulled them with it. It wrenched and tore the metal Path. The men flung themselves back and away. The body hit, ten tons of cold flesh and stone. The guns fired. The Monster lashed its armored tail, twitched its snake jaws, and lay still. A fount of blood spurted from its throat. Somewhere inside, a sac of fluids burst. Sickening gushes drenched the hunters. They stood, red and glistening.

The thunder faded.

The jungle was silent. After the avalanche, a green peace. After the nightmare, morning.

Billings and Kramer sat on the pathway and threw up. Travis and Lesperance stood with smoking rifles, cursing steadily.

In the Time Machine, on his face, Eckels lay shivering. He had found his way back to the Path, climbed into the Machine.

Travis came walking, glanced at Eckels, took cotton gauze from a metal box, and returned to the others, who were sitting on the Path.

"Clean up."

They wiped the blood from their helmets. They began to curse too. The Monster lay, a hill of solid flesh. Within, you could hear the sighs and murmurs as the furthest chambers of it died, the organs malfunctioning, liquids running a final instant from pocket to sac to spleen, everything shutting off, closing up forever. It was like standing by a wrecked locomotive or a steam shovel at quitting time, all valves being released or levered tight. Bones cracked; the tonnage of its own flesh, off balance, dead weight, snapped the delicate forearms, caught underneath. The meat settled quivering.

Another cracking sound. Overhead, a gigantic tree branch broke from its heavy mooring, fell. It crashed upon the dead beast with finality.

"There." Lesperance checked his watch. "Right on time. That's the giant tree that was scheduled to fall and kill this animal originally. He glanced at the two hunters. "You want the trophy picture?"

"What?"

"We can't take a trophy back to the Future. The body has to stay right here where it would have died originally, so the insects, birds, and bacteria can get at it, as they were intended to. Everything in balance. The body stays. But we can take a picture of you standing near it.

The two men tried to think, but gave up, shaking their heads.

They let themselves be led along the metal Path. They sank wearily into the Machine cushions. They gazed back at the ruined Monster, the stagnating mound, where already strange reptilian birds and golden insects were busy at the steaming armor.

A sound on the floor of the Time Machine stiffened them. Eckels sat there, shivering.

"I'm sorry," he said at last.

"Get up!" cried Travis.

Eckels got up.

"Go out on that Path alone," said Travis. He had his rifle pointed. "You're not coming back in the Machine. We're leaving you here!"

Lesperance seized Travis's arm. "Wait—"

"Stay out of this!" Travis shook his hand away. "This fool nearly killed us. But it isn't that so much, no. It's his shoes! Look at them! He ran off the Path. That ruins us! We'll forfeit! Thousands of dollars of insurance! We guarantee no one leaves the Path. He left it. Oh, the fool! I'll have to report to the government. They might revoke our license to travel. Who knows what he's done to Time, to History!"

"Take it easy, all he did was kick up some dirt."

"How do we know?" cried Travis. "We don't know anything! It's all a mystery! Get out of here, Eckels!"

Eckels fumbled his shirt. "I'll pay anything. A hundred thousand dollars!"

Travis glared at Eckels' checkbook and spat. "Go out there. The Monster's next to the Path. Stick your arms up to your elbows in his mouth. Then you can come back with us.

"That's unreasonable!"

"The Monster's dead, you idiot. The bullets! The bullets can't be left behind. They don't belong in the Past; they might change anything. Here's my knife. Dig them out!"

The jungle was alive again, full of the old tremorings and bird cries. Eckels turned slowly to regard the primeval garbage dump, that hill of nightmares and terror. After a long time, like a sleepwalker he shuffled out along the Path.

He returned, shuddering, five minutes

later, his arms soaked and red to the elbows. He held out his hands. Each held a number of steel bullets. Then he fell. He lay where he fell, not moving.

"You didn't have to make him do that," said Lesperance.

"Didn't I? It's too early to tell." Travis nudged the still body. "He'll live. Next time he won't go hunting game like this. Okay. He jerked his thumb wearily at Lesperance. "Switch on. Let's go home."

1492. 1776. 1812.

They cleaned their hands and faces. They changed their caking shirts and pants. Eckels was up and around again, not speaking. Travis glared at him for a full ten minutes.

"Don't look at me," cried Eckels. "I haven't done anything."

"Who can tell?"

"Just ran off the Path, that's all, a little mud on my shoes—what do you want me to do—get down and pray?"

"We might need it. I'm warning you, Eckels, I might kill you yet. I've got my gun ready."

"I'm innocent. I've done nothing!"

1999. 2000. 2055.

The Machine stopped.

"Get out," said Travis.

The room was there as they had left it. But not the same as they had left it. The same man sat behind the same desk. But the same man did not quite sit behind the same desk.

Travis looked around swiftly. "Everything okay here?" he snapped.

"Fine. Welcome home!"

Travis did not relax. He seemed to be looking through the one high window.

"Okay, Eckels, get out. Don't ever come back."

Eckels could not move.

"You heard me," said Travis. "What're you staring at?"

Eckels stood smelling of the air, and there was a thing to the air, a chemical taint so subtle, so slight, that only a faint cry of his sublimal senses warned him it was there. The colors, white, gray, blue, orange, in the wall, in the furniture, in the sky beyond the window, were . . . were. . . . And there was a feel. His flesh twitched. His hands twitched. He stood drinking the oddness with the pores of his body. Somewhere, someone must have been screaming one of those whistles that only a dog can hear. His body screamed silence in return. Beyond this room, beyond this wall, beyond this man who was not quite the same man seated at this desk that was not quite the same desk . . . lay an entire world of streets and people. What sort of world it was now, there was no telling. He could feel them moving there, beyond the walls, almost, like so many chess pieces blown in a dry wind.

But the immediate thing was the sign painted on the office wall, the same sign he had read earlier today on first entering.

Somehow, the sign had changed:

TYME SEFARI INC.

SEFARIS TU ANY YEER EN THE PAST.

YU NAIM THE ANIMALL.

WEE TAEKYUTHAIR.

YU SHOOT ITT.

Eckels felt himself fall into a chair. He fumbled crazily at the thick slime on his boots. He held up a clod of dirt, trembling. "No, it can't be. Not a little thing like that. No!"

Embedded in the mud, glistening green and gold and black, was a butterfly, very beautiful and very dead.

"Not a little thing like that! Not a butterfly!" cried Eckels.

It fell to the floor, an exquisite thing, a small thing that could upset balances and knock down a line of small dominoes and then big dominoes and then gigantic dominoes, all down the years across Time. Eckels' mind whirled. It couldn't change things. Killing one butterfly couldn't be that important! Could it?

His face was cold. His mouth trembled, asking: "Who—Who won the presidential election yesterday?

The man behind the desk laughed. "You joking? You know very well. Deutscher, of course! Who else? Not that fool weakling Keith. We got an iron man now, a man with guts!" The official stopped. "What's wrong?"

Eckels moaned. He dropped to his knees. He scrabbled at the golden butterfly with shaking fingers. "Can't we," he pleaded to the world, to himself, to the officials, to the Machine, "can't we take it back, can't we make it alive again? Can't we start over? Can't we—"

He did not move. Eyes shut, he waited, shivering. He heard Travis breathe loud in the room; he heard Travis shift his rifle, click the safety catch, and raise the weapon.

There was a sound of thunder.

1. How is the concept of process illustrated by "Sound of Thunder"?

2. Does everything really affect everything else?

3. What small incidents in your life have had major and longlasting effects?

4. What are the implications of referring to communication itself as a *process of processes*?

Communication as a Process of Processes

We describe communication as a process. Indeed, as the reading above shows, *it is a process of processes.* Several interactions are involved in each communication, and the outcome of the interactions is something new: new understanding and attitudes, behavior, and feelings, or some combination of these. The interactions occur almost instantaneously—so rapidly that we commonly think of communication as an event. But when we look closely, we can see the event is really a process involving many interactions. Let's look at them briefly.

Receiving sensations is a process. Nerve endings in your eyes, ears, mouth, skin, and nose all receive stimuli and transmit impulses to the brain, which then interprets the sensations. *Interpretation of sensations received* is a process. When the brain receives sensations, it identifies, classifies, evaluates, and manipulates the information. Then the brain sends messages to the rest of the body, directing responses to the sensations received. This is *responding to interpretations,* and it too is a process.

Communication is a process composed of many processes. Many interactions occur, each an essential part of the whole. A single interaction produces little communication; combined they create meanings. An example will illustrate. When Sara arrives at work in the morning, she is greeted by her partner, Raoul. "Good morning. How you doing today?" Sara *receives* the aural sensations (she *hears*), *sees* Raoul at his desk, *smells* his shaving lotion. The nerves that receive these stimuli transmit impulses to the brain, which *interprets* each different sensation. Sara thus recognizes the person, the situation, the smells, the words and grammar, and associates meanings with each. Because all fit into a familiar pattern, her brain is satisfied the situation is OK and directs a familiar *response.* "Fine. Nice day, isn't it?"

And as with all processes, although new outcomes result from each communication, the previous results aren't lost. For example, assume you have just learned something about a person close to you, and what you've learned contradicts what you previously believed about that person. In processing this new information, you might change your ideas, but you do not lose the knowledge you previously had. You add to ideas as you process new information. In this case, you'll probably continue the process on both intra- and interpersonal levels. When we see that communication is a process of processes, we understand the changes that constantly occur within us as a result of communication.

A useful way to visualize communication was suggested by one of our students. Think of an interlocking gear system: one set of gears could represent one communicator.

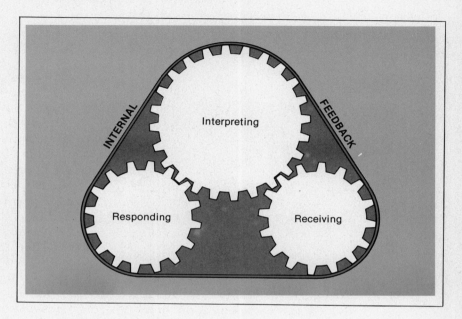

Then consider another communicator.

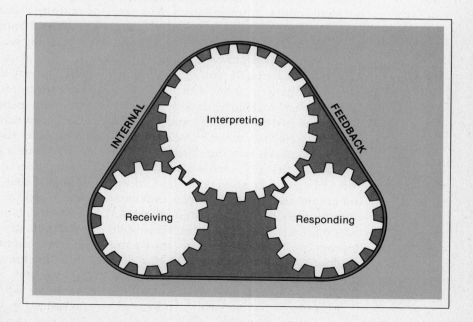

Note that all affect each other and the communicators interact through feedback.

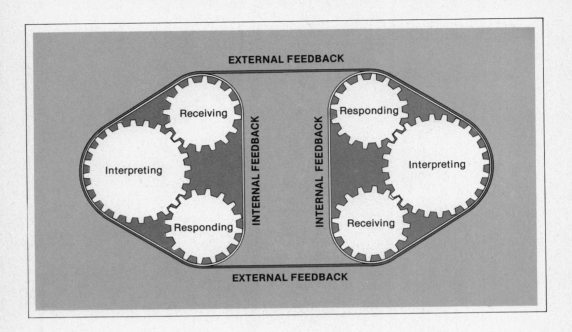

Of the communication processes, the ones most people are least aware of occur during interpretation of messages. Many people think, "I speak, you hear, therefore we have communicated." It's not that simple. Interpretation of sensations is quite complex. It involves *perception, symbolization, remembering,* and *thinking.* You learned each of these processes during the first few years of your life. They have by now become behaviors that occur on a largely unconscious level. If you're driving a car and a child dashes into the street, you jam on your brakes. You don't consciously think, "Brain, what do I do?" Receiving, interpreting, and responding occur almost instantaneously, and you don't consciously think through the interactions. Communication usually happens so fast, and the processes are so familiar, that you aren't aware of the interactions.

In the first part of this book we analyze these processes. We want you to become conscious of the various interactions that occur during communication. Then you can look carefully at your communication habits and assess their effects. You may find out that some patterns you learned during infancy and childhood are no longer appropriate. You can analyze your patterns, change them when appropriate, and better control your communication behaviors, thus gaining the most from each situation.

Let's now answer the question, What is speech communication? Many kinds of messages are sent, received, and interpreted as you communicate. What particular ones distinguish speech from other kinds of communication? For us, *speech communication is a process during which persons assign meaning to verbal and nonverbal symbols.* Let's look carefully at that statement.

process We have described above what we mean by "process." Processes are comprised of elements that interact in dynamic, ongoing relationships. Speech communication involves many elements (a source, stimuli, a receiver, sensory receptions, receiver interpretations and responses, noise, feedback, and a situation) and processes (reception, perception, symbolization, remembering, responding, and thinking) that interact.

during which This term indicates that assigning meaning happens *during* the process, along with other things. In other words, assigning meaning to symbols is not the only thing that happens. In speech communication many interacting processes occur, often simultaneously.

persons That persons assign meanings indicates that at least one participant in the situation must be human.

symbols Symbols are things that represent, or stand for, something else. Speech communication symbols include words, spoken or heard.

verbal and nonverbal In all speech, both nonverbal and verbal symbols are involved. We use the word "nonverbal" to refer to all nonword symbols. These include gestures and body actions, tone of voice, and the uses of objects, space, and time.

assigning meaning The process of using words and nonword cues to refer to something else is the process of assigning meaning. Symbols are useful in communication when source and receiver use them with similar referents.

Exercise: Making Models of Communication[4]

Objective: To apply your understanding of the processes of communication by creating a model that represents them.

Discussion:

Modeling is a common way of learning. At one time or another all of us have built models. Yours may have been model airplanes, cars, doll houses, trains, or sand castles on the beach.

But modeling is not limited to play. Aircraft engineers make models and test them in wind tunnels. Architects create scale models of buildings; auto manufacturers create prototype models of future

---

[4] Throughout the book you will have a chance to do exercises that will help you to better understand the principles you have been reading about. These will allow you to apply what you have learned to specific situations. In addition, there are further exercises and projects in the Student Activity Guide available for your use.

cars. Sculptors often make small forms of larger creations they plan to execute.

Naturally, no model can ever be totally accurate in representing a process. Still, creating a representation of it can highlight the significant aspects of all the processes involved and thus can be helpful in understanding them.

The kind of model you're asked to create is a symbolic, graphic, or three-dimensional representation of the communication processes. In the model, try to show what parts or elements are involved in the concept and how the parts relate to each other.

Many different models are possible. None will be perfect; each will have special qualities. You may want to refer to the suggested readings. You'll see how different writers have visualized the process.

Directions:

1. Working together in groups assigned by the instructor, create a model (graphic or three-dimensional) that seems to you to be representative of the speech communication process.

2. Your instructor may ask you to explain your model to the rest of the class.

LOOKING BACK

We all have reasons to study speech communication: to avoid or minimize breakdowns; to better understand how we use communication to relate to the rest of the world; and to learn how we use communication to attempt to satisfy many of the human needs we experience. This study can provide tools to help handle various communication situations, but it cannot provide simplistic answers, because communication is not a simple process.

Communication is described as a process of processes. It involves sending, receiving, and interpreting many stimuli. The communication processes include eight elements: (1) source; (2) stimuli received from the source; (3) receiver; (4) sensory receptors; (5) receiver's interpretations and responses to the sensations; (6) noise; (7) feedback; and (8) situation or context. To describe communication as a process suggests it is composed of interactions among many elements, and it is ongoing. Each part of the process interacts with and affects the other parts.

Three types of communication are distinguished by different situations: intrapersonal, interpersonal, and public. Intrapersonal communication takes place within you; it is your communicating with yourself. Interpersonal communication is direct one-to-one interaction. This usually occurs in situations involving two persons, or within a small group. Public communication occurs in a situation where a large number of people receive stimuli from primarily one source. Mass communication, sending messages via media to many widely separated receivers, is a special type of public communication. Speech communication is defined as a process during which persons assign meaning to verbal and nonverbal symbols.

Questions for Discussion

1. Why study speech communication?
2. What concept is suggested in Bradbury's "Sound of Thunder"?

3. What does "Sound of Thunder" suggest for understanding human communication?

4. What does it imply to describe speech communication as process?

5. What are the processes of speech communication?

6. What differences do you see in the three types or levels of speech communication?

7. After having read this chapter, do you have any new insights about the following conversation?

Scene:	Wife and husband after dinner in the living room. Husband is silent.
Wife:	What's the matter, dear?
Husband:	Nothing.
Wife:	What do you mean, nothing?
Husband:	Just what I said—nothing.
Wife:	You look upset about something.
Husband:	Do I?
Wife:	Yes.
Husband:	Come to think of it, I am a little annoyed.
Wife:	Over what, dear?
Husband:	You.
Wife:	But why?
Husband:	Because your nagging is driving me nuts!
Wife:	I was just concerned because you were so quiet.
Husband:	Martha, please go away and leave me alone.
Wife:	George, you give me a pain. If I don't ask you what's wrong, you accuse me of not giving a damn whether you live or die. If I do ask, you bitch that I'm nagging. As far as I'm concerned, you can drop dead!

Suggestions for Further Reading

ARANGUREN, J. L., *Human Communication.* New York: McGraw-Hill Book Co., 1967.

BARKER, LARRY, *Communication Vibrations.* Englewood Cliffs, N.J.: Prentice-Hall, Inc., 1974.

BARKER, LARRY L., AND ROBERT J. KIBLER, *Speech Communication Behavior: Perspectives and Principles.* Englewood Cliffs, N.J.: Prentice-Hall, Inc., 1971.

DEVITO, JOSEPH, *The Psychology of Speech and Language.* New York: Random House, 1970.

———, *Communication Concepts and Processes* (2nd ed.). Englewood Cliffs, N.J.: Prentice-Hall, Inc., 1976.

MORTENSEN, C. DAVID, *Basic Readings in Communication Theory.* New York: Harper & Row, Publishers, 1973.

PETERSON, BRENT D., GERALD M. GOLDHABER, AND R. WAYNE PACE, *Communication Probes.* Chicago: Science Research Associates, Inc., 1974.

2
The Pictures in Your Head
interpreting reality

goal:

To understand how processing sensations leads to human communication.

probes:

The material in this chapter should help you to:

1. Indicate the role each of the following interpretation processes plays in communication:

   Perception, pp. 27–39   Symbolization, pp. 40–46
   Memory, pp. 46–55   Recall, pp. 54–55
   Conceptualizing, pp. 47–48   Abstraction, pp. 48–51
   Evaluating, pp. 51–54   Thinking, pp. 55–62

2. Explain why perception varies among receivers, using the following concepts: experience, attention, socialization, expectations, physical condition. pp. 27–39

3. Explain the following principles of symbolization, showing how each influences communication:

   Symbols are both verbal and nonverbal. pp. 43–45
   Meanings are in people, not words. pp. 40–43
   Meanings are both connotative and denotative. pp. 41–43
   Ambiguity in using symbols is inevitable. pp. 40–45

4. Explain how storing interpretations in long-term memory instead of direct sensory input affects communication. pp. 47

5. Give an example of the "ladder of abstraction" principle, using a specific subject. pp. 49–51

6. Define attitude, distinguishing attitudes from behavior. pp. 51–53

7. Give an example of the five inferential processes, using a specific subject. pp. 56–60

All of our experiences with external reality come to us through our senses. When we "see" a person or an object, for instance, we experience an image because light waves are processed through our eyes and sensations are sent to the brain. When we talk, our speech communicates with others only because they receive sound waves and interpret them as words. Though human beings are born with the ability to receive sensations (stimuli) and to respond to them, the ways of interpreting the stimuli must be learned. As infants we did not inherit a store of meanings in our brains. We processed sensations at first without knowing any meaning for them. Only gradually did we learn to associate certain stimuli with specific meanings. For instance, we learned to identify "mother" by repeatedly seeing, hearing, and touching her. As specific stimuli repeatedly created similar sensations we learned what they "meant." Then we learned how stimuli differ, and sometimes what their causes and effects were.

In short, *we learn to interpret the sensations we receive through our senses; it is the interpretation process that makes communication possible.* The way we interpret the many sensations we receive is what makes interaction with others meaningful. For that reason understanding how we interpret is very important in understanding how communication happens. This chapter analyzes the interpretation processes. We look closely at four major processes of interpretation: perception, symbolization, memory, and other thought processes.

PERCEPTION

As you grew from infancy, you learned a very important skill: you learned to select and organize sensations so they would be meaningful. In other words, you learned to perceive. Because *perception*

27

The fly sat upon the axle-tree of the chariot wheel and said,
"What a dust do I raise!"

FRANCIS BACON

is learned, how you perceive will depend on your experiences. You
first learned what sensations "meant" by direct responses to pain or
pleasure, or by whether they satisfied specific needs. For instance,
the first time you sensed heat from a radiator, you didn't know it
would burn, or how painful that burn could be. After touching the
radiator, however, you knew. And then when you felt heat from an
iron or a stove for the first time, you didn't have to touch it to know
it would burn and hurt.

Experience Influences Perception

People perceive (interpret) sensations received using what they
have learned. Thus, if people have different experiences with stimuli, they will have different perceptions of them. Suppose, for instance, the first cat you knew was a bad-tempered Siamese. With a
child's curiosity, you reached out to touch it, and the cat's response
was a nasty snarl, a slashing paw and you got a painful, bloody
scratch. After that you'll perceive all cats as mean and dangerous
animals, at least until you have enough experiences with gentle cats
to change the early impression. On the other hand, if your first experience with cats was pleasant, you may still perceive them as
creatures to be petted and loved. You can undoubtedly supply
many examples from your own experience to illustrate this principle.

Not all people have the same experiences. That's a truism, of
course. But the logical conclusion based on that truism is too often
forgotten. If (1) perception is learned, and (2) what is learned depends on experiences, and (3) people don't have identical experiences, then *people will perceive the same things in different ways.*
Perception varies, so meanings constructed from sensations will
also vary. If you understand this, you can see one reason people
have communication breakdowns.

socialization

Socialization is a part of our experience, and many differences in
perception are due to this process. *Socialization refers to the process by which a child, born with behavior potentials of enormous
range, develops more limited behavior patterns.* Human infants at

first reveal few uniquely human behaviors. They act much like our primate relatives. But rapidly the behavior of humans is learned, from parents at first, then from peers and social institutions. The socialization of our eating behavior illustrates this process. Newborn infants suck a breast or bottle nipple. Later, when solid food is introduced, babies happily grab it with both hands and smear everything within reach (and much that is not within reach!). Countless corrections are required before a child can eat with a spoon. Slowly, knives and forks will be conquered. Most parents work hard to teach "proper" ways to eat. They don't want children to be messy or eat in socially disapproved ways. Finally, people can learn to dine with competence in elegant restaurants.

You may be thinking, "Hey, that's not always so. I have trouble deciding what all those forks and spoons are for." You're right, of course. The results of the socialization process depend on what groups do the socializing. Many children are not taught how to deal with ten-piece place settings; their socializing groups didn't think they needed that. And it's not just a matter of socioeconomic class. Henry VIII, though he was king of England, wouldn't have been prepared to cope with four forks. And one of us had a college roommate who was a Brahman Indian, heir to a fortune of several millions—she ate her rice with her fingers, perfectly acceptable behavior in her society.

The groups that provide most socialization for children are actually subsystems or micro-societies. The family is the predominant socializing group for most of us. It's a small society that is part of a larger one. We're first socialized to the "rules" of our family; then to neighbors' and friends' "rules"; then to those of socioeconomic reference groups as they exist in particular localities; then to a larger culture that may be identified as English, Italian, American, Black, German, Mexican, Jewish, Chicano, U.S. white middle class, . . . Some cultures cross national boundaries, others do not; still others exist as subsocieties within nations.

Socialization accounts for vast differences in approved behaviors from one society to another. Social groups, whether small primary groups or large reference groups, have widely varying "rules" that regulate the behaviors of people who belong. This issue will be discussed later in this book. At this point, we note it to show how many differences in perception are influenced by learning in the socialization process.

Expectations Influence Perception

Below you will find nine dots. Try the following exercise with them. Take a pencil and connect the nine dots in the square using four straight lines. Don't lift your pencil from the paper, and don't retrace any lines.

Try this puzzle several times before you give up. Could you do it? If not, it was because your previous experience and the words we used influenced your expectations. Your past experience and our verbal instructions caused you to perceive a square. With that perception, you probably tried to make the straight lines within the boundaries of the square. If you did, you found you couldn't accomplish the task. You have to perceive the dots differently to do it. (See page 64 for the solution.)

Here are other examples. These triangles below contain some common sayings. Read them aloud.

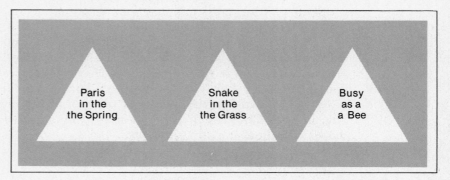

Paris
in the
the Spring

Snake
in the
the Grass

Busy
as a
a Bee

Now look carefully. If you didn't read two "the's" in the first two phrases and two "a's" in the third, you didn't perceive accurately. And if this happened, it was because your previous experience created an expectation to see them as you have seen them before. These examples illustrate the principle that *we interpret sensations received according to our expectations.*

Our language, after all, is a thought trap: when certain sorts of notions don't fit into its framework, they remain unrecognized. It's a monstrous handicap. We are so crippled we haven't even the words to think about all those thoughts that might have been.

WILLIAM HEDGEPETH

There are three factors involved in the influence of expectations on perception: emotions, language, and attitudes. Let's look first at the impact of emotions.

emotions

Our feelings strongly determine how we perceive sensations. One of our students supplied this excellent example. A fellow on his way home from work one night stopped by the neighborhood bar, and with some friends, got involved in a game of pool. One game led to another, and still another; and then it was an hour past the time he was expected home for dinner. When his wife called him to say, "Your dinner is in the oven: I'm leaving for the PTA meeting," his feeling of guilt for being late led him to perceive anger in her voice, whether she was angry or not. In a similar case, a teenager who had the family car for the evening returned home an hour late. Her guilty feeling influenced her to hear anger in her father's greeting, "Where have you been?" even though Dad was expressing more relief than anger. These cases also show the effect of previous experience in creating expectations. If in similar events in the past the wife or father had really been quite angry, an expectation of similar behavior is natural.

language

A second factor in the influence of expectations on perception is that *language itself creates expectations.* For example, look at this diagram. Do you see anything meaningful?

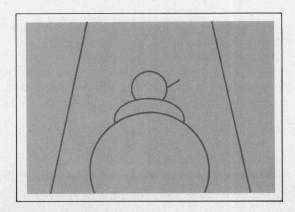

If not, try looking at it as a cooking utensil. Do you see it any differently? Next, see it as a weapon of war. Does your perception change? Now, can you see Winston Churchill smoking one of his favorite cigars? Finally, try seeing an animal. No luck? Well, can you imagine seeing Secretariat and jockey Ron Turcotte from the perspective of second-place Sham in the 1973 Kentucky Derby and Preakness?

Here's another example. Does this figure make any sense to you?

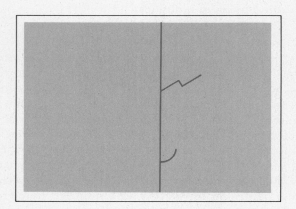

If not, can you see a foot soldier and his dog just passing the corner of a building? In each of these cases, language influenced your perception.

We can also cite verbal examples. Some of you may understand what the West Virginian meant when he said, "I'll be glad to carry you home." Many more will probably have the same mental image we did, of being physically hoisted into the arms of the gentleman for the trip home. Similarly, an English student visiting America one June found that his new passion for ice cream beaten up with syrup and milk could be indulged in New York by a milk shake, in Massachusetts by a frappe, and in Rhode Island by a cabinet—and they were all the same delicious drink!

The influence of language on perception (and vice versa) is strong. We discuss the role of symbolizing in stimulus processing shortly. At this point we want you simply to realize that language itself often creates expectations that affect how you perceive.

attitudes

Both language and emotions are involved in the third factor, the influence of attitudes on expectations. One research study illustrated

how strong this influence is.[1] During Roosevelt's administration
three groups were selected to hear a ten-minute speech that contained nearly equal amounts of pro- and anti-New Deal comments.
One group consisted of people who favored the New Deal; another
group was neutral; and the third opposed these policies. After the
speech, these listeners were given a test to see which of 46 specific
items they heard. The items included 23 comments that were favorable and 23 that were unfavorable toward the New Deal. The results reported below show how much listeners' attitudes influenced
what they perceived.

	Pro–New Deal	Anti–New Deal
	Items Recognized	
Favorable Listeners	16.1	9.9
Neutral Listeners	12.8	11.8
Unfavorable Listeners	10.9	13.0

These responses illustrate how people tend to see what they
want to see and hear what they want to hear. Attitudes are very important as a cause of perceptual variability. We discuss shortly their
role in memory and how they affect behavior.

Perception Is a Selective Process

Throughout life, people are constantly bombarded by millions of
sensations. At any one time you see more than you consciously see;
you hear more than you consciously hear; you feel more than you
consciously feel; you taste more than you consciously taste; and you
smell more than you consciously smell. To put it simply, *you must
select what you perceive.* Selectivity is influenced by attention, perspective, and physical condition, among other factors. We will look
at each of these three influences in turn.

attention

Stop reading for a minute. Focus on everything you can see around
you. Notice you can't see everything at once, and you always view
some surroundings with peripheral vision. Is the radio or TV on?
Were you consciously hearing everything on it, or were you push-
ing most of it into the background until just now? But you might
have noticed if the radio had quit, right? Or if your favorite artist
came on? How about the chair you're sitting on? Did you consciously feel it until we called attention to it? Probably not, unless

[1]Study conducted by Allen L. Edwards, "Rationalization in Recognition as a
Result of a Political Frame of Reference," *Journal of Abnormal and Social Psychology*, 36 (1941), 224–36. © 1941 by the American Psychological Association. Reprinted
by permission.

it's uncomfortable. But you would have noticed if it began to give way under you. Perhaps you're sitting in the student center while you read. Were you hearing the conversation at the table next to you? But if the voices increase in volume, or if you now pay *attention* closely, you may receive the sounds of voices and perceive some of the meanings.

People don't receive all the sensations it is possible to receive at any one time, nor do they consciously perceive all the sensations they receive. Both these factors are due to the role of *attention.* What is attention? It's a complex psychological process, hard to specify clearly. But it's important in communication. *We think of attention as an adjustment of the receiving senses.* For example, you pay attention when you look in the direction of someone you expect to speak, or to whom you are listening. You extend your hand to a person you expect to shake hands with. This we call *focal attention.*

You receive many sensations without focusing direct attention on their sources. This is referred to as peripheral or *marginal attention.* It can also be described as partial receptor adjustment. Many sensations are received through marginal attention. Much of the information you use to guide your life is received marginally. For example, if you cross an empty street while talking to a friend, you focus attention on the conversation, but you also give marginal attention to the street to watch for cars. If you become aware of how many times you use marginal attention, you will become more aware of why you and others behave as you do. We discuss many of these uses below, because awareness of marginal attention can help you control the ways your behavior influences others.

Finally, some stimuli are received at the level of *subliminal attention:* at a level of awareness that could not be perceived even if you focused your receptors. For example, you know a movie doesn't consist of a moving picture. But can you see the thousands of still pictures flashed on the screen so rapidly? No, you can't perceive the individual pictures, and you have the sensation of seeing movement, though you know you aren't. Similarly, television images are not the complete pictures that you perceive. They are pinpoints of light, moving so rapidly you don't perceive them individually.

Exercise: Lemons

Objective: To become aware of information usually gained marginally through sensory receptors.

Directions:

In groups of twelve, sit in a circle on the floor. The instructor will give a lemon to each class member. You will be given ten minutes to "become acquainted" with your lemon. Spend the first five minutes observing the uniqueness of your lemon visually; take the next five to become aware of the lemon by touch, with your eyes closed.

Next, form pairs; introduce your lemon to your partner by describing its particular characteristics. You should also exchange your lemons so that you do not limit your introduction to visual characteristics.

Now form groups of six. Put your lemons in a pile in the middle of each group. Close your eyes and find your lemon. Return to the original circle of twelve. Put your lemons on the floor in the middle. Have a member of the group distribute the lemons to the group. Begin passing them around the circle to the right, with eyes closed. When you receive your lemon, put it in your lap. Keep passing the lemons around until everyone has his or her own lemon. Discuss the experience, including the following questions:

1. Did you "see" more in your lemon when you began talking about it with a partner?
2. Could you improve your ability to identify by touch with practice? How might you do so?
3. What did closing your eyes contribute to use of the sense of touch?
4. What about *yourself* did you express as you described "your" lemon?

perspective

Look carefully at the photographs below. What do they seem to be pictures of?

Source: Reprinted courtesy *American Way,* inflight magazine of American Airlines. Photos by Norman Cousins.

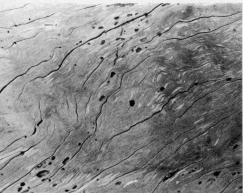

They are closeups of trees. From this perspective, trees look different. These pictures illustrate that *we interpret sensations according to our way of viewing the world, our perspective.* Have you ever stood on the overpass of a four-lane highway and observed how the lanes run together? You know they don't, but they appear to, don't they? Without previous experience, you wouldn't know this. Similarly, people in the fifteenth century perceived that the world was generally flat. They believed that somewhere, if the world ended, an edge must exist over which adventurous sailors were sure to sail, and go tumbling through space. Observation could lead us to similar perceptions of a flat world if we had had no experiences with globes and books and teachers. Not until we viewed a round earth through the astronauts' cameras were many of us provided with the perspective to confirm that the earth is indeed generally circular.

Source: *The Family Circus* by Bill Keane reprinted courtesy The Register and Tribune Syndicate, Inc.

A standard of living that includes running water and indoor toilets and excludes fur coats, steak for dinner, and automobiles would be perceived as luxurious by a starving Indian (either in New Delhi or Arizona). But from the perspective of a person born into the family of Joseph Kennedy, Sr., or John D. Rockefeller, that living standard would probably be perceived as marked by poverty.

physical condition

To read, you perceive marks that you interpret as words and process as meaningful. If you can't see well, you'll have trouble reading. You receive other sensations, too: sound, taste, touch, and smell. And your perceptions are influenced by how well your sensory receptors work. For example, most of us perceive the world using both eyes. Try examining the room around you with only one eye. How different does it look? Most of us perceive more space more quickly with two eyes. Is your depth perception impaired when you look with only one? For most of us, it is. People who have a physical impairment such as loss of hearing or sight perceive differently than others do. Have you ever tried to explain color to a blind person? Do you usually recognize your favorite food cooking when you walk through the kitchen door? But if you have a bad cold, you'll have difficulty identifying what is cooking by the smell. The food will taste different, too. The senses of a person who is fatigued or ill do not operate as well as possible. Have you noticed how your perceptions change when you are ill or in pain? Or that you listen less attentively when tired? Doctors have found that heavy smokers have a loss in the sense of feeling in their fingers. People who have quit smoking report that food tastes differently and new smells are noticed. All these points illustrate that *physical condition of receptors influences perception.*

During this discussion of perception, we have talked about perception without limiting ourselves to speech communication. We have done this to emphasize that you receive sensations continuously, from all your environment. As you do, you communicate with yourself. Your brain interprets messages received through your senses and sends messages back to the motor muscles. Touch a hot iron and your brain quickly sends the message, "move your hand." You perceive and respond almost instantaneously, because the message involves a "reflex" response.

On the other hand, touch a mink coat, and the cerebral part of your brain interprets. Several messages will be involved and no responses occur as quickly as the reaction to the burn. You may run your hand across the fur gently, responding to the softness, thinking how good it feels, how expensive it must be, or how nice it would be to have such a coat. You may wonder how many people you know have one, or if you will ever have one. Or you may withdraw your hand, feeling repulsed and thinking what a crime it is to slaughter tiny living beings just so rich people may show off their wealth.

Thus you see, perception and interpretation of sensations received in communication occur constantly as you process stimuli from both your external and internal environments. These important processes of communication are highly individual, resulting in many differences in perceptions of similar events by different people. We now turn to one factor causing these differences, the second process in stimulus processing, symbolization.

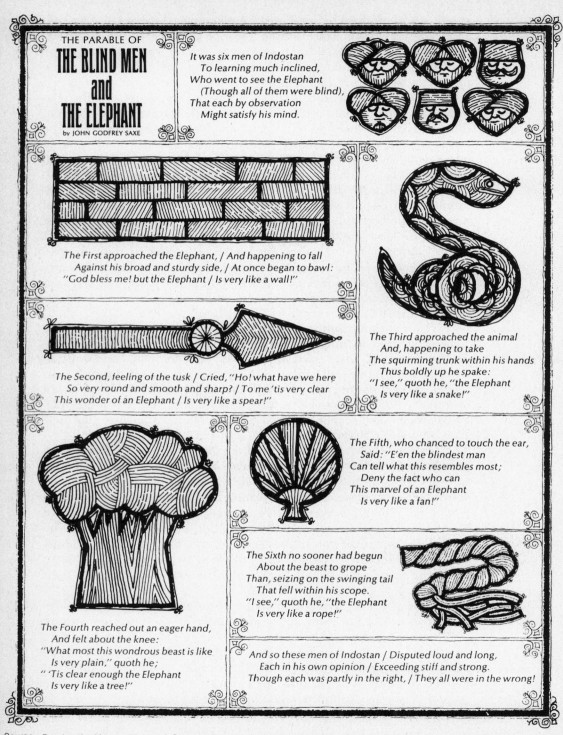

THE PARABLE OF
THE BLIND MEN and THE ELEPHANT

by JOHN GODFREY SAXE

It was six men of Indostan
To learning much inclined,
Who went to see the Elephant
(Though all of them were blind),
That each by observation
Might satisfy his mind.

The First approached the Elephant, / And happening to fall
Against his broad and sturdy side, / At once began to bawl:
"God bless me! but the Elephant / Is very like a wall!"

The Second, feeling of the tusk / Cried, "Ho! what have we here
So very round and smooth and sharp? / To me 'tis very clear
This wonder of an Elephant / Is very like a spear!"

The Third approached the animal
And, happening to take
The squirming trunk within his hands
Thus boldly up he spake:
"I see," quoth he, "the Elephant
Is very like a snake!"

The Fourth reached out an eager hand,
And felt about the knee:
"What most this wondrous beast is like
Is very plain," quoth he;
" 'Tis clear enough the Elephant
Is very like a tree!"

The Fifth, who chanced to touch the ear,
Said: "E'en the blindest man
Can tell what this resembles most;
Deny the fact who can
This marvel of an Elephant
Is very like a fan!"

The Sixth no sooner had begun
About the beast to grope
Than, seizing on the swinging tail
That fell within his scope.
"I see," quoth he, "the Elephant
Is very like a rope!"

And so these men of Indostan / Disputed loud and long,
Each in his own opinion / Exceeding stiff and strong.
Though each was partly in the right, / They all were in the wrong!

SYMBOLIZATION

> The essential function of language is that of taking an idea . . .
> that exists inside the head of a speaker, shaping it so that it can
> be transmitted, . . . then actually transmitting the message—and
> hoping that approximately the same idea will somehow miracu-
> lously reappear inside the head of the listener.
>
> The wonder of it all is not that the system does not work per-
> fectly, but that it works as well as it does.
>
> WILLIAM MOULTON

To a great extent, our ability to communicate equals our ability to
use symbols. Therefore, it's useful to look closely at this process.

What Is Symbolization?

The simplest definition of symbolization is that *it is a process in
which one thing is used to refer to or stand for something else.*
Some symbols are obvious and we recognize immediately that they
stand for something in addition to what we directly perceive with
our senses. For example, a wedding ring is not merely a circular
piece of gold; it's a traditional symbol of agreement between a man
and a woman. A flag is not merely a few yards of cloth on the end
of a pole; it's a symbol of a country or an organization. Although not
all symbols are so obvious, the definition applies to them all: *a symbol is anything that stands for something else.*

Some symbols confuse us because we think of them as things
rather than as symbols, when they are both things and symbols. The
clothes you wear are "things" in that they provide warmth and protection, but they also reveal certain things about you as you wear
them; thus they are also symbols. Similarly, the car you drive is a
"thing" that provides transportation, but it also indicates taste,
status, your concept of self, and perhaps even economic position.
Thus your car is also a symbol.

Symbolization has been called the process that distinguishes
humans from the other animals. As more is learned about animals'
communication systems, this popular concept is being questioned.[2]

---

[2] R. Allen and B. T. Gardner, "Teaching Sign Language to a Chimpanzee,"
Science, 165 (August 1969), 664–72, is one of the earliest reports of symbolic activity
by chimpanzees. Later reports include "The Education of S*A*R*A*H," *Psychology
Today,* September 1970, pp. 54–58; "Language in Chimpanzee?" *Science,* 178 (May
1971), 808–22; and "Teaching Language to an Ape," *Scientific American,* 227 (Octo-
ber 1972), 92–99; all by David Premack. Another study and rejoinder appeared in
Science, "Reading and Sentence Completion by a Chimpanzee," by D. M. Rum-
baugh, *et al., Science,* 182, (November 1973), 731–33; the rejoinder by J. L. Mistler-
Lachman and R. Lachman in *Science,* 185 (September 1974), 871–73.

But the questions raised are not whether the symbolic ability is important. The questions relate to whether other animals use symbolic systems we haven't learned to understand. No one doubts the importance of the symbolizing process.

The Meaning of Meaning

Among the most used symbols are words. Like all symbols, words stand for, or refer to, something else. Commonly you hear or say, "That word means . . ." What does that say? Have you ever thought what you mean by the word "meaning"? A word's meaning is not its definition. Though a definition is part of the meaning of a word, it is not all the meaning. You can define love, but that isn't its meaning, is it?

We use the word "meaning" to refer to the entire set of reactions that people assign to a symbol. Your "meaning" for a word is the sum total of reactions you have when you hear, read, or think about that word. Thus words have many meanings. *Meanings* fall into two different categories: *connotations* and *denotations.*

denotation

The denotations of a word are the objects or concepts referred to: the actual "things" symbolized. One denotation for the word "fire," for instance, is the rapid oxidation of organic matter. Another denotation is the flame itself. Other possible denotative meanings for the word "fire" are: the act of discharging a gun; dismissing an employee from a job; and igniting a skyrocket. You could add other denotations.

We often forget that most words have several denotations. Even simple words. "Chair," for instance, can refer to thousands of different kinds of objects. Have you ever tried to define chair? Try. A chair is ———. Fill in your definition. Compare it with others in class. Are there differences? Certainly. Denotative meanings often differ greatly from user to user. The 500 most commonly used English words have 14,000 different definitions! When symbols have different possible referents, they are described as ambiguous. Ambiguity is another way to label the difference between intended and received messages, and is a major problem of using symbols to communicate.

Exercise: Denotations

Objective: To recognize the wide variety of denotations that are possible even for concrete words.

Directions:

1. Write down as many denotations as you can think of for the word "frog."

2. Ask a friend to do the same thing.
3. Compare your lists, and combine them to see how many referents for the word "frog" you can call to mind.
4. Look up the word in a standard dictionary (not the small pocket size, one of the large ones found in libraries).
5. How many referents were listed in the dictionary that you didn't have?
6. How many referents did you find that were totally new uses of the word for you?

connotation

Most symbols also have connotative meanings. *The connotations of a word are the attitudes or feelings you have about the object or concept symbolized,* or about the word itself. For the word "fire," for instance, you probably have several different connotations, depending on the denotation you think of. The idea of a fire in a fireplace on a cold day, or of a campfire, will usually have favorable connotations. You probably like those things. The idea of a fire in the attic or basement, however, produces negative connotations. You dislike that kind of fire. To the firing of a gun, you probably have mixed connotative reactions. Is it being fired at a mallard or pheasant? If you like hunting, your connotation is positive. If you think hunting is a cruel, barbaric pastime, then you probably have a negative connotative reaction to the word "fire" in the context of "to fire a gun." Do you like fireworks on the Fourth of July or on New Year's Day? Then firing a skyrocket probably elicits positive reactions from you. But if you ever fired a Roman Candle that went off in your hand, the thought of setting off any fireworks is probably negative for you.

The important point to remember is that meanings, both connotative and denotative, are very personal and thus use of symbols is highly ambiguous. We will discuss this later.

Exercise: Connotations

Objectives: To become aware of connotative meanings. To recognize why people have different connotations for words.
Directions:
1. As you read the words in the list below, write down what your emotional response to each word is. Use the categories of favorable, unfavorable, and neutral to classify your responses.
2. Next, read the list to at least four other people, asking them each to write down how they respond to each word.
3. Compare the five sets of responses and discuss the following questions:
   a. To which of the words did most of you have similar connotative

responses? Were there any words to which all five responded the same? What explains the similarities?

b. Compare the words to which there were different responses. Were any of the differences because the person had a different denotation in mind? Which?

c. If you think of different denotative meanings for the words, does that change the connotative reactions? What other factors might explain different connotative meanings?

d. What are the characteristics of words that have neutral connotations? Did you and others have different connotative responses to numbers 3 and 5? People usually do. Why? If you did not, why not?

The list:

1. chair	8. peace	15. acid
2. grockett	9. love	16. nigger
3. pig	10. plaque	17. officer
4. Black	11. grass	18. Spic
5. ham	12. mother	19. Anglo
6. effish	13. Italian	20. WASP
7. rip off	14. desk	

Different Kinds of Symbols

Symbols can be divided into four basic categories: *verbal, nonverbal, vocal,* and *nonvocal.* We use the term "verbal" to refer to word symbols, and "nonverbal" denotes all nonword symbols. Vocal symbols use voice, but not necessarily to make words. Vocal symbols can be emotional cries such as screams, sobs, sighs, or groans. Ella Fitzgerald and Roger Miller use vocal, nonverbal symbols when they add nonsense syllables to song lyrics. Nonvocal symbols convey meanings through actions, objects, and other nonword means. A gesture without words is a nonverbal, nonvocal symbol. As you read this, you're reading verbal, nonvocal symbols. The picture below is another nonverbal, nonvocal symbol meaningful to most of us.

You might find the following diagram helpful in distinguishing among the kinds of symbols used in communication:

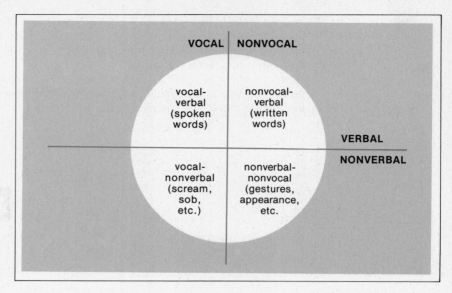

Some means of communication do not use all these kinds of symbols, but speech invariably uses at least three: verbal, nonverbal, and vocal.[3] To speak you use words and add voice, thus using vocal and verbal symbols. *You cannot speak words without adding nonverbal messages.* Voice quality, tempo, pitch, inflection, and volume are all nonverbal elements adding meaning to words. Because body movements usually accompany the use of voice, nonvocal elements are also involved in speech whenever communicators can see, touch, or smell each other.

Even when you write or read, you communicate with nonverbal symbols as well as verbal. Look at a letter you have recently received. Note the slant of handwriting, its legibility, its evenness, its size, the way words and letters are or are not connected. All these are nonverbal elements revealing much about the writer and the writer's mood. The layout and graphics of a printed page add to the meanings derived by the reader. A beginning journalism student quickly learns that where a story is placed on the page, the size and boldness of its headlines, and the white space surrounding the words are important factors. They all influence the total impact of the carefully chosen words. If this book contained very small print

---

[3]Those of you who will later study phonetics will learn that some speech sounds are described as "voiceless," but for an introductory text, we believe the distinction too technical to be useful.

with closely spaced lines, no pictures, no headings, and coarse paper, you'd receive a different set of messages from it than you do. So you see, even when you write or read, you communicate with nonverbal symbols. Nonverbal symbols are very important to effective communication because they are so often processed through marginal attention. We discuss nonverbal communication at length in Chapter 3.

Source: © King Features Syndicate, Inc., 1974.

Language as a Code

It's a language, not just symbols, that you use daily. If you had a very exciting experience yesterday and today you see a friend you want to share the experience with, you don't simply use words to do it. Certainly, you select certain words, but you also add nonverbal symbols. You arrange the symbols in a particular order and express them with particular inflections. You use more than words: You use a language.

Languages are systems of symbols. Words are the major symbols and a grammar makes the individual words useful. A series of single words has much less value in communicating than words that have been combined into meaningful sequence or arrangement. A grammar provides the "rules" that make word arrangements meaningful; grammar provides the code. *The, is, on, fire,* and *house* are five symbols you recognize and that individually make sense to you. But "The is on fire house" is a combination that communicates little. It doesn't fit your code. However, "The house is on fire" is meaningful. "Is the house on fire?" is also meaningful, though different. These last arrangements were meaningful because they followed "rules of word combination" (grammar) that you recognized.

Every human language is characterized by its own grammar. Speakers make judgments about meanings of a communication based on the grammar of the sentences. For example, "The is boy running" wouldn't be considered sensible by a native speaker of American English. But "The boy is running" would be meaningful. "The boy be running" would also be considered meaningful, but not "correct" according to the grammar of American Standard English. It would, however, be grammatical in American Black dialect.

If you know the grammar of your language it helps you interpret word relationships, and sentence meanings. The two sentences, "A detective hunted down the killer," and "A detective hunted the killer down," mean essentially the same. The person competent in English grammar will know what the sentence "Flying planes are dangerous" "correctly" refers to. However, what the speaker *intends* isn't actually clear, because the arrangement of the words makes sense but part of the grammar is not "correct." Some sentences are ambiguous even when the grammar is "correct"—for example, "The man decided on the train," and "They fed her dog biscuits." A decoder can assign several meanings to the sentences and needs more information to know the intended meanings.

People can communicate with each other with language because they know the code. They must know some of the symbols, the sound systems, and a minimum of grammar. In speaking, you use a process we call *encoding.* You assign meanings to words, use the rules of word arrangement to form sentences, and send verbal and nonverbal messages to try to communicate your meanings. Your receiver uses the process we call *decoding.* Meanings are assigned to the language and nonverbal cues received. To communicate by means of language, people must have similar acquaintances with symbols. If you don't share a code, you can't communicate with language. If you speak in Spanish and your listener "no habla Español," your communication will be ineffective. Careful encoding and decoding aid communicators in avoiding communication breakdowns.

MEMORY

I'm not sure what it means.
Why we cannot shake the old loves from our minds.
It must be that we build on memory/and make them more than what they were.

ROD McKUEN

Memory is the third major interpretive process that influences our communication. It may be the most important process in interpreting sensations received. Without memory, neither perception nor symbolization is possible. Memory enables us to communicate with words about things that are not present.

How Does Memory Function?

The brain can retain the sensory input it receives and put information into storage. We call that ability memory. Apparently, human beings have three different types of memory: *sensory information storage, short-term memory,* and *long-term memory.* Sensory information storage has a very short duration. It is the impression of actual sensory reception that you retain for a very limited time. To illustrate it, press your fingers against your arm and then lift them off. You retain the sensation of touch only briefly. Wave a pencil back and forth in front of your eyes while you stare straight ahead. Notice how an image of the pencil trails behind as the pencil moves. This is sensory information storage.

Of more importance to communicators are the short- and long-term memories. Short- and long-term memory differ from sensory information storage because actual sensory input isn't retained. *Interpretations* are stored in long- and short-term memory, not sensations. For example, when someone talks to you, you usually don't retain the sounds. Only if the person has an unusual way of pronouncing familiar words, or if strange words are used, will you remember sounds instead of words. Generally, you remember only some of the words. Mostly you remember ideas. You remember the interpretations or meaning of the actual sensations. And to create an interpretation to remember requires concepts.

conceptualizing

To conceptualize, you find the similarities in otherwise diverse objects, situations, or events. You assimilate information and conclude how sensations received are alike. When you associate words with concepts, you are able to store vast amounts of information rapidly and efficiently.

Most of the words in any language represent concepts. Words like "true," "square," "dogs," "liquid," "round," and "love" represent concepts. They select common aspects of things that are in many respects quite different and bring them together into a single perceptual framework. The things we regard as "true" are infinitely diverse, but the concept of truth allows people to select and connect similarities, so "that's true" is a meaningful statement.

From one point of view, concepts are condensations of past experience. Concepts bring together what a person has learned about many different things. Therefore, *concepts are ideas created by experiences.* The word "experience," as we use it, refers both to sensations received from external sources and those from internal sources. A sense of pain or pleasure is experience in this sense. Some things you experience by reading or hearing about them. Associating what you haven't directly experienced with what you have can create internally derived experiences. For example, you can experience a round world even if you never actually observe it from an astronaut's perspective.

Some experience, internal or external, is required to form a concept. To know red as a color, you had to experience the optical impression of redness. A person born blind couldn't have the concept, red, as others do. If you attempt to describe red to a blind person by saying "fire is red," the receiver might think of red as a sensation of heat. Can you imagine trying to describe the concept of snow to a person who has always lived in the tropics?

To a great extent, the concepts you learn are directed by the language you experience while you are growing up. Take for example the concept, tree. A speaker of English has a referent for tree, even though it denotes literally millions of different objects. Some Australian tribes, on the other hand, have no concept of tree. In their language is a concept for *jarrah, mulga, gum, palm,* etc., but no single word translatable to tree. If that is their only language, these Australians wouldn't see mesquite, oak, and the California redwood as being the same kind of thing. They don't fit into the same concept.

abstracting

To create concepts requires the ability to abstract. The selective process of conceptualizing is called *abstracting. Abstraction refers to the process of selecting elements from a reality to distinguish it from other things.* In abstracting, attention is paid to some qualities, leaving out others. To illustrate, look at a table. It is possible to focus on its color, shape, the objects on top of it, its height, the period of its design, composition, number of legs, quality of construction, or many other things. You could continue the list. Each feature represents a different abstraction. Abstraction uses a category system. As children learn language, they acquire the category systems of that language.

In abstracting, you attend to any of several aspects of a reality. The number of features you can consider depends on the range of experiences you have internalized. For example, a physicist has many concepts to use when analyzing the behavior of matter, but, faced with a stalled car, may find it impossible to conceptualize reasons why the car won't run. At the same time, a good mechanic will have many concepts about the stalled car, but would probably have difficulty with theoretical physics.

The Ladder of Abstraction. People use different "levels" of abstraction to fit parts of reality into concepts about it. Some selected features reflect observations. These can be applied only to specific objects or events. For example, in describing a particular person, you could say, "Frankie O'Mara is 5' 4" tall, has brown hair, green eyes, is 19 years old, lives at 1015 Oak Avenue." Other concepts are broader. They apply to groups or categories. Referring to Frankie as young, or slim, pretty or handsome, uses more general, abstract concepts.

These levels of abstraction can be illustrated by describing a pet named Muffet. The name, in this case, applies only to one thing. The word "Muffet" refers to a reality, not a concept. But by selecting specific features about this object, we can fit the reality into a concept. We can call her white, a terrier, a dog, an animal. We can create a ladder of concepts relating to the reality. We can say Muffet has short legs and long white hair. "Short," "legs," "long," "white," and "hair" are all concepts—fairly specific ones, but concepts nonetheless.

Calling Muffet a terrier uses a slightly broader concept. Referring to her as a dog, a mammal, and an animal uses increasingly broad concepts. Each one uses a higher level of abstraction, focusing on less specific features.

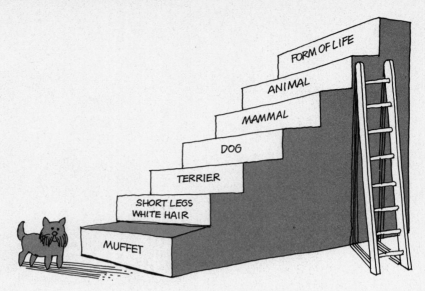

The "higher" it is on the ladder of abstraction, the farther a concept is from what can be verified by observation. To verify that Muffet has short legs and long hair, you need only look at her and know the verbal code. On the other hand, to verify that she is an animal, you must have concepts distinguishing between plants and animals. Words representing concepts high on the ladder are called abstract.

The higher a concept is, the more possible things it applies to. Therefore, the more abstract a word, the more ambiguity in its use. To illustrate, let's create another abstraction ladder. We have a friend named Joe. We can describe him as being 5′ 10″ tall, having dark hair and eyes. We could move higher on an abstraction ladder, and call him an Italian. At a still higher level, he's labeled as a human being. Then, you guessed it, another level joins Muffet's ladder.

"Muffet" and "Joe" are words we use to refer to one object. But the labels "dog" and "human" can accurately be attached to many different things. The word "animal" represents some features of both dogs and humans and can be applied to many more objects. Thus, *the higher on the ladder, the more ambiguous is the concept represented by a symbol.* Highly abstract concepts can accurately refer to more different things. This increases the possibility that people won't attach the same meanings, even if they share codes.

Words representing concepts high on the abstraction ladder

are called *abstract* words. Abstract words represent features that can't be seen. They refer to intangible things. Words referring to objects that can be seen are called *concrete*. *"Terrier," "Muffet," "Joe"* are concrete words. They refer to tangible things. *"Animal," "human," "primate"* are abstract words. Most words are abstract, making communicating more complex because of their great ambiguity. Moreover, some of the most used words are so abstract and so ambiguous that they cause many communication breakdowns. Words like "love," "inflation," and "prejudice" are very abstract and very common. They illustrate the ambiguity in common use. The next time you find yourself in an argument, analyze the words being used. Are you really arguing over what a word means, and not about the concept itself? You'll find that many arguments occur because of ambiguity in the words used.

evaluating

The memory system also involves evaluation. In processing sensations received, you often not only recognize sensations as familiar but also react with an assessment of *value*. Evaluation involves attitudes and values. Attitudes go beyond recognizing and identifying experiences as similar. They involve prediction. Values involve identification of some objects and events as having more worth than others, as being somehow better. Values and attitudes organize concepts into meaningful patterns, or systems.

We use the term *attitudes to refer to predispositions to respond to stimuli in particular ways,* while *values refer to deeply held beliefs regarding what is good.* We have noted earlier how attitudes influence perception. Some other implications of these concepts are also important in understanding how attitudes and values influence communication.

1. Attitudes and Values Are Internal States. Because they function internally, they can't be seen. Because attitudes and values are intangible, the concepts are very abstract. But abstract or not, they exist. For example, the love that you have for your husband or wife or boyfriend or girlfriend is very real, but it can't be seen. The love exists, however, and affects your value and attitude system. Even though not observable, these internal systems of evaluation help organize your reactions to events, people, things, and situations. These systems involve predicting how things happen, how they relate to each other, how they will happen in the future.

2. Attitudes and Values Involve Predispositions to Behavior. They aren't the same as behavior. To open a bottle of champagne is behavior; to have the attitude that you have an occasion worth celebrating is not behavior. Behavior is observable, and though it is often caused by attitudes and values, behavior is distinct from the internal states causing it. The internal states aren't observable. Suppose someone insulted your mother. Probably your values would be offended and negative attitudes would be activated. But lots of different behaviors might result. You might tell that person off, get angry, deliver a punch in the nose, or all three. But none of these three behaviors was itself an attitude. The attitude is your internal complex of beliefs and feelings that leads to the behavior. Though your values and attitudes regarding your mother may not change, the actual behavior in such a situation would depend on who did the insulting, where it happened, when, and perhaps other variables.

Behavior, as we use the term, is observable action. Behavior includes talking. The coding process—choosing which words to say—is internal, but expressing the words is an external act. It's observable. Thus, saying something is behavior. Values and attitudes are internal states about which people can and do make statements. Remember, however, the statements are not the attitudes. The statements are behaviors that reflect one or more elements of an attitude.

3. Attitudes and Values Vary in Intensity. A person can be moderately or very favorable toward someone else. You can like someone a little or a lot. The stronger the intensity, the more likely behavior will result. If you love your mother a lot, you'd react to an insult to her much more strongly than if you barely knew her.

4. Attitudes and Values Vary from Specific to General. Perhaps it's obvious that some attitudes are quite specific and some very general. For example, consider the situation of Roger, who believes himself quite well informed about music and who has general attitudes toward the arts that are very favorable. He plays the violin and generally likes music very much. He is predisposed to respond favorably whenever he encounters stimuli related to music. At a party recently, he heard a group discussing good music and joined them with interest. He found they were comparing Bruce Springsteen and Triumvirate, but that all considered both to be brilliant musically. He disagreed violently. This reflected his specific attitude toward a specific type of music, which was less favorable than his general attitude toward music.

The degree to which attitudes and values actually influence behavior depends on how intense and specific they are, and on the situation. Each different person creates a new situation. Behavior *tendency* and *actual* behavior will not always be the same. For example, take the case of Roger, given above. At the same party, he met a girl who played the flute in both a chamber music society and for a rock group. During the two months after the party, he dated her. He didn't change his negative attitudes about rock music, but he never said much about them when with her. Furthermore, he even attended a rock concert with her, something he had never done before.

5. *Attitudes and Values Organize Concepts.* They help create predictability in your world, and they help make sense of sensations received. Because of their strong influence in both perception and memory, attitudes and values are among the most important elements involved in processing sensations received.

Exercise: What's In An Attitude?

**Objective: To become aware of the components of attitudes and values
and how they interrelate.**
Directions:
   Before class on the assigned day, state the belief dimensions of at least ten different attitudes you hold toward the subject of religion.
Part I:
   1. In class, the instructor will divide the class into groups of two, based on the similarities of the lists.
   2. With your partner, compare your lists. Choose five statements that you both agree on. If you can't find five from the lists you already have, together state five you can agree on.
   3. For these, discuss the following:
      a. How did each attitude develop?
      b. How important is each?
      c. How does each relate to other attitude systems or values you have? State some basic attitudes that are related to these, and some that are not related.

Part II:

1. In class (perhaps on another day), the instructor will divide the class into pairs, this time combining people whose lists are very different.
2. With your partner, compare the lists and choose the two statements that are most different.
3. In a discussion, the two of you should answer the following questions:
   a. What different experiences led to the different attitudes? Are these attitudes recent or old?
4. Choose the attitude most important to each of you. Answer individually the following:
   a. What other things would I have to change in order to believe as this other person does?
   b. What would he/she have to change to believe as I do?
5. Compare your answers to #4 and discuss the differences.

Recall Is Reconstruction

> The mind is such a junkyard;
> it remembers candy bars
> but not the Gettysburg Address,
> Frank Sinatra's middle name
> but not the day your best friend died.
>
> ROD MCKUEN

Memory is more than a storage system. To be useful, stored information must be reconstructed. And the system of memory from which recall comes is not built as a pyramid with blocks. It's more than a pile of stimulus-response patterns. *Memory is a dynamic system that grows as you interact with your environment.* Think back to when you were learning about the Pilgrims landing at Plymouth Rock. Can you remember what you first learned about the event? Probably not. And whatever it was, certainly your concept of the event is different now. You've learned about other settlers, other religions, other reasons the Pilgrims came. You've learned more about the Indians and their relations to settlers both before and after the Pilgrims arrived. Your concepts have continually been elaborated. Recollections about Pilgrims, even if you never studied their landing again, would take into consideration things you've learned about related items. It's the same with all concepts you learn. As you gain more knowledge, memories are modified and elaborated as well as expanded. Thus, recall is reconstruction, not simply extracting from a storage bank.

The evolution of stored knowledge affects how you process new information. Obviously, the way you took in information as a child and the way that you store information now differs greatly.

For very young children, much more memorization takes place. But as we mature, we seek to understand sensations we receive. If adults don't understand information, they'll often reject it instead of storing it.

Memory, after early childhood, primarily fits new concepts into the pre-existing memory structure. The existing memory system is used to interpret, organize, and integrate new information.

The major memory difficulty for most people is *retrieving* stored information. Most of us have stored much more than we can easily recall. Remembering often operates without conscious direction by your brain, but you can improve your ability to recall by understanding the processes of recall. Recall processes seem to resemble those of problem solving. Let's illustrate. What did you have for dinner on the first Sunday of last month? Though it would be easier to answer "What did you have for dinner yesterday?" your brain probably uses similar operations to recall. The first thing you do is eliminate all questions about information you know you don't have. For example, if you were asked, "What kind of car did Thomas Jefferson drive?" you'd say, "Nonsense—cars didn't exist when Jefferson lived." You'd not so quickly reject the question, "What kind of car was John Kennedy riding in when he was killed?" The question about Jefferson seeks information you know you never had. The other is close enough to something you may have known that you won't reject it immediately. In many situations that require recall, the elimination processes happen so quickly and efficiently that you never notice them. Much stored information that you call up to help interpret events is retrieved with no effort at all.

Recall of events that happened long ago and seem to have faded from memory is more difficult. It combines logical reconstruction based on deduction of what must have been and fragmented recollections of what was actually experienced. When you consciously apply this problem-solving process, you can learn to use recall more efficiently. Perhaps most important, though, is to keep in mind that what you remember are interpretations. You'll then be in a better position to assess the accuracy of what you recall.

THINKING

The fourth major process that influences our interpretation of reality is thinking. In interpreting the stimuli you receive, you usually do more than recognize them as familiar. Several mental operations that we call *thinking* may be involved as you engage in further processing of sensations. Thinking is an inferring process. *When you infer, you examine possible explanations of external and internal realities and choose explanations to help you understand those realities.* You examine your existing concepts, seeing how information fits into them or how they relate to each other. You choose among the many possible meanings for sensations received and use the meanings to draw further conclusions about them. Inferring is a constant process in communication. Understanding how inferences work can help you communicate more effectively.

What Do Inferences Do?

> . . . segmentation of nature is an aspect of grammar—one as yet little studied by grammarians. We cut up and organize the spread and flow of events as we do, largely because, through our mother tongue, we are parties to an agreement to do so, not because nature itself is segmented in exactly that way for all to see.
>
> BENJAMIN WHORF

Thinking requires you to draw inferences. *Inferring* uses symbolization, perception, memory, attitudes and values to go beyond simply recognizing and predisposing responses to sensations. *To infer is to draw conclusions, conclusions of different kinds and levels.* Some express attitudes or a belief that a concept exists. Other conclusions require more conscious mental processing. They draw relationships a nong concepts. These include generalization, deduction, cause and effect, analogy and contrast and the creative processes.

Let's illustrate, using the picture below. You see a girl, grass,

Source: Sybil Shelton.

and a ball, among other things. Perception, symbolization, and memory allow you to recognize what the objects in the picture are. Now, look again. Is it summer? Is the girl about to go swimming? Is she having fun or expecting to? To have any answer at all for those questions, you must engage in further processing of the sensations received—i.e., infer. Let's examine more closely some of the thinking processes you might use.

generalization and deduction

Two basic directions of inference are possible. *Inductive thinking, or generalization, infers general conclusions from specific events.* In *generalizing,* you make predictions about a group of objects based on information about part of the group. For example, driving at 5 P.M. three or four times may lead you to conclude that traffic conditions are bad at 5 o'clock. Your generalization predicts on the basis of your three or four experiences that the general conclusion is probably true. The reliability of the general conclusion depends on the repeatability of the cases. If John is late two or three consecutive times, Janice may infer that he is late often, that he is inconsiderate, that he doesn't care about her opinion, or that he doesn't have a watch. As you see, several different generalizations are possible. What inference is drawn depends strongly on who is making it.

Generalizing categorizes the concepts people have. Perceiving objects, persons, or experiences as similar creates the class or category. The conclusion of similarity is the generalization. You can generalize, "All balls fit into the class of round objects"; or "All red balls fit into the class of red"; etc. The classifying process is not especially a matter of being accurate. Generalizations are simply a result of what features of an object or reality are attended to and perceived to be similar. We discuss some faulty generalizing processes in Chapter 3.

In deductive inferring we apply a generalization to a specific case. Don't let this term scare you—it's an impressive way to describe a type of reasoning that is very common (and also can be very often deceiving). It involves drawing a conclusion from two statements. One of the oldest examples of deduction is:

> All men are mortal;
> Socrates is a man;
> Therefore, Socrates is mortal.

In this reasoning process is a generalization, citation of a specific case inferred to belong in the category to which the generalization refers, and a conclusion that the essential element of the generalization applies to the specific case. Using the example of driving, you could reason deductively as follows: start with a generalization, "Driving is difficult at 5 P.M."; note "It's now 5 P.M."; and conclude, "Driving now would be difficult."

Look at that picture of the girl with the beachball again. You used both generalization and deduction if you answered yes to any of the questions we asked, even though the reasoning process may not be obvious. That's because you processed the information so automatically. Take a close look at your thinking. If you concluded she was having fun, you reasoned something like this: People who are smiling are enjoying themselves. This girl is smiling; therefore, she is having fun. Was it summer? Yes? To say yes, you may have thought, "Grass is green in the summer; the grass looks green; therefore, it's summer." Or perhaps, "She is going swimming; people go swimming in the summer; therefore, it's summer." In each case, you took a general belief you have, looked at a specific case, and decided the specific case fit into the general conclusion. In other words, you reasoned deductively.

Beyond that, however, previous experience led you to the general beliefs, so inductive reasoning was also involved. Why do you believe grass is green in the summer? Because you have experienced a few (or many) summers and the grass always turned green. Therefore, reasoning inductively, you conclude that grass turns green in the summer. You could follow a similar path to analyzing each of the inferential statements you make about the picture. If you think she's going swimming, it's because your previous specific experiences with beachballs lead you to generalizations about people who are holding them. Several thought processes enter into your conclusions about girls, beachballs, and swimming, so let's look at some other types of inferences to discuss some of those conclusions.

comparison and contrast

Another inferential process people use is *comparison and contrast. Using comparison and contrast, you focus on those elements you see as similar to or different from something else.* These inferences draw conclusions of similarity or difference. For example, if you tell a child who is swimming in a lake that an ocean is like a lake but much larger, you're asking the child to use comparison and contrast. Then the child can develop a concept of ocean without having seen one. Comparison concludes how concepts are alike. The reverse is contrast. You'd use contrast if you cited the existence of safety equipment on 1975 cars and its absence on 1965 cars. The contrast could result in inferring that developments in automobile safety have occurred during the decade.

How is the girl in the picture on page 59 alike or different from the one in the previous picture? Looking at this picture and thinking about that question, you automatically use comparison and contrast. Did you

Source: Sybil Shelton.

think, "How unusual for a teenage girl to have a football or to be planning to play football?" If so, again you used comparison and contrast.

cause and effect

Suppose you contrasted the gas mileage obtainable in '65 and '75 cars. This could lead to another kind of inference. Note first that '65 cars had no pollution-control equipment, unlike '75 models. Second, note that '65 cars got better gas mileage than '75 cars. You could conclude that emission-control devices reduce gas mileage. This is *cause-effect thinking*. Inferring from cause to effect relies on the belief that because one event happens something else will result. Cause-effect inferring suggests a conclusion that event A can cause effect B. We'll note in Chapter 3 how often such inferences can be in error.

Look at the picture above again. Did you wonder why that girl has a football? If so, you were searching for a cause to the effect. Did you wonder why it seemed unusual to you for a teenage girl to have a football? You were searching for a cause, a very natural behavior because you probably grew up in a culture that believes events have causes.

creative thinking

The final inferential process we want to mention is *creative thinking*. *Creative inferences enable you to add, subtract, and combine experiences to create new ideas.* This form of thinking is sometimes referred to as imagination. It is more than recollection and recon-

59

struction of experiences. It involves the reworking, re-forming, and remodeling of abstractions. It is a type of mental exercising with abstracted aspects of experience. These changes in images can go beyond experience. For instance, imagine a purple terrier with green stripes. You've never seen one, but you can imagine it. This is a simple example of imagination. Everyone has some ability to extend imagination beyond simply abstracting, to create thought beyond experience. Some have acquired or inherited abilities that are superior to those of most other people. Picasso's creative imagination, his use of line and form was very special; Jules Verne's analysis of the technology of the world and people of the future represented an extraordinary use of creative imagining.

Creative imagination is evident in daydreaming and fantasy, but it can be put to work with direction, which is the reason for most human progress. For example, having observed birds flying, people imagined themselves doing it. They attempted to model the birds' act of flight. At first the modeling was mirrorlike. People strapped on home-made wings and tried to flap them, jumping off buildings and cliffs. Eventually, as the creative imagination of more people was applied, flying machines were perfected until today, men have landed on the moon and returned.

Mental processes that create new concepts or abstractions from past experience are evident in our use of language. Words are created by people to represent new concepts. Adding prefixes and suffixes, for example, creates meanings beyond the previous uses of the symbols. The suffix *less* added to the words "help," "care," and "thought" creates totally different meanings for most of us. Words can also be combined to create new images. Take, for example, the three words, "never," "the," and "less." Put them together. You have "nevertheless," a word that is totally different from the individual referents of the three.

Creative uses of language can combine denotative and connotative meanings with startling effects. Imaginative uses of words often create powerful images beyond their literal referents. Note the following image from T. S. Eliot's "Love Song of J. Alfred Prufrock":[4]

> *The yellow fog that rubs its back upon the window-panes,*
> *The yellow smoke that rubs its muzzle on the window-panes*
> *Licked its tongue into the corners of the evening,*
> . . . .
>
> *Slipped by the terrace, made a sudden leap,*
> *And seeing that it was a soft October night,*
> *Curled once about the house, and fell asleep.*

---

[4]From *Collected Poems 1909–1962* (New York: Harcourt Brace Jovanovich, Inc., 1963).

This image is forceful and meaningful to anyone who has experienced a foggy night in a city. Creative thinking enables each of us to see experiences in new, often more interesting ways.

Try the following exercise. Create an explanation for the girls in the pictures on pages 56 and 59. Tell why they are in the yard and why they have the ball. As you do that, you're using the creative thinking processes. Compare your explanation with a group of your classmates. Note the wide variety of possible responses.

Exercise: Perception Box

Objective: To become aware of how interpretations differ and why.
Directions:
Your instructor will provide a box with a variety of small objects.

Each of you will have 30 seconds to observe the box, then 5 minutes to describe as completely as you can everything you saw in it.

Then, in groups of five, you will compare your lists and answer the following questions:

1. Were there any items all members of your group described exactly alike? Which ones? What communication principles explain the similarities?
2. Of the items listed by all of you, what differences were there in the ways they were described? What communication principles explain the differences?
3. What items were not remembered by members? What communication principles explain why some people didn't notice or remember these items?
4. What concepts were reflected in the different reports? Were varying levels of an abstraction ladder recorded?
5. Were any inferences recorded?

Exercise: What's in a Cup?

Objectives: To illustrate factors that create variability in stimulus processing. To compare symbols chosen to report sensations received. To illustrate types of inferences.
Directions:
1. The instructor will bring to class a cup nearly full of black steaming liquid and place it on a desk or stool in the center of the room.
2. You will be given 5 minutes to write all the perceptions you can become aware of, the symbols you can think of for it, and the inferences you can draw from it.
3. Your class will be divided into groups.

4. The groups will compare the perceptions listed and answer the following questions:
   a. Which differences were influenced by different experiences of observers?
   b. Which differences were influenced by different perspectives?
   c. Which differences were influenced by different expectations?
5. The groups will compare symbols chosen for the cup and/or its contents and compile lists of the ones that all seem to refer to the same concept. Later the groups will discuss how many different symbols in the entire class were used to refer to similar concepts.
6. Each group will attempt to create a ladder of abstraction using the symbols representing the cup and/or its contents. Later these will be compared to see how the abstraction ladders were alike or different.
7. A list will be compiled by each group of all the inferences each individual listed. Members should attempt to classify these as generalizations, deductions, comparisons, causal or imaginative inferences.
8. All the groups will share their results and discuss how the experience illustrates variability in stimulus processing.

The processes of stimulus processing were introduced in this chapter. Perception, symbolization, memory, and recall are used to assign meaning to sensations. Although all occur simultaneously and interact, affecting each other, looking at each process separately can help in our understanding of the total process. Perception, which is interpreting sensations received, is a learned process, and therefore infinitely variable. Perception is influenced by experience, the selectivity of attention and perceptual abilities, and the expectations, emotions, language, perspective, and socialization of the perceivers. Attention plays an important role in perception, especially in its selectivity. Attention is defined as a receiver adjustment, and the degree of adjustment can cause attention to be focal, marginal, or subliminal. Some stimuli are received at the subliminal level because it is not possible to perceive them individually at the rate they are received. Examples of this phenomenon are films and television.

Symbolization is the process of assigning meaning to symbols. Meaning is a reaction by a perceiver that the symbol stands for, or refers to, something else. Meanings can be classified as of two types: denotative and connotative. Denotative meaning is the referent thought of when the symbol is used; connotative meaning is the mix of feelings the user has toward the symbol. Although the connotative meaning comes partly from the feelings about and experiences with the referent, to a great extent it also comes from the feelings about and experiences with the symbol itself. Symbols are both verbal and nonverbal. Verbal symbols are words; nonverbal symbols are nonword symbols. Words become meaningful primarily by their function in language, a common code to those who understand the language. Language consists of words with widely agreed-upon denotations and rules of arrangement. The code of a language includes vocal and nonvocal cues that contribute to communicating far more with words than with the individual symbols.

All the mental processes depend on memory, which is the storage of information, and recall, which is the reconstruction of events based on the information input. Three types of memory exist, but long- and short-term memory are most important to communication. Both require perception, symbolization, and conceptualization. Concepts are condensations of past experience, categorizing experiences on the basis of similarities and differences. The ability to conceptualize involves focusing on certain features of objects or experiences to categorize them. Concept levels vary from descriptive statements appearing to report observations to high-level abstractions using very broad categories that refer to essences or qualities. Involved in conceptualization is evaluation, which is the formation of predictive categories called attitudes. Attitudes are defined as predispositions to respond to stimuli in particular ways. It's important to remember that attitudes are predispositions, not behavior. The behavior tendency—i.e., the predisposition—is largely dependent on the strength of the attitude, but the actual behavior in any situation will depend on the total setting as well as upon the predisposition. Recall is seldom total. It is largely a reconstruction process, influenced by time, intensity of reinforcement, and the relation of the information to prior categories in the interpretive and memory system.

Thinking is really an inferring process. It involves the further processing of sensations after their perception. Thinking involves several processes that draw relationships among concepts. Generalization categorizes and groups concepts together to create a broad predictive statement about the category. Other inferential processes include deduction, comparison and contrast, cause and effect, and creative imagination. Imagination is the process of adding to experience to create new concepts. Imagination is more than mental mirroring; it requires a reconstruction of experience.

Questions for Discussion

1. How do your experiences affect your perception?

2. What does the "selectivity" of perception suggest about communication?

3. What is symbolization?

4. What does it suggest to say "Meanings are in people, not symbols"?

5. What good does it do to realize the difference between denotative and connotative meanings?

6. "Lasting memories are interpretations." So what?

7. What does understanding the process of conceptualization contribute to understanding communication?

8. What does the "ladder of abstraction" tell you about communicating clearly?

9. What are attitudes and how do they affect your communication?

10. What is the role of inference in processing sensations received?

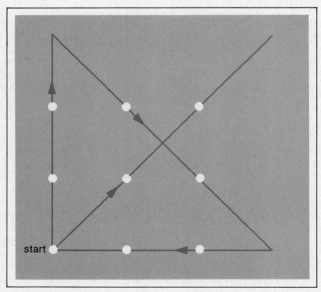

start

Solution to nine dots puzzle (p. 30).

Suggestions for Further Reading

BORAH, R. BRENT, AND SHEILA SHIVELY, *The Language Lens*. Englewood Cliffs, N.J.: Prentice-Hall, Inc., 1974.

BROWN, ROGER, *Words and Things, An Introduction to Language*. New York: The Free Press, 1958.

DEVITO, JOSEPH, *Language: Concepts and Processes*. Englewood Cliffs, N.J.: Prentice-Hall, Inc., 1976.

ESCHHOLZ, PAUL A., ALFRED F. ROSS, AND VIRGINIA P. CLARK, *Language Awareness*. New York: St. Martin's Press, 1974.

HAYAKAWA, S. I., *Language in Thought and Action* (3rd ed.). New York: Harcourt Brace Jovanovich, Inc., 1972.

LINDSAY, PETER H., AND DONALD A. NORMAN, *Human Information Processing*. New York: Academic Press, 1972.

MORTENSEN, C. DAVID, *Communication: The Study of Human Interaction*. New York: McGraw-Hill, Inc., 1972.

NEWMAN, EDWIN, *Strictly Speaking*. Indianapolis: The Bobbs-Merrill Co., Inc., 1974.

WHORF, BENJAMIN LEE, *Language, Thought and Reality*, ed. John B. Carroll. Cambridge: M.I.T. Press, 1956.

3

Pictures Out of Focus
problems in processing sensations

goal:

To learn how to avoid common causes of communication breakdowns.

probes:

The material in this chapter should help you to

1. Explain why it is important not to confuse words and things. pp. 58–70
2. Distinguish between the "intended" message and "unintended" messages in communication. pp. 71–72
3. List a statement of observation, a statement of inference, and a statement of judgment using a specific topic. pp. 68–76
4. Explain why "you cannot NOT communicate." pp. 77–78
5. Give an example showing how each of the seven categories of non-verbal symbols can communicate meanings. pp. 78–87
6. Explain how objects influence communication. pp. 83–86
7. Explain how knowing the functions of nonverbal symbols can help reduce ambiguity. pp. 87–90
8. Give an example illustrating an error using each of the following: pp. 91–93
   Hasty or unrepresentative generalization
   Faulty causal reasoning
   Inappropriate comparison
   Faulty deduction
   False alternatives

By this time in your life, thinking and communicating have become largely automatic for you. That's especially true of the basic processes you acquired in your first six or seven years. In most situations, you probably think and talk so easily that the several different processes involved seem automatic, and to talk about them at length may seem silly to you. But it is this very ease and familiarity that leads so often to communication difficulties.

When what you want to say is very important, and it's critical that you say it right, you probably find it more difficult to communicate. What are the right ideas to express? What are the best words to use to say them? What's the best way to say what I want to say? What am I really hearing? What is this person really trying to say to me? These are all familiar questions.

But also, haven't you been in ordinary communication situations when it all seemed so easy—then something happened, and suddenly you had communication problems? You misunderstood someone, or someone didn't get your point. Directions weren't followed. Someone's feelings got hurt. Something important wasn't done right, or wasn't done at all, because someone else didn't hear instructions the way they were intended. All these call up familiar scenes, right? Why? If it's all so easy, what goes wrong? Many things. The way people interpret sensations from the environment—the processing of stimuli—can lead just as easily to error as to accuracy. The processes of communicating can create communication barriers and breakdowns as well as satisfying exchanges with others. This chapter examines some of the causes of those barriers, some common errors in the processing of sensations.

Careless Interpretation of Verbal Symbols

Our use of language seems so effortless to most of us that we are led into some beliefs that upon examination turn out to be myths. We describe these as common confusions, and we will look at some of the most important ones now.

confusion of words and things

> What's in a name? That which we call a rose
> By any other name would smell as sweet;
>
> SHAKESPEARE

Our language often leads us to forget that our only contact with the world is through the sensory input we receive. We talk as if our *reactions* to the world outside us were the same as that world. We often fail to remember that a word is not its referent; that is, *a word is not the thing it represents.* Take a familiar example, your name. You can recognize without difficulty that you, the person reading this book, are not the name people use to represent you. If your name is lost in the registrar's office, the registrar will have to find it; but *you* have not been lost in the registrar's office. The relationship between you and your name is the same as the relationship between all words and the "things" they represent. Your name is a symbol used to represent you, but it is not you.

This confusion of words and things is particularly common in our language. Confusion is inherent in the use of the verb *to be.* The form *to be* equates the words with the reality. We often hear such sentences as, "My car is a compact," or "It is a luxury car," or "It is an import," as if the car and the words used to describe it were the same. You hear, "Mary is beautiful," or "Mary is dumb," or "Mary is a good cook," as if somehow the object Mary and the words referring to her were equal. You say, "It's hot today," or "It's stuffy in this room" as if your reactions to the air *were* the air.

These examples reflect a myth: that words have meanings. But *words don't have meanings, people do.* People associate meanings with words. The only connection between symbols and the concepts symbolized are the users. No necessary link between the word and what it refers to (its referent) exists. Ogden and Richards created a triangle of meaning to illustrate the relationship.[1] You may call an object a chair, while someone from France calls it a *chaise*. In Spain it would be referred to as *silla;* in Germany it's a *stuhl;* in Russia, a *стул*. In each case, no necessary or *real* connection exists between the words (the symbols) and the object. Only the users connect it. And the link is arbitrary, not necessary.

Confusion of words and things.

If you were to behave as if the word "chair" were the only possible way to describe the object, you'd be acting as if the word had meaning. That's really what happens when you act as if saying a word should make its referent clear to someone else. If someone accused you of cheating because you copied a friend's homework and you replied, "I didn't cheat. I didn't copy one thing on the test," you're acting as if words had meaning. What you did may fit the word "cheating" as some people use it, whether you call it

---

[1] C. K. Ogden and I. A. Richards, *The Meanings of Meanings: A Study of the Influences of Language Upon Thought and of the Science of Symbolism* (New York: Harcourt, Brace & World, Inc., 1923) was one of the pioneer publications in the study of semantics.

cheating or not. When we forget that meaning is in the user of the words, not in the words themselves, we're often guilty of the next common error, confusion of intended and perceived messages.

confusion of intended and perceived messages

> A common language is not a fail-safe system for understanding.
>
> ANONYMOUS

Commonly, people act as if the *intended* and *perceived messages* in communication should be the same. Often it's assumed that if a thought or feeling is expressed in reasonably clear language, it will be, or at least *should* be, understood. We describe this common assumption as the myth that ideas can be transmitted. But *ideas can't be transmitted.* In talking, you are a source of sensations that are received and interpreted by others. You send sounds, but you don't transmit the ideas themselves. You'll be understood only if a receiver associates meanings to sensations received similar to the ones you intended when you chose the symbols. Words and actions may be perfectly clear to one communicator, but too often it's forgotten that they are only symbols, and symbols don't mean the same thing to everyone who uses them. *Symbols must be received as sensations and require interpretation before they have meaning to anyone but their source.* Symbols are not the ideas themselves. It's decoding that determines whether or not the symbols communicate the messages intended. Most of us know that. We just keep for-

Confusion of intended and perceived messages. *Source:* © 1976, Archie Comic Publications, Inc.

getting it. When we talk as if receivers will always decode symbols as we intend, or when we act as if we decode exactly as others will, we're acting as if ideas can be transmitted.

Exercise: Intended and Perceived Meanings

Objective: To become aware that intended meanings may not be the same as perceived meanings.

Directions:

1. Ask four people to help you in a class project (not all at the same time).
2. Give them a piece of paper and ask them to follow your instructions to draw the design you see below. Give them any objects needed to draw the correct size — rulers, compass, etc.
3. Stand with your back to them as you give the instructions so that you can't see them as they draw. Give verbal instructions only. Answer no questions.
4. Collect the drawings and number them in the order they were made.
5. Compare the first drawings with the last. Were the last more accurate? Did your symbol choices become more precise?
6. How does this experience illustrate the differences between the intended and perceived messages?

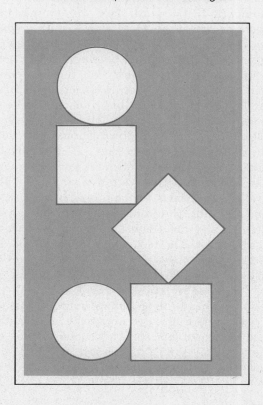

7. Did some receivers decode your intended messages more accurately than others? Why? Did you change or were they different?

confusion of facts and observations

> Language . . . though a useful and even indispensable tool, is a dangerous one, since it begins by suggesting a definiteness, discreteness, and quasi-permanence in objects which physics seems to show that they do not possess.
>
> BERTRAND RUSSELL

We believe a physical reality exists. It's there whether anyone receives sensations from it, talks about it, gives it a name or a meaning, or not. But when people see, hear, touch, smell, or taste things, they react to them and perhaps talk about them. Because those reactions use language, they are subject to the confusion of words and things. To try to avoid this confusion, we suggest that the term *"fact"* should be used only to refer to elements of physical reality, not to any statements. If the word "fact" refers only to observable, nonverbal objects or acts, then *facts exist separate from and irrespective of any sensations received from them or any statements made about them.* Distinguishing between facts and statements about them is important. It reminds you the *perceptions are not facts, but are interpretations of sensations received.* In other words, you can be sure a reality is there, but you cannot be sure exactly what it is. Perceptions are at best only guides to physical facts.

If you distinguish facts from observations, you won't be guilty of the common phrasing, "It's a fact that . . ." For instance, in referring to an acquaintance who has red hair, your language would reflect a confusion of fact and observation if you said, "It's a fact that John's hair is red." Many facts about John's hair exist, among them its existence and its color. But your statement was not a fact. It was a symbolic reference to John's hair and its color; it was a statement of observation, not a fact. The fact is the reality; your description of it is a statement of observation.

Distinguishing between facts and observations reminds you that *any use of language requires abstraction.* Recall from the discussion of symbolization in the last chapter: any statement about an object reports only certain features about the reality. Whatever you choose to say about an object, you have chosen *not* to say something else. When you say John's hair is red, you have chosen not to

Facts	Observations
1. Exist or happen in physical world	1. Are statements describing facts but are not themselves facts
2. Can be verified by one or more senses	2. Are limited to what can actually be observed

report that it may be long, curly, coarse, neatly combed, or many other things. Thus, all statements of observation are partly inaccurate, because all are incomplete.

A suggestion to use to remember this important feature of language is to think "etc." after statements of observation. The "etc." will remind you that because a fact is not the same as the statements about it, the statements can never report all there is to say about the fact. It may also remind you that some statements of observation are totally inaccurate.

confusion of observations and inferences

People not only regularly confuse facts and observations, they often can't distinguish inferences from observations. Verbal responses to facts can be classified into several kinds of categories, but for now, let's note three. These categories are *observation, inference,* and *judgment. A statement of observation uses symbols to try to describe the physical reality of an object or event.* A statement of inference goes beyond directly observed physical reality. It may relate the present to the future, or state relationships among elements of the physical reality. *Statements of inference connect the known or observed to that which has not been or cannot be observed.* They require thought beyond simple association of symbol and referent.

A statement of judgment also goes beyond reporting observations of physical reality. Judgments relate the reaction of the observer to objects or events. Judgments, like inferences, reflect a mental leap asserting what has not or cannot be observed. Indeed, *judgments are really just a type of inference that involves assessment of value,* of right or wrong, good or bad. One distinguishing characteristic of judgment statements is that they tell more about their source than about the item referred to.

Let's review examples of different kinds of statements, using the fact of John's hair. Statements of observation about it might include: it is red; it is parted in the middle; it is cut to an even length touching John's shoulder; it is straight. Some inferences are: unless

Facts	Observations	Inferences	Judgments (A Type of Inference)
1. Exist or happen in physical world 2. Can be verified by one or more senses	1. Are statements describing facts, but are not themselves facts 2. Are limited to what can actually be observed	1. Are statements that go beyond describing facts 2. Are not limited to observation; usually involve interpretation of something observed; involve mental processes beyond perception, symbolization, and memory 3. Often use abstract language 4. Cannot be verified by one or more senses; are tested by the consistency with which others draw similar conclusions from same data	1. Same as all inferences 2. Same as all inferences 3. Same as all inferences 4. Cannot be verified; result from personal value system 5. Attach value to things referred to 6. Tell more about the source than about the apparent referent

cut soon, it will be longer than his wife's hair; if he doesn't use a hair tie of some type, it will get in his eyes when he plays golf; its length might make it difficult for him to get some jobs. Judgments: his hair is too long; it's foolish for a grown man to wear his hair that way; it's a beautiful shade of red; it would look better on his wife; it gives him the look of Samson.

The distinctions among these three kinds of responses to facts are important. A common experience illustrates one of the simplest reasons why. Note the drawing below.

In this situation, Car A is proceeding up the street with the right of way and with a right-turn signal blinking. Car B is sitting at the stop sign, its driver wanting to make a left turn. The driver of Car B *observes* the right-turn signal of Car A and *infers* that it's going to turn right at the intersection. Acting upon this inference, Car B's driver pulls into the path of Car A, whose driver had been intending to turn into a driveway 100 feet past the intersection.[2]

---

[2] This example is found in William Haney, *Communication and Organizational Behavior* (Homewood, Ill.: Richard D. Irwin, Inc., 1967), p. 193.

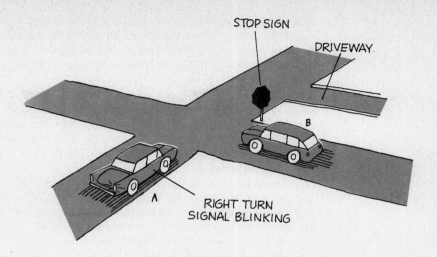

STOP SIGN

DRIVEWAY.

B

A   RIGHT TURN
SIGNAL BLINKING

To say the least, confusion of inference and observation in this case was costly. Other cases have resulted in more serious consequences when they occurred on freeways at high speeds. Avoiding confusion of inferences and observations can greatly reduce the ambiguity of communication.

Exercise: Inference-Observation Confusion

Objective: To practice distinguishing observations from inferences.
Directions:
1. Individually, complete the test following Story A, following directions carefully.
2. In groups, agree on the correct answer for each item. Discuss each item thoroughly to be sure you have no inferences labelled as observations.
3. When you are given the correct answers, note the reasons that you missed any items. Then complete the test that follows Story B.
4. Again, your group should discuss the items to agree on the correct answers, then you will be given the correct answers.
5. When both tests have been corrected, discuss the following:
   a. What unstated inferences led to incorrect answers?
   b. Why should inferences be distinguished from observations?

Directions for taking tests:
Assume that all information presented in the story is accurate. Mark statements either T, F, or ?. T means that the statement is definitely

true *on the basis of the information in the story.* F means that it is definitely false. ? means that not enough information is in the story to know whether the statement is true or false. If any part of a statement is doubtful, mark it ?. Answers appear on p. 95.

Story A

John and Betty Smith are awakened in the middle of the night by a noise coming from the direction of their living room. John investigates and finds that the door opening into the garden, which he thought he had locked before going to bed, is standing wide open. Books and papers are scattered all over the floor.

Statements about Story A:

1. Mrs. Smith was awakened in the middle of the night.   T   F   ?
2. John locked the door into the garden before going to bed.   T   F   ?
3. The books and papers were scattered between the time Mr. Smith went to bed and the time he awakened.   T   F   ?
4. John found the door to the garden was shut.   T   F   ?
5. Mr. Smith was not awakened by a noise.   T   F   ?
6. Mr. Smith did not lock the door to the garden.   T   F   ?
7. Nothing was missing from the room.   T   F   ?
8. Mrs. Smith was sleeping when she was awakened.   T   F   ?
9. The noise did not come from their garden.   T   F   ?
10. Smith saw no burglar in the living room.   T   F   ?

Story B

A businessman had just turned off the lights in the store when a man appeared and demanded money. The owner opened a cash register. The contents of the cash register were scooped up, and the man sped away. A member of the police force was notified promptly.

Statements about Story B:

1. A man appeared after the owner had turned off the store lights.   T   F   ?
2. The robber was a man.   T   F   ?
3. The man did not demand money.   T   F   ?
4. The man who opened the cash register was the owner.   T   F   ?
5. The store owner scooped up the contents of the register and ran away.   T   F   ?
6. Someone opened a cash register.   T   F   ?
7. After the man who demanded the money scooped up the contents of the cash register, he ran away.   T   F   ?
8. While the cash register contained money, the story does not state how much.   T   F   ?
9. The robber demanded money of the owner.   T   F   ?
10. The story concerns a series of events in which only three persons are referred to: the owner of the store, a man who demanded money, and a member of the police.   T   F   ?
11. The following events were included in the story: someone demanded money, a cash register was opened, its contents were scooped up, and a man dashed out of the store.   T   F   ?

NONVERBAL SYMBOLS

Careless or Unconscious Interpretation of Nonverbal Symbols

> Don't *say* things. What you *are* stands over you the while, and thunders so that I cannot hear what you say to the contrary.
>
> RALPH WALDO EMERSON

The errors of stimulus processing we discussed above relate to verbal behavior. Yet many of the problems in communication relate to nonverbal behavior. People are seldom consciously aware they receive, interpret, infer, and judge based on nonverbal symbols, but they do. You've heard, "A picture is worth a thousand words." In communicating, that's often true. Estimates vary, but a conservative conclusion is that 60 to 80 percent of the meaning in a speech communication situation is derived from nonverbal symbols.

Andy's right, of course. You don't have to say a word to communicate, nor does anyone have to say anything to you. You receive messages constantly from your nonverbal environment. And even if you prefer not to communicate with others, you cannot help it unless the fact of your existence is an irrelevant stimulus. *You cannot NOT communicate.* Silence, postures, facial expressions, even a person's absence, communicate. Suppose during a quarrel at your family dinner table over the use of the family car, you sit quietly

Source: © 1971 Daily Mirror Newspapers Ltd. ANDY CAPP, distributed by Field Newspaper Syndicate.

77

and say nothing. Your silence communicates, whether you frown, keep a straight face, smile, or get up and leave.

You can reduce possible mistakes in communicating nonverbal messages. Two important ways are (1) to know how to *encode* and *decode* nonverbal symbols and (2) to be aware of the *functions* of nonverbal symbols. We will discuss both of these now.

codes of nonverbal symbols

In this country, nonverbal communication is the primary means of communicating feelings. Most people in the U.S. find it difficult to talk about their feelings, so what we infer about how others feel is largely from nonverbal symbols.

Often nonverbal signals aren't decoded as their source intends; that's one reason they cause error. Interpreting nonverbal symbols should be done with great caution, but it usually isn't. Too much of it occurs without awareness. People constantly infer meanings from nonverbals, receiving and decoding nonverbal messages. But the messages are highly ambiguous. Because many nonverbal messages are received at the level of marginal, or even subliminal attention, they usually aren't consciously interpreted. People gain countless "impressions" nonverbally without even being aware of having received the messages. We hope as you read this book you become aware of the nonverbal symbols in your communication.[3]

Along with your increased awareness, however, we want you to beware. Recent efforts by researchers have increased knowledge of nonverbal "codes," but they remain far more ambiguous than verbal. Thus, in interpreting nonverbal symbols, you need to be wary of their ambiguity. Draw inferences from nonverbals with care, and be sure you distinguish observations from inferences.

Voice. Remember that 20 to 40 percent of the meaning in speech communication is derived from the language. Join your words with voice, however, and you will add about 20 percent more meaning. *Voice,* with its variable quality, rhythm, articulation, pitch, volume, rate, hesitations, and inflections, adds meaning to speech communication. Take the word "no" for instance. It has a clear meaning to you, right? Now say "no" and let your voice rise in pitch on the "o" sound. You made a question mark, no? Now say "no" emphatically. Raise the volume of your voice. Then raise the pitch. You have expressed three different kinds of exclamation points, haven't you? Now say "no" fast. Then say it with a long "o," such as "nooo." Then try "uh—no." Each different sound carried a different mean-

---

[3] Nonverbal messages could be classified many ways. No single category system is perfect. As with any category system, the purpose is to understand the phenomena being dealt with. We generally follow the classification system used by Mark Knapp in *Nonverbal Communication in Human Interaction* (New York: Holt, Rinehart and Winston, Inc., 1972).

ing without changing the language you used, didn't it? These are simple illustrations of how voice can add meaning to the verbal symbols in speech communication. You can think of many others.

Actions. Add another dimension. Imagine this face saying "no."

Then think of this one saying "no."

And this one:

And this:

These facial expressions demonstrate the category of nonverbal communication described as *action* or *kinesic* behavior.

Damn with faint praise, assent with civil leer,
And without sneering, teach the rest to sneer.

ALEXANDER POPE

Who can refute a sneer?

WILLIAM PALEY

Among the most important of kinesic behaviors are those associated with the face and eyes. But many others also affect communication. A conversation in which Mike said to Tony, "You will be sure to get that done, OK?" with a smile and a handshake would differ radically in meaning from one in which Mike pronounced the same words with a steady glare and a gesture toward the door. That case would, in turn, differ from Mike saying, "You will be sure to get that done, OK?" with a clenched jaw and a fist shaking in front of Tony's nose.

Facial expressions, including eye behavior, are probably the primary communicators of feelings. Facial expressions reflecting extreme emotions appear to be assigned quite similar meanings across all cultures. Similar recognitions of emotions have been secured across the world in response to pictures of faces with a smile or frown. Although attempts to prove that nonverbal behaviors are cross-cultural have not succeeded, the study of facial expressions does indicate some universal understanding of emotional messages.[4]

There's no art
To find the mind's construction in the face.

SHAKESPEARE

Actions can be classified in two categories: *overt* and readily observable, *covert* and less immediately obvious. Examples of overt behavior are numerous and familiar: shaking a fist, waving, pacing the floor, touching, holding up and using objects, pounding a table, gestures. The second group, being covert, are less observable, but sometimes convey more meaning. Because covert behaviors are not very easily controlled by their source, they send very honest messages. Muscle tension that reflects nervousness or anxiety is covert kinesic behavior. Similarly, a blush and shaking hands that reveal controlled

---

[4] Paul Ekman and Wallace Friesen, "Constants Across Cultures in the Face and Emotion," *Journal of Personality and Social Psychology*, Vol. XVII (1971), 124–29.

"Wipe that opinion off your face."

Source: George Dole. Reprinted courtesy *Parade* magazine, June 30, 1974.

anger or fear, or muscle tension due to impatience, are also covert actions.

Touch.   We give a special categorization to actions that are *touching* behaviors because they also involve personal space. Touching symbolizes many different things to people, but is almost always a very important source of nonverbal messages. Much evidence exists to show that infants require extensive touching experience to develop normally. Although the implication of this evidence is that touching continues to be an important aspect of communication throughout life, the subject has not been researched except in a few highly focused situations such as the sex research by Masters and Johnson.

Source: Freddy by Rupe, courtesy of Field Newspaper Syndicate.

Touching is a highly ambiguous communication symbol. A friendly pat, a playful push, or a punch can all be interpretations of the same behavior. The meanings of touching behaviors are strongly influenced by interpersonal relations and by culture. North American males, for instance, rarely embrace or touch one another. Shaking hands or vigorous shoulder patting is "permissible," but other kinds of touching communicate socially disapproved meanings. Notable exceptions exist, as when players during a football game frequently pat each other on the rear. Other sports competition and related locker-room behavior provides examples of male touching behavior that would be strongly disapproved in different settings. In contrast, an Italian wedding reception will present a startling experience to an unsuspecting non-Italian male. He will probably be hugged by more men than since he was a 6-year old at a family reunion. We cite these two contrasting examples to illustrate that the approved touching behaviors vary widely from age to age, social situation to social situation, and culture to culture. To be unaware of the group "rules" with respect to touching behavior is to fail to receive much information from nonverbal communication.

The use of touch frequently underscores family relationships. For example, in many families the embrace and kiss is very common, especially in the relationships between parents and children. This use of touch is probably an extension of the touching behaviors that were used during the years of infancy of the children. Whether this use of touch contributes to improved family relationships is a matter of speculation, although we believe touching behaviors create a helpful background for other nonverbal and verbal

Touching behavior.
Source: St. Louis Post-Dispatch. The Pulitizer Publishing Co.

communication. On the other hand, any activity repeated so often that it becomes a ritual can lose its meaning and become a negative influence in communication.

Touching behavior is similar in one important way to most other aspects of communication. No hard and fast rules can be set forth. Touching behavior is as much a matter of individual style as of culture and situation. Some people might find it quite natural to use a variety of touching behaviors, and for them touching communicates very effectively. However, they are still guided by situation and culture. Other people may attempt the same touching behaviors, but not find them natural or effective. They don't fit everyone's individual style. Within the limits of common sense and respect for others, you might experiment with touching behaviors. You may find they will contribute positively to your effectiveness as a communicator.

Personal Space. Related to action is the nonverbal communication of proxemics, or the use of *personal space.* Proxemics deals with the distance relationships among people as they communicate. It involves how close or far apart you stand or sit when talking with others and the other uses you make of space. Notice the behavior of people riding in elevators: they divide the space as much and as long as possible. That's the result of efforts to preserve distance from others in settings in which environment makes it difficult.

Anthropologist Edward Hall has studied personal distances and voice volumes that seem appropriate for people in the U.S., when they talk with each other.[5] Here is his guide to the various uses of personal space.

(intimate)	1. Very close (3–6″)	Soft whisper; top secret
	2. Close (8–12″)	Audible whisper; very confidential
(personal)	3. Near (12–20″)	Indoors, soft voice; outdoors, full voice, confidential
	4. Neutral (20–36″)	Soft voice, low volume, personal subject matter
(casual)	5. Neutral (4½–5′)	Full voice; information of nonpersonal matter
	6. Public distance (5½–8′)	Full voice with slight overloudness; public information for others to hear
(public)	7. Across the room (8–20′)	Loud voice; talking to a group
	8. Stretching the limits of distance	20–24′ indoors, up to 100 ft. outdoors; hailing distance, departures

[5] Edward Hall, *The Silent Language* (Greenwich, Conn.: Fawcett, Inc., 1959) pp. 184–85.

To illustrate personal space as communication, ask a question after one of your classes today while you are standing closer to the instructor than you normally would. Observe the reaction. We don't recommend trying this on your boss, because it's considered intrusion, and the "right" to do so is usually reserved for persons of higher status. Moreover, you should explain immediately afterward to your instructor that you were doing this for a class experiment. Intrusions of this kind usually create negative reactions.

Try this with some friends: engage in conversation standing at what feels to you a normal distance apart (2 to 5 feet). Then move in as close as you can before one backs away. Next, walk two or three feet further away and try to continue the conversation. Does that seem inappropriate for personal conversation? Talk with your friends about how they felt in the different spatial relationships. You might then try the same things with your parents. You'll find it interesting to compare the reactions of different people.

Comfortable personal distances vary greatly from person to person and situation to situation. How physically close we allow others to come to us depends on our relationships with them, our socialization, and our relationships with any others who may be around.

Proxemics also involves seating arrangements and other kinds of relationships among people in groups. How you seat guests at a party or a meeting or at dinner are matters of personal space and can create serious problems. Also involved is the concept of territoriality. Territoriality is shown, for instance, when you sit in the same chair in class every day, or when you park in the same slot in the parking lot, or ask the waiter for "your" table in a restaurant. If you think territoriality is not important, try this: go to a class early today and sit in "somebody else's" chair. Observe the reactions when the person enters. You could also observe this phenomenon by parking in the boss's parking spot today, but we don't recommend it. Territoriality also extends to personal objects such as belongings, assigned rooms, or lockers.

> We shape our buildings and afterward our buildings shape us.
>
> WINSTON CHURCHILL

Objects. Related to proxemics is a major category of nonverbal symbols: objects and their use. This group of symbols includes things such as decorations, furniture, clothes, jewelry, cars, houses, use of color, and so forth. Communicating through objects can be divided into two categories: *environmental and situational objects,* and *objects related to personal behavior and appearance.* Two identical chairs arranged thus:

will reflect and/or cause different relationships among those seated than would this arrangement:

In an office with desk and chairs arranged so the desk is between the chairs, you can conclude the desk "owner" establishes different personal distances from those who come in than the person who arranges the furniture differently. People can usually place the furniture in their homes and offices where they want, so it is meaningful to draw conclusions about people from the way they arrange furniture. Remember as you do, however, that often people can't affect the furniture arrangement. People are often uncomfortable in their offices and never know for sure why; occasionally it's a result of furniture having been arranged by a previous office occupant and never changed, or a result of immovable objects. On the other hand, furniture arrangement is often one of the nonverbal cues that contradicts the verbal.

Other elements about objects are often significant. An extra-long overstuffed couch covered with real fur communicates messages about its owner that differ from the messages "sent" by a Danish modern sofa with vinyl cushions. The messages communicated by driving a Mercedes 450SL and by driving a beat-up Volkswagen would be very different. Wear patched blue jeans and a tie-dyed tee-shirt and you will send different messages from that conveyed if you wear a neat brown suit, shiny shoes, and carry a briefcase.

How a person dresses, the objects worn or around the person, the efforts made by the person to transform an environment, all communicate countless messages about that person. Objects and their use are a valuable source of information in any communication situation.

Physical Characteristics.   Physical characteristics are body communicators that do not involve movement, such as physique, body odors, arrangement and/or length of hair, skin color, etc. These various physical characteristics are often assigned inappropriate meanings because just as with words, we forget that people cannot be equated with their physical characteristics. Physical appearances are partial indicators of personality or mood, but do not equal them. Moreover, we frequently stereotype by physical characteristics and then behave as if our inferences were observations. This frequently results, due to selective perception, in the stereotype "coming true."

Physical characteristics that are *stable* are appearances that are not readily changeable. Body type is a good illustration of a stable appearance that is assigned meaning by others. When we meet a man with an athletic build, we may be surprised if we find he doesn't like sports. One of us was recently hustled into thinking we had an easy tennis game when challenged by an overweight man with long grey hair and professional eyeglasses. This turned out to be a mistaken assumption, however, for we were badly beaten.

People not only expect certain behaviors from persons because of their body types, but they also expect personality characteristics. Of the three major body types (athletic, frail, and obese) you can easily report who in North American society would be expected to be aggressive, jolly, serious, nervous, intelligent, lazy, slow, etc. An attractive, well-built female is expected by some people to be sexy and not very bright—surprise is expressed if she speaks intelligently. Gloria Steinem receives this kind of reaction constantly. Moreover, this expectation influences some perceptions so strongly that many intelligent, educated, and attractive women report that in committees they are not listened to, while the same ideas expressed by men will be received positively.

People with particular body types often work long and hard to change their appearance to avoid these interpretations. Thousands diet constantly to avoid certain appearances and achieve others. Note the fortunes made by hucksters who promise to create a Charles Atlas from a skinny man or a Raquel Welch from a flatchested female.

The second type of physical characteristic is more *unstable* and easier to change. A man with long hair can choose to ignore that many people consider him a hippy or a dropout. But if he wants a job that requires it, he can change the length of his hair. Facial hair, color of hair, and facial appearance are all nonstable aspects of physical characteristics. That these characteristics are often adjusted in order to communicate is attested to by the several billion dollars spent every year in this country on cosmetics, in beauty salons and barber shops, and on plastic surgery.

> He had occasional flashes of silence, that made his conversation perfectly delightful.
>
> SIDNEY SMITH

Time. Time as a code in communication deserves special notice. Rate of speaking is an obvious example of meaning conveyed by time. But time is also involved when someone pauses before replying to a question, or when someone interrupts another speaker. How long it takes to reply to questions, comments, a letter, tells you a great deal about the answer. Time is concerned both with sounds and silences, and with combinations of both. Time may even be the element that makes rhythm, both of voice and of music, such a potent communicator.

Time is also an element in communicating relationships. How important it is to be "on time" for an appointment, for instance, depends on who the appointment is with, who made the appointment, whom you are, and the culture. The total success of an interview could be jeopardized by appearing fifteen minutes late, while an arrival of five or ten minutes before the appointed time could help create a supportive atmosphere. Time in the sense of the time of day is also a factor. Some communication events are better suited to the evening than to the morning, and vice versa. Most people can readily understand how time could influence a meeting scheduled shortly before dinner. An able communicator will be aware of the influence of time on communication, and will attempt to use it to his or her advantage. When time options are available, the most appropriate time should be chosen for events. Use of time is probably the most culturally bound of all nonverbal codes. You'll improve your own communication if you learn how the group or society you live in uses time.

functions of nonverbal symbols

Nonverbal symbols in speech communication serve various functions, and knowing these functions can help us reduce ambiguity in communication. Nonverbals can repeat, contradict, substitute for, complement, emphasize, or regulate verbal behaviors.

Repetition. If you were to say, "I see three reasons why we should take that contract," and hold up three fingers or write I, II, III on a chalkboard, you'd be *repeating* the verbal statement with nonverbal symbols to make your message clearer. Much action or use of objects, charts, and other visuals involves repetition to achieve clarity and recall of ideas.

Contradiction.   Contradictory nonverbal symbols can be illustrated by the following case: If a friend of yours says, "Oh, no, I'm in no hurry," but sits tensely on the edge of her chair, drumming her fingers while you finish getting ready, you won't believe the verbal message. You may not be sure whether the nonverbal symbols are intended to convey anger, irritation, or impatience, but you will be sure that the verbal symbols aren't accurate. Almost always, when verbal and nonverbal symbols contradict, the nonverbal will be believed. The old song, "Her lips tell me no, no, but there's yes, yes in her eyes" illustrates this contradictory nature of some nonverbal symbols. Contradictory messages are often intended by their source to be recognized. They can be used to employ sarcasm or irony. When you are told of the exploits of a friend and exclaim, "Oh, isn't that great!" with a tone of voice and facial expression that reflect enthusiasm and delight, you're nonverbally repeating or emphasizing the verbal message. But if the story you react to is that of a colleague of yours who has just botched up a job you spent all morning working on, you could say the same words with a voice and face reflecting anger, irritation, and disgust. The verbal and nonverbal messages would then be contradictory and you'd intend for the listeners to believe the nonverbal.

Substitution.   Often words seem inappropriate. In moments of extreme emotion, we may feel a need to substitute nonverbals for words. Grief or passionate disappointment are difficult to express with words. So we often employ touching behaviors or do something rather than using words. Lovers greeting after a long absence will fall into each other's arms and hug and kiss. You'll put your arms around the shoulder of a friend who has just lost a beloved relative. A lover, trying to say "I'm sorry" after a quarrel or thoughtless act, may send a dozen roses instead of calling or writing.

Complementing and Emphasis.   Most often, the nonverbal messages complement the verbal. Usually the dozen roses are accompanied by a card from the contrite lover. To a grieving friend we display sympathetic behavior and verbally express our shared sorrow. The lovers' hugs and kisses come at the same time as words that say, "I'm so glad to see you."

Nonverbal behaviors and other nonverbal symbols are complementary in that we use them to interpret the total message—the person sending it, the mood, the person's attitude, the total situation. Nonverbals tell us much about the words being sent and the person sending. If an instructor lectures a class in faded cutoffs and open sandals, sits on the desk and smokes right in front of a red "no smoking" sign on the wall, students probably won't use all those nonverbals to interpret the lecture. But they will draw conclusions about the instructor as a person and about his or her attitude toward the instructor role. The speaker's appearance, animation and gesture, use of pauses, and tone of voice all help you interpret not only the professor as a person and her or his attitude toward the subject but also the verbal messages. Some of these nonverbals complement in the sense of adding clarity to the words, and others complement in the sense of adding information about the message source. Both help you understand the total situation.

Sometimes nonverbals don't just complement, but emphasize as well. If you are angry and your face flushes, your voice quavers, and you shake your fists and pound the table, the nonverbals both complement and emphasize the verbal message. The listeners learn from the nonverbals not only that you are angry, but also *how* angry you are.

> I like a look of agony,
> Because I know it's true;
> Men do not sham convulsion,
> Nor simulate a throe.
>
> EMILY DICKINSON

Many nonverbals that complement and emphasize at the same time are described as *emblems*. Emblems are widely accepted symbols. The huge pictures of the donkey and elephant and the red, white, and blue flags that drape the halls at political conventions are all emblems. Other examples are clenched fists raised high while audiences sing the Black National Anthem or "I am Woman," the V sign with two fingers, the soul handshake, hardhats, the cross behind the altar in churches, the rings worn by married couples. When used in connection with verbal messages, emblems often serve both to complement and emphasize messages.

Regulation. Regulative nonverbals function most often as feedback. If a child pouts as a parent says, "No, you may not have any more cookies," the child is trying to get more cookies. Parents can recognize the message as an attempt to regulate their behavior, even though they may not respond as the child wants. If you're bored listening to a lecture, your face and posture may show it. This response should regulate the behavior of an instructor to somehow get you interested, though it often doesn't. Leaning back in your chair with crossed arms can communicate that you aren't interested in or open to the ideas you're hearing. A responsive speaker will react to this feedback, thus nonverbal messages regulate the speaker's behavior.

Explaining to a date why you are very late, you will need to watch the nonverbals to determine when or if you achieve the purpose of allaying anger. The nonverbal signs can tell you through the rest of the evening if you can, in fact, forget the bad start or if you must continue to accommodate for it. Nonverbals communicate feedback that regulates others' behaviors.

In later chapters of this book, much attention will be given to the use of nonverbal symbols to improve your communication in interpersonal and public communication situations. Now we turn to some of the common thinking errors that can cause communication breakdowns.

Exercise: Communicating Emotions

Objectives: To practice assigning meanings to nonverbal symbols.
Directions:
1. In groups of two you will attempt to communicate the meanings you assign to the words in the lists below.
2. First, Partner A will choose a word at random from the A list, and try to communicate the meaning to Partner B, using facial expressions only. If Partner B cannot successfully identify the emotion A intends to communicate, Partner A may then use any additional *nonverbal* messages (gestures, touching, objects, space, voice without words, etc.)
3. Partner B will next choose a word from the B list, and try to communicate its meaning to Partner A, using facial expressions only. Again, if facial expressions alone will not communicate the intended message, any additional nonverbals may be used.
4. Partners should rotate, choosing at random until they have completed the two lists.
5. Upon completing the lists, the partners should discuss and prepare an analysis of how meanings can be communicated through nonverbal messages and which ones are easiest for a receiver to understand as intended.

List A	*List B*
Anger	Resentment
Contentment	Disappointment
Sorrow	Happiness
Surprise	Grief
Impatience	Joy
Anxiety	Fear
Admiration	Love
Hate	Respect

As we noted in the last chapter, once you receive and interpret sensations, you usually think about the idea or feeling they evoked. These inferring (thinking) processes are subject to error as much as are the interpretations of verbal and nonverbal symbols. Let's examine some of the commonly found errors of inference.

hasty or unrepresentative generalization

You'll recall that generalizing is drawing a general conclusion based on several cases. One of the most common errors of reasoning is generalizing on the basis of too few or not representative cases. Some generalizations require only a few cases to support the inferences. To conclude that all green apples are sour because you tasted two or three that were sour is appropriate because the cases are unvarying and repeatable. Another way to describe this is to say that the elements generalized about are quite similar and do not have variable properties. If the cases are more variable, more are required to generalize. And often, even with many cases, the generalization will need to be qualified in some way. If you encountered three red-haired people with hot tempers, you might generalize that red-haired people are hot-tempered. This is an example of hasty generalization. Three cases aren't enough to draw inferences of similarity when you're talking about something as variable as people. You might qualify the generalization and conclude that *many* red-haired people are hot-tempered, but even then, using only three cases makes your conclusion weak.

Equally dangerous is generalization on the basis of unrepresentative evidence. The classic example of this was the big win predicted by the polls for Landon in 1936. The polls were taken by telephone. And thousands were called, so the generalization wasn't hasty. But in 1936, only high-income people had telephones, so the cases weren't representative of the entire population. Often we generalize about people on the basis of those around us, since most of us have limited social contacts. Thus, it is awfully easy to be guilty of unrepresentative generalizations.

faulty causal reasoning

Cause-effect reasoning infers that because of B, A happened. Errors in causal thinking are common because often items are related but not causally. Just because one event precedes another, it doesn't always cause the other. There is often a "calm" before a thunderstorm, for instance, but the calm doesn't cause the storm. It takes more to establish causal link than knowing that one event precedes another—but often we simply don't bother to look for more evidence.

Commonly, people confuse *correlation* with causation. Correlation shows a relation between two elements. A high correlation reports that when one event occurs another is also likely to occur. In the U.S., autumn and football games are correlated. But often correlated events lead people to conclude that one causes the other. And autumn certainly doesn't cause football! Just because one event regularly happens before another does not mean it causes the other. Today it is common to hear that using marijuana causes use of hard drugs, because most heroin addicts first smoked grass. As it is stated, however, this is a correlation, not causation. All heroin users probably also drank milk before they became addicts. We usually don't notice that correlation, and so you never hear anyone say that drinking milk causes heroin addiction.

To establish causation, another link in reasoning besides correlation needs to be established. Perhaps a common element causes people to use both marijuana and heroin. To establish logically that marijuana use causes heroin use would require evidence that *all* grass smokers become heroin users, or that no one who had *not* used marijuana ever became a heroin addict.

Causation is not nearly as simple as most of us believe. For one thing to *cause* another, two conditions have to be true. One is that the cause never occurs without the effect following it and the other is that the effect never occurs without a cause. Cigarettes alone, for instance, don't cause lung cancer. Many people smoke and don't get cancer. Moreover, some people who get cancer never smoked. For smoking cigarettes to be *the* cause of cancer, people who never smoked must never get lung cancer.

To be clear about causation, you need to distinguish between *necessary* and *sufficient causes*. Some elements like viruses that lead to colds are necessary causes. This means that you won't get a cold without the virus. A necessary cause is one that must be present or the effect will not occur. But often, necessary cause won't result in the effect. For instance, a virus isn't a total explanation for colds. Virus isn't a *sufficient* cause. Often a virus is present and a cold doesn't occur. Other conditions must be present before you'll get the cold. Sufficient cause will include any necessary factors and whatever additional factors must be present for the effect to occur.

inappropriate comparison and contrast

The common errors in using comparison and contrast involve comparing items that really aren't comparable. When you assume that two items are similar in all respects just because they're similar in some respects, you are making a common mistake. Here's an example: "British police don't carry guns and the rate of violent crimes is very low in England. Therefore, why do police in the United States need guns?" This assumes that British and U.S. populations are enough alike that they could be treated similarly.

We are all guilty of this kind of thinking when we assume that people should feel or behave as *we* do. We think, "It works for me—it should work for you." This isn't true of course, but we commonly behave as if it were. A valid comparison is based on items that are actually similar in the important aspects.

faulty deduction

In deduction we apply generalizations to a specific case. But when a case doesn't fit into the general category, or when the generalization is qualified, and we assume that it applies to the specific case, we are making an error. For example: Most students want to improve themselves. Because Jan is a student, he/she wants to improve. But Jan may not be in the "most students" category, so the conclusion may not apply to her/him. Since the generalization is qualified by "most," not enough information is available to apply it. After all, Jan may be in the "most students" category.

Probably, though, the most common error of deduction is starting with a faulty general conclusion. Suppose you reasoned as follows: Young people (under 21) are irresponsible; since Jan is under 20, she/he is irresponsible. The *deduction* is logically flawless, but the reasoning is in error because the general conclusion is false. Stereotyping is based on generalizations that are partly or completely inaccurate. Since stereotyping is very common, errors in deduction are quite common.

false alternatives

One common fallacy is "either-or," or *false alternatives thinking*. Often, people argue, "We must either do this or . . ." and they predict a dire outcome. Given a truly contradictory situation, a conclusion of either this or that is valid. It's either 8:00 A.M. or it's not. It's either 70 degrees Fahrenheit or it's not. The error occurs when this kind of thinking is applied to situations in which the alternatives are not truly contradictory. For example, you've probably heard, "He's either honest, or he's not." "It has to be done this way or not at all." "You're either for me or against me." "Either behave this way or you'll regret it." You could supply other common examples. In these situations, the concepts are not truly contradictory. Many different alternatives exist. Either-or thinking is invalid reasoning in most cases because most situations offer more than two possible alternatives.

Some common errors of interpretation lead often to communication break-downs. The first group has to do with careless use of *verbal* symbols. This involves: (1) confusion of words with things (when a communicator behaves as if the word or symbol were the actual reality); (2) confusion of intended with perceived messages (when a communicator forgets that each in-dividual's perceptual system varies, that meanings are attached by each individual within his/her own perceptual system, and that as a result per-ceived messages always differ from intended messages); (3) confusion of facts and observation (when a communicator forgets that sensory mecha-nisms are the only contact people have with the world; believes that some-thing "is" as each has perceived it to be; forgets that statements about an object or event are never the same as the object or event); (4) confusion of observation and inference (when a communicator forgets that inference requires a mental leap beyond observation).

The second group of errors involves the careless or unconscious in-terpretation of *nonverbal* symbols. Nonverbal symbols are classified into seven groups: voice, action, touching, physical characteristics, use of per-sonal space, objects, and time. Nonverbal codes are more ambiguous than verbal and are therefore subject to more varying interpretations. The wider variations cause many communication breakdowns. Perhaps more important as a cause of error is that nonverbal symbols are often unconsciously inter-preted. The errors are further compounded because people forget that non-verbal symbols are culturally bound to a large extent, just as verbal symbols are. Therefore, people often react to nonverbals from a communicator of another culture or subculture as if the nonverbals meant the same in all cultures.

Many communicators also fail to realize the functions of nonverbal symbols: to repeat, contradict, substitute for, complement, or emphasize verbal symbols, to serve as emblems, or to regulate the behaviors of people being communicated with.

The third group of interpretation errors involves common fallacies of thinking. These include hasty or unrepresentative generalization, faulty causal reasoning (confusing correlation with causation), inappropriate com-parison and contrast, faulty deduction, and false alternatives (either-or thinking).

Questions for Discussion

1. What are the effects of confusing words with the things they repre-sent?

2. Why are messages labeled "intended" and "perceived"?

3. Why is it a myth to believe that ideas can be transmitted?

4. Why should we avoid confusing facts with observations? And obser-vations with inferences?

5. Why are we not careful with our use of nonverbal symbols?

6. Can you give an example of times when you received communication from each of the categories of nonverbal symbols?

7. How does knowing the functions of nonverbal symbols reduce am-biguity?

8. Can you give an example illustrating each of the common errors of reasoning?

94

Answers to exercise on p. 75.

Story A

1. ? You do not know John & Betty are married, nor that they were in the same room.
2. ? John *thought* he did. That doesn't mean he did.
3. ? You don't know when the scattering occurred.
4. F
5. F
6. ? That the door is open doesn't mean it wasn't locked.
7. ?
8. ? Same as #1
9. ? You don't know where the noise came from.
10. ? You don't know what else Smith saw.

Story B

1. ? You don't know that the owner and the business man are the same person.
2. ? You don't know there was a robbery. Perhaps, the landlord appeared and demanded the rent.
3. F
4. ? You don't know the owner is a man.
5. ? Unlikely, but you don't know it didn't happen.
6. T This one is for morale!
7. ? The story says, "sped"; that doesn't necessarily mean ran.
8. ? While the last part of the statement is true, you don't know what was in the cash register.
9. ? Robbery?
10. ? There could have been 4 or 5 people; or only 3.
11. ? "Dashed out" isn't in the story.

Suggestions for Further Reading

EISENBERG, ABNER, AND RALPH SMITH, JR., *Nonverbal Communication.* New York: The Bobbs-Merrill Co., Inc., 1971.

FAST, JULIUS, *Body Language.* New York: Pocket Books, 1974.

HALL, EDWARD T., *The Silent Language.* Greenwich, Conn.: A Fawcett Premier Book, 1959.

————, *The Hidden Dimension.* Garden City, N.Y.: Doubleday, Inc., 1966.

HANEY, WILLIAM V., *Communication and Organization Behavior Text and Cases.* Homewood, Ill.: Richard D. Irwin, Inc., 1967.

KNAPP, MARK L., *Nonverbal Communication in Human Interaction.* New York: Holt, Rinehart and Winston, Inc., 1972.

LANGACKER, RONALD W., *Language and Its Structure.* New York: Harcourt Brace Jovanovich, Inc., 1973.

LORENZ, KONRAD, *On Aggression.* New York: Bantam Books, Harcourt, Brace & World, Inc., 1971.

MEHRABIAN, ALBERT, *Silent Messages.* Belmont, Cal.: Wadsworth Publishing Co., Inc., 1971.

4

How We See Ourselves
self-concept, the central attitude system

goal:
To understand how your self-concept affects your communication.

probes:
The material in this chapter should help you to

1. Explain self-concept in terms of thinking, feeling, needing, physical, and attitudinal facets. pp. 97–101
2. Describe the part played in the development of self-concept by early awareness of self, modeling, role playing, role taking, significant and generalized others. pp. 102–10
3. Describe one "significant other" in your life. pp. 106–7
4. Explain the five influences of self-concept in communication:
   Pygmalion effect
   Self-fulfilling prophecy
   Selective perception
   Self-disclosure
   Self-confidence
   pp. 110–22
5. Complete a Johari Window diagram of yourself in relation to a significant other and a person you have just met. pp. 114–118
6. Describe some ways to cope with speech anxiety. pp. 118–22

> The Caterpillar and Alice looked at each other for some time in silence; at last the Caterpillar took the hookah out of its mouth, and addressed her in a languid, sleepy voice.
>
> "Who are *you?*" said the Caterpillar.
>
> This was not an encouraging opening for a conversation. Alice replied, rather shyly, "I—I hardly know, Sir, just at present—at least I know who I was when I got up this morning, but I think I must have been changed several times since then."
>
> LEWIS CARROLL

WHAT IS SELF-CONCEPT?

In this chapter we focus on the most important variable in the communication process: you. You receive, perceive, and determine the meanings involved in all your communication. Who you are affects how you communicate. Nothing is more important in your communication than your self. But who are you? What are you? Who are you, *really?* It's not easy to answer, is it? You could respond by giving your name and occupation. But that's not you. You're much more than that. You are a physical being but you're also much more than that. You are also a concept, an image in your own mind. That image or concept includes your name and your perceptions of the important things you do and have done. "I am Mary Smith." "I am a student." "I am a plumber, lawyer, policeman, doctor, father, mother, wife, . . ." But your concept of self includes more than the roles you play. *Self-concept* also includes your feelings about your self and many other things. To illustrate some of these aspects of your concept of self, think about these questions:

How do you see your self?

How do others see you?

97   How do these perceptions affect you when you talk?

When introduced to others, how do you identify yourself?
How do you feel about your name?
How do you feel about your looks? Your skills? Your talents? Your intelligence?

How you answer these questions reveals *some* significant information about your self-concept. But very little. Let's go on. How would you complete the following statements?

I usually worry about . . .
I get angry when . . .
I'm happiest when . . .
. . . pleases me.
If I were an animal, I'd be . . .
If I were a color, I'd be . . .
If I were a national figure, I'd be . . .
If I could change my name, I'd choose . . .

These items all reveal some of you, some facets of your self-concept. They point out how much of you is beyond the physical self. They illustrate the breadth of your self. Self-concept involves these facets, and more. *We think of self-concept as all you think and feel about you, the entire complex of beliefs and attitudes you hold about yourself.* Your self-concept consists of all your physical, emotional, social, and intellectual perceptions of self.

Facets of Self-Concept

Self-concept is a complex system of many beliefs and attitudes. We like to compare the self to a many-faceted diamond. Each facet contributes to the brilliance and completeness of the whole stone, but each is a unit in itself. Many facets of self could be cited, but we'll examine five: the *thinking, feeling, needing, attitudinal,* and *physical.* Each of these, in turn, is composed of several facets, creating in each person a many-faceted self.

thoughts

Ideas and thoughts compose one facet of self. This is the cognitive, thinking self. This dimension of self provides reasons, observations, inferences, rationalizations, conclusions, and judgments. The thinking self is largely a verbal self. When you verbalize your attitudes, feelings, needs, and perceptions, you translate other facets of self into the thinking state of self. This self is the part of you that explains you to yourself and others.

feelings

Your self also has a feeling facet. This is the part of you that says, "Turn on the light; I'm afraid," or "I feel happy; I'm in love," or "Don't hurt me." Feeling responses are important aspects of self. As we mentioned in Chapter 3, our society frequently discourages the expression of the feeling self, but it exists whether it is expressed or not. The feeling dimension of self can make you physically sick, socially maladjusted, mentally incapable of functioning. When people recognize and accept feelings as real, legitimate, and normal, they can more effectively live because they've accepted one of the most important facets of self.

needs

Similarly important is the needing dimension of self. Each human being must have certain needs satisfied merely to survive, and other needs must be satisfied to exist in a social and personal world. People behave in ways to satisfy these needs. They perceive the world in terms of these needs. Of all the many phenomena that might be perceived at any one time, people usually select to perceive what is meaningful to them, which means they perceive those items that fill needs most unsatisfied at the time. Because needs strongly influence what we think and feel, our needs are an important component of self.

attitudes

What you value is an important part of your total self, as are your *attitudes*. Attitudes predispose you to respond in certain ways to specific stimuli. These predispositions rely heavily on your values.

How do you see your self?
Source: David S. Strickler— Monkmeyer.

Both attitudes and values determine much of what you are and how you see yourself. Values and attitudes vary widely among people, but for each person, values play a vital role in perception of self and determine many behaviors. For example, one person may hold the attitudes that religion is necessary to mental peace; that ministers do great service for society; that politics is dirty business and all politicians are on the take. Another person may believe that religion is a ripoff, and that ministers are parasites. This person may also see politics as necessary and politicians as mostly honest and hard-working. The first of these two people values religion and not politics; the second has a different set of values. Both, however, have a concept of self that reflects their own values and attitudes.

physical existence

Another facet of self is the physical. You have a physical existence, and a perception of yourself as a physical being. You may not be conscious of your body at all times, but the image you have of it is one of the strongest influences on the way you behave. If you see your body as fragile, you'll be more protective of yourself in dealing with the "outside" world than if you see it as husky and strong. If you see your body as ugly, you'll dress differently, walk differently, and sit differently than if you see yourself as attractive.

Each person has an individual rhythm, a characteristic way of moving. You might not always be aware of it, but the rhythm of walking, of handling objects, of gestures, reflects a unique pattern of accents and pauses in action for each person. This aspect of self is an essential part of the way you act toward others and respond to them. Personal physical mannerisms and ways of moving are important in identifying us as who we are. Most of us have had the experience of recognizing someone ahead of us in a crowd by noticing a familiar "something" in the way that person moved his or her body.

Your voice—its tone, inflections, the feel and sound of its production—is a significant physical dimension of you. Whether heard either from the inside by you or from the outside by others, your voice is often thought of as you. A young man we'll call Herb appeared at a speech clinic for help one day. Herb had been told that his voice was unpleasant, though he didn't understand why. When his voice was recorded and replayed for him, he heard it from the outside for the first time and couldn't believe what he heard. That high pitch had to be due to a faulty recorder; he *couldn't* sound like that! With therapy, Herb learned to drop his tone to a well-modulated baritone. Still, for several months, he frequently slipped back into his old voice because, perceived from the inside, it was what he identified as his. Only as he used the voice more and more did he accept the new voice patterns as part of himself.

Changing the voice involves changing a profound aspect of

self; that's one reason speech clinicians approach the task with great caution. Recently, police and other researchers have shown what we all know intuitively: that people can be identified by the sound of their voices. Voiceprints, like fingerprints, are unique and distinctive.[1]

Exercise: Your Many Selves

Objective: To become aware of some of your many selves.
Directions:

> The checklist of questions below relates to your many selves. *The answers to these questions are yours and need be shared with no one unless you wish to do so.* Complete the questions as openly and honestly as you can. Leave blank any that do not apply to you.

Cognitive Self
I believe that

1. religion is . . .
2. religion should be
3. politics is . . .
4. politics should be . . .
5. women are . . .
6. women should be . . .
7. men are . . .
8. men should be . . .
9. I am . . .
10. I should be . . .
11. democracy is . . .
12. democracy should be . . .
13. my wife/husband is . . .
14. my wife/husband should be . . .
15. my girl/boyfriend is . . .
16. my girl/boyfriend should be . . .

Feeling Self

1. I am happy when I . . .
2. I am sad when I . . .
3. Next Saturday night I want to . . .
4. Five years from now I want to . . .
5. My wife/husband makes me happy when . . .
6. My parents/children make me happy when . . .
7. My boy/girlfriend makes me happy when . . .
8. My wife/husband makes me sad when . . .
9. My parents/children make me sad when . . .
10. My girl/boyfriend makes me sad when . . .

Physical Self

1. I am attractive/handsome when . . .
2. My . . . is attractive/handsome.
3. My . . . is ugly.
4. My . . . is sexy.
5. I am ashamed of my . . .
6. I am proud of my . . .
7. I am unattractive when . . .
8. If I were a movie star, I could play the kind of roles that . . . does.
9. I look terrible in . . .
10. If I could change my looks I would . . .

---

[1] See Ross E. Steinhauer, "Voice Prints, a New Aid in Detecting Criminals," *Saturday Review*, LII (September 6, 1969), 56–59.

Voice and Movement Selves

1. I wish my voice were . . .
2. The pitch of my voice is . . .
3. The worst thing about my voice is . . .
4. The best thing about my voice is . . .
5. If I could change my voice it would sound like . . .
6. If I could change my walk, I would walk like . . .

HOW DOES SELF-CONCEPT DEVELOP?

Complex and many-faceted, *your self-concept is your central attitude system.* Because it is the single most important element in determining with whom you communicate, how you communicate, and for what purposes, *it has a major role in your communication behavior.* Thus, it's helpful to understand how the self becomes known and how the concept of self develops.

Self-concept is developed through your experiences. From your physical, emotional, social, and mental interactions with the world you live in, you develop a set of attitudes toward the being you call "me." In other words, throughout life as you communicate with the people and the environment around you, as you perceive those communications, you develop a concept of self.

The early years of childhood are among the most important in the development of self-concept. To understand self-concept and how it influences communication, we must examine those developmental years.

Infancy and Awareness of Self

In the early months of life, infants seem to have little understanding of their own bodies. Then they begin gripping, pulling, and tasting. Gradually they learn to reach for, grab, and hold objects and to put them into their mouths. Slowly children develop self-awareness. They learn to recognize the distinction between self and not-self, between their bodies and the rest of their environment. Self-awareness occurs as children learn to distinguish between sensations and the conditions that produce them. Only gradually do children learn to recognize and sort out body parts, name, feelings, and behaviors as integral parts of a single self. Slowly, they build a cluster of attitudes about that self, and begin to understand the meaning of "me."

Infants become aware of stable and changing parts of their environments. Appearance of certain objects and people becomes predictable and anticipated. Sights become recognizable and meaningful. Some events become associated with specific other events and feelings. Appearance of mother—even though the word isn't

102

Infants develop the first stages of self-awareness.
Source: Christy Park—Monkmeyer.

available to the infant—becomes associated with being fed or cuddled. Children learn the importance of the appearances of these persons and objects. Events are perceived in relation to the services or sensations they provide for the infant.

As their experience broadens, children learn to include things aside from self in their sense of personhood. They learn to distinguish mine from not-mine much as they learned to distinguish self

The experiences of early childhood are important in the development of self-concept.
Source: Mimi Forsyth—Monkmeyer.

from not-self. During this time, they also acquire language, which in turn becomes an important factor in development of self-concept. Children learn that a name identifies the self. They also learn the pronouns "mine," "me," "I," "you," and to associate the words with the concepts. "My" comes to include such things as home, possessions, groups belonged to, values held, and people. Children who identify parents or brothers and sisters are extending their sense of self. Likewise, they identify pets, toys, and other possessions as "theirs." This process of identification is the basis for expansion of the concept of self.

Awareness of Others

modeling

> All the world's a stage,
> And all the men and women merely players.
> They have their exits and their entrances;
> And one man in his time plays many parts.
>
> SHAKESPEARE

Now let's look at growing children. After maturing enough to recognize differences among people, what do they do? Well, at first in their play, they *model*—they simply imitate. They look at their environment and see people do certain things and they imitate those things. A friend, for instance, has a habit of leaning forward from the waist when laughing. She was never aware of this habit until she was around a 2-year-old niece. The niece was observed leaning over peculiarly several times during a family gathering; no one could determine the meaning of it until it was finally realized that she was imitating the aunt's laughing behavior. *Children observe their environment and model the behaviors around them.*

Children learn that certain behaviors are associated with certain people. They see behaviors repeated, and at this stage, they resemble monkeys. They play by repeating the behavior they have seen others use. In this *modeling*, children don't really understand why or what they are doing. They just see that some kinds of behavior are identified with some people, like Mommy and Daddy, and repeat or model those behaviors. Some of these behaviors become integral parts of self—for example, learning language. Children model the language behavior of parents and others they are around during the years of language development. A child growing up in Alabama models a totally different dialect from one in Brook-

Children model the behaviors around them.
Source: David S. Strickler—Monkmeyer.

lyn. The accent is almost totally acquired by modeling. Yet later in life, the Southern or the Brooklyn accents become essential characteristics of the two personalities and attempts to change the accent require major adjustments of self-concept.

role playing

Gradually, children learn to associate the behaviors they've connected to Mommy with more than the person, Mommy. They learn that the behaviors have a reason. They learn to interpret the behaviors as related to a role, mother. Children meet other people called mothers, and learn that other children have mothers different from their own; the concept of a mother role is learned. At this point, children can role play. In this sense, *role playing involves only an understanding that the behaviors are associated with the role.* It is acting out the observed behavior related to the role, and doesn't require understanding of the role itself.

A child can role play a police officer by simply having observed a police officer. He or she only needs to have seen that person do certain things: direct traffic, drive a police car, arrest people, wear a special uniform, etc. But this role playing isn't very empathetic, doesn't really include understanding of what the role involves. Maintaining order or enforcing justice wouldn't be meaningful role behaviors to the child. In role playing, children aren't able to anticipate events related to those concepts or to formulate responses different from the behaviors they've observed.

role taking

Finally, children acquire a *role-taking* ability. *Role taking is the act of interpreting behaviors and understanding the motivations re-*

lated to a particular role. Role taking is more than just repeating a behavior. It involves a subjective, internalized interpretation of that behavior. In role taking, children learn to anticipate the behaviors appropriate to a role and evaluate how they will behave in situations involving the role. When children who have reached this stage of self-development are asked, "Tell me what you are," they can respond, "a New Yorker, Catholic, Texan, Methodist, Jew, Negro, Italian, etc." They have *internalized* these roles.

Internalized roles become facets of self-concept, especially those roles perceived as important. For example, our society teaches children a boy role and a girl role, and that the two are different. These differences influence the way a child develops. Children are rewarded for taking the appropriate role and punished for not doing so. A girl who does not take the role of a girl may be derided as a "tomboy," and the boy who does not take the role of boy is called a "sissy."

Children identify more or less strongly with various roles. Two youngsters might each be raised to take both the role of Baptist and of football player. But for one the role of Baptist might be the most important influence in life and the role of football player merely a means to a college education. The other person might think of the role of Baptist as incidental and identify self primarily by the role of football player. The first might strive to become a minister, the other a Green Bay Packer, and the two will live vastly different lives. Role taking is of major importance in development of self-concept.

Others Provide the Looking Glass

significant others

Role taking doesn't happen to a child simply by association. The roles a child learns are strongly influenced by other people. Rejection or acceptance of a child's behavior by some people becomes very important in the child's interpretation of self. *The people of most importance in a person's life are called significant others.*[2] Significant others exercise a major influence on the development of a child's self-concept. The significant others early in life are usually parents or people who play the parent role. Others who live in the home—brothers, sisters, aunts, uncles, grandparents—are also important. Friends, other relatives, and teachers may later become significant others. Children actively seek rewards and acceptance from their significant others. You've surely heard children say repeatedly, "See what I did, Mommy," or "Daddy, watch me! watch me!"

---

[2] Original development of this concept was by George Herbert Mead in *Mind, Self and Society* (Chicago: University of Chicago Press, 1934).

The efforts for rewards from significant others don't stop with childhood. All people seek praise and reinforcement from those who are important to them and will not be so concerned about rejections or criticisms by those who are not important. Significant others are people with whom an individual, of any age, has an important relationship. Your significant others are people you look to for interpretation of your successes and actions. Some students, for instance, consider their classmates the most significant people in school and are rewarded most by the other students' evaluations of their performance. Other students react to teachers as the most significant others in school, and seek evaluations of performance from teachers, giving little importance to the opinions of classmates. Whoever they are, as important sources of rewards and punishments, significant others exert major influences on a person's developing self-concept.

generalized others

As infants mature, they realize that parents, sisters, and brothers aren't the only people in their lives. Growing children also seek interpretations of self from persons other than the family and close peers. In this process, they internalize attitudes from casual friends, teachers, and distant relatives as well as from the significant others, and develop general attitudes of what other people think about them. These attitudes create a composite evaluation derived from what is described as

Significant others influence self-concept. *Source:* Paul S. Conklin—Monkmeyer.

the *generalized other*. *The generalized other is the composite view you have of others' views of you.*

Larry receives inputs from tests, teachers, friends, and parents, mostly saying he hasn't done as well as they expected. All these interpretations are reflected in Larry's conclusion, "I'm not a very good student." This conclusion is not a simple description of self. It reflects his perception of the attitudes of many others. It is a composite evaluation that reflects the generalized other. Larry derives the evaluation from interacting interpretations of many people, some significant to him and some not.

The model of a looking glass is illustrative. Because growing children can't see themselves directly, they need other people as mirrors to provide the images. But self-concept is not merely a mirror reflection of others' views. In the same way that children pick and choose among possessions, they can select among the images of self offered by others. Children learn to evaluate their own behavior in terms of its consequences. Part of those consequences are rewards from other people, to be sure. But other consequences are measured by results. If someone says, in reaction to your behavior, "That was a dumb thing to do," or "That was really terrific," you can decide which opinions you accept and which you reject. You don't always agree or accept the evaluations of others. The people around you influence but don't totally control your self-concept. The child, as a growing individual, becomes able to look into the mirror and accept or reject images presented there by others.

You not only accept and reject images seen in the looking glass provided by others, you magnify or reduce parts of the image. You aren't a sponge. You interpret the images you see in the view of others. Behavior is more than a response to what happens to you. It results also from how you interpret and feel about what happens. Ability to reject or modify images in the mirror of others' views varies according to the stage of a person's development. The less mature a person is, the less stable is the concept of self. That's why the reactions of significant others at very early ages of life have such important and longlasting effects on self-concept.

Image Making Changes the Mirror

> There will be time, there will be time
> To prepare a face to meet the faces that you meet!
>
> T. S. ELIOT

face making

Once a certain stage of development has been reached, you begin to go beyond receiving and reacting to others' interpretation of you. You start trying to affect their interpretations. *You behave strategically to influence how others think about you.* People learn to construct or create the images presented to others. This behavior sometimes is described as *face making* or masking.[3] If you want to be thought of as a certain type of person, or as having certain characteristics, you'll behave in ways that project those images, even if the images are not altogether accurate reflections of how you see your "actual" self.

A medical doctor, for instance, attempts to project an image of being considerate, concerned, knowledgeable, trustworthy, and having a high degree of competence and control over the situations being dealt with. In some cases, a doctor may really not care about the individual, or know what the diagnosis ought to be. But a doctor learns not to project an uncaring, unsure image. A doctor who isn't sure of a diagnosis knows that fear and anxiety could be created by letting the patient know, and that it could harm recovery. The doctor intends to project a "face" or "mask" of competence and knowledge.

This kind of presentation of self is sometimes warranted. Masking strategies are often required in daily interactions. Salespersons must appear interested in the customer even if they aren't; parents try to behave supportively toward children even when they don't feel like it; you act respectfully toward your boss even if you don't feel respectful. Face making seems demanded in many roles of life, but we don't recommend it as a dominant strategy in your interpersonal behavior.

To understand the development of self-concept you need to be

[3] Erving Goffman, *Encounters* (New York: Bobbs-Merrill, 1961).

aware of how face making influences the process. After repeated face making, people sometimes *believe* the masks they've been putting on. If you project a particular image of self long enough, you often no longer realize that you started out just masking or playing a role. As a result, this strategic presentation of your self becomes irretrievably mixed with other beliefs about self. Continual and habitual repetition of masking may create a situation in which the person comes to believe the mask. When that happens, the mask is as much a part of self-concept as the physical self or any other facet of self.

Lifelong Development

Finally, remember, your self-concept is not static. Its many facets grow and change with all your experiences. Changes are fewer and usually less dramatic after the end of adolescence, but self-concept can and does change throughout the rest of your life. Changes in education, occupation, lifestyle and/or social milieu can set in motion forces that change people in many ways. Critical events often change self-concept. In the U.S., reaching 40 or retirement often causes drastic changes. Losing a job, a longtime mate, close friends, or relatives can alter a concept of self radically. Similarly, positive experiences can help people gain positive self-acceptance. Perhaps you've had the elating experience of leaving home for college or moving to a new community and thinking, "Now I'm free to become what I really want to be. No one has any expectations of me, no one is conditioned by the masks I've worn. I can become a new me." Indeed, it's possible, though not easy, to change the masks, take new roles, and alter your concept of self.

HOW DOES SELF-CONCEPT INFLUENCE COMMUNICATION?

Your self-concept is the most important variable in communication. Without it, you do not communicate as a human, only as an organism. With it, you interpret your behaviors, your environment, and the relationships between your selves and your world.

Self-concept develops through communication experiences, but it also strongly influences those communications. Let's note specifically five of those influences: the Pygmalion effect; the self-fulfilling prophecy; selectivity in exposure, perception, and retention; the willingness or hesitancy to self-disclose; and the creation or lack of self-confidence.

As we have seen, your self-concept develops in part through others' appraisals of you and of the social positions you hold. If a significant group of people regard you as a leader, or as a follower, you're likely to see yourself the same way. In adopting the attitudes and behaviors expected of you, you receive reinforcing feedback, and the effect spirals. Reinforcement leads to repeated behavior that is reinforced, and so on. This is called *the Pygmalion effect.*[4] The term comes from the Greek myth in which Pygmalion fell in love with a statue of a beautiful woman and the statue came to life. Most people are familiar with the modern version of the myth—the musical "My Fair Lady." In this play, Professor Higgins sees that Eliza Doolittle can become more than a common flower girl; she responds to his expectations with behaviors reinforced by Higgins, his mother, and Colonel Pickering. In the process, she is transformed from a street urchin to a lady of social grace and charm.

We recall a student a few years ago who was elected to chair a group of about fifteen students for a class project. This student appeared to be a shy, quiet person, but he did such a remarkable job leading the group that he won the support of all. After the assignment was completed, the instructor complimented the young man for his great job. He responded, "You know, I was scared to death. I didn't think I could do it. But then I got to thinking about it and figured that if they thought I could be a leader, I'd *act* like a leader, even if I had to fake it. I took charge like I had all the confidence in the world, a real snow job. Then, you know, a strange thing happened. The others in the group began to treat me as if I really *was* confident. They seemed to expect me to have the answers. Pretty soon I didn't know which was the fake me and which was the real me."

Both Eliza Doolittle and this student illustrate an important point about self-concept: *others' expectations influence our behavior toward them, and our behavior influences our self-concept.* We all tend so see ourselves as we think others see us. Expectations exert a major influence on interpersonal communication. This effect is so powerful that psychologists have demonstrated that it is often a variable in experiments. What the experimenter *expects* to happen has been shown to influence the outcome of the experiment. Similarly, what teachers expect students to do influences the students'

---

[4] The most recent and accessible discussion of the Pygmalion effect is found in Robert Rosenthal, "The Pygmalion Effect Lives," *Psychology Today* (September, 1973), pp. 56–63.

performances on tests, and what counselors and parents expect of children influences their behavior in school and other aspects of life.

The Self-Fulfilling Prophecy

The conscious awareness of self makes the Pygmalion effect more than a matter of simple reinforcement, however. Everyone interprets all experiences, attaching meaning to events experienced. The personal meanings create self-expectations. The self-expectations in turn influence future behavior. *You tend to behave as you expect yourself to behave.* We describe this effect of self-concept as the *self-fulfilling prophecy.*

Do you see yourself as a good student? You will probably study diligently, attend class regularly, and participate actively. As a result, you fulfill your own prophecy; you get good grades. Or do you think of yourself as a poor student? You may cut classes, not do assigned work, and as a result do poorly in school. Do you see yourself as attractive? Then you probably spend a lot of time getting dressed each day, styling hair, choosing the right combinations of clothes. You are probably also quick to meet new friends of the opposite sex. Do you see yourself as good in history but poor in math? Then you probably are an alert, vocal, and influential member of your history class, but in algebra you are indifferent, silent, and confused. The principle is that people tend to behave in ways that confirm their expectations of themselves. People create prophecies and then fulfill them.

Selectivity

Because the filter is there in each of us, self-projection is a basic bodily process that operates not only in all our speaking but in other kinds of communicative behavior.

WENDELL JOHNSON

The examples of self-fulfilling prophecy illustrate other ways in which self-concept influences communication. *Our view of self influences communication behavior because it influences what messages we expose ourselves to, how we perceive them, and what we remember.* The self-concept is the filter on the lens through which we see the world. How we interact with others depends on what passes through the filter of self-concept.

selective exposure and perception

Do you see yourself as friendly, easy to get along with, and enjoyable in social situations? Then you will perceive a party as an event to be enjoyed. But if you believe yourself to be shy, not good at conversation, and socially awkward, you'll perceive that party as an event to be avoided if possible, endured if not. You'll try not to go, perceive it as painful if you must go. Our self-concept determines what situations, and thus what communications, we expose ourselves to.

If you think of yourself as athletic, you probably watch games, participate, and pay attention to sports news. You discuss players and games with like-minded friends, and remember facts about players and teams. On the other hand, if you don't like sports, you may see games as endless, boring bits of nonsense. When people talk sports, you tune out; you skip the sports section of the paper, and turn to something that interests you more. You screen out some messages and admit others based on self-concept.

selective retention

We not only tend to expose ourselves to events and people we see as matching or appropriate to our self-image. We also remember most readily those things that fit. We retain things according to how they affect or relate to our self-concept. We all know people who seem to remember everything about a particular sport. They can recall specific plays in specific games from years ago, along with statistics, players' first, last, and middle names, and many other details. In contrast, another person will remember every movie Clark Gable ever made, the name of each character he played, and where he spent each honeymoon. Self-concept plays a major role in such variances of memory.

Self-expectations influence future behavior.
Source: Mimi Forsyth —
Monkmeyer.

Self-concept influences the people we choose to talk to, what we talk about, what we decide to listen to, and what we remember. It is probably the major cause of *selectivity in exposure, attention, perception, and retention* of communication.

Self-Disclosure

Self-concept also influences our communication with others in that it creates or limits our ability to be open and honest with others. To know self is perhaps the most important knowledge we can have to improve communication, while at the same time, to communicate with others is perhaps the most important way we can gain knowledge of our selves. During successful counseling, Carl Rogers has discovered that people become increasingly aware of their real feelings as they share information about themselves. With self-disclosure, self-concept comes closer to the actuality. When the self-concept and the person's experiences are adequately matched, a person is more open to new experiences, has less defensiveness, and is more accurately aware of self and others. And when people are realistically aware and positively accepting of self, they are more likely to be open and honest with others. In other words, *positive self-concept leads to willingness to self-disclose. At the same time, self-disclosure leads to improved self-concept.*[5]

the Johari window

One way to show the relationships between self-concept and self-disclosure is to use the Johari Window.[6] The Johari Window is a representation of the degrees of openness and awareness a person has regarding self. One-half represents the aspects of self that are public—i.e., that are shared with others. The other half represents the aspects not shared.

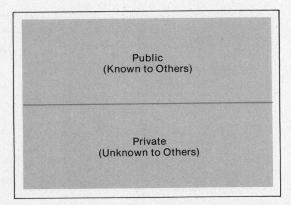

Dividing the window the other way separates aspects of self that are known from those that are unknown.

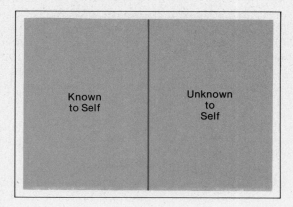

Impose one on the other, and you have a window with four sections.

KNOWN UNKNOWN

OPEN BLIND

PUBLIC

PRIVATE

HIDDEN UNKNOWN

---

[5] A student interested in pursuing this concept can review many of Rogers' writings that are easily accessible in paperback. Two books of readings in communication contain articles by Rogers: *Bridges Not Walls* edited by John Stewart and *Communication: Concepts and Processes* edited by Joseph A. DeVito, both listed in the readings list at the end of Chapter 1.

[6] So named after its originators, Joseph Luft and Harry Ingham. The best discussion of the Johari Window can be found in J. Luft, *Of Human Interaction* (Palo Alto, Calif: National Press Books, 1969).

The four sections can be described as the open area, the blind area, the avoided or hidden area, and the unknown area.

1. The area of free activity, or *open* area, involves behavior and motivations known both to ourselves and others.
2. The *blind* areas are things others can see in us but that we ourselves are unaware of.
3. The avoided or *hidden* area includes things we know but do not reveal to others, such as a hidden agenda or matters about which we have sensitive feelings.
4. The area of *unknown* activity is that area of behaviors and motives that neither the individual nor others are aware of. Sometimes these influence our behavior and we become aware of them later; and some things we never become aware of.

The open part of your window is where you'll find the masks or "faces" mentioned earlier. Often we believe, for many reasons, that what we see as our "real" self is not appropriate to the situation. We think others won't like it, or it's out of place, or we don't want others to know. So we project a face for the situation or person. We put on a mask so what others see is what we want them to see. What we're covering with the mask is in the *hidden* quarter of the window. For example, suppose Ron hates being overweight, yet doesn't want people to know this.

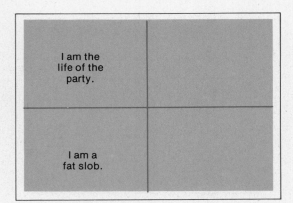

When the face making has become so habitual that we no longer realize it, the mask may appear in the blind quarter of the window. That is, others may recognize the behavior as masking, but we don't. A good example of this is a person who feels inferior (has what is sometimes labeled an inferiority complex), and acts like a snob. Often this person will find ways to run other people down and may not even recognize what he/she is doing. A perceptive receiver (box A below) of this kind of communication will recognize the behavior as masking even when the source doesn't. Another person, however, may not recognize the behavior as masking (see box B).

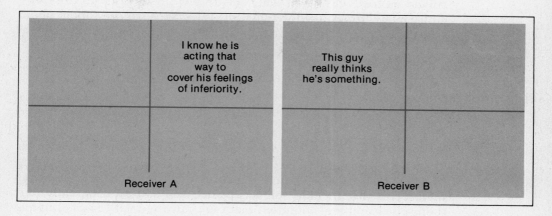

The public side of each person's window is different. A few things about people are known to all who are acquainted with them, such as physical appearance and manner of dress. Even a stranger can know that. Other things are known only to a few people. Certainly, openness is related to relationships with others, not just self-concept. The better you know someone, the more intimate the relationship, the wider is the open area of the window.

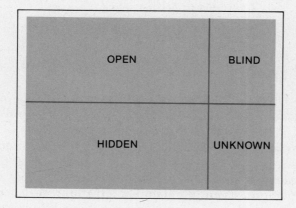

Try completing a Johari Window describing your relationship with a close friend, and another illustrating what you'd share with a stranger or a supervisor. Notice how different they are.

Self-disclosure and self-awareness are closely related. The more we are able to disclose about ourselves, the better we are likely to know ourselves. Self-disclosure is not the same as self-awareness, but helps lead to it. On the other hand, self-awareness that is positive and accepting leads to self-disclosure and a willingness to reveal oneself in situations in which the other person is perceived as trustworthy. In later chapters we refer back to this principle many times. Willingness or reluctance to be open about ourselves and our feelings significantly affects interpersonal communication.

Self-Confidence

relates to self-esteem

How you see yourself is a major factor in the confidence with which you approach communication situations. Some people have a self-concept that can be called positive. They have attitudes about themselves that include self-acceptance and self-esteem. They like themselves and feel confident that they can cope with most communication situations. On the other hand, people with a negative self-concept have attitudes toward self that are predominantly negative. They don't like themselves very much, have little self-esteem, and usually lack *self-confidence.* They feel uncomfortable on many occasions, and often feel unable to cope effectively with important or unfamiliar situations.

> Self-trust is the first secret of success.
>
> RALPH WALDO EMERSON
>
> What you think of yourself is much more important than what others think of you.
>
> SENECA

Either attitude toward self will affect the way you communicate. A person with self-esteem will experience a minimum of speech anxiety, and will have little difficulty in talking with people in most situations. Even in unfamiliar situations, that person will be able to deal with the uneasiness that usually comes with the strange or unusual. A person who has negative self-image, in contrast, will find any communication situation a source of great anxiety. This person, depending on the degree of anxiety, will have reactions that range from nervous hesitation all the way to nausea. Some people choose to cope by completely avoiding situations. They'll never give speeches, ask favors or willingly talk to the boss. They may

Self-confidence.
Source: Caraballo — Monkmeyer.

even cross the street to avoid meeting someone with whom they'd feel obligated to talk.

Certainly, a negative self-concept isn't the only factor related to nervousness or speech anxiety, at least when the communicator is faced with unfamiliar or important situations. Other facets of self are related, as are aspects of the situation. You might feel quite comfortable and capable of coping in some situations and with some people, and quite uneasy and incapable in other situations, or with other people. We have all had moments when we felt we couldn't handle a communication situation. Who hasn't experienced the sweaty palms and short breath that come, when say, we have to stand up and talk at a meeting, or go to a job interview, or have a conference with the boss? Still, it's generally true that the more positive your self-concept, the fewer communication situations that will produce serious anxiety.

coping with lack of self-confidence

We all encounter situations when we don't have as much self-confidence as we'd like. For that reason, we examine why these situations are uncomfortable and suggest several ways to cope with them. Think about the following statements for a minute:

1. Fear is bad and undesirable.
2. Fear is a sign of weakness or inferiority.
3. Brave people do not have fear; only cowards are afraid.

4. Self-confidence means not having fear.
5. Self-confidence eliminates fear.

Did you recognize these as untrue or half-true? If not, you're not unusual. These are common misconceptions about fear, and these mistaken beliefs interfere with the ability of many people to cope with anxiety in communication situations. Too many people understand neither the nature of fear nor how to deal with it. They may even believe that fear and self-confidence are mutually exclusive. But they aren't. Let's examine why.

We think of *fear as a biological process through which a person develops adequate energy to do a job* when the job is very important. Fear is thus a normal condition when a person faces a difficult task or an important job. And fear, it should be recognized, does not result only from threats to physical well-being; it also results from threats to psychological well-being.

Fear mobilizes an organism, whether a human being, or another animal. If a deer, for instance, smells a mountain lion, instant fear mobilizes the animal for self-protection. Instinct says, "Move— move *quickly*." But running at full speed requires a great deal of energy. Fear is the energizer that calls on the body nerves and muscles and the chemistry needed to mobilize rapidly. Fear is thus useful. It is often useful for human beings. You've heard of cases in which a person lifted an automobile to rescue someone trapped underneath, or bent iron bars on a window to escape a burning building. Fear was what called forth an extra supply of adrenalin and supplied that extra energy. Similar reactions happen to people when they face a communication situation they fear. Their heartbeat speeds up, and their hands get sweaty (often a cold sweat), they have trouble breathing, their mouth gets dry, they get butterflies or cramps in the stomach. These are all manifestations of the same physical process that allows the deer to run away from the mountain lion or the human being to lift an auto off an injured friend. Nervous energy results from fear in varying amounts, depending on the situation. It's a natural reaction. Realizing that fear is natural is the first step in learning to cope with it.

If fear is a natural reaction in some situations, how are self-confidence and fear related? Recall how fear functions: it mobilizes the energy to accomplish important tasks. If the tasks are important, then failure to complete them has harmful results. Self-confidence won't eliminate fear of the potential harmful results. Indeed, if energy is needed to accomplish the tasks, self-confidence *shouldn't* eliminate the fear. What self-confidence can do is reduce the level of anxiety caused by the fear, and thus make it possible to behave in ways to avoid harmful consequences.

We use the term *self-confidence* to refer to the ability of an individual to predict, with fair accuracy, that what needs to be done to eliminate any potential harmful results of a situation will or can be done. This is how self-confidence relates to self-concept. Positive self-concept won't enable you to predict in every situation that you can accomplish what needs to be done to avoid harm. Other factors may be involved. But it will enable you to predict positive consequences in many situations, and thus reduce the intensity of fear or anxiety.

To illustrate the differences in ways people might approach a fear-producing communication situation, let's look at reactions of two different people to the same situation.

An instructor asked a student, Aaron, to see him after class. Immediately Aaron thought, "No one else has been asked to stay. What have I done?" His heart started pounding, and his face felt flushed. His hands got sweaty, and he had butterflies in his stomach. Nervously, he went to the instructor after class. The teacher asked if he would participate in a panel discussion before the local Junior Chamber of Commerce. Extra credit was offered Aaron for the activity. Aaron's butterflies got worse. His heart pounded so loudly he was sure the instructor would hear it instead of the strange tense voice that stammered out, "I—I can't. I—I have a part-time job and I have to work every evening."

After leaving the classroom, Aaron felt terrible. What was the matter with him? The teacher must have thought he was a real jack not to accept the opportunity for extra credit. The worst thing was that he didn't even have a job! Aaron had let fear drive him away from receiving extra credit because he lacked the self-confidence to predict he could do well enough to avoid failure.

When Ross was faced with the identical situation, he behaved differently. True, his first reaction was also anxiety. However, when he thought about it, he decided he knew the subject well enough, and besides, there'd be that extra credit. He concluded, "I'm sure I can do it so I don't embarrass myself or anyone else. In fact, I'll bet I can do a pretty good job!"

As the time for the discussion got closer, he got butterflies again, especially when he worked on the assignment. But at the Jaycee meeting, he was "up" for the event. His heart was pounding, he was anxious, his hands were sweaty. But he knew what was happening to him, so the fear didn't grow worse, feeding on itself. He was confident that he would perform adequately. He'd have to move around a little before the discussion started to use up some of his extra energy, and he'd probably still have shaky hands at first. But as soon as he got into the discussion, his energy would be useful as he talked and listened to the others. It would help him sound enthused and interested, and improve his reaction time in responding to questions and ideas raised by others.

The differences are obvious. Both students had fear. Ross, however, had positive enough self-concept in that situation that he knew he could get prepared and perform adequately. He could predict positive results. He also knew what to do in the situation to focus the extra energy into channels that would help, instead of interfere, with his accomplishment. Ross knew that his physical manifestations of fear could be controlled. He recognized his fear as natural, and did what we all can learn to do: used that energy to prepare for the situation. He planned for the task, planned some physical activity right before he had to speak, and welcomed the extra energy to help him do the job well. Moreover, his attitude itself helped reduce the harmful effects of excessive fear. By understanding the physical manifestations of fear, he didn't let them create more fear, leading to more effects in a vicious spiral. In addition, by doing the job instead of running, Ross confirmed his ability to predict accurately that the results would not be harmful. Thus, he increased his self-confidence in handling similar situations in the future.

Accepting and completing communication tasks that cause anxiety for you can improve your ability to cope with them. Each successful communication makes further successes more probable. Using your knowledge of self-concept and fear, you can accept fear for what it is: natural and useful. You can then channel it to your benefit instead of using it to run, or letting it feed on itself and grow to unmanageable proportions. Repeated successes in dealing with speech anxiety can increase your positive attitudes toward yourself. As a result you'll gain many other benefits of improved self-esteem.

Physiological Signs of Fear	*Coping with Fear Symptoms*
increased pulse rate	analyze the situation
increased perspiration	*how serious are the consequences?*
dry mouth	*can I handle the job?*
shaking hands and knees	recognize fear as natural
shortness of breath	*don't let effects spiral*
nervous stomach	prepare adequately
	visualize positive results
	plan physical movement to use up excess energy

Self-concept, one of the most important variables in the communication process, is defined as the entire complex of beliefs and attitudes you have about yourself. Self has many facets, five of which are discussed in this chapter: thinking, feeling, needing, attitudes, and physical facets. Self-concept develops through a person's communication experiences. Beginning in infancy, one first develops an awareness that self is distinguished from the rest of the world, and this awareness grows to an identification with objects and events in the environment. Basic feelings of self-worth, security, and ability to cope with the world develop during the period of infancy to five years. Major stresses on self-concept come again at adolescence, and thereafter the concept of self stabilizes considerably, though it is constantly subject to change with new experiences, especially when major changes in life occur.

A child acquires an ability to identify self with various roles in life, first through modeling those around, then through role playing, and finally, with a realization of what the role is supposed to be, a child becomes able to take roles. Children acquire much of their understanding of their selves and abilities through the reactions of significant others to them. Later they acquire a concept of how generalized others view them. Sometimes children (and adults) create faces or masks, projecting an image to the outside world that may not be consistent with what they perceive themselves to be. Such masking behavior sometimes becomes confused with the prior concept of a real self and the individual fulfills the prophecy of the image.

Self-concept influences communication in five ways that interact in a sometimes spiralling effect. The Pygmalion effect is the tendency for a person to become what significant others see her/him as. The self-fulfilling prophecy is a tendency to become what you expect yourself to be. Self-concept is one major cause of selective exposure, perception and retention, determining to a large extent what people expose themselves to, what they perceive and remember of what they are exposed to. Self-concept affects the tendency to disclose important things about self. A person with acceptance and esteem of self will be more likely to be open and honest in communications with others and less closed and guarded in interpersonal interactions.

Finally, self-concept relates to the self-confidence with which you approach communication situations. Self-confidence, the ability to predict that what needs to be done to eliminate any potential harmful results of a situation will or can be done, is improved by positive self-concept. Having self-confidence will not eliminate fear caused by potentially harmful situations, but will improve your belief that you can handle those situations and avoid harmful results. Self-confidence and understanding of fear and its effects can contribute to reducing the intensity of fear and improving your ability to cope with anxiety producing communication situations.

Exercise: Disclosing Your Many Selves

Objective: To assess your willingness to self-disclose.
Directions:
1. Refer to the items completed in the Many Selves exercise on pp. 101–2.
2. How free would you feel to disclose how you completed each statement?

a. Consider the following persons:

mother	employer
father	supervisor
girl/boyfriend	sister
wife/husband	brother

Which persons, if any, would you, *willingly, without hesitation,* share how you completed each of the items?

3. If you would hesitate to share your responses on some of the items in the Many Selves exercise, use the following scale to indicate how willingly you would share each answer:
   1 — would tell if asked
   2 — not sure
   3 — would prefer not to tell
   4 — would refuse to tell or would change statement before telling

4. What relationships do you see between your self-concept and your willingness to talk about any of the responses?

Questions for Discussion

1. What is self concept?
2. Why is it more accurate to speak of many facets of self than of a single self?
3. Can you explain six processes in the development of self-concept?
4. Name and cite examples of five ways in which self-concept influences communication.
5. What positive steps can you take to reduce the intensity of the effects of fear in communication situations?

Suggestions for Further Reading

ALLPORT, A. W., *Becoming.* Princeton, N.J.: Princeton University Press, 1954.

BLUMER, HERBERT, *Symbolic Interactionism, Perspective and Method.* Englewood Cliffs, N.J.: Prentice-Hall, Inc., 1969.

FREUD, SIGMUND A., *A General Introduction to Psychoanalysis.* New York: Buni and Liveright, 1920.

GERGEN, KENNETH J., *The Concept of Self.* New York: Holt, Rinehart and Winston, Inc., 1971.

GOFFMAN, ERVING, *The Presentation of Self in Everyday Life.* New York: Doubleday & Co., Inc., 1959.

GORDON, C., AND K. J. GERGEN, eds. *The Self in Social Interaction,* Vol. I. New York: John Wiley & Sons, Inc., 1968.

HAMMACHECK, DON, *Encounters With the Self.* New York: Holt, Rinehart and Winston, Inc., 1971.

JOURARD, SIDNEY, *The Transparent Self.* Princeton, N.J.: D. Van Nostrand, Inc., 1964.

LAIR, JESS, *I Ain't Much Baby, But I'm All I've Got.* Greenwich, Conn.: Fawcett Publications, Inc., 1972.

LEISLEY, W. J., AND D. B. BROMLEY, *Person Perception in Childhood and Adolescence.* New York: John Wiley & Sons, Inc., 1973.

MEAD, GEORGE H., *Mind, Self and Society,* ed. Charles W. Morris. Chicago: University of Chicago Press, 1962.

MUUSS, ROLF, ed., *Adolescent Behavior and Society: A Book of Readings.* New York: Random House, 1971.

ROGERS, CARL, *On Becoming a Person.* Boston: Houghton Mifflin Co., 1970.

ROSENBERG, MORRIS, *Society and the Adolescent Self-Image.* Princeton, N.J.: Princeton University Press, 1965.

Key To Words and Phrases

Abstracting: the process of focusing on parts of a whole to form a mental concept that distinguishes the whole from other things

Attention: an adjustment of the receiving senses

Attention, focal: focusing the receiving senses on stimuli

Attention, marginal: receiving stimuli in the margin or periphery of receiving senses (as seeing in the "corner of your eye")

Attention, subliminal: receiving stimuli below the conscious level; receiving sensations that could not be consciously perceived even by adjusting the receiving senses from marginal to focal

Attitude: a predisposition (or tendency) to respond to stimuli in one way rather than another

Cause-effect thinking: an inferential process that concludes one event causes another one

Communication: the process of assigning meaning to sensations received

Communication, elements of: (1) source, (2) stimuli, (3) receiver, (4) sensory receptors, (5) receiver's interpretations and responses, (6) noise, (7) feedback, (8) situation

Communication, interpersonal: direct interactions between communicators on a one-to-one basis or in small groups

Communication, intrapersonal: the communication of a person with him/herself; the processing of internal feedback

Communication, mass: public communication transmitted by electronic or mechanical means to people who are widely dispersed

Communication, public: many people receive messages primarily from one source

Communication, speech: a process during which persons assign meaning to verbal and nonverbal symbols

Communication breakdown: occurs when messages are not received or are perceived by receivers in a different way from that intended by senders

Comparison and contrast: the process of inferring that events, objects or persons are like something else (comparison) or different from (contrast) others

Correlation: a relationship between two elements; often confused with causation

Creative thinking: a process of drawing new conclusions by adding, subtracting, or substituting elements in thought processes; use of imagination

Decoding: describes the process of deciding what verbal and nonverbal messages received during speech or written communication mean

Deduction: an inferential process that involves applying generalizations to specific cases

Encoding: describes the process of choosing words, grammar, appropriate voice patterns and behaviors to express an intended message

Facemaking: the tendency to create an image that you want others to perceive as you (often called a face or a mask)

Fact: an element of physical reality that is an observable, nonverbal object or act

Feedback: the link that connects source and receiver; a receiver's response *as perceived by the source* of stimulus to which it is a response

Generalizing: an inferential process that draws general conclusions from one or more specific cases

Generalized others: the composite picture you have of how other people view you

Inferring: a thinking process that draws conclusions based on observations and synthesizing information; cause-effect, comparison and contrast, creative imagination, deduction, and generalization are all inferential processes

Interpretation: the processes by which people organize, explain and otherwise make the sensations they receive meaningful

Language: a communication code consisting of words, vocal patterns, syntax and grammar. Many such codes exist

Meaning: the entire set of reactions a person has to a symbol

Meaning, connotative: the attitudes or feelings a person has about the event or object (referent) a symbol represents; sometimes connotations are related to the symbol as well as the referent

Meaning, denotative: the event, idea or object to which a symbol refers; the referent (i.e., the "thing" referred to by a word)

Message, actual: the actual stimuli in a communication situation

Message, intended: the ideas and understandings that a source in a communication situation wants receiver(s) to have

Message, perceived: the ideas and understandings receiver(s) get from stimuli in a communication situation

Modeling: repeating or copying behaviors without understanding them

Perception: the process of selecting, organizing and assigning meaning to stimuli

Process: a series of events that interact to create something new, which in turn becomes another element in a series of events that also interact to create something new, and so on in an ongoing sequence

Proxemics: study of how use of personal space communicates meanings and influences interpersonal communication

Pygmalion effect: the tendency for people to become what significant others expect them to be

Receiver: the person or organism that receives communicative stimuli

Referent: the concept, event or object to which a symbol refers

Response: any reaction to sensations received: many include awareness, understanding, changed attitudes, and/or behavior

Role: the behaviors expected of people who occupy specific positions in a social system; sometimes the word identifies the position

Role playing: performing or acting out the behaviors perceived as associated with a social position or "role"

Role taking: internalizing the behaviors associated with a role so that it is identified with, as when a person says, "I am a student"

Selective exposure: choosing, consciously and unconsciously, the people, objects and events to which a person exposes her/himself

Selective perception: choosing, consciously and unconsciously, the stimuli to attend to in any situation and the interpretations to apply

Selective retention: choosing, consciously and unconsciously, what will be stored and recalled from experiences

Self-concept: the total set of beliefs and attitudes you have toward your self; your central attitude system

Self-confidence: the ability to predict that what needs to be done to eliminate any potential harmful results of a situation will or can be done

Self-fulfilling prophecy: the tendency to

create or perceive what is expected, or to become what a person expects to become

Sensation: the impact of stimuli on the senses (the basic sensations in communication are sound, sight, touch, smell, taste)

Sensory receptors: the senses plus the related physiological elements that transmit sensations to the brain and central nervous system

Significant others: the people of most importance in a person's life

Situation: the total external and internal environment in which communication takes place

Socialization: the process of establishing socially acceptable behavior patterns as children grow from infancy to adulthood

Source: the person or environmental agent from which communicative stimuli originate

Source/receiver: any person involved in speech communication

Statement of inference: a statement that goes beyond reporting observations; it relates present to future, the known to the unknown, or states relationships

Statement of judgment: an inference that applies values

Statement of observation: a statement that reports perceptions of a fact

Stimuli: elements or events that cause a reaction by one or more of an organism's senses

Stimulus processing: the processes of receiving, interpreting, thinking about, and responding to sensations received

Symbol: anything that stands for or refers to something else

Symbolization: a process in which one thing (event, object, word) refers to, or stands for, something else

Symbols, abstract: symbols with nonconcrete (intangible) referents; that refer to qualities or attributes instead of objects; that refer to concepts concentrating essential qualities of several other (more specific) concepts. The degree of abstractness varies from high to low

Symbols, concrete: words with tangible referents; that refer to objects rather than qualities

Symbols, nonverbal: all nonword symbols, including the use of voice

Symbols, nonvocal: symbols that do not use voice

Symbols, verbal: all words, written and/or spoken

Symbols, vocal: symbols made with the voice, including but not limited to words

Value: a deeply held belief in the "goodness" or "worth" of ideas, objects, or events; a sense that the opposite or absence of what is good is bad or wrong

The Interpersonal Circuit

A popular song suggests, "People who need people / are the luckiest people . . ." Perhaps it should be added that we all need people, but not all of us can develop the interpersonal relationships necessary to satisfy this universal human need.

In Part Two, we discuss the communication behaviors that can lead to satisfying interpersonal relationships. First we examine the processes of interpersonal perception, then turn to a discussion of the purposes for communication. Understanding the reasons why people communicate involves understanding human motivation, trust, and defensiveness. All three topics are covered in some detail in Part Two. The final chapter in this part introduces several techniques and habits that can improve listening skills. These skills can be useful to communicators in many different situations, so you should not think of them as limited to interpersonal communication. You'll find many techniques discussed in Part Two that will also apply in group and public situations, but they are essential for effective interpersonal communication.

5

How We See Others
interpersonal perception

goal:

To understand the factors affecting interpersonal perception.

probes:

The material in this chapter should help you to

1. Explain why perception of people is more complex than perception of other stimuli. pp. 131–36

2. Diagram the "many selves" identities and explain how they influence communication. pp. 133–37

3. Describe the role of appearance and language in interpersonal perception. pp. 137–39

4. Explain how labeling and stereotyping influence interpersonal perception. pp. 139–44

5. List the four conditions that are the major sources of interpersonal attraction and illustrate how they operate by describing how those conditions influence your relationship with a friend. pp. 145–49

6. Explain the influences of stereotypes, perceived homophily and high credibility in communication. pp. 149–55

> Perceptions are not of things but of relationships. Nothing, including me, exists by itself—this is an illusion of words.
>
> HUGH PRATHER

In a popular movie, *Eye of the Beholder,* five different people interact with an artist in one 24-hour period. Each sees a different person. One sees a man about town who has a winning way with women, one sees a gangster, one a madman, one a thoughtless, immature boy, and one a killer. As the viewer later learns, the artist is none of these things, but his encounter with each person has led to the varying perceptions. Similarly, any politician can testify that many different perceptions exist of her or his every behavior. The same person is considered, depending on the viewer to be a saint, sinner, criminal, savior, pragmatist, opportunist, realist, prisoner of labor, slave to Wall Street, on the make, on the take, and so on and on. Choose any politician you want; you'll probably find that he or she will tell you she/he has been called each of those names at one time or another.

These differences are because *interpersonal perception* is a highly individual, highly complex process. The complexity is inherent because *perceiving people requires that you attribute characteristics to them as you actively interact with them.* Interpersonal perception, ultimately, is a process of interpreting people, and in interpreting we infer qualities and traits that people have. In this chapter, we want to examine the interaction processes in which interpersonal perception occurs, discuss some major factors that influence the interpretations, and finally call attention to some perceptions that strongly affect communication.

When observing objects or nonhuman elements in your environment, you can usually do so without serious distortions of perception. Separating inferences and observations of objects is relatively simple, if you remember to do it. But neither of these statements is true when you are perceiving people. Distortions are common, and inferences are indelibly imprinted on observations. That's because when you first encounter someone, whether a new acquaintance or an old friend, you don't just observe. You infer many things that are very abstract: among them personality, character traits, feelings, attitudes, and motivations. Moreover, as you communicate with people, they react. And this adds another element to the interpretation.

Interacting with Others

> The person always eludes our grasp; it is never static. It refuses to be confined within concepts, formulae, and definitions. It is not a thing to be encompassed, but a point of attraction, a guiding force, a direction, an attitude, which demands from us a corresponding attitude, which moves us to action and commits us.
>
> PAUL TOURNIER

The problem in perceiving people is that they don't stand still, either literally or figuratively. You don't just observe people—you interact with them. Because of the interactions, you interpret changing and abstract stimuli. During interpersonal perception, the potential interpretations are infinitely numerous. But even though people present infinite stimuli, you must select a limited number from vast amounts of information on which to base your communications. And *in interpersonal perception, the communication influences the perceptions at the same time as the perceptions influence the communication.*

People are constantly changing. What you are today is not the same as what you were yesterday, nor the day before, nor the week, month, or year before. The change from one day to the next is real even if not major. People are much like the water in a river. If you stand on a bridge and look at the water underneath for several days in a row, it may appear that you're viewing the same water, but you're not. The river may have the same name but the water is different. Similarly, the person you view today is in some way, however small, different from the one you may have seen yesterday. Yet in interacting with people, we tend to create a set of beliefs and attitudes about what people are, and each time we encounter them, we expect to perceive the same person.

interacting with many selves

Because your only contact with the world outside your skin is through your senses, *you communicate with your perception of a person and not the actual person.* A difference always exists between the person you interact with and your perception of that person. That is, of course, also true for the person communicating with

Interpersonal perceptions vary. *Source:* The Bettmann Archive.

you. A result is that *many selves are present in each interpersonal interaction.* To illustrate, take an example of two friends communicating, Saul and Sandi. Who are the many selves in the interaction? For starters, there are Saul and Sandi.

SAUL   SANDI

But Saul is communicating with his perception of Sandi and Sandi with her perception of Saul.

And because each person's concept of self is not the same as the actual self, there is also Saul's perception of Saul and Sandi's perception of Sandi.

The many selves don't end with these six parties in the interaction, however. Saul would like Sandi to see him in a certain way, so he attempts to create a face that he wants her to perceive; and the same is true for Sandi.

Finally, Sandi has a perception of how Saul sees her and Saul has a perception of how Sandi sees him.

As the discussion of the many selves in communication illustrates, when you interact with another person, you are really interacting with yourself. When so many stimuli are present that you can focus on only a small part of them and must perceive vast amounts of information at a marginal level, it's *you* who selects which to focus on and which to accept marginally. When more stimuli are present than it is possible to perceive, it's *you* who selects which ones to perceive and which not to perceive.

Moreover, any interaction between people makes demands on both participants. When encounters with other people make demands on you, it's *you* who perceive what those demands mean to you and how you feel about them. When you observe objects, you may observe and infer impassionately. But when you observe people, you usually must react; and when you do, it's *you* who interprets what the reaction means, how it affects you, and thus how much feeling and emotion influence the perceptions of that person.

> When Peter meets Paul, Paul's behavior becomes Peter's experience; Peter's behavior becomes Paul's experience.
>
> R. D. LAING, H. PHILLIPSON, A. R. LEE

Finally, once you have had some experience with other people, you create interpretive categories for them. These categories are often called *personalities*. You then develop attitudes toward the categories, or personalities, and apply these attitudes toward each person you encounter. These attitudes create expectations. People expect certain kinds of behavior from mothers, fathers, women, men, sisters, uncles, teachers, police officers, salespersons, friends, bosses, waiters, truck drivers, college students, etc. *You* are the person who brings these set expectations regarding kinds and types of people to interpersonal interactions. Because we know that expectations and experience both influence what we perceive, we know that we perceive other people according to our interpretive categories about them. We know that we assimilate new perceptions in terms of the systems we have learned for interpreting the world. We use our own categories for people to interpret them and frequently perceive what we expect to perceive. Indeed, a major problem in interpreting people is that *perceiving people requires us to interact with ourselves in the process.*

136

Exercise: My Me and Your Me Are Not the Same Me

**Objective: To become aware of the differences between your per-
ceptions of you and others' perceptions of you.**

Directions:

1. Complete this exercise with a partner whom you completely trust
   and are very close to: a friend, wife or husband, mother or father,
   brother or sister. Any of these would be appropriate. Just be sure
   that you feel totally comfortable sharing this information with the
   person.
2. Fill out the two left-hand columns of chart #1. (Provided in the Activity Guide.)
3. Ask your partner to complete the left-hand column of chart #2.
4. Compare the three sets of responses. Discuss the items with your
   partner. What are the differences? What are the reasons for the differences?
5. After the discussion, complete the right-hand column and ask your
   partner to complete the other column on his/her chart.
6. Prepare to discuss these questions in class. Were there any changes?
   How did your discussion affect your responses? What changes might
   exist in the chart if you were to do this with a stranger?

FACTORS INFLUENCING INTERPRETATIONS OF PEOPLE

> We construct the people we perceive . . .
>
> JOHN STEWART

Many factors play a role in the processes of attributing characteristics to the people we interact with. We will discuss three: appearance, use of language, and interpersonal attraction. You'll note that
in each case the verbal and nonverbal elements interact, whether
we are interpreting a person we know well or someone we are
meeting for the first time.

Appearance

Perhaps the best illustration of the influence of interpretive categories in interpersonal perception is the role of physical appearance. *Perceptions of people are influenced by attitudes toward
physical characteristics and appearance.* Information from appearance comprises the first perceptions you process when you interact
with a person. Therefore, physical appearance largely determines

your initial impressions of a person, whether you are interacting for the first or hundredth time. When you first see someone you think is beautiful, bad, sharp, sexy, intelligent, angry, happy, or sad, you interpret appearance and make evaluations about the person.

Most people have had the experience of meeting someone and reacting with a feeling of, "I don't like that person" without really being able to identify anything specific as the cause of the impression. This is because we react largely to appearance, including body language, at a marginal or subconscious level. Similarly, we often perceive changes of mood or attitude in people we know well based on our marginal or subconscious perceptions of their body language.

Many physical characteristics are stereotyped, and the stereotypes vary from culture to culture. Cultural norms in part dictate what features are more important, and how they will be evaluated. For example, men in this country are evaluated as short or little if they are under 5'8", while in some countries this height is tall. Women are evaluated for their measurements in certain ratios, and until very recently a woman with a large bust was automatically stereotyped as not being too bright. (Unfortunately, this is still operative for many people.) These stereotypes are based on stable characteristics. Other aspects of physical appearance are more variable. Perceptions based on hair length, color, whether it's curly or straight—all are likely to vary with current fashions or personal whims. Similarly, manner of presentation is also an important, though variable, factor in interpersonal impressions. A person who is frowning may be perceived as sad, moody, or angry. A person who is slumped over or slouching may be perceived as unenthusiastic or lazy. Though the attributions vary from person to person, many elements in body language influence interpersonal perception.

Physical appearance is processed on at least two levels. At the first, physical elements are categorized according to observations, such as height, weight, color. Then inferences are made from these observations. The inferences are often evaluations, such as "pretty" or "ugly," "smart" or "dumb," "aggressive" or "timid," "nervous" or "confident." Judgments about personality are often made largely on the basis of physical appearance. Whether evaluations are based on personal perspectives or cultural biases, or both, they're made to a large extent unconsciously.

Physical appearance is only one element in the interpersonal perception process. How influential it is varies with how important appearance is to the perceiver, the past experience of the person, and the success the perceiver has had in the past in accurately predicting attributes that people have. Some people are accurate readers of body language and have an "intuitive" ability to assess others. The ability is not really intuitive of course; it's a learned ability to use body language, along with other factors, both conscious and marginal, to accurately interpret the person being perceived.

Use of Language

Another factor influencing perception of people is the way they talk. The grammar of every language involves vocal elements as well as appropriate uses of words and word arrangement. When someone uses language according to what the perceiver believes is "proper" or "improper" grammar, perceptions are influenced. A native speaker of a language makes inferences about people based on which words are used, whether or not the rules of arrangement are followed, and the ways in which the words are vocally expressed.

dialect

Anyone who flies from Boston to Atlanta and listens to people talk in both cities becomes aware of differences in American English. This variability is commonly described as a *dialect* difference. *Dialect refers to a language variant used by a group of speakers perceived as different from the general language community.* Dialects are geographic, social, or ethnic, and involve differences in the use of words, sounds, and syntax.

Differences in the use of language lead to evaluations. For example, after hearing a person speak, you may infer that he/she is from the South. Depending on your attitudes, this leads to other inferences. If the speaker is a woman and you have an attitude that Southern women are coy and empty-headed, you'll tend to project these attributes onto the person. Similarly, if the speaker is a politician or a sheriff, your beliefs about Southern politicians or sheriffs will influence your interpretation of the person. The influence of dialects in perceiving people is strongest in identifying whether others are similar to or different from you and your own speech community. People within a particular region or community may not be able to describe exactly how another's speech differs, but they easily recognize when it's non-native. Nor must these differences be from one part of the U.S. to another. In many metropolitan areas, natives of one community can tell which part of town someone is from simply by listening for a while. Once perceived, differences in language activate attitudes or prejudices the perceiver has toward the area from which the speaker comes.

Perceived differences in speech cause people to attribute factors of personality, intelligence, or competence to the speaker. One study that illustrates this process asked listeners to rate speakers heard on an audio tape.[1] The speakers used language of five different speech communities. Those perceived as Eastern were rated high on intelligence and competence, but low on warmth and friendliness. The opposite was true of speakers with Southern speech. These ratings illustrate that people attribute personal characteristics to and evaluate each other on the basis of language use.

Related to these perceptions are those of appropriateness of roles. Persons with various educational, ethnic, social, or sex characteristics will be attributed different abilities. In a study similar to that cited above, various speakers were rated regarding what occupational level was considered the highest each could achieve.[2] Very few Blacks, Southerners, or lower-class women were perceived as having the capability of becoming a bank president. These ratings, of course, were not due to language alone, but most people will perceive a Black female with speech characteristics of upper-class New Englanders as more competent than her sister who speaks the language of a ghetto on Chicago's south side or the Delta in Mississippi.

DIFFERENCES IN THE USE OF LANGUAGE

indicators	marker	stereotyped element
a speech or language element that is used in a distinct manner by a particular speech community without conscious recognition by either natives or non-natives that it is different.	an element of which natives and non-natives are both aware, even though the use varies among natives.	stigmatized word uses that are noticed especially by people outside the speech community, who apply prejudices associated with the word or phrase usage.
For example, according to the specific area of the country, eggs are cooked in frying pans, skillets, or a spider.	*For example, the "Southern" accent varies greatly from Virginia to Tennessee to Louisiana, but clearly marks Southerners as different from "Yankees."*	*For example, Black English use of the verb* to be, *as in "I be going," is stigmatized as substandard by many whites.*

style

The effects of language use in interpersonal perception are not limited to differences of dialect. *Differences in language use also identify the degree of formality perceived in the communication situ-*

---

[1] Unpublished manuscript by Wayne Dickerson, Professor of Socio-linguistics, University of Illinois, 1974.

[2] Ibid.

ation. These are described as differences of style. Styles vary greatly, depending on relationships, situations, and other factors. Using inappropriate style will influence the perceptions of those interacting with the speaker.

Five styles of variable formality are usually described.[3]

Frozen
Formal
Consultative
Casual
Intimate

These five styles range from highly formal to very informal. Frozen style is used with strangers or in ritual situations. Formal style is found most often in one-to-many speeches or in work situations. At the other extreme, among family and close friends, people use an intimate style. The decision to use any of these styles results in many choices that must be made by the speaker. The choices involve differences in words used; the degree of formality of the expressions (whether sentences are completed or not, how carefully the words are articulated); and appropriate changes in nonverbal behaviors.

Styles of address illustrate this point well. Use of titles (Dr., Mr., Ms., Mrs., Miss, Professor, Captain, Lieutenant, Sir) is necessary in the frozen and formal settings. Titles may also, depending on the social rules, be used in consultative settings. Among friends, titles will be dropped and first names or nicknames used. Among

THE FIVE STYLES OF VARIABLE FORMALITY
(spoken by a receptionist at work to a client of the company)

Frozen: Good morning, Sir. May we be of assistance?

Formal: Yes, Mr. Marcus, Dr. Clementi is expecting you for a three o'clock appointment. Let me tell her that you have arrived.

Consultative: Mr. Marcus, Dr. Clementi just took a long distance call. She won't take long. Can you wait just a minute?

Casual: Jerry Marcus, how great to see you again! Why haven't you been to see us lately? We've missed you.

Intimate: Luv—you're early. It's not three yet, and you know the boss never sees anyone before the appointment time.

---

[3] The names for the five styles are from Martin Joos, *The Five Clocks* (New York: Harcourt Brace Jovanovich, 1967).

intimates, special forms of address, such as babe, dear, honey, sweetheart, common only to the intimates will be used. Yet when an argument or the formality of the situation calls for it, intimates drop the special address and use the same form of address as for friends, sometimes even reverting to titles. We well remember a friend who addressed her husband as Mr. when she was angered.

Toward the more formal end of the continuum, speakers choose words with special care, paying attention to grammar and pronunciation. Formal styles also call for more elaboration because less previous information is shared by the speakers. Formal styles cause more hesitations in speakers who are not comfortable in such settings, and usually require controlled emotions, with pitch, rate, and volume being maintained at moderate levels. All these factors vary from speaker to speaker and situation to situation. But the relationships between language, speech, and situation are generally those reflected in the following diagram:[4]

RELATIONS OF SPEECH COMMUNICATION STYLE AND OTHER VARIABLES

Situation	Style	LANGUAGE FEATURES				
		Concern for Speech	Syntactic Complexity	Vocabulary	Nonverbal	Comfort and Ease
Unknown Receivers	Frozen	↑ High	↑ High	↑ Wide	↑ Low Use	↑ Low
Important Receivers (one or many)	Formal					
Acquaintances or Associates	Consultative					
Friends	Casual					
Intimates and Family	Intimate	↓ Low	↓ Low	↓ Low	↓ High Use	↓ High

When a person uses the "appropriate style," inferences are drawn accordingly. He or she is perceived as competent, at least to the extent that the ideas are also perceived as competent and prejudices do not interfere. When people use a style considered inappropriate to the relationship between the communicators or to the situation, perceptions are influenced according to how important appropriateness is to the perceiver. The perceiver infers whether or not the style is deliberate and why, or decides if it is accidental because the source is ignorant or incompetent. Whatever is concluded, perceptions of the person are influenced.

---

[4] Adapted from Dickerson, *op. cit.*

> If my theory of relativity is proved successful, Germany will claim me as a German and France will declare that I am a citizen of the world. Should my theory prove untrue, France will say that I am a German and Germany will declare that I am a Jew.
>
> ALBERT EINSTEIN

Labeling behaviors are another way language use influences interpersonal perception. *We use labeling to mean attaching a word to a person as if the word were the person.* Examples: John is stupid; Mary is beautiful; Dick is sneaky; Pat is smart; Mother is unfair; Father is unreasonable. The labels we attach to people express the category we perceive them to fit. Once people are categorized, the label brings to mind a set of expectations we have about the people in the category. Thus, through selectivity of perception, the labels influence what we perceive. Remember that *we tend to perceive what we expect.* As an illustration, consider the following exchange between three bricklayers, Bill, Bob, and Bruce, at work on a hot Friday afternoon in July. Bill and Bob are planning a weekend outing together. They label each other as friends, but they don't think of Bruce as their friend. Bill inadvertently fouls up a line, causing all three to have to go back, tear out, and re-lay the wall they were working on. Bob says, "Bill, you s.o.b., that was a dumb move! Why don't you pay any attention to what you're doing?" Because Bob is labeled as a friend, the words are perceived as friendly and Bill agrees with a sheepish grin, "Yeah, I guess I was at the lake already. Sorry." Had Bruce chided Bill with exactly the same words, Bill's response would have been anger and defensiveness, perhaps worse. Bill's label for Bob determined what the words were expected to mean and how they were perceived. When Bill labels Bob as a friend, he perceives that Bob's actions toward him are friendly.

Stereotypes.   Labels that reflect stereotypes have a very strong influence on perception. Generally, stereotypes refer to characteristics of groups, but the process of *stereotyping projects the attributes of a group onto an individual.* When a person perceived as part of a stereotyped group is encountered, the perceiver projects the stereotyped characteristics onto the individual. Because stereotyping heightens the effects of selective perception, its influence in interpersonal perception is very strong.

Stereotypes are not necessarily derogatory, though they're usually thought of that way. For example, beliefs that men are logical thinkers, professors are intelligent, Jews have strong family ties, are all stereotypes, just as are attitudes that women are irrational, Blacks inferior, Jews money-mad, or cops obsessed with their authority. Generalizations and stereotypes, whether favorable or unfavorable, are often abusive to accurate perception. Strong connotative meanings are usually suggested by stereotypes, affecting the interpretations of a person perceived to fit a stereotyped category. Using the words "Polack," "Nigger," "Honky," "Jap," or "Wop" to describe a person will carry a strong connotation. No one needs to add the adjectives perceived by the labeler: dumb, inferior, sneaky, greasy. These connotations are suggested merely by use of the label, and the perceiver generally projects and sees these characteristics.

Exercise: Perceptions of Others

Objective: To illustrate the effects of appearance and language on interpersonal perceptions.

Directions:

1. Pick out a person you do not know in the library, student center, at work, or in a cafeteria or lounge.
2. Observe the person for a few minutes; then assess her/him according to the scale at the end of the exercise. Mark with a B each item you think fits the person.
3. Engage the person in a conversation for at least 15 minutes. You may tell him/her the conversation is for a class assignment. Seek information about occupation, interests, and hobbies, groups belonged to or identified with.
4. Then assess the person again, according to the same scales. Mark the scales with an A this time.
5. Discuss the ratings with the person to determine the accuracy of your perceptions.
6. Be prepared to discuss this experience in class. Plan to deal with answers to the following questions:
   a. How much change was there in the *before* and *after* ratings?
   b. On what did you base the *before* ratings?
   c. What labeling conclusions did you draw before the discussion?
   d. What was your accuracy of rating, according to the point of view of the other person?
   e. What language uses by the person led you to your conclusions?

Employed	— — — — — —	Unemployed
Occupation is employee-worker	— — — — — —	Occupation is manager-professional
Highly educated	— — — — — —	Little education
Friendly	— — — — — —	Unfriendly
Interested in sports	— — — — — —	Not interested in sports
Nonathletic	— — — — — —	Athletic
Irreligious	— — — — — —	Religious
Doesn't like hunting, fishing, camping	— — — — — —	Likes hunting, fishing, camping
Married	— — — — — —	Unmarried
Likes dogs as pets	— — — — — —	Doesn't like dogs as pets

A third factor that influences us in interpreting people is interpersonal attraction. *Interpersonal attraction describes the positive regard people have for other people.* When persons are "attracted" to each other, a bond exists. Both have a positive "feeling" toward each other. Attraction, like beauty in the eye of the beholder, is determined by the individuals. A person who has qualities that are attractive to many people is said to have "charisma." Whether it exists to a great or small degree, interpersonal attraction is an important element in interpersonal perception. It creates friendships and relationships, influences whether they are lasting or short-lived, helps determine the amount of pleasure derived from the communications.

People are attracted to others for many reasons. The major sources of interpersonal attraction are appearance, proximity, reciprocal liking, and attitude similarity. These are usually involved in combination. In the following pages we'll discuss the influence of these factors in creating attraction and thus in affecting interpersonal perception.

appearance

The initial condition for interpersonal attraction is usually physical appearance. An attractive appearance is an individual preference, and what is attractive to individuals varies widely. But whatever is perceived as a pleasing physical appearance is an important first element in creating interpersonal attraction. Although everyone knows the wrapper doesn't guarantee the quality of the contents, it contains lots of promises. The billions spent annually on advertis-

Interpersonal attraction. *Source: (left)* The Bettmann Archive; *(center, right)* Springer/Bettmann Film Archive.

ing, packaging, cosmetics, fashion, and hair styling demonstrate that the look helps sell the product, whether the product is an object or a person. Physical appearance, however, is usually only an initial means of getting someone's attention or high evaluation. Alone, it rarely maintains interpersonal attraction.

Attractiveness based on physical appearance is influenced both by cultural variability and personal preferences. People have individual preferences as to what qualities are necessary for someone to be physically pleasing. Chris may prefer slender blonde types while Sandy may be partial to athletic-looking, dark people. Hair color, body build, facial characteristics, and other physical elements vary in importance to different people. At the same time, however, these preferred qualities are affected by cultural standards. Cultural norms of appearance account for a 19-year-old girl liking the long hair of her boyfriend while her parents describe him as looking like a bum. Cultural boundaries set certain characteristics above others as important aspects of attractiveness. The U.S. standard for a beautiful woman looks puny or undernourished to people of some cultures.

proximity

A second source of interpersonal attraction involves the accidental or intentional use of proximity. Distances between people influence interpersonal attraction. *Accidental proximity* refers to physical closeness over which you have little control. For example, you have little to say about selecting your neighbors unless you're willing to move whenever you get a new neighbor you don't like. At work you come into contact with people as your jobs relate. You seldom can control work associations. Thus, in many situations how close you are to others is accidental.

The rules of living dictate certain associations, and a frequent result of those associations is liking. The more often you come in contact with people, the more likely you'll be attracted to them. Research indicates that a person placed in neighboring settings with others is likely to develop a positive attitude, or lessen an already negative one. It's simpler to get along with persons you work with or live near. One coping reaction to those you dislike is to ignore or stay away from them. Keeping close contact with enemies is a stressful situation that people usually try to avoid. Assault and homicide statistics demonstrate the seriousness of not getting along with people in close proximity.

Though close distance doesn't guarantee people will be attracted to each other, it's usually a necessary condition for friendship. Close distances offer greater opportunity for shared experiences and exchanges of personal information. Notice yourself in classes. You may become friends with people whose seats are next to yours. Chances are less that you'll become well acquainted with those who sit on the other side of the room. It's difficult to create relationships without some proximity. Although some prolonged pen-pal relationships exist, and some result in intimacy between the writers, frequent contact is generally required for liking to develop.

Intentional proximity results when you make a special effort to be near someone you find attractive. If you've seen someone in class you like the looks of, you may move your customary seat to be close enough to get acquainted. Or you may try to leave the room at the same time, or request work reassignments to be near someone you would like to get to know.

reciprocal liking

Reciprocal liking is a basic element in interpersonal attraction. If you become aware that someone likes you, then your evaluation of her/him is apt to move toward liking. A positive evaluation from one person engenders a similar response from the other person. Liking people can prompt you to focus attention on them; their liking of you becomes the catalyst for you to consider liking them. How often have you heard, "He/she likes you," and then paid more attention to that person than you otherwise would have?

This reciprocity hinges on two factors. First, the person extending the reinforcement (liking) must be someone you are willing to be attracted to. If not, you'll rationalize or justify the disliking. Second, the recipient of liking must not have a low self-concept. People with low self-esteem often regard people who dislike them more favorably than those who like them.

attitude similarity

Similar attitudes can produce increased liking or interpersonal attraction. Attitude similarity relates to interpersonal attraction in two ways: first, *people are attracted to others who share their attitudes.* When you meet someone who shares your interests, you find it pleasing. Shared interests are usually rewarding. Conversations with strangers are less awkward when you discover you have something in common. Talking to someone who doesn't share your attitudes and interests can be boring. People who cannot share interests have less attraction for each other.

The relationship of attitude similarity and liking is often an unpredictable one. It's not accurate to say that people must have similar attitudes to like each other. People of opposite interests can be attracted to one another by appreciation of the differences. However, a degree of similarity is helpful in attraction. Once liking occurs, it's a "chicken-egg" argument as to whether persons are ini-

People are attracted to people who share their attitudes. *Source: (left)* Henry Monroe—Design Photographers International; *(right)* Delmor Lipp—Design Photographers International.

tially similar or if the similarity is created by interaction. Liking a person can create attempts to share important attitudes.

The second relationship of attitude similarity to interpersonal attraction is that *liking can create perceptual distortion in favor of similarities*. When people like each other they often assume similarity in interests and attitudes. You expect friends, for example, to have attitudes toward common acquaintances that are like your own. In most cases, people are dismayed if they learn their friends don't like the same people they do. Try to remember the last time someone reported to you that a mutual friend made a statement you disagreed with. Wasn't your first reaction to think, "Oh, that wasn't quite what she/he meant"? If so, it was a natural reaction. As people focus on people they like, they perceive similarities and selectively disregard attitudes or characteristics that are different.

Exercise: Why Do I Like People?

Objective: To examine how the factors of interpersonal attraction affect you.
Directions:
1. Pick out a person you like very much and one you do not like.
2. Using the scale provided at the end of the exercise, assess how many of the factors of interpersonal attraction are involved in each relationship.
3. Discuss the following questions with a group of your classmates:
   a. Do your ratings appear to confirm the relationships indicated in the reading about the relationship between the four factors and interpersonal attraction?
   b. If so, how?
   c. If not, why not?
   d. Can you think of other factors involved in interpersonal attraction?

Physical Appearance

Is pleasing to me. — — — — — Is not pleasing to me.

Proximity

I associate with as much as I can. — — — — — I avoid whenever I can.
I must be around a lot at work/home/school. — — — — — I don't need to be around very much.

Attitude Similarity

Religion is like mine. — — — — — Religion is different.
Is interested in same things. — — — — — Is not interested in same things.
Political views are like mine. — — — — — Political views are not like mine.

Reciprocal Liking

Likes me. — — — — — Doesn't like me.

EFFECTS OF INTERPERSONAL PERCEPTION IN COMMUNICATION

As we pointed out earlier, communication transactions and inter-personal perception are interactive. Communication transactions cause interpersonal perception, while at the same time our perceptions of people cause us to communicate in particular ways. Interpersonal perception and communication not only interact, they have interacting effects. No amount of analysis can separate them. Still some interpersonal perceptions have such a powerful effect in communication interactions that we need to single them out for special notice. We will mention three: *stereotypes, homophily, credibility.*

Stereotypes

As noted above, stereotyping influences interpersonal perception because we project attributes believed characteristic of a group onto individuals perceived as being part of the group. We see in the individuals what we expect them to exhibit as a result of this group membership. Having thus projected, our communication behavior is affected.

stereotypes and cultural biases

Stereotypes affect communication most strongly when cultural biases are associated with the stereotype. When we have attitudes toward cultural or ethnic groups that are either negative or positive, such attitudes affect how we communicate with persons identified with these groups. If a person believes that Blacks are lazy and dumb, Mexican-Americans are violent, Irish drink too much, Southerners are big-

149

ots, women are irrational, New Yorkers cold and unfriendly, Californians radical, and so on, the belief will affect how he or she will talk to people identified with the group. A person holding these negative attitudes will make a strong effort to avoid any communication at all with individuals they fit. If communication cannot be avoided, it will be marked by coldness, hostility and/or suspicion. If in contrast, the person believes that Black is beautiful, Irish are warm and sociable, Southerners are the only remaining bastian of true Americanism, and so on, opposite effects occur. Communication with persons identified with the group will be welcomed, enjoyed, and warmly responded to.

Stereotyping thus not only affects how we perceive people, it is also one of the strongest influences in how we communicate with them. Far too often stereotypes are based on incomplete or inaccurate knowledge about the group to which the stereotype is applied. Moreover, even if the stereotype were totally accurate, the individual identified as a member of the group probably does not possess all attributes of the group. In most cases where stereotyping affects communication, both conditions are true. Stereotypes are usually only partly true, if at all, and the individuals do not reflect every characteristic of the identified group.

The only useful way to approach communication when stereotypes are involved is to treat the stereotype as an hypothesis. Hypotheses are considered tentative, to be tested and rejected if the evidence doesn't confirm them. Stereotypes should be thought of the same way. Think of any generalization you hold about a group as tentative: tentative as a conclusion and tentative as to whether it applies to an individual member or not. It will then be less likely that the stereotype prevents potentially valuable communication or makes you communicate with attitudes that guarantee negative outcomes.

Homophily

This concept was mentioned above without using the term, homophily. *Homophily refers to the degree to which communicators are similar in attributes,* such as attitudes, values, socioeconomic status, and appearance. Obviously, two dimensions of homophily exist: actual and perceived similarity. The two need not be the same. You can, for instance, perceive someone who may *actually* have the same education as you as being on a very different level. In some aspects, such as appearance, perceived and actual similarity are usually close. In other aspects, as discussed above under the heading of attitude similarity, perceptions may be quite different from reality. For example, newlyweds often discover in the first weeks of marriage they were wrong in assumptions about each other. Attitudes and habits they thought were similar turn out to be quite different. Because of differences between actual and perceived similarity, many marriages founder.

At this point, however, we are mainly concerned with *perceived* homophily (similarity).[5] Perceiving a person as homophilous will be due to appearance, language, and behavior, usually in some combination. Whatever the reasons you conclude another person is like you, once the interpretation has occurred, several effects on communication follow.[6] Communication between people who perceive themselves as homophilous will be more frequent, more effective and as a result, will have a tendency to increase the actual homophily.

We can note, in reverse, the effects of the absence of homophily in communication. We communicate less frequently and less effectively with people who are different or are perceived as different from us. As interaction decreases both in amount and effectiveness, nothing occurs to increase the perception of homophily, even if we are, in fact, similar to or become more like the other person.

Of course, homophily doesn't have to be total. You can perceive someone as like you in some aspects and unlike you in others. To have a strong effect on communication, the perceived similarity should be relevant to the situation. We discussed that idea above under attitude similarity. If two people are discussing football, their attitudes toward religion would probably not affect the interactions. But if one is very interested in football and perceives the other as not being interested, it will affect the interaction.

A final set of effects of homophily involves the other effect of interpersonal perception we want to discuss, credibility.

Credibility

One of the very important perceptions of people that we have is whether they are credible or not. Credibility refers to how believable a person is. We define the term, *source credibility, as a receiver's evaluation of the believability of a source in a particular sit-*

---

[5] You may wonder why we use the complicated language, when homophily is synonymous with similarity. We use the term, *homophily,* to familiarize you with a word that is becoming common in the research literature in explaining effective persuasion and opinion leadership. You should also be aware, if you wish to read further in the area, that *heterophily* is the term used to describe the degree of difference between communicators.

[6] Everett M. Rogers and Dilip K. Bhowmik, "Homophily-Heterophily: Relationships Concepts for Communication Research," in *Speech Communication Behavior Perspectives and Principles,* ed. Larry L. Barker and Robert J. Kibler (Englewood Cliffs, N.J.: Prentice-Hall, 1971), pp. 206–25.

uation. Credibility is high or low according to whether a person is considered by the perceiver as believable in this situation. When a communicator is perceived to be credible (believable), communication is strongly affected. Credibility of a communicator is not a simple perception. People are believable, depending on several other perceptions.

bases of credibility

Credibility primarily originates from receiver perceptions of a source's character and competence. Perceptions of honesty, friendliness, and pleasantness provide credibility based on character. Persons perceived as dishonest, unfriendly, and unpleasant are usually low in credibility. Credibility based on competence comes from being perceived as reliable, informed, qualified, and intelligent. Persons perceived as unreliable, uninformed, unintelligent, or inexpert lack credibility based on competence.

These elements vary, primarily because they are all based on receiver perceptions. Credibility isn't global. One receiver or group may consider a person competent, while another receiver or group may see the same person as incompetent. Perceptions vary also because of the topic or situation. People at work, for instance, perceived as an authority regarding the job may not be seen as informed or expert regarding politics. Certainly, high ratings on one scale have some effect on the others, but the effects vary. Being perceived as honest won't cause a person to be seen as an expert on every topic. Being an expert in one topic won't guarantee a person will be thought of as expert on others, or considered honest.

Whether receivers like a person seems also to be related to credibility, but this depends very much on the situation. You may like a friend very much, but your friend may have no credibility at all regarding how to repair your car. On the other hand, you may know an auto mechanic whose personality you don't like, but in whose honesty and mechanical ability you have complete confidence. On a question of how to repair the car, the disliked mechanic will have higher credibility than your friend. On the other hand, given two equally skilled mechanics, one you like and one you don't like, the former will probably have higher credibility. How much a person is liked is probably more important to credibility in interpersonal than public communication, though that is not invariably true. Perception of credibility is highly situation-bound.

Other factors are also involved in credibility, at least in some situations. The first of these is *poise* or *composure.* To be seen as poised is to be perceived as in control of your emotions. If you're seen as poised, relaxed, and confident in contrast to being nervous, tense or uptight, you'll gain in this dimension of credibility. Still, if you are unemotional in a situation where you'd be expected to have feelings involved, it will not add to perceived credibility. Display of emotion can add to perceived honesty. This factor is as situation-bound as other dimensions of credibility. Generally, however, being perceived as having your feelings under control would be considered positive, especially in group or public situations. A second factor is described as *dynamism.* This is to be perceived as aggressive, bold, and extroverted, rather than meek, timid, and introverted. Though also influenced by situation, neither extreme of this continuum seems to contribute strongly to credibility. This may be a dimension on which you gain most from being perceived as slightly to the extrovert side of the middle. If you are perceived as either highly extroverted or introverted it seems to interfere with believability. The chart below illustrates the scales that are sometimes used to measure the credibility dimensions. The scales illustrate the factors of credibility.[7]

Example of Credibility Scales

Honest	— — — — — — —	Dishonest
Friendly	— — — — — — —	Unfriendly
Trustworthy	— — — — — — —	Cannot be trusted
Pleasant	— — — — — — —	Unpleasant

Competence

Reliable	— — — — — — —	Unreliable
Informed	— — — — — — —	Uninformed
Qualified	— — — — — — —	Not Qualified
Intelligent	— — — — — — —	Unintelligent

Composure

Poised	— — — — — — —	Anxious
Calm	— — — — — — —	Uneasy

Dynamism

Aggressive	— — — — — — —	Meek
Bold	— — — — — — —	Timid
Extroverted	— — — — — — —	Introverted

---

sources of credibility

Several factors contribute to perceptions of credibility. Receivers' prior knowledge, halo effect of associations, environment, verbal

---

[7] The actual items on the scales vary. You should also know that when the scales are used, the positive elements are not always on the same end of the scale. They are reversed from side to side in a random manner.

and nonverbal message variables all have effects. Remember, we perceive others largely as a composite, drawing inferences on appearance, environment, and behaviors as well as language. No ultimate guidelines exist to indicate how much of each dimension is perceived from which factor. The effect of any factor (language, nonverbals, environment, associations) in creating credibility varies according to the situation, but all have some effect. The effect of each of these is how it is perceived in relation to the dimensions of credibility. What people know about you prior to any situation doubtless influences how they perceive your credibility in that situation. If you are known to be associated with respected authorities or opinion leaders, it will have an effect upon the initial perceptions of your competence. The converse is true, also. Associations with those not respected for knowledge or competence can have adverse effects on your perceived competence. In addition, of course, perceptions regarding character, competence and dynamism all result from what a person does and says. Manipulation of the environment, appearance, behavior, all will influence perceptions of the various dimensions of credibility.

effects of credibility

Sources who are perceived as high in credibility receive favorable treatment, both in total perceptions as people and in acceptability of what they say. People expose themselves more, listen with more attentiveness, remember longer, and are more likely to believe a highly credible source.

Beyond these effects, people perceive credible sources as more homophilous. Receivers often assume and even amplify similarities between themselves and highly credible sources. A highly credible person might say something contrary to what is expected or believed by a listener, but selective perception often results in the statement not being heard; or in distortion and modification so the statement is consistent with the expectations. Receivers usually aren't aware of these selective distortions, but they occur.

Similarly, messages from low credibility sources are often negatively distorted, with the degree of distortion depending on how intensely the receiver dislikes or distrusts the source. Attitude change in response to messages from highly credible sources is faster than for low. People spend less time considering actions proposed by highly credible sources.

You can see, therefore, how stereotypes, homophily, and credibility are interactive perceptions. Similarly easy to see is how strongly all three can affect communication. You'll hear reference to these important concepts several times in this book. What we perceive about people influences whether we talk to them, what we say to them, the attitudes we have while we talk with them, what we are willing to talk to them about, how much we are willing to listen to them, and how much we are willing to accept of what we hear from them. These elements are involved whether the communication is between two individuals in a private conversation, or at the other extreme of the audience size, if you are talking via television to millions.[8]

Exercise: Assessing Credibility

Objective: To understand the elements affecting credibility.
Directions:
1. Think back to a recent situation in which you were persuaded to do something. Choose a situation in which the person really persuaded you. In other words, don't choose a time when you really were wanting to do something and a person just happened to suggest it at the appropriate time.
2. Using the scales on page 153, assess the credibility of the persuader.
3. Now, think of a recent situation in which someone unsuccessfully tried to persuade you to do something.
4. Using the same scale, assess the credibility of this persuader.
5. Your instructor may lead the class in a discussion of what factors contribute to credibility, asking that you share the two assessments of credibility that you made.

---

[8] The study of interpersonal perception, including homophily and credibility, is relatively recent in development. The sources cited in the readings list suggest several places in which you might pursue the most recent research in this area.

Interpersonal perception is the process of interpreting the people with whom you interact, of drawing inferences about them. It is a complex process for several reasons. First, perceptions influence communications at the same time communications influence perceptions. Also, in perceiving people, a perceiver must process a vast amount of data—thus *selective* perception is very influential. Much data is not processed at all or only marginally perceived. Moreover, the perceiver's self becomes strongly involved in interpersonal perception. The self is what selects which data are perceived and what interpretations are drawn. The perceiver is interacting with the person being perceived and is thus interacting with a perception, not just with an external object. Finally, in perceiving other people, many different selves influence the perceptions.

Ultimately, interpersonal perception is a process of attributing characteristics to a person. Three factors play a major role in the attribution process: physical appearance, use of language, and interpersonal attraction. Physical appearance is a major influence because it is the first information processed about a person and is the basis for many stereotypes that are then projected onto the person. Use of language is a major influence through both speech and word choice. Labeling is the process that makes use of language so important in interpersonal perception. As labels are applied to people, perceivers expect to see the behaviors and attributes that confirm those labels. Because the selectivity of perception applies in interpersonal perception as much if not more than in all perceiving, perceivers tend to see what the labeling leads them to expect.

Stereotyping, a form of labeling, is probably most damaging in interpersonal perception because emotions are usually attached to the labels and thus tend to influence selectivity very strongly. All labels should be considered as hypotheses to be tested rather than conclusions to be predicted as probably true.

The final influence on interpersonal perception discussed was interpersonal attraction. Interpersonal attraction describes the process by which people develop positive regard for each other. Four factors influence the development of interpersonal attraction: physical attractiveness is in the eye of the perceiver but is influenced to a large extent by culturally determined attributes of beauty. Self-concept is also a major factor in what a person perceives as attractive appearance. Proximity can be either accidental or purposeful. The relation of accidental proximity to attraction is twofold; people have more opportunities to learn about and share with people they are close to, and people generally find it easier to like those they must be around than to dislike them. Purposeful proximity is when one party or the other creates opportunities to be close to someone they believe to be attractive. Reciprocal liking operates to influence interpersonal attraction because it focuses attention and operates to reward the person to whom attention is directed. Reciprocal liking does not tend to create attraction for persons of very low self-concept, because they respond more positively to people who dislike them than those they perceive as liking them. Attitude similarity increases interpersonal attraction because it rewards the persons involved and operates to increase proximity as well as shared interests.

Three elements, stereotypes, homophily, and credibility, are interpersonal perceptions that have strong influences on communication. These three elements each interact with perception, in that each is a perception resulting from communication, and that in turn affects the subsequent communications. Stereotypes that are negative can either prevent or distort communication, as can perceived absence of homophily or low credibility. On the other hand, favorable stereotypes, perceived homophily, or high credibility can lead people to communicate more often and more effectively.

Questions for Discussion

1. Why is perceiving people more complex than perceiving objects?
2. Who are the many selves in each interpersonal transaction?
3. How do the many selves affect communication?
4. How do language, appearance, and stereotyping influence interpretations of people?
5. What is interpersonal attraction and how does it influence interpersonal perception?
6. If a person is perceived as homophilous or highly credible, how does that influence communication?

Suggestions for Further Reading

BYRNE, DONN, *The Attraction Pardigm.* New York: Academic Press, 1971.

DOUGLAS, JACK, ed., *Understanding Everyday Life.* Chicago: Aldine, 1970.

GIGLIOLI, PIER P., ed., *Language and Social Context.* Baltimore: Penguin, 1972.

HASTORF, ALBERT, DAVID J. SCHNEIDER, AND JUDITH POLEFKA, *Person Perception.* Reading, Mass.,: Addison-Wesley, 1970.

HEIDER, FRITZ, *The Psychology of Interpersonal Relations.* New York: Wiley, 1958.

JOOS, MARTIN, *The Five Clocks.* New York: Harcourt Brace Jovanovich, 1967.

LAING, RONALD D., *et al., Interpersonal Perception.* New York: Springer, 1966.

LINDZEY, GARDNER, AND ELLIO ARONSON, eds., *Handbook of Social Psychology.* Reading, Mass: Addison-Wesley, 1969.

McCALL, GEORGE J., *et al., Social Relationships.* Chicago: Aldine, 1970.

STOTLAND, EZRA, AND LANCE CANON, *Social Psychology: A Cognitive Approach.* Philadelphia: Saunders, 1972.

SUDNOW, DAVID, *Studies in Social Interaction.* New York: Free Press, 1972.

TAGIURI, RENATO, AND LUIGI PETRULLO, *Person Perception and Interpersonal Behavior.* Stanford, Calif.: Stanford University Press, 1958.

WALFAM, WALT, AND RALPH FASAED, *Study of Social Dialects in American English.* Englewood Cliffs, N.J.: Prentice-Hall, 1974.

WARR, PETER B., AND CHRISTOPHER KNAPPER, *The Perception of People and Events.* New York: Wiley, 1968.

6

Why We Communicate

goal:

To be able to use our understanding of communicators' purposes and motivations to improve communication.

probes:

The material in this chapter should help you to

To be human is to share your thoughts and feelings with others. How often the excitement of experiences is heightened by telling someone else. Keeping thoughts to yourself makes them seem wasted. Could you spend two hours today not communicating with anyone? How about a whole day? Small wonder that the harshest punishment in prison is still solitary confinement! We need and want to talk with other people for many reasons. This chapter examines some of those reasons.

Communication, like almost all behavior, is motivated, or goal-directed. Communicators have goals or purposes they want to accomplish. Knowing these purposes can help you understand communication. If you can discover the purposes in your own and others' communication, you can prevent yourself from behaving in ways you don't want to either as source or receiver. Understanding the purposes for which people communicate can help you interact with others more effectively.

PURPOSES ARE USUALLY MULTIPLE

> Our reasons for speaking are ego-centered and intrapersonal, as well as socio-centered and interpersonal—for example, we speak for self-assertion, self-identity, and self-fulfillment, as well as for reducing tensions, establishing social contact, and controlling our environment.
>
> THOMAS SCHEIDEL

Most, if not all, communicators have three different sets of purposes. These *purposes are related to self, to the subject, and to the other participants.* For example, when you say, "Please close the door," you may be communicating to satisfy a personal need for privacy (a purpose related to self); and/or to create the reality of a closed door (a purpose related to subject); and/or to express or establish a relationship with the person addressed (a purpose related to others). Even in this simple case you had multiple purposes. In most cases every person in a communication situation has at a minimum three interrelated purposes. These purposes may be either hidden or open, and both sources and receivers have purposes.

Hidden or Open Purposes

Communication purposes are both hidden and open. Open purposes are apparent to all participants. In the example above, the open purpose is to get the door closed. But often, one or more purposes are hidden from one or more of the communicators. Why do you want the door closed? You may not tell the person you're talking to. You may not even know all the reasons yourself. What personal need will a closed door satisfy for you? Why did you ask the other person to close it? Why didn't you do it yourself? What is your purpose related to that person? People often have goals they don't disclose, both for talking and listening. These are called *hid-*

Communication purposes are both
hidden and open.
*Source: (below)*Mini Forsyth—
Monkmeyer; *(upper right)* Hugh Rogers—
Monkmeyer *(lower right)*; Sam Falk
—Monkmeyer

den purposes. Hidden purposes are among the most significant in communication.

> Man is the only animal that blushes—or needs to.
>
> MARK TWAIN
>
> The true use of speech is not so much to express our wants as to conceal them.
>
> A paraphrase of S. BUTLER

Source and Receiver Purposes

It's also important to remember that *a communicator has purposes both as a source and as a receiver.* When you *talk* to ask for information, you *listen* with the purpose of understanding the information. Occasionally, you say and do things to influence others' behaviors. Sometimes you listen to influence others. It's easy to think of speaking as purposive, but remember that listening is equally purposive, whether you are aware of the purposes or not. In this chapter, we analyze reasons you may have for engaging in an interaction with others. In later chapters, we look specifically at purposes you may have for speaking in public situations or for listening in various settings.

PURPOSES RELATED TO SELF

Let's look now at four purposes related to self that communicators have: to satisfy personal needs; to reinforce self-concept; to structure time; and to express tension, emotion, or anxiety.

Satisfaction of Personal Needs

Perhaps the fundamental purpose in all communication is to satisfy personal needs. An analysis of human motivation by Abraham Maslow provides a structure for understanding human needs.[1] We will discuss each of the levels of Maslow's hierarchy.

---

[1] Data on "Hierarchy of Needs" (pp. 35–46) *Motivation and Personality*, 2nd edition, by Abraham H. Maslow. By permission of Harper & Row, Publishers.

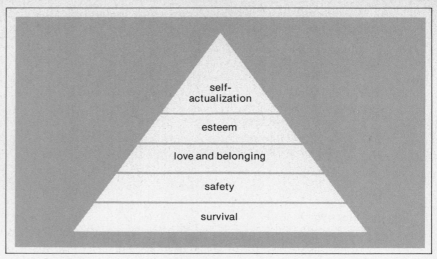

A hierarchy of needs.

survival

> Self-preservation is the first law of nature.
>
> S. BUTLER

At the first level are survival needs. To survive, *certain basic physiological needs must be satisfied.* These include provisions for shelter, food, water, air, reproduction—all the basic requirements necessary to sustain life. In a human being, an estimated 21 trillion cells are organized into a system that has to survive; and although the biological person is a tough, adaptable organism, it has limitations. The average person cannot survive without oxygen for longer than ten minutes, without food for longer than thirty days, or without water for more than six days. Nor can most people survive body temperatures that vary more than ten degrees above or below 98.6° F, or too many days without rest. The need to maintain a constant internal environment provides some of our most basic, though often unnoticed, motivations for communication.

Our psychological needs, though less important to survival, often explain our responses to physical needs. For instance, someone trying to lose pounds to achieve a "socially desirable" appearance may not eat even when hungry. Some people fast for other reasons, also. The socialization process that teaches people acceptable means of satisfying physical needs creates social needs. These psychological needs are powerful motivators. Most people learn to seek social-psychological satisfactions with the same intensity they apply to satisfying survival needs. These psychological needs involve the next four categories of the Maslow hierarchy.

safety

After survival needs come the needs related to safety. Safety needs are primarily a mental extension of survival needs, a fear of not having physical needs met. One reason people need a house, for example, is a fear of freezing in winter. This is a mental extension of a survival need. *Safety needs motivate behaviors to create a feeling that physical needs will be satisfied in the future.* Safety needs could also be labeled *security* needs. Preferring familiar working methods over new patterns of work, wanting insurance against poverty in old age or illness, wanting savings accounts, job security, or nearby police and fire protection are all examples of safety (security) needs. A person whose security needs are not met will have little time for behaviors related to other needs.

love and belonging

In Maslow's third category are the needs for love and for belonging. A *human being needs to identify with someone or something, to feel a sense of belonging, and of love.* Perhaps love and belonging needs should be considered as two separate subgroups: to love and to establish interpersonal relationships are one; to belong and to identify with others are the other. Both relate to needs people have for being affectionately related to other people.

The first subgroup involves both the need to give and to receive love. This group of needs explains families, communes, and people living together in all kinds of arrangements. It explains why family ties stretch across thousands of miles and decades of time.

The second subgroup refers to a need for a sense of *identity.* The desperate search for ethnicity as "Americans" at the time of the colonial War for Independence 200 years ago illustrates this point. The early Americans couldn't consider themselves English any more. They'd broken governmental ties, and thousands of people from other nations had joined them. They had to create an identity as Americans. The same thing is happening today. Blacks, Indians, Chicanos, and many other minority groups are searching for roots, for identity in their ethnicity. Some people describe one of the major problems in the U.S. today as our rootlessness and high mobility. Many people have lost the sense of identifying with a locale, a neighborhood, a place to belong.

esteem

At the fourth level in Maslow's hierarchy are esteem needs. These needs relate to status and to respect from others and self. They involve more than the need to belong. They include *a need for self-*

acceptance, a need to be esteemed by others, to be accepted with positive attitudes, and to be well-regarded. Included in this category are needs for achievement and mastery (which lead to self-esteem), and for respect, attention, and recognition from others. Satisfaction of these needs leads to self-confidence, worth, a feeling of usefulness.

Two subgroupings are useful to clarify the nature of these needs. First, and perhaps most important, are the needs for positive acceptance of self. Satisfaction of the need for self-esteem is important to the fully developed human. But seldom is it possible to have positive acceptance of self without the satisfaction of the second group of esteem needs, the needs for esteem by others. Thus, esteem of at least a few significant others is probably necessary for full satisfaction of both subgroups of needs in this group.

self-actualization

At the highest level of needs are behaviors relating to *self-actualization. Self-actualization relates to reaching the full potential of the individual* — to use Maslow's words, "to become everything one is capable of becoming." For instance, some people need to write poetry, or to paint, or to build things. Some seek power, others knowledge; and the list could extend infinitely. Self-actualization needs relate to the human quality of satisfaction with self. Some people require creative activities; others need to manipulate and control their environment. For example, work may be a survival or safety need for some people, but for others it becomes a source of self-actualization. For them work is important, not for the income it produces, but because such people must feel useful and productive to feel fulfilled. Leisure for them may be uneasy and anxious because they only know how to satisfy self-actualization needs through work.

Exercise: Motivation

Objective: To practice identifying motivations.
Directions:
1. Choose two advertisements for some product. Select each ad from different media: newspapers, magazines, radio, television.
2. Identify the needs the advertisers are trying to appeal to in selling the products.
3. On the assigned day, bring the ads or a description of them to class.
4. Be prepared to explain the needs you think the advertisers are appealing to, and explain how the advertisers were trying to use them.

categories are interrelated

You may have difficulty distinguishing clearly among Maslow's categories of needs. Each might seem to blend into the next, especially if you try to think of examples. That's because the categories overlap, and because the actual hierarchy of a person's needs at any precise time varies. Seldom at any one time are all physical needs satisfied, much less all psychological needs. The interrelations among satisfied and unsatisfied needs create a very complex motivation situation. The categories are not clear-cut, nor are they related to each other as building blocks.

It's only generally true that needs "higher" in the triangle don't motivate a person until those below are satisfied. Certainly people in physical danger don't usually worry about self-actualization or belonging, but sometimes they do. Some people go on hunger strikes to dramatize opposition to war or the plight of their fellows. Mahatma Gandhi literally starved himself to achieve independence for India in 1948. Sometimes parents deliberately put themselves in physical danger to save a child. Sometimes pride will make people refuse welfare and endure physical deprivation to satisfy self-esteem or self-actualization needs.

Studying the categories in the Maslow hierarchy can help you understand the various causes of human behavior. But be sure to keep in mind that *rarely if ever does a single need motivate any single behavior.*

Reinforcement of Self-Concept

Another way to view the purposes related to self is to realize that *communication is used to reinforce our concept of self.* Self-concept, you will remember, refers to the total complex of beliefs and attitudes you have about yourself. While self-concept involves more than a singular position, at its foundation it consists of a negative or a positive view of self and of self in relation to others. Once a person has acquired one of these basic ways of viewing self in relation to others, interpersonal interactions are required to confirm the position. Therefore, communications are structured so that they will reinforce the concept of self. If you pay careful attention to your own and others' communications, you'll see how often this is true. You'll also be able to understand why so much behavior can't be explained in rational terms, because many people are actually communicating to reinforce a negative concept of self.

Structuring of Time

If a people are to create enough predictability in interpersonal interactions that communication can be relied on to reinforce a self-concept, structured use of time is required.[2] Time, at least that

---

[2] Based on pp. 115–25 (hardbound edition) *I'm OK—You're OK* by Thomas A. Harris, M.D. Copyright © 1967, 1968, 1969 by Thomas A. Harris, M.D. By permission of Harper & Row, Publishers. Harris is the primary source for this discussion of time,

shared with others, cannot be allowed to pass in a random, unstructured way, because people cannot then reliably predict the outcome of interactions. Most of us find ourselves uneasy, for instance, when we face a day when we have planned nothing to do. When that happens, we begin to plan. We structure our time. We decide things to do so that our behavior and that of people around us can be planned and predicted. Four patterns of structuring time can be described.

rituals

Ritual communication is perhaps the clearest example of structuring time. We describe rituals as *socially programmed use of time when everyone agrees to do the same thing*. Ritual communication is talk that communicates, but is not primarily motivated by communicating the verbal message.

Rituals are of all kinds: religious, family, business, social, bedroom. Religious rituals are perhaps the most familiar to most of us. At church we complete rituals, repeating words and actions not because we perceive the words themselves as communicating, but because the rite as a whole communicates. When you go to a party, or meet friends socially for a few minutes between classes, ritual communication often occurs. Exchanges of pleasantries, greetings, or formalities structure the time involved so that outcomes of interpersonal interactions are predictable. The predictability is what makes rituals comfortable forms of interaction. Participants know the outcomes and thus avoid the discomfort of the unexpected or the unknown.

activities

Activities are also programmed uses of time, but usually the people in the interaction do the programming; they don't merely accept externally established social patterns. *Activities are ways of structuring time and effort in accomplishing purposes with reference to external reality*. Activities are found in all aspects of life: work, play, keeping house, and many others. The distinguishing element about activities is that they deal with external reality, usually producing or creating something. Though much human interaction occurs in activities, little interpersonal sharing is required. Activities permit, but do not require, intimacy among the people engaged.

---

although his book is indebted as is this discussion to Eric Berne, *Games People Play* (New York: Grove Press, 1967). Harris describes five "patterns" of using time. We have chosen to cite four since the pattern described as intimacy by Harris is essentially an unstructured use of time.

Pastimes are semi-ritualistic interactions arranged around a single subject. They differ from rituals in that they aren't socially programmed behaviors. Outcomes of pastimes aren't as predictable as rituals. They differ from activities in that they do not create or produce. Their primary object is to *pass time,* typically beginning and ending in either rituals or activities. Pastimes occur in conversation before church, meetings, work. They also occur during social affairs and at work. Pastimes are forms of social probing as a way of selecting friends or maintaining acquaintances. Eric Berne has named some of the common pastimes, and you'll recognize many of them instantly: General Motors (comparing cars), Who Won, Kitchen, Wardrobe, How To, How Much, Ever Been To, Do You Know, and Whatever Happened To. Pastimes, like activities, may lead to intimacy, but do not require it.

games

We're now going to spend a little time to introduce you to a concept involved in time-structuring that we think you may later wish to pursue with further reading.[3] The word "games" as it is used here refers to *a patterned series of communication transactions with well-defined and predictable outcomes.* The definition comes from the writing of Eric Berne, who is generally considered the person responsible for developing the study of human behavior called Transactional Analysis.[4] Transactional Analysis (popularly called TA) studies individual behavior by describing how people communicate. TA also relates to the game-playing activities that explain much communication. We describe the concept of game playing because it is a very useful way to examine some interpersonal communication that otherwise seems unexplainable.

Communication games are *ways of using time by people who need to interact with others for rewards, but whose attitudes toward self and others prevent them from participating in real, honest, or intimate communication with others.* Such games are maneuvers. They have predictable patterns, and predictable outcomes. Indeed, it is the predictability of outcome that induces game players to stay at it. Games are intended to create specific results and when they do, this reinforces the game player's behavior, causing it to be repeated.

---

[3] You'll find several sources in the readings list at the end of this chapter. We suggest you begin with Dr. Berne's book, *Games People Play.*

[4] Transactional Analysis studies human behavior by analyzing communication transactions. A transaction, as defined by Berne, is a communication and the response to it. ibid., p. 29.

Common games are easily recognizable. For example, consider a person who gets a new outfit and asks, "How do I look?" Some people who ask that are honestly seeking an opinion or are wanting approval. Others aren't. The game player, for instance, will take whatever answer is given and turn it to the purpose of the game. This player might say, "Oh no, I really don't look good. You're just flattering me." Or "You're just saying that to make me feel good. You don't really mean it." Or, if the reply was, "I don't really like it very much," a game player may respond, "You never like anything I pick out. You're always running me down."

Games are played primarily by people who have negative self-concept, or who have negative views of other people. They engage in the game for the purpose of reinforcing their self-concept or their view of others. This reinforcement is described as the payoff. Because the outcome of a game is predictable, players gain the reward

Source: *More Peanuts*, Vol. I, by Charles M. Schulz. © 1953 United Feature Syndicate.

(payoff) each time the game is played. Payoffs vary. Probably the most common payoffs are reinforcement of self-concept by setting oneself up for failure, or reinforcing a negative view of others by making them fail.

You can probably identify several game players you know, perhaps including yourself, after reviewing the short summary of common games at the end of this chapter.

Expression of Tension, Emotion, or Anxiety

A seldom-realized communication purpose is found in what we call expressive speech. *Expressive speech communicates, but is not motivated primarily by the intent of conveying meaning or influencing others.* The purpose is primarily to satisfy personal needs for expressing feelings. If you hit your finger with a hammer, you'd probably use expressive speech. When you respond with four-letter words to rude treatment by a waiter or a salesperson, you've used expressive speech. You spoke primarily to express feeling. The nonstop talker is a person who communicates, but the main purpose of talking does not relate to subject or behavior of the other communicators. The major purpose of nonstop talkers is expressive. They talk to relieve tension, to eliminate silence, to express feeling, or to get rid of anxiety.

People often engage in expressive speech without recognizing they've done so. They often think they intend to influence others when the primary purpose is expressive. Have you ever said, "I'm going to give him a piece of my mind," and then did just that? Then later realized that your behavior didn't influence the other person in the way you'd hoped? If so, you didn't achieve the purpose you thought you wanted because of the way you vented your feelings. You used expressive speech. You said what you thought. But it was the desire to *express* feelings that primarily motivated your communication, not your desire to influence the other person's behavior. Had the desire to influence been the major purpose, you'd have chosen your words more carefully, probably more temperately.

Expressive speech.
Source: Michal Heron—Monkmeyer.

Exercise: Purposes

Objective: To practice identifying communication purposes.
Directions:
1. Refer to the dialogs on page 3 of this book.
2. See if you can identify the purposes related to self that each communicator has.
3. What game playing purposes do you see in these cases?
4. Which of the purposes you identified were hidden and which were open?
5. Be prepared to discuss your answers to these questions in class.

PURPOSES RELATED TO SUBJECT

Perhaps the most obvious communication purposes are those related to the subject. When we talk, we intend the words we use to express our meaning. We have an idea we want to communicate. We may attempt to *explain* the idea, or *clarify* or *amplify* it; we may want to develop an argument or *prove* a thesis; we may want to *narrate* a story or *tell* an anecdote. Whatever the idea or subject of our talk, we have some purpose related to it.

Similarly, when we listen, we have subject-centered purposes. We may listen for the purpose of learning about the ideas, assessing the argument, or evaluating the behavior urged upon us. Both source and receiver have purposes related to the subject of the communication.

Recall the first example cited to illustrate the many communication purposes people have, asking a person to close the door. The purpose related to the subject in that situation was the idea: the source wanted a closed door. Assuming a positive response, the receiver may have agreed with the subject-centered purpose and closed the door. Or if not favorable to the idea, the receiver may have asked, "Why?" In either case, each person had an intent with reference to the subject of the communication.

Whether the communication involves satisfying personal needs, reinforcement of self-concept, or structuring time — whether you are engaging in a ritual, an activity, a pastime, a game, or establishing relationships with others — in every case your talk involves a subject. Whatever you intend to say about your subject is the subject-centered purpose for communicating.

PURPOSES RELATED TO OTHERS

The final area we want to discuss is purposes related to other communicators. We describe these as either instrumental or relational.

170

Instrumental Purposes

Instrumental purposes have to do with the behavior or reaction you want from others. In the case of the closed door, your instrumental purpose was to get another person to behave in a particular way. The "why" purposes may have involved a relationship or satisfied a personal need. The instrumental purpose was to activate a particular behavior.

The following are all examples of instrumental purposes: getting receivers to understand something they didn't previously; giving them information they didn't have; securing or intensifying their belief in some idea; and activating a particular behavior. These purposes all involve a desired reaction from other people. Often these purposes are described in terms of the communicator wanting to inform, persuade, entertain, or gain action. Often, you'll act as receiver of messages to fulfill an instrumental purpose. A supervisor may listen to an employee's grievance with great empathy in order to encourage the person to keep working even though unhappy.

Relational Purposes

> This desire for interpersonal fusion is the most powerful striving in man. It is the most fundamental passion, it is the force which keeps the human race together, the clan, the family, society.
>
> ERICH FROMM

Earlier in this chapter, we discussed communication with a purpose of establishing predictability in interpersonal interactions, which is usually one of the purposes of interpersonal communication. But *communicators are also trying to establish or maintain a particular relationship with one another.*

Interpersonal relationships can be placed along a five-category continuum that ranges in interpersonal sharing from much to little. The type of communication and level of sharing depend largely on the relationship each communicator wants with the other(s).[5]

---

[5] The discussion of levels of relationships here is based largely on John Powell's *Why Am I Afraid to Tell You Who I Am?* (Niles, Ill.: Argus Communications, Inc., 1969), pp. 50–85.

ritual relationships

The first level of relationship is ritual. *In ritual communication, little interpersonal sharing is required.* People brush, but don't really touch. They talk to each other, often without hearing. The maintenance person, for instance, who comes to our building every day replies to a "Hi" or "Good afternoon" with "All right." A security guard answers the same greeting with, "Fine, thank you." The response is ritual. It's irrelevant that no one asked about the person's health. The content of the greeting is irrelevant. The response is to acknowledge our presence, and the ritual is important, but the content is not. When you greet someone in the morning, "How are you?" you are seldom really asking for information. It's a ritual. The greeting acknowledges the existence of the other person, or lets you make contact with those around you.

Ritualized relationships include social situations that require you to speak and interact with people in a prescribed manner. For example, you may feel terrible some morning when you arrive at work, wanting only to be left alone. But if the boss comes by and engages in pleasantries, you probably respond similarly, though you'd rather not. The relationship is ritualized and demands your response.

People engage in social rituals of all kinds, and do so often without being fully aware of the role of ritual in the communication. Noticing it and being aware of its value can assist you in communicating effectively when ritual is appropriate and avoiding it when it's not.

objective relationships

> ... even the spoken word itself can become a thing if it adopts the neutral and objective tone of information ...
>
> PAUL TOURNIER

A second level of interpersonal relationships is objective and externally oriented. *This type of communication involves reporting observations and some inferences that describe how you perceive your environment.* Personal reactions to the environment are not included in this level of relationship. Joe Friday's famous, "Just the facts, ma'am," reflects objective relationship. A doctor's diagnosis or a police officer's report illustrates this kind of communication. The content can be terminal cancer or murder, but the communication will use objective statements just as if the report were of a bruised knee or a bent fender. In this kind of relationship you simply report, objectively, what happened, or is happening, outside you.

Very little personal sharing occurs. Only as your personal interpretive system shapes your perceptions are you as a person involved in this kind of relationship. Much communication in work situations involves objective relationships.

evaluative relationships

A third level of relationship involves evaluation. In this kind of relationship *you communicate about ideas and judgments.* Encounters involve personal sharing at this level, because you report not only your observations but also your evaluations. Because ideas reflect the people who hold them, you share something of self when you share evaluations and judgments.

Still, this relationship tends to be "other"-oriented. "I believe that ..." usually is a statement that describes someone or something else. It refers largely to things and people other than self, reporting reactions in terms of a belief. *Evaluations only indirectly reveal how you feel.* A perceptive receiver can learn much about you from your judgments, but the sharing of self is not intentional. You probably only want receivers to relate to the ideas and not analyze what feelings the judgments imply. This may be the most common interpersonal relationship most of us have.

shared feelings

A fourth level of relationships involves *sharing feelings, communicating how you feel about situations, events, ideas, and people.* At this level you really begin to share yourself with others. Communicating at this level is an important step in deepening relationships, because when you report a feeling rather than a judgment, two things happen. First, because an important aspect of self has been shared, trust can grow. Second, because you do not judge the others or events in the situation but simply report reactions, the effects in others differ greatly. For example, note the differences in the following exchanges:

Judgment	Feeling
"You're not thinking clearly."	"I don't understand what you just said."
"You shouldn't behave that way."	"I feel angry when you act that way."
"You are bothering me."	"I need to concentrate on my work right now and an interruption upsets me because it breaks my train of thought."
"You are beautiful."	"I feel good when I look at you."

In each case, the judgment concentrates on the other person and evaluates the behavior. Reporting feelings also tells your reaction, but it doesn't necessarily imply evaluation of the other person, though a *defensive* person might interpret a feeling as an evaluation.

For each of the contrasting remarks above, many more feeling responses are possible. Let's take an example and illustrate:

Judgment	Feeling
"I think that you are beautiful."	"I feel ugly."
	"I feel inadequate."
	"I feel jealous."
	"I am proud of you."
	"I am suspicious of you."
	"I am threatened by you."

You might find it useful to try phrasing other feeling responses to the other examples above. Most of us are not so honest in our responses. We find judgment more comfortable because it appears to describe the other person, and doesn't openly share information about us. A perceptive listener can see through the judgment to some of our reactions; but seldom are all the feelings apparent, even to a perceptive listener.

You need to reach this level of sharing for relationships to become really personal. If you don't share your feelings, they can, at best, only be inferred by others. The inferences may not be complete or accurate. Friendships, distinguished from acquaintances or business relationships, require some of this kind of sharing. The more completely feelings and reactions are shared, the deeper the friendship can become.

I was angry with my friend;
I told my wrath, my wrath did end.
I was angry with my foe;
I told it not, my wrath did grow.

WILLIAM BLAKE

Often people stay in an evaluative relationship because it's easier to state judgments than feelings. But you should remember that just because feelings aren't communicated doesn't mean they don't occur. If you feel inadequate, jealous, threatened, or hurt by someone, the feeling exists whether you talk about it or not. And often, when such feelings are not stated, especially between two people who must regularly interact at work or home, negative feelings build up. This backlog of unexpressed feelings creates enormous emotional loads in relationships. The load of feelings from previous encounters is often brought into each meeting, making situations explosive that otherwise wouldn't be. As one popular poster puts it, "When I repress my emotions, my stomach keeps score." Repressed emotions cause more than ulcers and physical ailments: they can damage interpersonal relationships. When feelings aren't shared, much that is positive in a relationship is lost and much that is negative is allowed to grow. This can cause communication breakdowns, terminations of friendships, or continual conflicts in interpersonal relationships.

To be honest, however, we need to point out that a relationship that involves shared feelings is not without its dangers. If both or all people involved don't have this willingness to share as a purpose, resistance and rebuff may be encountered. Moreover, some people can't handle the feelings of others. They are so used to evaluative, objective, and ritual relationships that they can't or won't relate on any other level. Purposes usually need to be shared for a relationship to reach the level of shared feelings.

intimacy

The fifth level of relationship is intimacy. This is the kind of interaction found in most deep and lasting friendships. *This kind of communication involves complete and absolute openness and honesty.* Feelings are shared, totally. Parties in an intimate relationship have no secrets from one another about their feelings. Each accepts the other person as that person is.

We need to emphasize here that we're talking about interpersonal intimacy, which may or may not include physical intimacy. Physical intimacy can occur in ritualized, objective, and/or eval-

Intimacy.
Source: Mimi Forsyth—Monkmeyer.

uative relationships. But it may not be related to shared feelings at all. Here we're referring to the kind of relationship that shares feelings on a personal level with no limitations, whether physical intimacy is involved or not.

The kind of communication needed to reach intimacy must express shared feelings, of course. The essential difference between intimacy and shared feelings is the complete openness involved. And few, if any people relate to each other on an intimate level all the time. Obviously, it's not appropriate much of the time. But for friends, close fellow workers, and family, it results in the deepest and most rewarding relationships. *Trust* is required to attain this level of openness between people. For that reason we devote the next chapter to the conditions that make it possible for trust to develop in interpersonal relationships.

Purposes are defined as the intentions people have for communicating. Purposes are not always clear, and seldom do people have only one purpose for each communication. Purposes may be hidden or open; and they operate for both the source and receiver of messages. Communicators generally have at least three purposes: these are related to self, to the subject, and to others. One communication purpose related to self is probably in all communication—it is the satisfaction of personal needs. The personal needs are classified according to the Maslow hierarchy as needs for survival, safety (security), love and belonging, esteem, and self-actualization. Generally, a person is motivated by unmet needs at the bottom of the hierarchy before those higher in the structure cause behavior, but the ratio is not constant. The state of a human being at a particular time sometimes causes the hierarchy within an individual to be different from the usual hierarchy. Communication purposes related to self also include an intent to reinforce self-concept, to structure time, and to express emotion or anxiety.

Purposes related to the subject may be to explain, amplify, clarify, prove, narrate, or accomplish some change in the objective reality of the environment. Both source and listener have subject-centered purposes. Purposes related to others fall into two categories: (1) instrumental—what you want to accomplish in terms of another person's behavior or beliefs; and (2) relational—the relationships you wish to establish with others. Relationships range along a continuum of varying amounts of intimacy from rituals, through objective, evaluative, shared feelings, and intimacy.

Exercise: Assessing Purposes

Objective: To practice analyzing purposes in your own communication. Directions:

1. Pick out the communication interaction that was most significant of all you engaged in during the last week.
2. Analyze the purposes you and the other person(s) had for engaging in the interaction. Try to assess purposes related to self, subject, and others, as well as all hidden and open purposes.
3. You might find the following outline helpful:

A. Situation
B. Purposes related to self   *Me*   *Other*
   1. need satisfaction: What
     needs?
   2. reinforce self-concept?
     how?
   3. structure time: how?
   4. expressive?
C. Purposes related to subject
D. Purposes related to other
   1. instrumental? what?
   2. relationship? how?

Exercise: Relationship Statements

Objective: To practice making statements establishing different kinds of relationships.

Directions:

1. For each of the following situations, prepare three different responses: one that would be classified as objective, one that would be described as evaluating, and one that is sharing feelings.
2. Identify each statement as to which type of relationship it is attempting to establish.
3. Prepare to share and discuss your responses in class.

Situation I:

You are shopping with a friend who has just tried on a suit that retails for $150. The friend says, "How do you like it?"

Situation II:

You and your husband/wife/girlfriend/boyfriend are planning an evening out. She/he suggests that you eat at a place you do not like.

Situation III:

Your instructor has given you a take-home final exam. A classmate who has been having trouble in class asks if he/she may see yours after you have finished it.

Questions for Discussion

1. What purposes related to self might communications have?
2. How can you identify the purposes related to self that might be in a communication exchange?
3. What purposes related to subject might communicators have?
4. What purposes related to others might communicators have?
5. Is ritual communication useful? How?
6. Given examples of communication situations, can you phrase responses that would illustrate each of the types of relationships with others a communicator might have?

APPENDIX TO CHAPTER 6

GAMES PEOPLE PLAY[6]

The following brief catalog of games is based on Eric Berne's description in *Games People Play*. The term, games, as used here, refers to a patterned series of communication transactions. Most are totally serious and, for players, hard work. Though the outcomes are

---

[6] This section is based on Eric Berne, *Games People Play* (New York: Grove Press, 1967). Reprinted by permission of Grove Press, Inc. Copyright © 1963 by J. P. Lippincott Co.

often painful, they are also rewarding; players (other than innocent, first time victims) wouldn't be in the game if they weren't. The rewards are various: momentary relief from the unhappiness of an "I'm Not OK" position by winning small victories that make it more bearable; confirmation of "You're Not OK" positions by showing again and again how awful other people are; structuring time and relations between two people so they are predictable, so the outcomes of interactions can be known, thus reducing the terror of unpredictability in the world, and sometimes so that the danger of intimacy can be avoided. Relations involving real intimacy, not just physical intimacy, require openness of the self. For the person in an "I'm Not OK" position, intimacy creates a fear of showing others that "I'm Not OK," because of fear of evaluation. Even though the game is not fun, it is usually better than isolation. Games can serve any or all these purposes for players.

These common games are listed under two headings: life and family games. Many more could be included, and if you find this summary interesting, you'll want to examine Berne's book and some of the other sources cited.

Life Games

see what you made me do

This game has two degrees. As a life game, it may require another person who is playing I'm Only Trying to Help You. The classic player of See What You Made Me Do projects decisions onto others; and thus is able to project the consequences of these decisions onto others. Then if the result is bad, the See What You Made Me Do response is an excuse for the bad result, and the person need not take or accept responsibility for the result. For example, if Tom is trying to decide what to do on tonight's date, and cannot or doesn't want to decide, he defers to Mary. "What shall we do tonight? Go to a movie, or something else?" She makes the decision. If the show is good, "Fine," and Tom will consider the choice a good one. If it turns out to be a bad show, too expensive, or they can't get in because they were too late, the blame is on Mary. She made the choice. "See What You Made Me Do." The payoff is not having to decide or take the blame of a bad or inaccurate decision.

This is often a marital game. Father or Mother lets the other one make all the decisions regarding the kids. Then, when one of the kids gets into trouble, doesn't do well in school, or does poorly in some way according to the parent's viewpoint, the response is, "See what *your* kid has done now." The common joke illustrates:

when Johnny gets good grades, Dad is proud of *his* kid; when Johnny flunks math, "He takes after his mother." Another version of this game is You Got Me Into This. See What You Made Me Do — You Got Me Into This is often a covert marital contract. "You got me into this" suggests the other person is to blame for one's misfortunes. When both married partners prefer not to accept responsibility for their choices to live with each other, the "see what you made me do — you got me into this" contract is the basis of remaining together.

kick me

This game is like placing the sign on a card on your desk, "Don't Read This." To anyone who sees it, the urge to do so is almost irresistible. The Kick Me player walks around wearing an invisible sign that says, "Please don't kick me," which is really a veiled invitation to do so. The payoff is that when people do Kick Me, it proves what the player knew all along: either I deserved it; or people can't be trusted. For example, Joe brings his attractive new girlfriend around his friends. He warns them not to get any ideas. The aim is to see who can be provoked into making a play for his girl. The payoff is when the friend asks her for a date. Joe can then say, "Why does this always happen to me?"

The Kick Me player always claims "My troubles are the worst," and behaves in a way to insure it. People who fall prey to con games are often Kick Me players. People who have "secrets" and voluntarily disclose the important information with the words, "Keep it to yourself; this is not to go any further," know the temptation will be too great. That is why it's told. When it's revealed, as Kick Me was sure it would be, the person now can go to a third party, probably a mutual friend, and say "See what happens to me! I knew that _____ couldn't be trusted. People are no damn good."

alcoholic (addict)

Some life games are deadly, and this is one of the most. In this game, the central role is the Alcoholic or the Addict. This dangerous game is often played to a fatal conclusion with major impact on other game players involved. In this game, as many as five players can be involved, though it usually begins with only two. The main role besides Alcoholic (Addict) is the Persecuter, typically played by wife or husband. As the game develops, other roles are added. The Rescuer is someone who cares, like the family doctor, a friend or social worker who recognizes the illness and tries to be of assistance. The Patsy is often also involved when the main player reaches the down and out state and someone else needs to supply the drug. Finally, sometimes a Connection is also involved. This is a professional supplier of the drug. This role is, distinct from the others, a professional; the person is in the game purely for the commercial benefit. When the Alcoholic (Addict) can no longer pay, or in the course of a single bout has had too much, the Connection opts out.

In many situations, supporting roles of Persecuter, Patsy, and Rescuer are all played by the same person, usually a family member: husband, wife, child, parent. The wife who undresses her husband at 3 A.M. when he comes home too drunk to crawl into bed, who picks up his hot checks, withdraws from all social contact because she is ashamed, works to pay the family bills, calls in sick for him when he has too much of a hangover to get to work, makes excuses to the family (and the husband who does the same for a wife) is playing the Patsy. Then when the wife accuses, sobs, claiming he wouldn't drink like this if he really loved her and his family, complains about having to work and pay all the bills, bitching and crying about the bill collectors who continually hound her, she is engaging in the Persecuter role. She may be the Rescuer also, seeking to get her husband to the doctor, hiding his alcohol, trying to get him to do things that will keep him away from liquor and those bad companions. Rescuers must watch their role very carefully or they become Patsy. Getting the Alcoholic (Addict) to a doctor can be very close to bailing him/her out of jail repeatedly.

The maneuvers of the Alcoholic (Addict) are difficult to understand in terms of a payoff, unless the perspective on life positions is kept in mind. The payoff of this game is the hangover itself, and in the continually deteriorating life. The Alcoholic (Addict) is working out in the most deadly form an I'm Not OK-You're Not OK script. In the early stages of the game, the hangover itself is the payoff. The punishment is needed to reinforce the position, "What a Heel I Am!" Guilt needs to be satisfied by punishment. Thus if the hangover isn't enough punishment, the Persecuter will be provoked into providing more punishment by scolding, crying, and so on. As the disease progresses to its fatal conclusion, the degrading of the person provides the punishment. The person learns to hate him/her self more and more, which naturally provides the excuse for more drinking, which provokes more guilt, requiring more punishment that requires more drinking, etc. This game continues in a death-dealing spiral unless some kind of intervention either alters the game or the script.

Payoffs for the other players in this game may seem even more difficult to discover than those for the Alcoholic (Addict). The Persecuter may be playing You Got Me Into This, or See What You Made Me Do. Rescuers may be playing I Was Only Trying to Help. Though the most common form of this game involves alcohol or some other addictive drug, it can be played with less obvious addictions. Obesity may well be a form of this game, as well as other forms of self-destructive behavior.

Family Games

corner

This game illustrates more clearly than most how games really involve manipulation of one player by another, or both by each other. The paradox of Corner is that it consists of an apparent refusal to play the game of a partner. The situation of Corner can perhaps best be illustrated with an example. Wife suggests that husband and she go to a movie. Husband agrees. In conversation, wife mentions a project that needs doing, such as buying a new living room suite. This is a provocation because she knows that he just recently told her their finances were strained and asked that she not bother him with any unusual expenses right now, at least not for a few months until they get caught up on a few bills. It's a bad moment to bring up the problem and she knows it. He responds as expected with anger.

An alternative form may be that he brings the discussion around to the subject of shabby furniture so that he knows it would be very difficult for her to avoid mentioning that they need the new living room suite. Since the discussion about money puts him in a bad mood, wife takes offense and says, "Well, then perhaps you'd better go without me." Husband takes her literally and goes out, alone. She was cornered. Her husband knew that all she really wanted was to be reassured that he did indeed want her company in spite of her bringing up the unpleasant subject. But he had her cornered and could act upon it.

A variant of Corner is often played between parents and children. Situations are set up so that whatever a child does is wrong. A good example is when a child is urged to be helpful around the house. Then when the daughter helps mother with the dishes and breaks one, she is criticized for being so clumsy. Or son helps father work on the car to be helpful as father has requested. But the youngster gets grease on the seats and Dad yells at him, just as he would have had the boy shown no interest in being helpful. This double-bind type of game is referred to as Dilemma Type of Corner.

Close to Corner is the game of Lunch Bag. In this case a family member who can well afford to eat lunch out will make sandwiches and take them to the office. With this kind of behavior, saving money and time, how can anyone in the family be extravagant? It's a way to corner them into similar kinds of behavior or provide the basis for criticism if they don't act the same way.

if it weren't for you

To play this game a player marries someone who will restrict his/her activities. The person desires to be dominated and the restriction gives several payoffs. One is that being dominated supports the complaint "If It Weren't For You," I could have done so many things. The domination usually prevents the player from doing something he/she would be afraid to do anyway, but this way the player doesn't have to admit the fear. Another payoff is that complaints make the dominant partner uneasy, and the player gains from the partner's guilt feelings. The guilty partner often compensates with gifts and other benefits for the domination. Also, domination often leads to quarrels, thus reducing sexual intimacy.

Another version of this game is the son who lives with his mother. He reaps many advantages of the arrangement: she keeps house, feeds him, washes his clothes and in other ways waits on him. He likes the arrangement or he wouldn't be there, but he uses the game to make unfair demands because he has the upper hand over the parent.

uproar

In Uproar, the players vary, but the main idea is that one or the other or both provoke a fight to avoid intimacy, especially sexual. The classic game results in cases where a domineering father has a sexually inhibited wife and unacceptable sexual feelings toward his maturing teenage daughter. Often because he cannot even bear to recognize such thoughts, he provokes a fight the minute she enters the door, criticizing her dress, the way she walks, her companions, anything about her, but primarily anything that provokes him sexually. She responds, naturally, with defense of her behavior, and father is irritated, becoming more critical. She responds more heatedly and the clash erupts. One or both escape into a private room, slamming doors emphasizing their separateness, or escape out of the house. The anger provoked by the uproar enables the two to live together.

Uproar can be played between any two people who are trying to avoid sexual intimacy. It's a common ending of other marital games. Under appropriate circumstances, it can result in a daughter leaving home early, marrying to escape, or other forms of escape by innocent victims. A married person who fears or dislikes sexual intimacy can use Uproar to prevent it. When a husband or wife cannot use other games for avoidance of physical intimacy, the Uproar will do the job.

COPING WITH GAMES

An important guide to living and communicating effectively is Socrates' injunction to "Know thyself." That is the reason this section is included in this book. Understanding your motivations helps you communicate better. Transactional Analysis is one means of studying human motivation. The person who wants to learn how to cope with games that people play should remember first of all that in games both parties are often, if not usually, playing. Both are often receiving payoffs from the transactions. In discussing games, we aren't always, not even usually, talking about innocent victims.

Games have important payoffs for players. Players have learned these games as ways of coping with the world. However unpleasant the game may be for the player, it is how that person has learned to get through parts of life. Some people learn to play games when interacting with others to satisfy often very deep-seated needs. A game may appear pathological, but the result of having the game destroyed might be worse for the individual.

If you are an innocent victim of games, learn to identify them early and choose not to play. Just say "Count me out," and seek friends who don't play games. If you are playing some games yourself, try to discover why. What are the payoffs for you? You can learn healthier ways of interacting with others. Learn to communicate more honestly and openly. Then, with people you really care about, you can move toward lasting, satisfying, game-free communication.

Approach identification of games that *other* people play with extreme caution. Remember, games are how some people defend themselves against the world as they perceive it. Should you be anxious to apply your newfound knowledge to straightening out the lives of others, you'll simply be guilty of playing a game yourself, and a game with very dangerous outcomes. We caution you with the words of a familiar poster, "Human Beings, Handle With Care." Most of us have our hands full improving our own communication. We need to start there, not with others.

Suggestions for Further Reading

ARGYLE, MICHAEL, *Social Interaction.* Chicago: Aldine, 1969.

BASLOOPER, THOMAS, AND MARCIA HAYES, *The Femininity Game.* New York: Stein & Day, 1974.

BERNE, ERIC, *Games People Play.* New York: Grove Press, 1967.

————, *What Do You Say After You Say Hello?* New York: Bantam, 1972.

DECHARMS, RICHARD, *Personal Causation.* New York: Academic Press, 1970.

DEROPP, ROBERT S., *The Master Game.* New York: Dell, 1974.

HARRIS, THOMAS, *I'm OK — You're OK.* New York: Avon, 1973.

MASLOW, ABRAHAM, *Motivation and Personality.* New York: Harper & Row, 1970.

————, *Toward a Psychology of Being.* New York: Van Nostrand Reinhold, 1968.

SCHEIDEL, THOMAS M., *Speech Communication and Human Interaction.* Glenview, Ill.: Scott Foresman and Company, 1972.

SPIEGEL, JOHN, *Transactions, The Interplay Between Individual, Family and Society.* New York: Science House, Inc., 1971.

STEINER, CLAUDE, *Games Alcoholics Play.* New York: Grove Press, 1971.

————, *Scripts People Live.* New York: Grove Press, 1974.

SUDNOW, DAVID, *Studies in Social Interaction.* New York: Free Press, 1972.

7

Trust and Defensiveness in Communication

goal:

To learn how to use trust and supportive behavior to improve communication.

probes:

The material in this chapter should help you to

1. Define trust and describe how it can develop in a relationship. pp. 187–95
2. Explain why trust improves interpersonal communication. pp. 188–91
3. Explain why defensiveness limits the growth of trust. pp. 187–201
4. Describe the behaviors characteristic of defensive climates and give an example of each. pp. 196–202
5. Distinguish between intentional and unintentional feedback. pp. 203–4
6. Distinguish between directive and nondirective response statements. pp. 204–6
7. Indicate the purposes for which you might choose to use directive and nondirective feedback. pp. 206–7
8. Given a situation, give examples of both directive and nondirective feedback to achieve specified goals. pp. 202–8

Effective interpersonal communication involves many elements, but relationships are perhaps the most important. Many causes of breakdowns and many of the barriers to communicating effectively have minor effects if good relationships exist between communicators. In contrast, the clearest, most unambiguous, and most accurate messages cannot prevent breakdowns if poor relationships exist.

This chapter is devoted to an examination of two of the most important factors in creating interpersonal relationships: trust and defensiveness. We discuss the causes and effects of both factors, and then analyze how feedback can affect both.

TRUST IN INTERPERSONAL RELATIONSHIPS

We ended Chapter 6 by observing that trust is necessary if communicators are to feel free to share their feelings openly and honestly with each other. We suggested that trust is required before people will open themselves to others sufficiently to develop intimate interpersonal relationships. We now turn to the discussion of what trust is, how it develops, and how it can contribute to satisfying interpersonal communication.

What Is Trust?

Trust is a familiar word, subject to varying and usually vague denotations. As we use the word, trust involves three elements:

1. You expect behavior by another person that can have either beneficial or harmful consequences
2. You realize that the consequences depend on the other person's behavior
3. You have confidence that the other's behavior will have the desired consequences (predictability)

Source: © King Features Syndicate, Inc., 1974.

For clarification, consider an example. The title of a popular book, *Why Am I Afraid to Tell You Who I Am?*,[1] refers to the countless "masks" and "faces" people wear to keep those they associate with from knowing their innermost feelings and thoughts. The author cites a friend's answer to the title question: "Because if I tell you who I am, you may not like who I am, and it's all that I have." This comment illustrates the absence of trust. The speaker has a personal need to be liked (No. 1 above), and realizes that liking is the other's to give or withdraw (No. 2 above). This demonstrates the first two elements required for trust. The third element, confidence in desired results, is missing. The speaker isn't confident the other person will like him if he is truly open and honest in revealing his feelings or thoughts. Without this confidence, trust does not exist; and communication between the two is not open.

What Are the Benefits of Trust?

Is trust always appropriate? Indeed not. Good reasons often exist for people not to be open or completely honest with others. Trust in another person is often not justified. But for the most satisfying interpersonal relationships, trust is required.

If you trust someone enough to reveal important feelings, thoughts, and behaviors, several benefits occur. One is that trust improves interpersonal communication because it opens channels. It improves clarity of message sending and receiving and increases

---

[1] John Powell, *Why Am I Afraid to Tell You Who I Am?* (Niles, Ill.: Argus Communications, 1969).

the chances of communicators accomplishing their purposes. Under-standing other people, their differences from you, their attitudes, beliefs, and perspectives is often difficult. It's nearly impossible to develop understanding if other people won't tell you how they perceive, feel, and think. If you don't understand a person you're communicating with, you'll find it hard to determine where that person is "coming from," which often results in communication barriers. *Trust opens the lines of communication.*

As trust leads you to disclose important things about yourself to others, it *also helps you understand yourself better.* This is a second benefit of trust in interpersonal communication. Opening up to people who are important to you is probably the best way of improving your self-awareness and understanding.

Finally, *without trust, the development of significant, intimate interpersonal relationships is unlikely.* This may be the most important effect of trust. Without trust, the relationships themselves, not just the communication, will be impaired. When communicating

> Trust is so powerful because it is hooked up to the self-fulfilling prophecy, which says that what you expect from the world is about what you get.
>
> JESS LAIR

Trust opens the lines of communication *Source: (left)* Hugh Rogers—Monkmeyer; *(upper right)* Pro Pix—Monkmeyer; *(lower right)* Michael Kagan—Monkmeyer.

Without trust the development of intimate interpersonal relationships is unlikely.
Source: David S. Strickler—Monkmeyer.

with someone you feel is not being open and honest, you're likely to respond the same way. As a result, relationships not built on honesty tend to be superficial, shallow, or short. Interpersonal relationships void of trust will seldom reach the level of shared feelings and never the level of intimacy.

Intimacy and sharing feelings involve telling another person how you really feel. This is difficult if you fear that person's evaluation and possible dislike of you. It becomes almost impossible without trust. People invent all kinds of rationalizations for avoiding communication at these levels. They say, "If I tell my true feelings, I'll hurt another person," or "I won't be accepted," or "It wouldn't be appropriate," or "It will make others dislike me." But when

Trust develops when communicators perceive each other as trustworthy.
Source: Mimi Forsyth—Monkmeyer.

190

people refuse to reveal their feelings, they fail to reveal some of the most important information people need to relate to each other. Intimacy requires complete and total honesty. Without trust, this degree of honesty cannot be reached.

The logic is compelling: open, honest communication about feelings and self is required for deep, longlasting friendships, but openness and honesty are not likely without trust. Thus the importance of trust in creating satisfying lives is hard to overestimate.

How Does Trust Develop?

If trust is so important, how is it developed? It's not sufficient to say, "Be trustworthy." That's not only superficial, it's inaccurate. *The key to development of trust is that communicators perceive each other as trustworthy.* And by now you realize that this is the difficulty. For some people perceiving others as trustworthy is easy. Some people believe that everyone is basically "good." These people tend to trust everyone until specific experiences remove individuals from the general rule. Others believe that all people are basically "bad" and will behave to harm others. These people distrust everyone until specific experiences exempt a few persons from the general category. Naturally, these mistrustful persons are often closed and guarded in their communication.

As a rule, most people develop trust on the basis of specific experiences. They may have learned to expect certain types of personalities to be trustworthy. For example, generally, ministers and doctors are expected to be trustworthy, and some people also expect trustworthy behavior from teachers, police, and counselors. At the same time, other people have had experiences that created the opposite expectations. They do not trust ministers, doctors, police, or teachers, and would never go to a counselor for fear of being betrayed. You can see that trust is usually specific, not general. You'd probably trust the police to come when you report a burglary, even though you might not trust the officer to refuse a bribe if it were offered. You might trust a police officer you know personally, but not trust the police generally, or vice versa.

Simply put, *trust develops on the basis of communication experiences with individuals and others believed to be in similar categories.* Less simply, trust develops when you've communicated with a person or group of people and found all three elements of a trust relationship to exist. A close look at those relationships will reveal three specific communication behaviors that help to create trust relationships. Let's analyze them one at a time.

> I would like to propose, as an hypothesis for consideration, that the major barrier to mutual interpersonal communication is our very natural tendency to judge, to evaluate, to approve or disapprove . . .
>
> CARL ROGERS

Acceptance is the ability to relate to another person without judgment and without attempts to control. Acceptance is the attitude that the other person is a worthy individual as a human being. Carl Rogers, to whom much of our thinking in this area is indebted, describes the attitude of acceptance as positive regard. One who expresses positive regard prizes an individual as a person "regardless of his particular behavior at the moment." An accepting person believes other people are worthy as individuals simply as what they are. An accepting person perceives others realistically and accepts all their characteristics, both liked and disliked.

Accepting others does not mean you have to like their behavior, however. That's an important concept. Acceptance is of a person, not necessarily of that person's behavior. When you accept a person, you recognize that behavior results from internal and external forces on that person when the behavior occurs. This doesn't necessarily mean that you must accept that person's behavior or its consequences. It does mean *not judging* the *person* just because behaviors are disliked. You relate to another person with acceptance when, even while disapproving the behavior, you communicate regard for the person. Acceptance leads to trust because it increases the confidence a person has that your behavior will have positive consequences for her/him.

Acceptance is the ability to relate to another person without judgment.
Source: Mimi Forsyth—Monkmeyer.

Acceptance is not an easy attitude to acquire; it's a behavior very foreign to most of us. We are quick to evaluate and slow to accept. Perhaps that's why many of our interpersonal relationships are less effective than we desire. Absence of acceptance tends to destroy trust and leads quickly to closed, distorted communication. When we don't behave with acceptance, we tend to judge and criticize. These are undesirable consequences of communication for most people. Thus they destroy trust.

> I accept this person, . . . I affirm the person I struggle with: I struggle with him as his partner, I confirm him as creature and creation.
>
> MARTIN BUBER

> The major part of life is acceptance of others, and yourself.
> JESS LAIR

empathy

A second behavior helpful in creating trust is *empathy.* To have *empathy is to experience the feelings of another person.* It's a sense of knowing how another feels. Empathy is not the same as sympathy. Sympathy usually means "feel sorry for." Empathy means to "feel with" another. You can empathize with positive feelings just as with negative ones, while sympathy is usually extended only to persons with problems. To empathize with another is to experience his/her world. When you sense another's feelings and attitudes as if you had experienced those feelings or attitudes, you are empathizing. Empathy can be thought of as the ability to put yourself into other people's personalities. It's the ability to see as another sees, hear as another hears, feel as another feels. But empathy always retains the "as if" quality, for in reality, no one can get "inside the head" of another.

It may be true that you can fully empathize only with internal states you have experienced. If you have never loved, it's probably difficult to empathize with someone who is in love, and even more difficult to empathize with someone who has lost a loved one. But a person who has loved could probably empathize with a person who has lost a parent, or wife, or husband. Having experienced love, it would be easier to sense how you'd feel without it. To aid in developing trust, however, complete empathy really isn't needed. Often more important is communicating a sense of empathy. That you care about or want to share a person's feelings is often as important as totally sharing that person's world.

Empathy contributes to trust.
Source: Hugh Rogers—Monkmeyer.

Empathy is different from many behaviors that pass as empathy. Often, you've heard, "I understand what the problem is" or "I understand why you behave as you do." And perhaps understanding is present. But that's not empathy. This kind of "understanding" involves evaluation, judgment. Empathy is a response that "knows." It feels with another; it isn't evaluation.

Empathy contributes to trust because it helps communicate the attitude of acceptance. Acceptance without empathy could be perceived as indifference, an "I don't care about you" attitude. People usually perceive indifference as undesirable. To create trust, acceptance of another person must include empathy for that person.

> . . . when someone understands how it feels and seems to be me, without wanting to analyze me or judge me, then I can blossom and grow in that climate.
>
> CARL ROGERS

honesty

Finally, in creating trust, you should be *honest.* Because feedback is only effective as perceived, acceptance and empathy may be offered but not *perceived.* Or they can be perceived wrongly—acceptance can be interpreted as uncaring, uninvolved, or unreal; and empathy seen as pretended or intentionally sarcastic. No insurance against such perceptions exists, but honesty comes closest. *Honesty in interpersonal relationships is the foundation of trust.* If you do not respond to others as you really are, you're "face making" or "masking."[2] Being honest is being free from deception, removing the mask.

[2] You'll recall the discussion of face-making in Chapter 4.

Now, let's be honest with you. Practicing honesty in interpersonal communication is not simple. We're aware, as you are, that many times we find ourselves in situations that seem to require deception. Often we believe that to avoid hurting someone, or to achieve some goal, we must be less than totally honest. With some people and some goals, that's probably right. But if you examine those situations carefully, you'll find that the need for deception usually exists because acceptance and empathy are missing. When acceptance and empathy are present, honesty will cement the relationship and lead to trust.

Honesty is probably the major behavior that creates trust. For instance, don't you often find yourself trusting a person who is outspokenly biased and opinionated more than you do one who refuses to express an opinion? That's because if you know the opinions are strong enough to produce behavior based upon them, you know enough to predict a person's behavior. You then have *the major condition for trust, predictability.* You can have confidence that the person will behave as you expect. Given a predictable set of behaviors, you know those conditions under which you can expect either beneficial or harmful consequences. Unpredictability destroys the third condition of trust. Honesty helps create predictability.

Another reason honesty is important in interpersonal relationships is that being honest with others requires you to be honest with yourself. If you share important things about yourself with someone else, your understandings of self will be verbalized in a way that may never otherwise occur. Aren't your thoughts and feelings much clearer when you've put them into words? Using another person as a sounding board clarifies thoughts and feelings. Because you can't hear yourself the way others do, their feedback will give you fresh perspectives on your own thinking.

You can see that honesty in interpersonal relationships helps to create trust in at least two ways. First, others believe that how you react to them is your real reaction. They'll accept that you're not hiding important thoughts or feelings from them, and believe they can predict your behavior in situations that might affect them. Second, you'll understand yourself better. With that understanding you'll be better able to predict and control your own behavior in interpersonal situations.

> I have to be free and able to say my thoughts to you, to tell you about my judgments and values, to expose to you my fears and frustrations, to admit to you my failures and shames, to share my triumphs, before I can really be sure what it is that I am and can become.
>
> JOHN POWELL

When communication does not result in trust, it often causes defensiveness. *Defensive behavior results when a person perceives a threat in a situation,* and usually it negates the three essentials for trust. Defensive behavior is not accepting, not empathetic, and seldom honest. Defensive people usually devote so much attention to protecting themselves that no time or energy is left for understanding others.

Causes of Defensiveness

Research on *defensiveness* by Jack Gibb demonstrated six kinds of behavior that cause people to have defensive reactions.[3] These behaviors are listed below. Also listed are opposite behaviors that are characteristic of groups without defensive climates. As you examine the list, think about your communication behaviors. How does your usual pattern of sending feedback fit into the list? Can you see ways in which you create defensiveness in others? Do you often engage in behaviors that are supportive? Which climates are more typically used by the people you feel really comfortable with?

BEHAVIORS CHARACTERISTIC OF DEFENSIVE AND SUPPORTIVE COMMUNICATION CLIMATES

Behaviors Resulting in Defensive Climates	Behaviors Resulting in Supportive Climates
1. Evaluation	1. Description
2. Control	2. Problem orientation
3. Strategy	3. Spontaneity
4. Neutrality	4. Empathy
5. Superiority	5. Equality
6. Certainty	6. Provisionalism

---

evaluation vs. description

Evaluation is passing judgment on others, assessing blame or praise. Evaluation involves making moral assessments of others, questioning their standards, values, and motives. Its opposite is description. *If you are descriptive, you are nonjudgmental.* You ask questions that are perceived as genuine requests for information. You present feelings, events, perceptions. You do not ask or imply

---

[3] The first publication of this research was in Jack R. Gibb, "Defensive Communication," *Journal of Communication,* Vol. XI (September 1961), 10–15.

that the receiver should change behavior or attitude. To give descriptive feedback is to be *perceived* as accepting. We emphasize "perceived" because evaluation is so common that what you may not intend as evaluation can be perceived that way. "Did you say that?" might be perceived not as a simple request for information but as an attack on veracity or intelligence.

Evaluation can be of ideas or of persons. Some people, however, are not able to distinguish the two. When you evaluate an idea they've expressed, they feel you're evaluating them. In many situations it's important that you express evaluations of ideas only if you at the same time state support for and acceptance of the person. To distinguish between evaluating a person and ideas, you need also to distinguish between your own observations and inferences. Ability to project the attitude of acceptance while evaluating ideas is one of the most delicate and difficult skills of interpersonal communication. Can you think of anyone who has this ability? What can you learn from this person?

control vs. problem orientation

Control behaviors are those aimed at trying to get others to change themselves or to change their attitudes, opinions, or behaviors. If you try to control others, you try to restrict the choices available to them, or to influence their behavior in making choices. Control behaviors imply evaluation, for the effort to change others implies they are now inadequate. Trying to control others also displays lack of acceptance. If you accept people as they are, you won't try to change them. You'll behave in ways that allow them to decide what changes in themselves they want to make.

Problem orientation is the opposite of control. It involves communicating a desire to work together to define problems and seek solutions. With problem orientation you avoid suggesting that you have all the answers. Instead, you indicate that you have no preconceived solutions. If you are problem-oriented, you allow the other person to set his/her own goals, to make choices and evaluate her/his own progress toward those goals. It implies that if you are in a situation in which you need common goals, you will work together toward setting goals and deciding how to meet them.

Defensive and supportive climates. *Source: (left)* Hugh Rogers—Monkmeyer; *(right)* Sybil Shelton.

strategy vs. spontaneity

Strategy involves use of tricks or manipulation to influence others' behavior. To be perceived as having hidden purposes, to have private, unrevealed motives, to be using communication for unstated personal benefits, is to be seen as using strategy. Gibb defines strategy in a different way than is usually used. Strategy usually is used to refer to what we use the word "control" to mean. In the context of communication climates, strategy refers to trickery and hidden manipulative behaviors. A comment of the television personality, Archie Bunker, serves as an excellent definition of strategy in this sense. When asked how he'd accomplished a particular feat, Archie said, "You get others to do what you want by promising to do something you ain't got no intention of doing."

The opposite of strategy is spontaneity, and the essence of spontaneity is honesty. *To be perceived as straightforward and free from deception is to be perceived as spontaneous.* People who show spontaneity demonstrate that they have no hidden motives. Behaving spontaneously gains all the benefits of honesty discussed above.

neutrality vs. empathy

Neutrality is the communication climate of impersonality. It expresses a lack of concern for the other person, a detached "other-person-as-object" attitude. This label "neutrality" is another one that is used differently in the context of communication climates. People often use neutral to mean objective. Objectivity is closer to the climate of description as we defined it. *To be neutral, as the word is used here, refers to the absence of empathy.* Empathy respects the worth of people in "knowing" their feelings. Empathy is accepting behavior, accepting that the feelings, emotions, and attitudes people express are real and believable from their own perspective. Neutrality is the absence of that attitude. It is an "I don't really care what happens to you" attitude.

superiority vs. equality

If you create a climate of *superiority you communicate an attitude that you are better than others in some way;* that you have more status or power or are higher in economic or intellectual levels, or in other ways. The attitude of being superior in any respect usually results in some degree of defensiveness in those you communicate with. If others sense that you feel superior to them, it can prevent their perceiving honestly expressed attitudes of empathy or problem orientation.

198 Equality is the climate that counters superiority. *Equality is*

willingness to interact with mutual trust and respect, and to attach little importance to differences in skill, status, wealth, power, beauty, etc. Differences among communicators are probably inevitable. People are seldom truly equal in any qualities. But a climate of equality de-emphasizes differences, and emphasizes the value of the separate qualities all parties bring to the communication situation. A climate of superiority stresses the differences, and degrades the value of the less able, poorer, or less attractive. Because differences in abilities, skills, and wealth are common, it's important to communicate the attitude that you attach little value to the differences if you want to reduce defensiveness in people you communicate with.

certainty vs. provisionalism

Certainty suggests what it implies, an attitude that the speaker has all the answers. A person with certainty appears dogmatic, usually needs to win arguments rather than solve problems, sees ideas as "truths" to be defended, not hypotheses to be explored. A person with certainty seldom listens to others' ideas. The opposite climate is provisionalism. A climate of *provisionalism communicates a willingness to reconsider behavior; to consider the possibility of being in error.* The basic attitude of provisionalism is investigation rather than advocacy. Provisionalism is a willingness to say, "Well, I could be wrong."

Effects of Defensiveness

> The opposite of this openness is a kind of "defensiveness," which hears only what it wants to hear, according to its own preconceived structure and bias, . . . The defensive person cannot be a growing person because his world is no bigger than himself and the circle of his horizons is closed.
>
> JOHN POWELL

Defensive communication is personally oriented and usually results in badly distorted perceptions. If you are preoccupied with defending yourself or your own point of view, you'll only half listen to others. As a result, the intended messages of those you communicate with are usually quite different from your perceived messages. High levels of defensiveness result in many incorrect perceptions and low communication accuracy.

Defensiveness can reach such extremes of hostility that communication is not just distorted and impaired, but hostile. Hostility can result in complete communication breakdown, even physical aggression. Our students who are police officers repeatedly tell of family arguments that break into violence. Indeed, approximately 25 percent of police calls are in response to family disturbances. Most cases in which hostility erupts are preceded by long periods of defensive behaviors by all family members involved. Acceptance, empathy, and honesty were missing; supportive behavior was rare; and communication breakdown was the predictable result.

RELATIONSHIPS OF TRUST AND DEFENSIVENESS

Several observations about communication climates are now in order. First, usually no climate discussed above occurs undiluted. *Usually, a little of both defensive and supportive communication shows up in interpersonal interactions.* When the different climates function together, as they often do, they partially neutralize the effect of each other. In some situations, you may be evaluated by a person you consider an equal who has your best interests at heart. If a trust relationship exists you might not react defensively to evaluation in that situation.

Second, *whether any communication causes defensiveness or trust is determined not by the actual message, but by how messages are perceived* by the receivers. You might intend to be supportive, but unless your behavior is perceived as supportive, you're not being supportive. You may think you are trustworthy; indeed, you may *be* trustworthy; but if a receiver doesn't see you that way, you won't be trusted.

You should constantly check the perceptions of those you communicate with, and use feedback to correct your behavior to be consistent with your intentions. Communication climates will usually have the results described above, but the context, the entire situation, affects the outcome. The results of any communication depend on the participants' level of defensiveness and concept of self, as well as on the influence of time, setting, previous experiences, and previous specific interactions with you.

You doubtless know someone who is so personally defensive that no amount of supportive communication by you could eliminate the threat that person perceives in a situation. This receiver can perceive provisionalism and description as neutrality or strategy and will view you with suspicion instead of trust, no matter how supportive your communication may actually be. If a receiver doesn't perceive empathy, acceptance, and honesty in you, any efforts to reduce defensiveness may instead cause it. As an illustration, look at the column we have added to Gibb's list. It shows how a generally defensive person might perceive supportive communication, or how it might be perceived by a person who doesn't believe you are honest.

Behaviors Resulting in Supportive Climate	Supportive Behaviors Perceived by Defensive Person
1. Description	1. Paternalistic
2. Problem orientation	2. Crisis-ridden
3. Spontaneity	3. Rude, overbearing
4. Empathy	4. Sarcastic, insincere
5. Equality	5. Patronizing
6. Provisionalism	6. Indecisive, sneaky

Often a defensive person has a negative self-concept and is not capable of feeling self-esteem. Thus, a threat is perceived in most situations. Messages sent by this kind of person are seldom open, nor are messages openly received. Coping with people of low self-esteem usually requires constant efforts to counter defensiveness, and even with effort you won't always succeed.

Third, *in reducing or avoiding the creation of defensiveness, the recommended attitudes must be genuine.* It's possible to verbally assert a supportive attitude but nonverbally demonstrate the opposite. Because nonverbal messages are usually perceived as more honest than verbal ones, they are crucial in creating either defensiveness or trust. It's possible to be verbally descriptive while clearly sending evaluation messages nonverbally. You can display dogmatic actions, such as crossing your arms, standing with hands on your hips, while asserting provisionalism. Saying, "It's up to you," in a voice that indicates it isn't really, communicates judgment, not provisionalism. Asserting equality while sitting at the head of the table, dominating the conversation, or invading others' personal space will convey the impression of superiority, not equality.

You should be aware of nonverbal cues usually associated with each climate so you can avoid contradictory verbal and nonverbal messages. Nonverbals in these situations are ambiguous, but knowing which behaviors generally convey which impression can help you avoid creating contradictory impressions. You may find the following chart helpful in remembering the nonverbal behaviors associated with defensive or supportive climates:[4]

---

[4] This list of nonverbal behaviors is adapted from Linda and Richard Heun, in *Developing Skills for Human Interaction* (Columbus, Ohio: Charles E. Merrill Publishing Company, 1975), pp. 82–83. Recall that several sources were cited at the end of Chapter 3 for you to pursue if you find the area of nonverbal communication of special interest.

SOME NONVERBAL INDICATORS OF COMMUNICATION CLIMATES

Defensive Behavior | *Supportive Behavior*

CERTAINTY

extended eye contact
crossed arms
hands on hips
dogmatic voice

PROVISIONALISM

nodding head
head tilted to one side
eye contact

SUPERIORITY

extended eye contact
hands on hips
large desk in office
formal setting
higher elevation
invasion of personal space

EQUALITY

warm colors
slower body movements
leaning forward
eye contact
same elevation
close personal distance

EVALUATION

extended eye contact
pointing
hands on hips
shaking head
shaking index finger

DESCRIPTION

slower body movements
leaning forward
eye contact

NEUTRALITY

legs crossed away
monotone voice
staring somewhere else
cool colors
leaning back
body distance of 4½–5′

EMPATHY

pleasant background sounds
closer personal distance 20–36″
eye contact
warm colors
legs crossed toward
nodding head
leaning toward

CONTROL

sitting in focal seat
hands on hips
shaking head
extended eye contact
invasion of personal space

PROBLEM ORIENTATION

comfortable personal distance
legs crossed toward
leaning forward
eye contact

STRATEGY

SPONTANEITY

leaning forward
legs crossed toward
eye contact
animated natural gestures

USE OF FEEDBACK

Feedback is an element of communication that can increase the level of either trust or defensiveness, depending on how it is used. Effective use of feedback can help prevent communication breakdowns and improve interpersonal relationships, while failure to use feedback effectively can interfere with communication. The following situation illustrates.

A foreman walking down the line told a machine operator, "Better clean up around here." Ten minutes later, the foremen's assistant phoned, asking, "Say boss—that bearing Sipert is working on—isn't it due up in engineering pronto?"

"You bet your sweet life it is. Why?"

"Well, Sipert claimed you said to drop it and sweep the place up. I thought I better make sure."

"Listen," the foreman flared, "Get the dummy back on the job. It's GOT to be ready in 20 minutes."[5]

What the foreman had in mind was for Sipert to take a minute or two to wipe up some oily waste on the floor, a fire and accident hazard. The employee had perceived a message quite different from that intended by the foreman. More effective use of feedback by either of the two could have prevented the misunderstanding. With a clearer understanding of how feedback functions, you too, can learn to use it to improve your communication.

Types of Feedback

Several classifications of the types of feedback can be made. We'll discuss four: intentional and unintentional; directive and nondirective.

intentional and unintentional feedback

You'll recall we use the term "feedback" to mean a receiver's response as perceived by the source. Because feedback exists only as perceived, much *feedback* is *unintentional.* Thus, *what you intend by a response may not be what the feedback is.* Feedback is what the originating source perceives of your response. Distinguishing between *intentional* and perceived messages is critical to use of feedback. Just as a word is not equal to the thing it represents, as discussed in Chapter 3, so the response to a message isn't the same as someone's perception of the response.

Differences in actual and perceived responses aren't the only source of unintentional feedback. Many nonverbal responses to messages aren't consciously intended by the responder. Thus, when they are perceived, these responses become unintended feedback. When you listen to others, you respond nonverbally, even if you don't say anything. Some nonverbal cues are barely perceivable but often they lead others to draw inferences about your responses that you didn't intend. For instance, has someone ever made you nervous and you didn't want him/her to know it? And yet you were

---

[5] Taken from the Foreman's Letter, February 8, 1950, published by the NFI, a division of VISION incorporated.

betrayed by shaky hands, uneasy eye contact, and tense facial muscles? Blushing can show anger or embarrassment when you'd rather it didn't. Respondents to lie detector tests don't intend that the questioner learn they are lying, but nonverbal cues often betray them. Even without electronic aids, a skilled interrogator can perceive cues of dishonest replies in a person who intends that just the opposite be perceived.

But be sure to be aware that nonverbal feedback isn't always unintentional. You often *intend* that nonverbal messages be perceived. Nonverbal messages are often used to communicate things you feel it's not appropriate to express verbally. You use eye contact, head movements, and facial expressions rather than saying, "I'm listening," or "That's right." Similarly, nonverbal messages in tone of voice can add sarcasm to words that otherwise would communicate a totally different message. You can say, "Isn't that great!" in a way that means it isn't great at all. Your voice would nonverbally convey the intended message. But if a receiver missed your sarcasm and believed the verbal message, you'd get unintentional feedback.

As you communicate, keep in mind how much feedback is unintentional and ambiguous. Take care not to act on feedback messages unless you're certain of their accuracy. Probe further to find out what responses mean. Use the corrective function of feedback. Be prepared to deal with reactions indicating that others have perceived your responses differently from the way you intended. As both a source and a receiver, you need to be constantly alert to use feedback to correct errors due to unclear or unintentional feedback. Using nonverbal codes, it's important to recall they're even more ambiguous than verbal ones. For example, nonverbal signs of anger and frustration are difficult to distinguish, as are those of understanding and agreement. Yet, because a communicator has less overt control of nonverbal responses, they are often more accurate feedback than verbal. When verbal and nonverbal messages contradict, the nonverbal probably reflect the feeling response of the communicator and perhaps therefore reflect the "real" response.

directive feedback

Responses can be classified as either directive or nondirective. *Directive feedback communicates an evaluation by the responder to either the source or the message.* Suppose, for example, you go with a friend shopping for new clothes and ask for your friend's opinion of a suit you've tried on. If your friend replies, "It's terrific," that's a directive response. Directive feedback can be either positive or negative. Your friend's comment, "terrific" would be positive if you like the suit. A nonverbal response of a frown and shaking head would be negative, and would also be directive.

Directive feedback may also be perceived as either rewarding or punishing. Usually positive feedback correlates with reward, but be careful of thinking it always does. A teacher singling out a youngster for praise when the student knows that classmates will resent the special treatment might not perceive the positive feedback as rewarding. Similarly, a teenager who's earned and enjoyed a reputation as the head tough in the neighborhood will consider negative feedback from the local police rewarding. Whether feedback is positive or negative can be determined from the verbal content of the statement; but whether it is rewarding or punishing depends entirely on the perceiver.

nondirective feedback

Feedback called nondirective is response perceived as nonevaluative. It is descriptive, stays as close as possible to the "facts." Nondirective feedback describes or questions, and avoids judgment. It relies on questions and statements of observation; it focuses on "how I see it" rather than "how it is." Phrases such as "It appears to me . . ." or "Here's what I said . . ." or "My feelings are . . ." indicate nondirective feedback. Questions that seek more information or that attempt to bring perceived and intended messages closer together are nondirective feedback, as are the following: efforts to cause another communicator to talk more or think further about what's being discussed; verbally giving encouragement to continue talking; nodding your head with an interested facial expression to create the same effect; paraphrasing what the other person says to check accuracy, with words such as "Is this what you mean?" or "Do I hear you saying . . .?"; repeating part of the original message—"Only two people got an A?" "You want to quit school?"

You can now easily see what directive feedback refers to. This is response perceived as evaluative. *Anything you do or say in response to messages received that is perceived by the source of the message as an evaluation of it is referred to as directive feedback.* Questions, failure to answer, words of approval, all can be perceived as evaluations, whether you intend that they are or not. And when perceived as evaluations, they are directive feedback.

Although nondirective feedback avoids giving evaluation, it doesn't mean you stay totally uninvolved. Nondirective feedback may include reporting your reactions. It's description, not evaluation, when you make clear that you are describing your feelings (distinguished from *opinions*, as indicated in the last chapter). This is true if you concentrate on your reactions and do not describe the feelings about the other person and her/his behavior. For example, if you react to someone's behavior by saying, "That sure was a dumb thing to do," you would be giving a directive response. But if you say, "That made me feel angry," you are reporting a reaction and it's nondirective. If on that shopping trip noted above, you asked, "How's this suit look?" and your friend responded, "Who's the designer?" that's nondirective. If the shopping pair are husband and wife, and one responds to the question with, "How much does it cost?" it's nondirective, although the questioner may infer a directive response.

When to Use Directive and Nondirective Feedback

Nondirective feedback is useful when you want to learn more about the source, or assist the source to draw conclusions without relying on your opinions. Parents and teachers who want youngsters to learn to think for themselves and to accept the consequences of their own behavior need to learn to use nondirective feedback. If you want others to make their own decisions, to rely on their own judgments, you'll want to use nondirective feedback.

In some communication situations, the decision about what kind of response to use is not complex. If someone asks, "What time is it?" the appropriate answer is easy to determine. If you know, you say. Most often, however, it's not so simple to decide the best response to a message. You will often have opinions about events and people, but it's not always useful to express them. Directive feedback is useful only in cases in which evaluation is appropriate, though often people evaluate without considering the result of doing so. We're suggesting you'll use feedback more effectively if you act differently. Before responding evaluatively, be sure that stating an opinion will be useful. Sometimes, indeed often, it's harmful. Suppose John is dating Emily, a full-time student who also works twenty hours a week. On Saturday night, they're going to the biggest dinner dance of the year together. Saturday afternoon she spends her entire week's paycheck to buy a new outfit and get a fancy hairdo. When he arrives that night, she asks with anticipation, "How do you like my new outfit?" Now, if he likes it, the answer is easy. But suppose he doesn't? Does he give his opinion just because it's asked for? A lot of factors are involved in the decision. What is the level of their trust relationship? Will his verbal response, if nondirective, be perceived as directive-negative? Will his nonverbals contradict the verbal? Is he capable of responding on the feeling, not opinion, level? Was her question really a request for his opinion or was it really intended to seek reinforcement or reward of her behavior? All these things must be consid-

> I can tell you who I am, report my emotions to you with candor and honesty, and this is the greatest kindness I can extend to myself and to you. . . . It is another thing to set myself up as judge of your delusions.
>
> JOHN POWELL

ered—and quickly—before he responds, or his long silence will be negative directive feedback.

The best *guidelines for deciding when to use directive feedback are two: be sure you understand the message before responding;* and *make sure giving an opinion will accomplish your purpose before giving it.* Learn to recognize when evaluation will interfere with the goal you're seeking as a communicator. As we've noted throughout the chapters on interpersonal communication, nothing special is gained just by stating an opinion. Sometimes, being directive is less effective, even when you're attempting to secure attitude changes in others.

Seldom is either directive or nondirective feedback used exclusively. In most situations both are used. Most interpersonal communication includes giving opinions, drawing and reporting inferences, asking questions, and stating observations. Unintentional and intentional feedback occur simultaneously; verbal and nonverbal feedback messages accompany each other; so too are directive and nondirective feedback often mixed.

LOOKING BACK

Trust is required for any interpersonal relationship to reach the level of intimacy found in the stage of complete openness. Trust involves three elements: expectation of behavior by another person that could have either beneficial or harmful consequences for you; realization that the consequences depend on the other person; and confidence that the other's behavior will have the desirable consequence. Trust in interpersonal relationships has several consequences: increased tendency to self-disclosure; improved communication due to consequent openness; and increased opportunities for the development of intimate, long-term relationships.

Trust develops on the basis of specific communication experiences with a person or persons perceived to be in the category of trustworthy people. Three behaviors are important in creating trust: (1) acceptance, which is relating to others with positive regard, not with evaluation or attempts to control, even when behaviors of the other may not be liked; (2) empathy, the ability to identify with the feelings of others; (3) honesty, which is being free from deception, and is the most basic requirement for building a relationship with trust.

Communication can also create defensiveness. Defensiveness occurs whenever a communicator perceives threat in the situation, and it results in closed, guarded, distorted communication. Six behaviors have been identified as likely to result in a defensive climate: evaluation, control, strategy, neutrality, superiority, and certainty. The opposites of these behaviors tend to reduce defensiveness. These are description, problem orientation, spontaneity, empathy, equality, and provisionalism. These sets of behaviors seldom appear unmixed. They often are mixed into conversations so that they counteract and partly neutralize each other. The important factor is how behaviors are perceived, not how they are intended. Some receivers are so defensive that they perceive threat in all situations, whatever the behavior. The supportive attitudes must be genuine because nonverbal messages that contradict verbal messages will be perceived as being more truthful than the verbal statements.

The element that completes the interpersonal circuit is feedback. Not all responses are feedback, just as not all feedback is intended. Some messages are perceived when they weren't intended, just as some were intended but not perceived. Thus a distinction is made between intentional and unintentional feedback. Communicators need to question and paraphrase to assess the similarity between intended and received messages. Feedback can be classified in two other ways, as directive and nondirective. Nondirective feedback is not evaluative. It describes, reports what is observed or felt, asks questions, and avoids judgments. Directive feedback gives judgment and opinions. Directive feedback should not be used until you are certain that you understand clearly what is being responded to. Thus, most situations call for both directive and nondirective feedback.

Exercise: Feedback

Objective: To illustrate the effects of directive and nondirective feedback.
Directions:

Before class on the assigned day, do steps 1, 2, 3, and 4 with a topic of your choice.
1. Engage a friend or relative in conversation. Don't tell that person you're doing it for a class assignment. Try to send only directive feedback.
2. Engage another friend or relative in conversation. Again, do not reveal it is for a class assignment. This time, send only nondirective feedback.
3. Engage in a third conversation, again, not telling that it's for class. In this case, send only directive feedback that is negative. After the conversation, you may want to indicate that it was for an assignment.
4. Analyze the differences in the communications and see if you can relate any of the differences to the different types of feedback.
5. Come to class prepared to discuss the differences and similarities among the three conversations.

Exercise: Using Feedback

Objective: To practice identifying goals for sending feedback and choosing appropriate responses to achieve those goals.
Directions:
1. For each of the three situations below:
   a. Identify a goal for responding;
   b. Indicate whether you would use directive or nondirective feedback to achieve the goal;
   c. Indicate what you would say in order to achieve the goal, using the chosen type of feedback.
2. Be prepared to share your responses in class.
Situation I:
Your supervisor has given you a task to complete. After looking it over, you decide it will take at least 10 hours work; it is now noon and you are expected to have the job completed by 10 A.M. tomorrow.

Situation II:

You and a friend have just met for a Friday night of relaxation. You were planning that the two of you would go to one or more of the local places where a band is playing for an evening of dancing, but you hope not to spend more than two or three dollars for the whole night. Your friend greets you with, "Hi, hey there is a great movie downtown. Let's go to that, O.K.?"

Situation III:

You are shopping with a wife/husband/girlfriend/boyfriend who has just tried on an outfit that you do not like at all. She/he says, "How do you like this? Doesn't it look great?"

Questions for Discussion

1. What is trust and what are the essentials for it to develop in a relationship?

2. What is the value of trust in interpersonal communication?

3. What communication climates interfere with the development of trust?

4. How does defensiveness interfere with communication?

5. What behaviors lead to defensiveness and which can help reduce it?

6. What are the functions of feedback?

7. Give examples of both intentional and unintentional feedback.

8. What are the differences between directive and nondirective feedback; do you know when to use each?

Suggestions for Further Reading

BROWN, CHARLES, AND PAUL W. KELLER, *Monologue to Dialogue.* Englewood Cliffs, N.J.: Prentice-Hall, 1973.

DEVITO, JOSEPH A., *The Interpersonal Communication Book.* New York: Harper & Row, 1976.

GOFFMAN, ERVING, *Interaction Ritual.* New York: Anchor Books, 1967.

JAFFE, JOSEPH, AND STANLEY FELDSTEIN, *Rhythms of Dialogue.* New York: Academic Press, 1970.

JANDT, FRED E., *Conflict Resolution Through Communication.* New York: Harper & Row, 1973.

JOHNSON, DAVID W., *Reaching Out: Interpersonal Effectiveness and Self-Actualization.* Englewood Cliffs, N.J.: Prentice-Hall, 1972.

LENNARD, HENRY, AND ARNOLD BERNSTEIN, *Patterns in Human Interaction.* San Francisco: Jossey-Bass, 1970.

LUFT, JOSEPH, *Of Human Interaction.* Palo Alto, Calif.: National Press Books, 1969.

POWELL, JOHN, *Why Am I Afraid To Tell You Who I Am?* Niles, Ill.: Argus Communications, 1969.

STEWART, JOHN, *Bridges Not Walls.* Reading, Mass.: Addison-Wesley, 1973.

8

The Effective Receiver

goal:

To be able to receive messages more effectively.

probes:

The material in this chapter should help you to

1. Explain the benefits of goal setting in listening. pp. 212–16
2. Set appropriate goals for various receiving situations. pp. 212–14
3. Prepare to listen effectively in different situations, whatever your goal. pp. 218–22
4. Be able to listen empathically when the situation requires it. pp. 222–24
5. Be able to identify and understand the main ideas of messages received. pp. 220–22
6. Apply the steps of critical listening to messages when appropriate. pp. 224–30

Most of us listen with less than 50 percent accuracy. Messages are misheard or not heard more often than they are received correctly. And most of us remember less than 50 percent of what we do hear. How tragic this is when satisfying our needs depends so heavily on listening effectively!

Listening skills can improve communication in almost every setting. They can improve both understanding and remembering of information. They can aid in establishing interpersonal relationships on every level from ritual to intimacy. Listening well can help you evaluate messages from people who want to affect your behavior and beliefs. Listening well can also help you as a sender of messages. Listening skills help you learn what verbal and nonverbal messages will be appropriate and clear to your receivers. Even when you're job seeking, listening can help you as much as speaking.

This chapter contains many suggestions to help you improve your communication through listening, whether you need to use it at home, at work, in the classroom, or when deciding how to spend your money.[1]

Seven out of every ten minutes that you and I are conscious, alive, and awake we are communicating verbally in one of its forms; and our communication time is devoted 9 per cent to writing, 16 per cent to reading, 30 per cent to speaking, and 45 per cent to listening.

RALPH NICHOLS

[1] For the framework of this chapter we are heavily indebted to Linda and Richard Heun, with whom the materials were developed. In addition, anyone who writes about listening skills owes a special debt to Dr. Ralph Nichols, who pioneered the study of how to improve listening. For his landmark work with Leonard Stevens see *Are You Listening?* (New York: McGraw-Hill, 1957).

GOAL SETTING

Whenever you communicate, as noted in Chapter 6, you have *purposes.* Too often people think only of the purposes for talking. In this chapter, we consider the purposes you have as a receiver. To do that, we need first to examine some of the differences in receiving situations.

Levels of Receiving

Situations in which you are a receiver vary widely. For different situations, different *listening* behaviors are appropriate. Listening situations fall along a continuum that runs from minimum receiver involvement to maximum involvement:

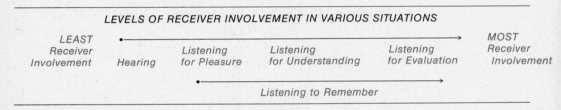

LEVELS OF RECEIVER INVOLVEMENT IN VARIOUS SITUATIONS

LEAST Receiver Involvement ← Hearing — Listening for Pleasure — Listening for Understanding — Listening for Evaluation → MOST Receiver Involvement

Listening to Remember

hearing

Hearing is little more than being in the range of and receiving sound. Little personal involvement is required. You may not even be aware of sounds you hear unless they're called to your attention. Background music and environmental sounds are heard, not listened to. If you keep your radio on or become used to typewriters and conversations in the office, or traffic outside in the street, you won't usually even notice hearing the sounds.

Input on the level of *hearing* has little imprint on your memory and doesn't require conscious decoding, though it does affect you. Noise or pleasant music in the background can influence moods and interactions. Research shows that family arguments occur more often when noise is in the background. Many businesses have learned that pleasant background music improves workers' efficiency, and that high background noise can increase fatigue and error.

listening for pleasure

Listening for pleasure involves more personal involvement than hearing. You receive input more consciously when you listen for pleasure, and you actively decode, usually by classifying. Differences, changes, similarities are heard and noted. Listening to music

212

Listening is affected by
selectivity of inputs.
Source: Hugh Rogers—
Monkmeyer.

is a familiar example of this situation, but speech is also often received at this level. You may listen to a pleasant voice, to poetry, to television and radio, or engage in casual, social, or ritual conversation at the level of listening for pleasure.

listening to understand

Listening to understand requires a higher degree of involvement. To understand what you're receiving, decoding is consciously controlled. You try to decode as accurately as possible, seeking to understand all messages received, both verbal and nonverbal. You consciously focus attention and feedback to bring the perceived and intended messages as close together as possible. Listening to understand may be the most common listening situation. It occurs with friends and family in informal settings; at work in dozens of different settings, both formal and informal; in school talking to classmates or listening to professors' lectures; in our roles as citizens receiving political and public communication, and as consumers.

We distinguish two levels of listening for understanding: *active* and *empathic* listening. In active listening, you are most interested in understanding a verbal message. You assess the speaker because understanding the person sheds light on the ideas. You use this kind of listening every day as you go to class and listen to the professor lecture. In empathic listening, you use the verbal message to understand the speaker. Your effort is to understand with the person, to see the world as that person sees it. In *empathic listening*, you use understanding of verbal messages as a means of assessing how the speaker feels about what is being said. An example of this kind of listening could be your attention to a friend explaining his/her difficulties in passing a required course.

listening to evaluate

Listening for evaluation also requires high receiver involvement. Many of the aspects of listening to understand are involved. Certainly you want to understand the speaker and the verbal messages before evaluating the messages. You want to consciously control decoding so that intended and perceived messages are similar. You note nonverbal as well as verbal messages, the person as well as the words. The major differences between listening for understanding and for evaluation are that when listening to evaluate you want also to *analyze* the messages you receive and assess their credibility and value to you. This kind of *analytical* listening occurs when someone is attempting to influence your beliefs or your behavior. When they do, you must critically assess the messages before responding.

listening to remember

Whether you listen to understand or to evaluate, you usually try to maximize what you remember. Remembering is necessary in both situations and will require special efforts from you. Whether you're listening to a sociology lecture, a friend explaining personal problems, or a salesperson's pitch for you to buy a product, you need to remember the important aspects of the messages.

Why Set Goals?

People don't usually decide what level of listening is appropriate for each situation. We do usually try to decide why we are giving a speech, or trying to get someone to do something. Less often in casual or interpersonal conversations do we think of our goals. Even more rarely do we set goals for listening. That's unfortunate, because goal setting can help us all become better listeners. What are some of the benefits of setting goals as receivers?

focusing receiving behaviors

Conscious awareness of a goal helps you behave in ways calculated to achieve that goal. In other words, if you know where you want to go, you'll be more likely to get there. *The main value of goal setting to a listener is that it helps you focus your receiving behaviors.* To use the simplest example, you can hear people better if you look at them while they talk. People can focus attention on any given stimulus only briefly. Effective listening thus often requires constant refocusing of attention. Doing this—constantly attending to someone or something with mind, eyes, ears, and the rest of your body—is hard work. It requires extra energy. In situations like this, where the listening task is demanding, goal setting can help you *want* to exert the extra effort required.

Focusing receiving behavior to
attain a goal.
Source: Mimi Forsyth – Monkmeyer.

selecting inputs

A second reason goal setting can make you a better receiver is that *listening is affected by the selectivity of perception.* In any given experience you can attend to many different things, and cannot possibly focus on every possible stimulus. So you must select from among many competing stimuli. Specifying a listening goal increases the chances that you'll select the inputs needed to achieve it. Goal setting helps you ignore distractions and irrelevant stimuli.

assessing listening efforts

A third value of goal setting is that *it provides a meaningful way to assess your listening efforts.* Especially when your purposes include gaining information, understanding someone or some idea, or evaluating messages, you can use a listening goal to assess your success. Commonly, after a discussion with a friend, or after listening to a speech or a program, people react with such feelings as "I liked that a lot," or "That was awful." If the goal in that situation was to gain pleasure, the "I liked it" response is perfectly appropriate. But if understanding or evaluation was required, "I didn't like it" is not a very useful reaction. If you have a goal in mind, you're in a better position to measure your success. More importantly, you'll be able to begin to assess why you achieved or why you failed to reach your goal. Comparing outcomes with goals provides a way to learn how to listen better next time.

shifting listening level

Fourth, *specifying a goal helps you know when it's necessary to shift from one level of listening to another.* Sometimes in the middle of a situation, you'll find you need to change the level of your involvement. Occasionally, when listening to someone—a teacher, preacher, friend, husband, wife, parent, child—you get tired of listening and "tune out." You daydream or think about something else, reducing your level of participation to the level of hearing. On the other hand, sometimes you're listening for pleasure and become aware that someone is trying to influence your behavior. Then you must quickly shift your focus, and increase your involvement in the listening process. Listening to radio and television often requires these shifts because of the insertion of commercials into entertainment and news programs. Equally often, perhaps, interpersonal situations call for these shifts. A pleasant lunch, golf game, or coffee break conversation often turns into an effort by someone to influence your behavior.

avoiding inappropriate behaviors

Finally, *having a goal in a listening situation can help you avoid behaving in ways that will achieve contrary results*. Remember, you are always both source and receiver in communication. If your goal for listening to someone is to develop a trust relationship or reduce defensiveness in a relationship, you need to control both your receiving and sending behaviors to avoid creating climates that have opposite results. For example, do you know a person who frowns when concentrating? Many people do. Suppose a supervisor is listening intently, trying to understand an employee who's explaining a complicated interpersonal conflict in the office. During the concentration, the supervisor had better not frown! If that supervisor is aware of both goals—understanding the message and being supportive to the person—she/he will avoid frowning, leaning away, or giving other nonverbal responses that would interfere with accomplishing either goal. Many similar cases could be cited. *Knowing your goal for listening can help you be more effective both as source and receiver.*

Aids to Goal Setting

It's not always easy to determine your goals as a receiver. Situations aren't always clear, and usually multiple purposes are involved. As a listener, you need to recognize that your role is an active, not a passive one. Three questions can help identify your specific needs in each situation. Ask:

1. What do I want to get from this situation?
2. What outcome do I need (want)?
3. How do I want to affect the others involved in this communication?

By answering these questions, you can determine appropriate goals for each listening situation and develop a plan of responding to help achieve them. Although you may frequently fail to achieve your goals completely, you will increase your chances of listening effectively if you have one or more goals in mind when you listen. When you find yourself in a listening situation without having a set goal, formulate one while you listen. Figure out *why* you're receiving. Always remember that to listen effectively you should know clearly what your goal is.

Exercise: Listening Diary

Objective: To become aware of different listening situations you commonly encounter.

Directions:

1. A form for this exercise is included in Activity Guide. If that isn't available to you, create a form that divides the day into 30 minute segments and allows you to identify the type of listening you do in each time period.
2. Choose one weekday and one weekend day.
3. Mark with #1 when you are simply hearing; #2 when you are listening for pleasure; #3 when you are listening for understanding; and #4 when you are listening for evaluation. When a situation shifts from one level to another, as from pleasure to evaluation, you will need to use both the appropriate numbers.
4. You may be called on in class to report the amount of time spent each day in each of the various situations and to discuss some of the following questions:
   a. Did you find it difficult to distinguish some of the situations?
   b. Is it common to encounter a need to shift the level of your involvement?
   c. Which level of listening is most common for you?
   d. Do you feel that sometimes you could more appropriately listen for understanding when you usually evaluate?
   e. Which situation is the most difficult for you? Why?

LISTENING TO UNDERSTAND AND REMEMBER

> Perhaps 80% of my work depends on my listening to someone, or on someone else listening to me.
>
> EXECUTIVE, MANUFACTURING FIRM

Appropriate behaviors to improve listening vary. Some receiving behaviors are more appropriate when you want to gain and retain information. Others are more suited to situations in which you must evaluate. Some behaviors apply to direct interpersonal interactions; others apply when listening to public and mass communication.

The suggestions in this section relate to behaviors appropriate for all situations when your goal is to understand either a message or another communicator.

Preparing to Listen

Often, the listening situation is one that you know about in advance—for example, a required lecture. In such a case, you can prepare in fairly obvious ways. First, *be physically prepared to listen.* Active listening is hard work. It takes a lot of energy. If you know ahead of time that listening will require a high level of involvement from you, you can try to be rested physically. Try to avoid important listening events when you are fatigued. Listening requires extra effort if you have to overcome either external or internal distractions.

Second, *be mentally prepared to listen.* If possible, determine your goals in advance and prepare accordingly. Think about the situation and subject to be covered to determine when it's necessary to gather prior information. In some cases, when prior information is needed and you aren't able to secure it, you can protect yourself by deciding you will delay your response until you secure the needed information. Another step in mental preparation is to determine the personal value of the situation for you. Finding personal value in the outcome can provide motivation for maintaining the high energy level needed to listen well.

Active Listening

use listening speed efficiently

Words we hear can be decoded at approximately 400 words per minute, while most people speak at less than 150 words per minute. An effective receiver uses the difference in speaking and decoding time, while poor listeners do not. The excess listening time, com-

Active listening requires mental and physical preparation
Source: Lida Moser Design
Photographers International.

bined with the shortness of the attention span, make concentration a special problem in listening. When you have extra time, and cannot focus on a single stimulus for very long anyway, maintaining attention is difficult. Poor listeners either completely waste the extra time or drift into daydreaming. You can use the time in more useful ways.

> To understand people, I must try to hear what they are *not* saying, what they perhaps will never be able to say.
>
> JOHN POWELL

Interpret Relevant Nonverbals. The difference in speaking and decoding time can be used to relate ideas to one another, using nonverbal cues to understand speakers' motivations, attitudes and feelings. The nonverbal messages can help you assess both the message and the source. They can help you draw inferences related to these important questions:

1. Why did the speaker say that?
2. How does the speaker feel about her/himself?
3. How does the speaker feel about me and our relationship?
4. How does the speaker feel about the verbal message?

The skill of interpreting messages is crucial to effective listening. People indicate needs, desires, feelings, intentions, and many other important things through nonverbal communication and sometimes *only* through nonverbals.

Ignore Distractions. The most common distractions are your own mental arguments with what you're hearing, or emotional reactions to a person's appearance or other nonverbals. *Guard against distortions caused by emotional reactions* to such things as loaded words, dialects, appearances, or ideas that conflict with your attitudes and values. When you're seeking to understand a person and his/her ideas, you need an open mind, and the ability to listen even when there are distractions. Otherwise the selective processes of perception and retention will greatly reduce your listening efficiency. Research has shown that poor listeners may best be distinguished from good listeners by their degree of receptivity to new ideas.[2] Controlling your mental and emotional responses will help

---

[2] Charles Kelly, "Empathic Listening," in *Small Group Communication: A Reader,* ed. Robert S. Cathcart and Larry A. Samovar (Dubuque, Iowa: William C. Brown Co., 1974), pp. 340–47.

you understand the entire message more accurately. If you search for denotations intended by the source instead of reacting emotionally to loaded words, your perceived messages will be closer to the intended meanings of the source.

Use Feedback to Check Understanding. Even if you're in a situation in which evaluation of a message is needed, you should try to fully understand before you evaluate. If possible, use verbal feedback when you don't understand something. Ask questions and paraphrase to check the accuracy of received messages. Don't just repeat. It's seldom useful just to say, "Do you mean . . .?" and repeat the speaker's exact words. The words will just be decoded as they were originally encoded, and no check on your decoding accuracy will occur. *Paraphrasing is more helpful because it requires that you encode a new set of words to express the meaning you decoded.* This enables the speaker to indicate how close your perceived message was to the one she/he attempted to encode.

Sometimes you can check understanding by asking, "What do you mean by . . .?" But this question may be interpreted as an attack by a defensive speaker. Only where the meaning of a word used by a speaker is clearly not indicated by the context is a direct question of that kind best. Generally it's more effective to paraphrase, saying something like, "Do I hear you saying that . . .?" and fill in what you heard expressed in your own words.

Avoid Evaluation Unless Necessary. If you avoid evaluation until you're sure you understand the intended message, you'll have a better basis when evaluation is really necessary. Try not to fall into the common habit of evaluating when it's not necessary. Many situations don't really call for it. As we noted in the last chapter, judgments may be the major barrier to interpersonal understanding. They are probably also the major barrier to effective listening. When it's necessary, of course, you must critically analyze messages. But unless evaluation is necessary, good listeners avoid it.

recognize source goals

Often you can't decide your receiver goals or the appropriate kinds of responses until you have decided what the source's goals are. You need to learn what these goals are as quickly as possible in the receiving situation.

Listen for Stated Goals. If the goal of a source is to share information, that's usually indicated openly. It's often announced before the occasion, especially in the case of lectures, meetings, and work sessions. In more casual, interpersonal situations, direct reference to a "topic" may be made at the outset of a conversation, often immediately after introductory comments or informal greetings. For instance, "Hey Joe, did you hear about the sale at the bookstore?" or "Did you see Carol's new car?"

Use Verbal and Nonverbal Cues to Identify Unstated Goals. In situations where a communicator wants to change your attitudes or influence your behavior, the purpose will probably be stated less overtly. Even when someone openly states an intent to persuade you, it's seldom done at the outset of a message or a conversation. Usually a lead-in, a pitch, or an introduction is given before the actual aim is stated. This is especially true when people are selling or soliciting. Alertness can help you note early cues to decide what the person's goal is. If someone with a briefcase knocks at your door and begins, "Could I take a moment of your time? What a lovely home you have . . ." you'd wisely guess it was a salesperson. Someone who telephones to "ask a few questions about your reading habits" *may* just be taking a survey, but more likely you'll get a sales pitch for magazine or newspaper subscriptions. In some situations in which the apparent goal of a source is entertainment or casual interaction, hidden purposes may be involved. If so, set your listening goal accordingly.

Check Inferences Regarding Goals. Whenever you infer what another person's goal is, be wary of your inferences. When possible, ask direct questions to check out your conclusions. The answers can help you decide quickly whether to listen or to end the conversation. When direct feedback isn't appropriate, nonverbal cues can help you decide what others' purposes are. Pauses often occur right before or after the reason for talking is stated. *A change in volume and rate of speaking, a shift in body position, use of more direct eye contact, all signal important purpose statements.* Environment, situation, and the previous knowledge you have about the person can help you make fairly reliable inferences regarding a communicator's purpose. Many verbal and nonverbal symbols should be interpreted as you decide what a source's goals are.

identifying main ideas of messages

Look for the Central Idea. After identifying the purposes of the source, search for the main point or idea. This is called a *thesis* or *central idea* in a speech or lecture, but remember that *most communication has a main idea* whether it takes place within a formal public speaking situation or in an informal exchange among several people. Effective listening requires that you recognize the main ideas of the person to whom you're listening.

Look for the Basic Thought Structure. When you are listening, don't try to remember everything that is said: concentrate on the central idea and the major supporting ideas that relate to that main point. Distinguish between these major supporting ideas and lesser details. Don't concentrate on the details. Seek a structure in what you hear and concentrate on the major ideas.

Use Both Verbal and Nonverbal Cues. Both are indicators of what the speaker considers important. Verbal indicators of main ideas include direct reference to the point by transitions. The speaker may say, "The first important idea is . . ." "Another important point is . . ." "Furthermore, . . ." "And finally, . . ." These transitions often highlight important ideas. Repetition is also used to emphasize important points. If something is repeated several times, you can safely conclude the source considers it important.

Position is a nonverbal indicator of an important idea. Communicators usually state their most important ideas at the beginning or the end of their message, or both. Other nonverbal indicators of important points usually accompany the verbal messages. These are similar to the cues you use to pick out purpose statements: change in volume or rate of speaking, usually slowing down; pauses before and after a point; change in body position; or maintaining eye contact for a slightly longer period of time just before or after making the statement.

mental review aids retention

You can mentally *summarize the main ideas as you listen.* When you identify a main idea, utilize a key word or phrase to remember it. Then use your excess decoding time to restate and summarize as you hear each new major supporting idea. Restatement not only helps clarify the speaker's overall message, it improves your retention of the ideas. You may occasionally want to take notes for later reference, but relate the note taking to your goals. Don't try to take complete notes because that will interfere with your listening. Moreover, it's seldom useful to write down everything you hear. If for some reason you need more detailed information, get a tape recorder. Usually, it's best to do what journalists do: use your memory to expand brief notes immediately after the event.

Empathic Listening

The differences between *active* and *empathic listening* are more of intent than of technique. *An empathic listener tries to hear the messages as the source is hearing them.* Carl Rogers defines it as seeing "the expressed idea from the other person's point of view, to sense how it feels to him. . . ."[3] In listening empathically you'll do much

---

[3] Carl Rogers, "Communication: Its Blocking and Its Facilitation," in *Communication Concepts and Processes,* ed. Joseph DeVito (Englewood Cliffs, N.J.: Prentice-Hall, Inc., 1971), pp. 182–88.

the same thing as you would while listening actively. You'll try to be mentally and physically prepared, avoid distractions, pay attention to nonverbals as well as words, identify source goals and main ideas. You do these things to help you see how the person you're listening to sees things.

try to see source's perspective

When you listen empathically, you seek answers to the questions, Why does that person say that? What does it mean to him/her? Only by understanding others' points of view, by sharing their perspective, can you understand *with* people, rather than understand *about* them. That's what the empathic listener tries to do.

> If you really understand another person in this way, if you are willing to enter his private world and see the way life appears to him, without any attempt to make evaluative judgments, you run the risk of being changed yourself. ... The risk of being changed is one of the most frightening prospects most of us can face.
>
> CARL ROGERS

Difficulty of Listening Empathically. Empathic listening isn't easy. It's easier to concentrate on understanding the verbal messages. Getting "inside" the mind of another person is much harder. In the first place, you never really can see things as another does. You can only approximate the perspective of someone else. More serious as a barrier, however, is that most of us don't really *want* to see things from another's point of view if it differs in any significant way from our own. That's because if we allow ourselves to see things as someone else does, we'll see things differently, and thereby run the risk of being changed. Trying to enter into another's world without evaluating it can threaten our own attitude and value systems. This becomes even more difficult because it usually occurs with reference to matters in which emotions are involved. *Empathic listening is most needed when emotional involvement is highest.* But the very emotion we bring to the situation interferes with the effort to see things as someone else does.

Finally, it is difficult to listen empathically because of the fear most of us have of being judged. Situations calling for empathic listening are usually interpersonal interactions in which immediate responses are required. To really understand with others, we must move from the level of interacting evaluatively and relate on a feeling level. But will the others react on the feeling level also? We fear they won't. So, expecting a nonreciprocal response, we often avoid empathic listening. We find it hard not to judge for fear of being judged ourselves.

In spite of the difficulties, though, in many situations we'd benefit from listening empathically. Interpersonal interactions seldom move to the feeling or intimacy level without this level of openness and effort to understand one another. Further, the qualities practiced in empathic listening are of value in all other kinds of receiving situations. If you learn how to see the world through the eyes of others, you'll be in a better position to interact with them even in situations in which evaluation of the messages is necessary. Empathic listening is the best way to assess the motivations and hidden purposes that others may bring to the communication situation. When you must listen critically, you can do it best when you thoroughly understand the message. Skills of empathic listening help you gain this understanding.

Exercise: Listening to Understand and Remember

Objective: To practice skills of listening to understand and remember.
Directions:
1. Your instructor will provide you with the opportunity to hear several five-minute speeches. Listen without taking notes, attempting to apply the skills of listening to understand and remember.
2. For each speech:
   a. Pick out the central idea or main goal statement.
   b. Attempt to determine the main idea or main point structure of the speaker, using a key word or phrase to identify each.
   c. Compare what you perceived as the main idea and main supporting points for each speech with a group of your classmates.

LISTENING TO ANALYZE AND EVALUATE

Often, your goals as a receiver require that you do more than understand a message. You often need to assess the accuracy of information presented, to determine the reasonableness of conclusions, to evaluate inferences, judgments, and suggestions regarding how you should believe or behave. In these cases, you need to analyze and evaluate.

We call this critical listening and we believe critical listening skills are important to you. You are constantly faced with making choices and decisions. One estimate suggests that each person in the U.S. becomes aware of eighty-eight advertising messages every day. Each of us also encounters countless interpersonal efforts to influence our behavior. Because it's impossible in this complex world to experience everything directly, each person depends on others

Critical listening.
Source: Irene Bayer—Monkmeyer.

for information and assistance in decision making. Assessing that advice is one of the uses of critical listening.

Critical listening involves three skills: (1) assessing the values motivating those we listen to; (2) distinguishing facts, observations, and inferences in the messages received; and (3) using relevant criteria to assess conclusions.

Assessing the Values That Motivate Messages

Assessing values involves three steps:

1. Identifying the values of those you're listening to
2. Comparing these values to your own
3. Assessing the appropriateness of acting upon a message based on these values.

Values are central in each individual's perceptual system, and even though they are taken for granted by most of us, they strongly influence our behavior. As we have seen in earlier chapters, values influence how people feel, what they believe, and what they do. Values also influence how they perceive and interpret messages received. Therefore, the first step in critical listening is to assess the values that motivate the message.

Often it's difficult to discover values in others' messages because values are seldom verbalized; they are implied. Sometimes

225

direct feedback can be used to determine a speaker's values. In conversations you can ask, "Why do you believe that?" Other times you have to make inferences. One way to make these inferences is to ask yourself, "What would *I* have to believe to say that?" For example, to evaluate the message, "Be sure to see the movie *Deep Throat*," you need to know why the source valued the experience. Your prior experience with the person can help you determine values, but it's never simple.

Sometimes you'll find it difficult to understand another's values because they're so different from your own. Perhaps it's an area of your value system you haven't previously given much thought to, or a situation with which you've had no experience. Perhaps the values are so vastly different from your own that you can't even conceive someone could think this way. In these situations you may need to switch back to the behaviors of active listening. You may need to learn and understand more before evaluating. Unfortunately, in these cases, people usually prejudge and then choose not to listen at all. By rejecting messages from those whose values differ vastly from yours, you can miss opportunities to grow and expand your horizons. We have noted that people too often perceive a threat in opening themselves to new ideas and new values, and close their minds to new experiences. Hasty prejudgment is a common cause of poor listening, and can be avoided by withholding judgment until the message is clearly understood.

We aren't suggesting that you decide what values are motivating the messages you receive so that you can avoid or reject everything you hear that is based on values different from your own. We believe all of us should be ready at all times to reconsider the appropriateness of our values. Moreover, we know, as we indicated above, that good listeners are open to new ideas. Rejecting anything based on new or different values is a poor listening habit and robs us of much valuable information. What we *are* suggesting is that you should be aware of the values motivating the messages you receive. If you are, it helps you decide how to respond whether your own values are reinforced or changed.

Discovering the values that motivate messages is useful in any interpersonal interaction. It helps identify differences among people that might not otherwise be clear, and explains differences for which no reason seems to exist. When participants are open with each other, discussing differences in values contributes to more effective communication. At the same time, searching for the values underlying a message can lead to acceptance of an idea or behavior that might otherwise have been rejected. For example, suppose you don't like the idea of strikes. But if you find that the person urging a strike is doing so because of unfair treatment of laborers, you might listen to a message you'd otherwise have rejected.

Other skills of critical listening are distinguishing facts from statements about them, and distinguishing statements of observation from inferences. You'll be a better listener if you remember that *a statement of observation isn't identical with the object or event being observed.* Observations vary because attention, perception, and retention are selective. No statement can claim to report all that is knowable about an object or event. Recall also that *statements of observation can't be made about future events.* "The sun will rise tomorrow," is not a statement of observation. It's an inference: a very likely inference to be sure, but still an inference.

Statements of observation can be verified by others using the same senses. Verification is the test of observations, but often you cannot verify others' observations. Then you must decide whether to accept others' observations as accurate. You must decide, "Am I willing to trust this person's observations?" In these cases, assess the qualifications of the person making the statements. Ask yourself:

1. Is the observer reliable?
2. Is the observer biased?
3. Was the observer in a position to see what is claimed?

Sometimes you must risk accepting observations from others, but when you do, remember the observers' perceptions are always subject to distortion. Observations aren't always reliable.

An inference, you'll remember from Chapter 3, is a mental leap, a mental connection of one thought with another or others. Inferring injects more of the person's perceptual system into the conclusion than observing. Thus, *inferences are more likely to vary from person to person and are more subject to error than observations.* You need standards for evaluating inferences. We call these standards *criteria* and want to suggest how you can use them in critical listening.

Using Criteria to Evaluate Inferences

Most people evaluate messages through a "good-bad" "right-wrong" type of evaluation, based on unstated standards. These abstract evaluations are not as useful as applying relevant criteria. Evaluation by criteria raises evaluation beyond the typical "I disagree," "I don't like it" responses. If the criteria are stated as questions, then evaluation of the inference is done by seeking appropriate answers. Potential criteria are many and varied, and which to use in each situation depends on the specific messages being evaluated.

227

The following questions can be used to apply criteria appropriate to most situations.

is the source qualified to draw the conclusions?

The criterion that *a source should be qualified* should be applied to most messages. For example, we agree that a highly successful musician is qualified to comment on music trends over the past twenty years, but we would question her or his authority to give opinions regarding medical advances for the same years. All people have a right to their own opinions, but you should avoid accepting judgments by those who have little or no background in the area of the conclusion.

Another way to apply this criterion is to ask, *"Is the source in a position to see what he/she claims to see?"* If you claim to have seen or heard something, you must have been in a position to have made the observation. Otherwise, you aren't qualified. To be an acceptable witness in an auto accident case, you have to have been where you could see it happen. An illustration of this principle was a classic defense by Abraham Lincoln. A woman claimed to identify a defendant as the burglar she saw in her backyard at night. Lincoln proved she couldn't see his face, because it was the night of a new moon. With no moonlight, she couldn't have seen what she claimed to see, and her testimony was rejected because she was not qualified.

does the source have a vested interest in sending the message?

This question applies the criterion that *sources should be unbiased.* It asks if the source has anything to gain personally by taking a position on an issue. Is there a vested interest involved? Having a stake in the message outcome doesn't automatically disqualify a person from being an influential authority, but it certainly does suggest the likelihood of intentional or unintentional bias. Be aware of and guard against these source biases. A yes answer to this question should arouse your suspicion of the source's conclusions.

Be properly skeptical of everything a salesperson says about a product, for instance. Believing football stars who advertise cars, when you know they've been paid for their endorsement, violates this criterion. On the other hand, if you find a person testifying against a viewpoint of personal benefit, it's important evidence. This is called *reluctant testimony,* and is usually worth listening to. Speaking against a point of view that would bring benefit personally is strong evidence of a speaker's sincerity.

is the evidence relevant to the conclusions?

Often, statements offered as evidence have no real relevance to the conclusions. For example, in asking you to vote for a senatorial candidate, a source may tell you, as evidence, that the candidate has a lovely family. Is that bit of information really relevant to the issue of becoming a senator? It should have little influence on your decision of whether to vote for the person or not. When an advertisement suggests you should buy a headache remedy because three out of four doctors surveyed recommended the ingredients it contains, this doesn't tell you the doctors have recommended the product. The ad contains evidence more relevant to the purchase of aspirin than to the product advertised.

Applying this criterion, that *evidence should be relevant to the inference supported,* will lead you to reject all inferences based on irrelevant data.

is there contrary evidence to that presented?

Do some facts exist that would qualify or negate the inferences in the message? Take the senatorial candidate as an example. If you knew that the candidate's children were vandals kept out of juvenile court only by the politician's influence, and that the candidate's family received support from the underworld, you might feel that this evidence negates the claim that this person has a lovely family. Someone who argues, "Have a smoke, I see no harm in it; no one I know got cancer from smoking," fails to mention all those smokers who died of cancer that he didn't know. When you reject inferences on this basis, you have applied the criterion that *contrary evidence invalidates an inference.*

is sufficient evidence presented to justify the claim?

An inference concludes what isn't known based on what is known. It implies the existence of observations on which the inference is based. This question asks whether or not the observations are sufficient. Is there enough basis to draw the inference? If not, the inference has not met the criterion that *evidence should be sufficient,* and the inference should be rejected.

does the message contain invalid or inadequate reasoning?

Inferences require a mental leap. This question asks if the leap is logically sound. If it's not, the conclusion should be rejected, because it does not meet the criterion that *reasoning should be valid.* To apply this criterion, recall the common errors in reasoning introduced in Chapter 3. Identify the kind of reasoning you're hearing. Is it generalization? deduction? cause-effect? comparison and contrast? use of false alternatives? Once you've identified the basis for the conclusion, you can assess it, using the guidelines for accurate reasoning given in Chapter 3.

is there overreliance on propaganda techniques?

Much fallacious reasoning results from *overreliance on propaganda devices*. You've probably been introduced to these devices before this course. A list at the end of this chapter will review them, if not. The devices include the use of bandwagon techniques, half-truths, card stacking, glittering generalities, name calling, labeling, transfer, testimonials, "plain folks" language, and loaded words. Most rely excessively on emotional appeals. When you see or hear these techniques, you should see a red flag. Be especially critical of messages that rely excessively on emotional appeals. Certainly, emotional appeals are necessary and useful, but a source who relies excessively on emotion may do so because of weak logic.

Propaganda devices and overreliance on emotional appeals should serve as warning signals to you to apply even more rigorously the other tests of evidence and reasoning. You shouldn't reject a message just because it's emotional, but neither should you allow emotional appeals and propaganda to suspend your examination of the evidence and reasoning in the argument.

LOOKING BACK

Goal setting is important in listening. Listening situations vary, ranging in degree of listener involvement required from hearing through listening for pleasure, listening for understanding, to listening for evaluation. Goal setting assists the listener in purposeful focus of attention. It provides motivation for expending the necessary energy, a method of assessing accomplishment, a means of determining when it's appropriate to shift listening levels, and a way to know how to avoid behaving in ways that interfere with goal achievement.

Active listening is needed for situations of listening for information and evaluation. It involves mental and physical preparation; recognition of the speaker's goals, concentration on the speaker's ideas; ruling out irrelevancies in the message, in the nonverbals, and in the environment; utilizing the rate differences in speaking and decoding to summarize, relate, and restate main ideas; and use of relevant nonverbals to help interpret the verbal messages. An active listener tries to understand completely a speaker's main idea and supporting reasons before evaluation.

Empathic listening is another level of listening to understand. It involves trying to understand what another person is saying from that person's point of view. Empathic listening requires that a person employ the techniques of active listening, but for the purpose of trying to see the world as the speaker (source) sees it instead of just for understanding the ideas of the message. Empathic listening involves understanding why the person believes as she/he does. Empathic listening is difficult because it is difficult to drop our own perspective for a different one; because of the risk inherent in opening ourselves to others' understandings; and because of the fear of being judged by others. But it is valuable as a prerequisite to effective critical listening and is necessary in developing close interpersonal relationships with others.

Critical listening involves identification of values that motivate messages to understand why the messages are sent; distinguishing observations and inferences to assess accuracy of messages; and using criteria to evaluate inferences. The criteria include assessment of source qualifications and bias, the relevance, adequacy, and accuracy of evidence, and acceptability of the reasoning process. Inadequate reasoning may be caused by confusion of correlation and causation, using false alternatives, confusion of facts, inferences and observations, or overreliance on propaganda and emotional appeals. Propaganda usually uses excessive reliance on emotions and when the listener recognizes this approach, the evidence and reasoning should be subject to even more careful examination than usual.

Exercise: Critical Listening

Objective: To practice the skills required to evaluate messages.
Directions:
1. Below are three messages. For each of them answer the following questions:
   a. What is the speaker's goal?
   b. What are the basic values on which the message is based?
   c. What are the important inferences I am expected to accept if I do or believe as the speaker wants?
   d. What are the appropriate criteria to use to evaluate this message?
   e. Applying the criteria, is the message acceptable?
   f. What further information do I need to fully evaluate the message?

Message I:
A student who sits next to you in the history class meets you a few minutes before class starts. "Hey, have you voted in the Student Senate elections?" When you say you haven't, the person replies, "Well, you'd better. You know the Senate is working very hard to get the pass-fail system adopted here at the college, and the Barker candidates haven't come out very strongly in favor of it. The Brinkman party, however, has an entire slate that supports pass-fail grading strongly. You wouldn't have to take all your classes pass-fail, but you would at least have that option, which is more than we now have. Come with me after class. Let's go vote for the Brinkman candidates."

Message II:
You are talking with a friend about what classes to take during the next semester. You may take one elective and must decide which English teacher to take composition from. The friend says, "Listen,

this ecology course is great. We go on field trips, and visit places, and haven't had a single test all semester. It's a breeze, nothing to it. And as for English—well, I don't know. This prof I have makes us write a theme every week. What a drag. You sure don't want to get Jones.''

Message III:

You are listening to a speaker who is urging you to support the Right to Life constitutional amendment. The speaker's basic argument is that abortion is murder because any fetus is a human life. The speaker argues, therefore, that abortion should not be acceptable under any circumstances.

PROPAGANDA DEVICES

Device	*Method*
BANDWAGON	Argues: "Since everyone else is doing it (or buying it) you should too."
HALF-TRUTHS	By telling only part of the information, leaves an impression that is inaccurate; e.g., advertising that "three out of four doctors surveyed recommend the ingredient in Anacin," without pointing out that the recommended ingredient is common aspirin.
CARD STACKING	Presents only one side of the evidence to support a particular position.
GLITTERING GENERALITY	Applies concepts that have powerful positive connotations—for example, "motherhood," "morality," "decency," "fairness"—to the idea being urged.
NAME CALLING	The use of words in a manner intended to arouse powerful negative connotations, usually to depict another person or a group as inferior or bad; e.g., calling busing a conspiracy or attacking the opponents of busing as racist.
LABELING	The use of words to categorize a person or a group under a single heading, frequently negative; intentionally selects one aspect of the person or group being labeled.
TRANSFER	Introduces one subject or topic that is highly respectable or popular, and then moves into other areas in an effort to transfer the positive attitude onto the new topic.
TESTIMONIAL	Uses a source of authority as evidence for ideas and positions, often in areas in which the person is not really an authority; e.g., Bob Hope advertising Texaco products.
PLAIN FOLKS	Presents the source or authority as a person who is really simple and humble, a person just like your neighbors, a person who is innocent and trustworthy.
LOADED WORDS	The use of words that will stir strong emotional responses either supporting the position of the advocate, or to attack the position of opponents

1. How do listening situations differ?
2. What are the benefits of goal setting in listening?
3. Distinguish between the receiver behaviors of active and empathic listening.
4. Distinguish between facts, observations, inferences, and judgments.
5. What steps are involved in assessing values as you listen critically?
6. List the questions asked in using criteria to evaluate inferences and indicate how the questions would have to be answered for inferences to be acceptable.

Suggestions for Further Reading

BARKER, LARRY L., *Listening Behavior.* Englewood Cliffs, N.J.: Prentice-Hall, Inc., 1971.

BROCKRIEDE, WAYNE, AND DOUGLAS EHNINGER, *Decision by Debate.* New York: Dodd, Mead and Co., 1963.

BARBARA, DOMINICK, *The Art of Listening.* Springfield, Ill.: Charles C Thomas, 1971.

DUKER, SAM, ed., *Listening: Readings.* Metuchen, N.J.: Scarecrow Press, 1966.

FEARNSIDE, W. WARD, AND WILLIAM B. HOLTHER, *Fallacy: The Counterfeit of Argument.* Englewood Cliffs, N.J.: Prentice-Hall, Inc., 1959.

NICHOLS, RALPH G., AND LEONARD A. STEVENS, *Are You Listening?* New York: McGraw-Hill Book Co., 1957.

THUM, GLADYS, AND MARCELLA THUM, *The Persuaders: Propaganda in War and Peace.* New York: Atheneum Publishers, 1972.

WEAVER, CARL H., *Human Listening.* Indianapolis: Bobbs-Merrill, 1972.

Key to Words and Phrases

Acceptance: the ability to relate to another person with positive regard, without judgment or attempts to control

Climates of communication: refers to various attitudes in interpersonal communication situations; can contribute to or reduce defensiveness between communicators

Climate of certainty: characterized by dogmatism, by communication that indicates the person has all the answers; increases defensiveness; is the opposite of provisionalism

Climate of control: characterized by attempts or desire to control behavior of others, to restrict that person's ranges of choices in belief or behavior; increases defensiveness; is the opposite of problem orientation

Climate of description: characterized by nonjudgmental communication; reduces defensiveness; is the opposite of evaluation

Climate of empathy: characterized by identification of the communicator with others, or by attempts to experience how others feel; reduces defensiveness; is the opposite of neutrality

Climate of equality: characterized by attitudes that differences between communicators are of little importance, and indicate willingness to interact with mutual trust and respect; reduces defensiveness; is the opposite of superiority.

Climate of evaluation: characterized by judging others and their behavior, involves either positive or negative opinions; increases defensiveness, especially when negative

Climate of neutrality: characterized by impersonal communication that indicates a lack of concern for the person(s) communicated with (used in this sense does not mean objective); increases defensiveness

Climate of problem orientation: characterized by willingness to join others in working together toward commonly agreed upon conclusions; reduces defensiveness

Climate of provisionalism: characterized by willingness to reconsider behavior and opinions, by absence of dogmatism; reduces defensiveness

Climate of spontaneity: characterized by straightforward, honest communication that is free from deception; reduces defensiveness

Climate of strategy: characterized by use of tricks or manipulation to influence others; increases defensiveness; the opposite of spontaneity

Climate of superiority: characterized by attitudes that the person communicating is better than others in one or several ways; increases defensiveness

Credibility: the degree to which a person is perceived as believable, varies with each situation

Defensiveness: behavior that occurs when a person perceives a threat in a communication situation; usually includes lack of openness; often involves dishonest, hostile and aggressive communication

Dialect: a language variant, used by a group of speakers, that is perceived by those who speak the language as different from the general language community; dialects may be regional, social, or ethnic

Feedback, directive: perceived responses that convey evaluation by the responder; may be nonverbal as well as verbal

Feedback, intentional: feedback messages that are perceived as their source intended

Feedback, nondirective: responses that are perceived as nonevaluative; verbally, responses that are intended to be nondirective take the form of statements of observation or questions

Feedback, unintentional: feedback messages that the responder does not intend to send or that may be perceived differently from how they were intended

Homophily: describes the degree to which communicators are similar in attributes, such as attitudes, values, status, appearance, etc.

Interpersonal attraction: the amount of positive regard, of liking, that exists between people

Interpersonal perception: selection and perception of stimuli received from people so as to interpret their qualities and traits; attributing personality and character to individuals

Labeling: to attach a word to a person as if the word were the person and then treat the person accordingly

Listening: a process, occuring on different levels, of receiving and interpreting communication

Listening, empathic: a high level of involvement in listening; is primarily an attempt to fully understand the source of messages received

Listening, hearing: receiving sound, but with little conscious processing

Purposes for communication: goal(s) sought by communicators; reasons for talking and listening; usually involve at least three goals, those related to self, to subject, and to others

Ritual communication: communication in which the verbal messages are less important than the form and the fact that the interaction occurs

Stereotyping: projecting the characteristics believed to be descriptive of a group onto individual members of the group

Trust: being confident of ability to predict a beneficial result in a situation where another person can behave either in ways that are beneficial or harmful to you, and where you cannot control the outcome

part 3

Communication Within Groups

In our daily lives, we communicate constantly within groups. We work in groups; we play in groups; most of us *live* in a group. Yet we often pay little attention to the dynamics of group communication. Few of us recognize how we can make group experiences more satisfying.

In this section of the book, you will be introduced to several concepts that will help you understand the different types of groups and how they function. In Chapter 9 we examine how characteristics of groups influence communication within them. Chapter 10 is concerned with how decisions are made in group situations. In Chapters 11 and 12 we deal with behaviors that increase communication effectiveness in two specific types of groups—the family and the work situation. With an understanding of group principles and practice in applying communication skills in groups, you can function more effectively in the many groups to which you belong.

9

Group Characteristics, Relationships, and Communication

goal:

To understand how group characteristics and relationships affect communication within groups.

probes:

The material in this chapter should help you to:

1. Identify the major purposes of groups and illustrate how purposes affect communication by giving examples. pp. 238–40

2. Indicate the differences between public and private groups that affect communication. pp. 240–42

3. Illustrate how size is a major factor influencing communication within groups pp. 242–47

4. Describe the inter-relationships among characteristics of groups that affect interdependence and cohesiveness. pp. 247–50

5. Distinguish between role expectations and role performances. pp. 251–52

6. Demonstrate an awareness of how roles, norms, and status affect communication by citing personally experienced examples pp. 251–56

7. Cite both internal and external norms that have affected your communication within some group. pp. 254–56

> A group is not to hide in.
> A crowd? Go ahead and hide.
> The difference is "being heard"
> vs. "being part of a herd."
>
> CHARLES WILKINSON

Human beings are social creatures. We spend most of our waking hours in groups, large or small. Our jobs, our play, our family life, all take place mostly in groups. But a *group* is more than a collection of individuals. When we refer to a group, we are talking about a communication system in which a series of interactions among members determines the structure and identity of the group.[1] Individuals in a group communicate directly or indirectly with one another, thus creating the group. At the same time, the

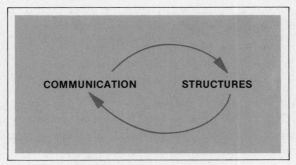

Group communication and group characteristics interact and affect each other.

---

[1] The word *group* is defined by different people in many ways. No definition is perfect, for the concept is very abstract, and cannot be made specific. This definition is chosen because we find it useful. It encompasses all kinds of groups: large and small, structured and unstructured, permanent and temporary, and so on.

Group communication is our most
common communication situation.
Source: (above) Tom Tracy — The Stock
Shop; *(upper right)* Mahon —
Monkmeyer; *(lower right)* Mimi Forsyth —
Monkmeyer.

elements of a group affect communication within it. This interactive
nature of group communication creates a complex set of relationships. An understanding of these relationships can help you improve your ability to communicate effectively in groups. To help
you achieve that understanding, this chapter discusses the characteristics and relationships that affect communication within groups.
We will cover type and size of group; members' interdependence
and cohesiveness; roles and norms. In later chapters specific applications of group communication are covered.

TYPE OF GROUP

Many different kinds of groups exist, and several classification
schemes could be used to illustrate the differences. We classify
groups according to purpose, length of existence, and whether or
not their interactions are observed by outsiders.

Purpose

Four types of groups with recognizably different purposes can be
noted: social, therapeutic, task, and a combination of these.

238   *Social groups* usually exist for the members' personal social

239

*Group
Characteristics,
Relationships,
and
Communication*

A group's structural properties, ... may create problems and may provide solutions to other problems of communication. Viewed the other way around, many properties of a group are outcomes of its communicative practices.

THEODORE NEWCOMB

satisfactions: to provide recreation, pleasure, enjoyment. Though tasks may be involved, the basic reason social groups exist is social. Fishing clubs, country clubs, camping organizations, card players in the student center, and neighborhood coffee klatches are examples of social groups.

Therapeutic groups provide physical or psychological therapy for individual members. Alcoholics Anonymous, Synanon, encounter, and sensitivity groups are examples of therapeutic groups.

Task groups exist for the specific purpose of accomplishing a job or set of tasks. Task groups exist independently and also are found within larger groups. Subgroups that are task groups are found within both large and small organizations, such as churches, social clubs, and places of work. The vast majority of people work in institutions or organizations that use task groups, whether they sell, teach, build, or distribute; whether they work in the private economy or for the government, for charitable organizations or for themselves; whether they work for profit, commissions, salary, or personal satisfaction.

The purpose of the group often varies from the purposes individual members have for belonging to the group. A social group, identified by the purpose of the group, may be considered a task group by some members. For example, some people belong to a country club for the business contacts they make there. Similarly, some people belong to work groups, not for income, but to satisfy self-actualization needs. Differences between member and group purposes may influence communication greatly, as discussed below.[2]

Some groups have combinations of purposes. One of the *combined-purpose groups* is the family. Whether your family is a large, close clan, the nuclear-type family more common in the U.S. today, or one of the commune-style group families, you have probably experienced the family as a group. Moreover, your family is probably a very important group in your life. For that reason we devote Chapter 11 to analysis of communicating in families. Remember, however, most of the information in this chapter also applies to family groups. Another combined-purpose group is a growth group, such as a college class in which groups are given tasks to accomplish and individual members also expect to achieve growth.

---

[2] See pp. 248–49.

The purpose of a group is a major influence on the kind of communication that occurs within it. Purpose helps determine which communications are acceptable and necessary and which are frivolous, irrelevant, or unacceptable. Knowing the purpose of a group will help you know what to say and do in that group. Recognizing that purposes vary can also help you identify the source of some groups' communication problems.

Length of Existence

The length of time a group expects to exist influences the communication within it. Groups may be casual, temporary, or permanent.

Casual groups are usually of accidental composition and last only a few minutes or hours. A group convened to hear a speaker and suggest solutions to a community problem would be a casual group. A group of witnesses to an accident convened to give testimony or a group of friends playing bridge in the student center between classes are other examples of casual groups.

Temporary groups are more common. Such groups meet to accomplish a specific task. They exist long enough to complete the task, and then are disbanded. A mayor's committee appointed to recommend solutions for a specific problem or a bridge group that forms for the duration of a semester are examples of temporary groups.

Permanent groups are such as churches, corporations, fraternities, or service clubs. They remain in existence even though membership changes through the years. Temporary groups exhibit strong tendencies to become permanent. Committees often find reasons to continue their existence long after their original purpose may have been fulfilled. An example is the March of Dimes Foundation, which was originally established to aid the battle against polio; when it did this successfully, it went on to adopt new goals.

A group that has existed for a long time may develop maturity, which influences the group's communication. (See p. 252.) New or casual groups have communication patterns different from those of older groups. When members do not expect to be together long, they behave differently. They may engage in rituals and never communicate beyond the level of objectivity or evaluation. Little real sharing or intimacy will be expected or even permitted in a group of brief duration.

Relation to Outsiders

A group may be considered public or private, depending on whether or not outsiders observe the group. In *private groups,* the interactions among the members do not occur in front of audiences.

241

*Group
Characteristics,
Relationships,
and
Communication*

Most task groups are private. Note that the word "private" does not imply closed membership, however. Not all private groups have closed memberships. By private we mean groups whose member interactions are not open to observation by outsiders. Such groups often involve interactions with people outside them—or representatives may be designated to do this. But they don't conduct their business in front of audiences. Because most groups are private, most of our attention here is directed to the study of communication in private groups.

In *public groups,* the interactions among the members are "open" to outsiders in the sense that they can be observed. Examples of this kind of group might be a panel of experts convened to discuss a question on a television program; a board of directors of a company meeting in open session; a board of education holding its monthly meeting or a city council. Public groups consist of people interacting in front of an audience to conduct various kinds of business. In such a group the audience frequently interacts with the group. Communicating in public groups is complex because both interpersonal and public aspects of communication are involved.

SIZE

The size of a group strongly influences communication within it. Some groups are quite large: for example, the Democratic or the Republican party, the Methodist or the Catholic church, General Motors or IBM. Members of these groups are widely separated and interactions among them are indirect. Still, affiliation with the group influences members' behavior, primarily because such large groups function as reference groups. By *reference group* we mean a group that a person uses to guide behavior and belief, one with which a person identifies but need not actually belong to. For instance, a pre-med student can identify with the AMA but may not actually belong. Members use reference groups to evaluate their own behavior. Some even use reference groups as the source of their opinions. For example, a student who is a union steward was asked his opinion about a recent city council action. His reply was, "I think what the union thinks, and the 688 Council hasn't discussed that yet. So I don't have an opinion."

Each of us has many reference groups, some consciously chosen and some acquired through the socialization process. Ethnic groups, nations, states, regions, religions, political parties, socioeconomic classes, and many other groups become reference groups for us as we recognize an identification with them. The identification may be physical, social, emotional, or all three. A group does not function as a reference group for you unless you recognize an identification with one or more of the group's characteristics. A reference group is a powerful influence on your communication whether you are with members of the group or not.

Many groups are not so massive but still are considered large groups: for example, the Democratic or Republican party organization within a city, a particular church, the local Chevrolet plant, or one city's branch of Bell Telephone. These groups function as reference groups, as well as directly influencing members.

Communication Patterns

Styles and types of communication in a group are often determined by its size. In small groups all members can interact with one another on a one-to-one basis, but that is not true of larger groups. Patterns and networks are needed to channel communication in larger groups, as we discuss in Chapter 12. A small group with sufficient time usually develops direct communication among all members. The following diagram illustrates lines of communication that reflect direct interpersonal communication among all members:

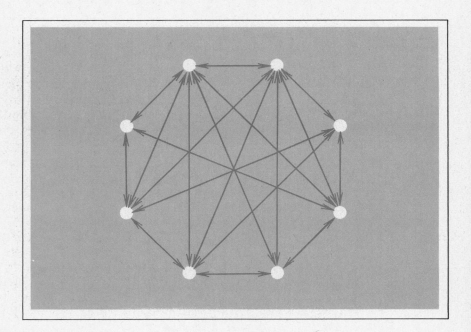

A larger group does not develop direct interpersonal communication among all members. Leaders emerge, and communications are largely directed to and from these leaders.[3] The resulting communication patterns within a large group might look like this:

---

[3] Communication and group leadership are discussed in Chapter 10.

243
*Group
Characteristics,
Relationships,
and
Communication*

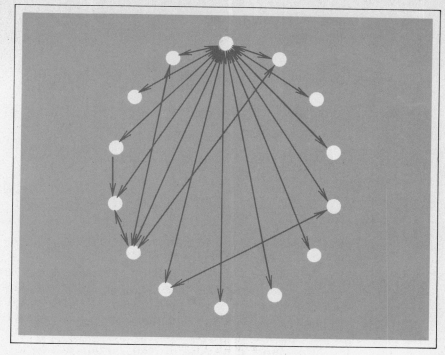

Many variations are possible, of course. In some large groups, member-to-single-leader communication patterns do not develop. Instead, several small groups emerge, each with a spokesperson to communicate among the subgroups.

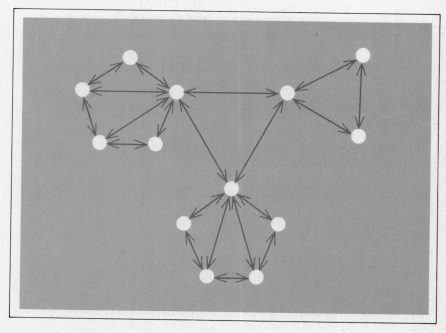

Public groups interact with each other and for an audience.
Source: Sam Falk—Monkmeyer.

Most groups are free to form communication patterns as they mature. These groups might be committees, task forces in which members have equal or nearly equal status, or social organizations of many kinds. In other situations, groups are more rigidly limited in the communication patterns permitted.

Communication patterns may be imposed by external or internal forces. External forces include both physical and psychological restrictions. For example, work teams may be created by the physical layout of desks and offices, or by appointments made by supervisors, or both. Committees are often created and their communication patterns influenced by appointment of their chairperson. Internal factors include the several group characteristics discussed below, as well as interpersonal attraction, attitudes, and habits of members. If you enter an organization with the belief that you shouldn't directly talk with people of high status, or that you should speak to a president only when spoken to, this will restrict your communication behavior.

Four *patterns of communication* can be described: all channel, the wheel, the Y, and the chain. The figure below illustrates these patterns in small groups. The actual number of members in groups with communication patterns like these is usually much larger.

A person at the beginning of a communication *chain* has some control over the communication of every member, but not in the same way the person in control in the Y or *wheel* might have. The hub of the wheel has access to all members. The fork of the Y directly interacts with three out of four members. Members in all-channel communication patterns can interact directly with all other members, while persons in a chain interact with only two and each must assume any messages will be passed on accurately.

244

245

*Group
Characteristics,
Relationships,
and
Communication*

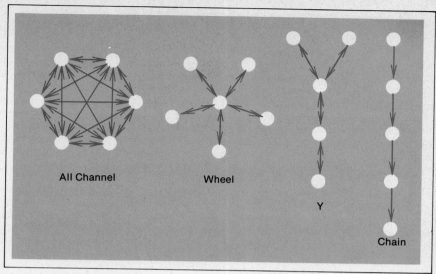

Patterns of communication.

People occupying different positions in each of these patterns are influenced differently. A person in a central position will find it easier to lead and become an influential decision maker. That person has direct access to more information and more opportunities to influence others, and will be able, other factors being equal, to communicate more effectively and have more impact on other members. As a result, persons in a central position are more likely to be satisfied with the group than are those in less pivotal positions.

Communication patterns influence the accuracy of the communication involved. A small group with all-channel interaction will have more accurate communication because of increased amounts of feedback and opportunities for all members to share information. Communication through *gatekeepers*[4] is subject to much more screening than is the all-channel communication pattern. Thus, the chain pattern has barriers to accurate communication. Communication along a chain is described as *serial communication.* Usually serial communication receives the same treatment that messages did when you played the games of "telephone" or "rumor" in your earlier schooldays. Passing messages from person to person usually results in at least some distortion. The following "report" of the expected appearance of Halley's Comet illustrates the distorting effect of serial communication.[5]

---

[4] *Gatekeeper* is the term used to describe a person who has the power to control and regulate the flow of information through channels of communication.

[5] "Permutation Personified," *Boles Letter* (E. D. Boles and Associates, 1962).

A colonel issued the following directive to his executive officer:

"Tomorrow night at 2000 hours Halley's Comet will be visible in this area, an event occurring only once every 75 years. Have the men fall out in the battalion area in fatigues, and I will explain this rare phenomenon to them. In case of rain, we will not be able to see anything, so assemble the men in the theater and I will show films on it."

Executive officer to company commander:

"By order of the colonel who was in fatigues at 2000 hours tomorrow evening, the phenomenal Halley's Comet will appear above the battalion area. If it rains, fall the men out in fatigues and march to the theater where the rare phenomenon will take place, something which only occurs once every 75 years."

Company commander to lieutenant:

"By order of the colonel who was in fatigues at 2000 hours tomorrow evening, the phenomenal Halley's Comet will appear in the theater. There is absolutely no explanation for this unusual event, and it is for that reason that the colonel is going to explain it to you in full. In case of rain in the battalion area, the colonel will give another order, something with occurs every 75 years."

Lieutenant to sergeant:

"Tomorrow at 2000 hours, the colonel will appear in the theater with Halley's Comet, something which happens every 75 years. If it rains, he will order the comet into the battalion area."

Sergeant to squad:

"When it rains tomorrow at 2000 hours, the phenomenal 75-year-old General Halley, accompanied by the colonel, will drive his Comet through the battalion area theater in his fatigues."

This report is, of course, fictitious and exaggerated. That such distortion in communication is common, however, can be attested to by anyone who has been involved in a large organization. You can verify this problem with your own experience if you've ever been involved in a non–face-to-face communication and attempted to establish exactly what it was that person X said to person Y and how the message was then sent to person Z.

Networks and patterns of information both result from communication and affect it. Communication patterns and their effects are situational. One pattern works in some situations when others do not. Sometimes a pattern is required by the circumstances, as in organizations. An employee who failed to follow established patterns for worker-union-management communication would probably be reprimanded by both union and management.

Especially in mature groups, habits influence communication. *Once a communication pattern is established in a group, it tends to become an expected pattern for messages among members.* The influence of patterns can be either positive or negative. Efficiency is increased when everyone knows who to talk to first about what. But sometimes, communication patterns persist past the circumstances that fostered them, and efficiency is impaired.

247

Group
Characteristics,
Relationships,
and
Communication

Exercise: Serial Communication

Objective: To recognize and assess ways to prevent problems in serial communication.

Directions:

1. Class will be divided into groups of six and will draw lots for positions A, B, C, D, E, and F.
2. All but person A and F of each group will be sent outside the room. Person A of each group will be given a message by the instructor.
3. Person F, using the form provided, will be given the message in writing, and will record any omissions, additions, or distortions to the message made in this or following transactions.
4. Member B of each group will be called back into the room and A will orally transmit the message he or she received to B. Members receiving messages will not take notes.
5. Member C, D, and E will each be called back—in turn, one at a time—and the message will be transmitted from B to C, then from C to D, and finally from D to E.
6. When member E has received the message, he/she should write down what was received. Each final message will then be compared to the others, and all will be compared to the initial message as A received it.
7. The class will then discuss—as a whole or in groups—how the transmissions could have been changed to improve the accuracy of serial communication.

INTERDEPENDENCE AND COHESIVENESS

Interdependence and *cohesiveness* affect communication within groups. *Interdependence refers to the extent members need each other to achieve group and individual goals,* while *cohesiveness describes the forces that influence members to choose to remain in the group.* Cohesiveness gives group members a sense of belonging, a feeling that the group is a unit and not merely an aggregation of individuals.

As with all group characteristics, interdependence and cohesiveness are variables. Either may be present in great or small degree, and it is even possible for one to be high and the other low. Although the two characteristics affect each other, they do not cause each other, nor are they caused by the same factors. The presence or absence of either, however, will affect the amount and kind of communication that occurs within a group. If cohesion is high, members probably want very much to be part of the group, derive great satisfaction from their membership, and devote energy and time to acquire and defend their membership. If cohesion is low, members of a group do not feel close to each other, and have little attachment to the group. Some interdependence is always needed or a group will not exist, but the amounts can vary. High interdependence usually results in cooperative communication that is task-oriented. Low interdependence among group members reduces the amount of communication among them and may also result in less cooperation among the members.

If we could describe precisely the communication behaviors that result in high interdependence and cohesiveness among groups, this would simplify the task of learning how to improve your communication in groups. But this is not possible. Factors affecting both interdependence and cohesiveness may be external to the group and you may have no control over them at all. At the same time, some factors affecting both characteristics may be internal to members in the sense that their personal attitudes, perspectives, and values affect members' behaviors toward each other. These personal characteristics may also be beyond your control. Many factors that affect interdependence and cohesiveness can be influenced by members' communications, however, and we want to discuss some of them here—namely, group and members' agreement on goals, maturity and control, and attractiveness and satisfaction.

> If you don't know where you are going, you will end up somewhere else.
>
> LAURENCE PETER

Agreement on Goals

Interdependence results partly from relationships among group and members' goals. The *group* goal is what the group is expected to achieve. Some groups exist to fulfill the personal needs of the members, some exist to produce goods, some to provide services, others to sell products or services. Groups might exist to solve problems, make or implement decisions, make or administer laws, or provide social activities. The list could go on and on. Group goals are often multiple and are not always agreed upon by all members.

Group goals often differ from individual members' goals. Members' goals are the reasons each person has for belonging to the group. Most group associations are matters of choice, and people join groups for many reasons. For example, the goal of one person in a church may be to worship as he/she believes correct. Another person's goal may be to impress neighbors and boss; a third may attend church to seek companionship; a fourth may seek self-fulfill-

249

Group
Characteristics,
Relationships,
and
Communication

ment by providing service and leadership; and a fifth may want reinforcement for beliefs and attitudes. People often have several goals for group membership, not just one, and commonly they share the group goal but have additional personal goals. Differences among group and member goals are often sources of communication problems in groups.

harmony of goals

Member goals can be either complementary or antagonistic. *Complementary goals* exist when each member can only achieve her/his individual goals if other members achieve theirs. *Antagonistic goals* exist when one member can reach individual goals only when others do *not* reach theirs. An example of complementary goals could be created in the classroom by your instructor if you were divided into groups for a task and told that none of your group could get an A on the project unless all did. Antagonistic goals could be created if the instructor said that only one member of each group could get an A, only one a B, one a C, and the others would flunk. Antagonistic goals cause competitive, often defensive communication.

Though not all members in a group need have identical goals, some degree of agreement is necessary. The greater the agreement, the more likely that cohesion will be high and that members will work together effectively. Individual goals that differ from or conflict with group goals, or that are antagonistic to other members' goals, can reduce or eliminate chances of accomplishing the group goal.

> Those who organize a group try to make the reality correspond as closely as possible to their images of what it should be like, but since the organizers have different images, compromises are always necessary.
>
> ERIC BERNE

Attractiveness and Satisfaction

Attractiveness and satisfaction, both related to cohesiveness, also influence group communication. Attractiveness may be of individual members or of the group. A person may want to belong to a certain country club because of the people who belong to it. You may be attracted to the people in a church, a bridge club, or service organization and join these groups because of interpersonal attraction. In other cases, the group itself may be attractive. You may believe in a group's goals, or be impressed by what it is or what it has accomplished. People often join churches, service clubs, professional associations, even the companies where they work for these reasons.

Group members must have at least minimal satisfaction — with the group, with others in it, or with its product or productivity — to remain in a group. The degree of satisfaction required to retain membership varies according to the purpose the individual has for belonging.

Needless to say, higher levels of attractiveness and satisfaction usually result in higher levels of cohesiveness, while interdependence tends to improve all three. The relationships among these characteristics, however, are not causal. Neither attractiveness nor interdependence automatically result in cohesiveness. The relationships are interactive, and are affected by the other group characteristics, as well as by external forces.

Maturity and Control

Maturity and control also affect communication within groups. Maturity is not the same as age of a group, though the two are related. *Maturity requires establishment of group norms, roles, and interaction patterns among members.* When members know group norms, and understand and are comfortable with their roles and the interaction patterns of the group, maturity exists. Maturity makes communication among members easier, more comfortable, and usually more efficient. In immature groups much more effort must be devoted to maintaining the group and to developing needed roles, norms, and interaction patterns. In new groups members must become acquainted, develop trust in each other, and grow accustomed to a pattern of relationships. Similar strains on communication occur in older groups adjusting to new members. Old members are often wary of newcomers who may bring in different or disruptive ideas or behaviors. And newcomers, until they learn the roles, norms, and accepted behavior patterns, are often defensive in relating to established members. As maturity in a group grows, less effort is required to maintain the group, and open communication is easier.

The degree of control in a group also influences members' communications. *Control refers to the influence a group has over its members' behavior, its own environment, and its task.* You should recognize that these three elements are different, even though they are related. Control influences members' morale and commitment to the group. If members must behave as the group requires, but can dictate the task of the group and are free from environmental restraints, their communication will differ from a situation in which other external or internal forces limit freedom. Whatever its source, the existence or absence of control affects the type of communication. To understand all the factors affecting group communication, you need to be aware of the influence of control on the members of a group.

While all group characteristics affect communication within groups, none are more important than the effects of roles, status, and norms. These factors directly affect the degree to which communication is open or closed, pleasant or unpleasant, accurate or inaccurate, successful or unsuccessful.

Role

> All the world's a stage, And all the men and women merely players. Each in his own time assumes many parts.
>
> WILLIAM SHAKESPEARE

Role is an important concept in understanding group communication, though the word is used with many different meanings. One search of journals and books revealed forty different uses of the word.[6] Problems arise because role is a complex, highly abstract concept. Sometimes the term refers to positions in social relationships. For example, you commonly hear of the roles of mother, father, husband, wife, son, daughter, parent, student, teacher, employer, employee. You could go on listing many other common social roles. More accurately, we think, these words refer to a *set of behaviors expected of people who occupy specific positions in a social relationship.*

role expectations and performances

We use the term "role" to refer to the behaviors expected of persons perceived to occupy particular social positions. But because the expectations differ, it is never possible to state precisely what a particular role is. Because a role consists of expected behaviors, it can be identified only by those holding the expectations. For example, the role of mother can't be defined simply by listing a set of behaviors. Many different mother roles exist. Roles relate both to specific situations and specific people. Expected and actual behaviors are also both involved in the concept of role.

You should consider both role expectations and role performances to understand the effects of role in communication. By *role performance* we mean how a person actually behaves in a social position. Only in very stable social structures will role performances

---

[6] Lionel Nieman and James Hughes, "The Problem of the Concept of Role—A Re-survey of the Literature," *Social Forces*, 30 (December 1951), 141–49.

conform closely to role expectations; and only in very stable social structures will members agree on role expectations. For example, look at the social position called parent. We could agree fairly easily on a way to divide the population into two groups, parents and nonparents. We would not so easily agree on the role of a parent. How is a parent to act? What behaviors are expected of parents? What should they avoid doing? Most people have a set of expectations regarding parents' behavior, but they'll rarely agree with everything that other persons expect of parents. Lack of agreement about roles, however, doesn't make them any less real. Each person, each group, and each society expect certain behaviors from people they call parents, and each reacts strongly to people who violate the expectations. Even though people seldom agree on a particular role, their *expectations are powerful influences on the communication of those who are perceived to take the role.*

Each group develops role expectations of its own. Most churches, for example, have a minister. But the Catholic priest role differs from that of the Episcopal priest, which differs from the role of a Presbyterian pastor, which in turn differs from that of a pastor in the Lutheran church. Moreover, within each subgroup of any system, particular roles develop. The congregation of a Methodist pastor in a small Midwestern town will not expect the same behaviors from their minister as will the congregation of a Methodist pastor in a large church in New York City.

Groups, whether large or small, are also affected by the role expectations of their society. The influence exists because some parts of the social structure operate as reference groups for other parts. The parent role in a particular family, for instance, grows from the personal experiences of both husband and wife with their own parents, and those of their friends. But role expectations of the larger society also affect how a family perceives the parent role.

role changes

Especially in small groups, and in large groups over long periods of time, *role performances influence role expectations.* For example, one family expects the person in the role of mother to cook, clean the house, and wash the dishes and clothes. Then a change in the family situation occurs and the mother goes to work at a full-time job. Some tasks previously expected of her will be assumed by the children and the father of the household. New role expectations result.

Over time, a whole society can change a set of role expectations. The wife role in the U.S. is an excellent example. The role of wife is vastly different today than it was in 1930. Not only have career expectations changed and the range of choices widened, a vast change in other kinds of expected behaviors has occurred. The sexual advances a husband might expect from his wife

253

*Group
Characteristics,
Relationships,
and
Communication*

today would have brought shock and horror in 1930. Moreover, we can safely predict that by 1990 the role of wife in this country will differ greatly from what it is now.

A specific set of role performances within groups relates to accomplishing group purposes. Analysis of these roles is included in the discussion of leadership in Chapter 10.

Exercise: Roles

Objective: To become aware of the roles you perform and the expectations relative to the roles of people with whom you associate.

Directions:
1. List all the roles you can think of that you perform in a typical day.
2. Choose the two roles that most influence your daily behavior.
3. Identify the most significant people (two or more) who communicate with you in that role chosen in #2.
4. List the expectations that you perceive these people (listed in #3) have for your behavior.
5. Show the list you made in #4 to the people. Ask them to confirm your listed expectations or to explain to you how their actual expectations differ.

status

Roles especially affect communication when another aspect of social positions is considered. In most social structures, different positions are accorded different levels of status or esteem. *Status refers to the rights, privileges, or esteem given to occupants of social positions.* Some positions have high status, others low. When persons having different status talk with one another, the attitudes of both often interfere with communication. Indeed, one recommended attitude for combating defensiveness in communication is to approach others as equals. But often, perhaps even usually, people do not communicate as equals. They approach each other from varying status levels. When the higher status of one threatens another of lower rank, defensiveness can result. Other barriers to effective communication in groups result from differences in status. Those of low status may resent whatever special rights or privileges those of higher status have and that resentment can close communication channels and distort messages. Status differences may even determine what group members may say to each other. Some types of messages are acceptable between peers, for instance, that would not be acceptable between those of different rank. Two supervisors can say to each other what they couldn't to an employee; two students can discuss what they'd never talk about with the professor.

Some expected behaviors are standardized to the extent that they become norms. *Norm refers to a standard of expected behavior for which a social penalty is paid if the standard is violated.* Norms may be held by an entire society, or subgroups within the society. These norms influence communication. You may choose to follow, ignore, or flaunt social norms, but in every case your actions relate to them. Even when you attempt to show that the larger society's norms don't restrict you, they influence your communication.

norms: internal and external

Norms may be internal, meaning they develop within a group, or external, meaning they are imposed on the group by a larger group or by the entire society. External norms result from collective attitudes of large numbers of persons who establish standards for a particular group or society. To illustrate, norms in most societies and groups relate to how people dress. Many social groups prescribe an approved style of dress for certain situations. For example, some high schools and religious colleges have strict dress codes that require men's hair to be cut to a certain length, women's skirts to be a certain distance below the knee. These are external norms imposed by external boards. In contrast, many schools don't have a strict dress code, but internal norms still regulate dress. For instance, at our college, no external dress codes exist. Students wear what they wish: bluejeans, cut-offs, mini-skirts, or suits and ties. But norms still exist. If students appeared without clothes, they would not be acceptable either to teachers or classmates. Members of the group share these norms with the larger society. Similar norms would cause men to be ridiculed for wearing skirts or women to be ostracized for wearing bikinis to work.

Norms may extend across an entire social group, or may develop within subgroups. Again, norms at our college illustrate. The expectation that everyone should wear clothes extends throughout the college. But groups within the college dress according to different norms. The art student's "uniform" of faded, paint-spattered blue denim might be adopted by a law enforcement student only if that person were assigned to the narcotics squad. The norm for dress of some Black male students, which allows hats, silks, and sequins, shocks some white students.

effects of norms

Choosing to ignore social norms leads to penalties from people who adhere to them. The penalties vary according to the strength of the norm, the extent of the violation, and its applicability to a particular situation. Nudity, for example, can get people arrested in some places, but it will bring paying patrons to a movie or burlesque

255

*Group
Characteristics,
Relationships,
and
Communication*

house, and has brought a fortune to the creator of *Playboy.* Arriving at work, at school, or at your neighborhood supermarket in your pajamas won't get you arrested, but you'll have difficulty engaging anyone in a conversation, even about the weather. Arrive dressed according to the norm for that situation, however, and you'll be ignored or talked to depending on your wishes. Even though the pajamas might be entirely decent and even attractive, social norms do not permit you to wear them to the supermarket.

The degree of pressure to conform to norms depends on both the individual and the group. Usually a person will participate in a group, either formal or informal, because of a felt need for belonging to it. The need doesn't have to be strong. For instance, a decision to join a group of classmates standing in the hall before a class doesn't usually reflect a strong need, and violating the norms of that kind of group brings little penalty. But if you join a group, having a strong need for its approval, the pressure on you to conform to its norms will be strong.

Few people want to participate in a group in which others feel they do not belong, so need for belonging induces most members to communicate in ways acceptable to the group. Group norms affect what may be discussed, as well as the verbal and nonverbal style of expression. Profanity is acceptable in some groups, criticized in others, and totally rejected by still others. Not too long ago discussing sex was taboo in any group that included both men and women. Personal space between men and women that is acceptable in one group will violate norms of sexual behavior in another. Norms even extend to what opinions may be expressed. Some groups accept people who have opinions different from the group norm; others do not. A person who says that busing is needed to achieve equality in the educational system might be accepted, though disagreed with in some PTA groups. In others the person might be branded, ignored, or asked to leave.

Clothing illustrates both internal and external norms.
Source: Focus — The Stock Shop.

If group members hold attitudes strongly enough, members who disagree with the norm have a choice: giving in to the group norm at least to the extent of modifying stated opinions or keeping quiet, or not belonging. In less extreme situations, some people employ the fine art of disagreeing in tactful and acceptable ways and still remaining acceptable to a group. Others find it necessary to conform to secure group acceptance. Either way, the group's norms affect the communication within it.

LOOKING BACK

Most interpersonal communication takes place within groups; thus it is important to understand how groups affect the communication within them. A group can be defined as a communication system in which successive interactions between members determine structure, identity, and content. The characteristics of groups affect the communication within them and the interactions in turn affect the characteristics. This interactive nature of groups makes them complex entities, and communication within them complex.

Many types of groups exist; they can be distinguished by their purpose as task, therapeutic, or social groups. Some important groups, especially the family, have elements of all three and will be studied separately. Groups may be classified as casual, temporary, or permanent, according to the length of their existence. Groups are also either public or private, depending on whether or not outsiders view their interactions and interact directly with them. Groups also vary according to the purposes they fulfill for their members. Individual member goals are not always the same as the group's, but they can't diverge too far or the individual will choose to leave or be expelled by the group.

Other characteristics that vary greatly and affect communication within groups include size, interdependence, cohesiveness, and related variables. Size is a major determinant of the amount, type, and patterns of communication within a group. Large groups affect interpersonal communication most often as reference groups. Interdependence is a variable that describes how much group members need each other to fulfill individual goals. When group members have complementary goals, the interdependence will be high, but if individuals have antagonistic goals low interdependence will result. Cohesiveness describes the forces that influence members to remain in the group. It involves attractiveness, satisfaction, maturity, and control.

Finally, important influences on communication within groups come from roles, status, and norms. Roles, defined as behaviors expected of persons in specific social positions, are meaningful largely in reference to specific groups because they differ from group to group. To fully understand the effects of role on communication, both role expectations and role performances must be considered. They interact and affect each other. Status affects relationships, especially when roles have different status. Related to roles are norms. These are standards of expected behavior for which a social penalty is paid if violated. Norms are both internal—that is, developed within the group—and external—imposed on the group from without. Norms affect communication whether they are accepted or rejected.

257

*Group
Characteristics,
Relationships,
and
Communication*

Exercise: Group Characteristics

Objectives: To become aware of the characteristics of a group you belong to.

Directions:

1. Name a group to which you have belonged for at least a month.
2. Describe this group according to the characteristics introduced in this chapter:
   a. purpose
   b. length of existence
   c. public or private
   d. goals
   e. agreement between member and group goals
   f. size
   g. communication patterns
   h. interdependence
   i. cohesiveness
   j. internal roles and status
   k. internal norms
   l. external norms that affect the group

Questions for Discussion

1. How does the purpose of the group affect communication within it?
2. What effects do goals have on group communication?
3. Describe how size, maturity, control, attractiveness, and satisfaction affect group communication.
4. How do roles, norms, and status affect communication within groups?
5. What is the difference between role expectation and role performance?

Suggestions for Further Reading

BALES, ROBERT, *Interaction Process Analysis*. Reading, Mass.: Addison-Wesley Publishing Co., 1967.

CARTWRIGHT, DORWIN, AND ALVIN ZANDER, *Group Dynamics*. New York: Harper & Row, 1969.

CATHCART, ROBERT, AND LARRY SAMOVAR, *Small Group Communication: A Reader*. Dubuque, Ia.: William C. Brown Co., 1974.

JOHNSON, DAVID, AND FRANK JOHNSON, *Joining Together: Group Theory and Group Skills*. Englewood Cliffs, N.J.: Prentice-Hall, Inc., 1975.

LUFT, JOSEPH, *Group Processes: An Introduction to Group Dynamics*. Palo Alto, Cal.: National Press Books, 1970.

ROSENFELD, LAWRENCE, *Human Interaction in the Small Group Setting*. Columbus, Ohio: Charles E. Merrill, 1973.

WEICK, KARLE, *The Social Psychology of Organizing*. Reading, Mass.: Addison-Wesley Publishing Co., 1969.

10
Making Decisions in Groups

goal:

To understand the factors that assist groups in making decisions.

probes:

The material in this chapter should help you to:

1. Explain why agendas help groups making decisions. pp. 259–61
2. Cite the advantages and disadvantages of three common forms of making decisions: majority rule, compromise and consensus. pp. 267–69
3. Given a specific discussion situation:
    choose the most appropriate type of agenda;
    prepare an appropriate agenda for the discussion;
    indicate the best form of decision making to attempt to use in the situation. pp. 261–69
4. Explain how conflict or competition can both aid and hinder groups in making decisions. pp. 269–73
5. Define the words *leader* and *leadership;* and distinguish a leaderless group from one without leadership. pp. 273–76
6. Be able to identify and use the functions of leadership. pp. 275–76
7. Describe two contrasting styles of leadership and explain how each relates to the climate and task leadership functions. pp. 273–81

> ... our very ability to experience, to decide, and to control our own behavior through our decisions is dependent in many subtle and involuntary ways on our relationships and interaction with our fellows.
>
> A. PAUL HARE, EDGAR BORGATTA, ROBERT BALES

Groups of all kinds have at least one thing in common—decisions are constantly required. Whether the group is a family, a church committee, a poker club, or a history class—whether it is temporary, private, casual, or therapeutic—decision making is required. In this chapter we examine factors to help you improve the quality of decision making in groups you take part in.

AGENDAS AND PURPOSES

When decisions must be made within a group, an *agenda* is of great benefit. We think of an agenda as *a plan or procedure the group agrees to follow*. Both the speed and quality of decision making can be improved with the use of a planned agenda.

Reasons for Agendas

To set an agenda, a group agrees on a procedure or outline to follow in moving toward its final decision. Failure to agree on such a plan is perhaps the most common reason that group discussions often wander aimlessly and fail to achieve group goals efficiently. Groups need agendas for several reasons.

259

There is always an easy solution to every human problem—neat, plausible, and wrong.

H. L. MENCKEN

examine problems before solutions

Several problems can result from not setting an agenda at the beginning of meetings when decisions are required. Some people always want to begin by suggesting their pet solution to the problem. That causes other suggested solutions and debate over everyone's favorite idea instead of a cooperative effort in seeking a decision. The worst thing about such debate is the failure to examine causes first. Arguing over the best solution without first deciding what are the sources and dimensions of the problem is a good way to waste time and polarize groups needlessly.

avoid hasty solutions

Another problem arises from not starting a discussion by agenda setting. Sometimes everyone quickly agrees when a solution is introduced at the outset. Then important considerations about the cause of the problem, or implications of the decision, may be overlooked. Quick agreement is often the result of superficial consideration of the total situation. The decision probably relates to complex issues or a group wouldn't be given the task of deciding what to do about it. If the group jumps immediately to a solution or to debating the pros and cons of pet solutions, important aspects of the total situation remain unexamined.

clarify group goals and procedures

Agendas are especially helpful because they aid in clarifying group goals. Individual members' personal goals may not be the same as others in the group. Agenda setting provides time to discuss and agree upon group goals. It also helps members to become aware of and/or agree to a plan to follow in achieving that goal. The agenda will serve as a means to guide use of time throughout the discussion. It also aids in focusing attention on relevant and important issues, and in excluding talk related to irrelevant issues.

cope with hidden agendas

Sometimes members have personal goals that differ from group goals and which are not revealed. These unstated personal goals are called hidden agendas. Some individuals belong to groups not for the purpose of achieving the group goal, but to use the group to achieve their personal goals. They use the group as a vehicle for personal purposes. Sometimes these personal goals are open and do

Decision making in groups. *Source: (left)* John Zoiner—The Stock Shop. *(right)* Focus—The Stock Shop.

not interfere with group goals. For example, at work Frank may say to the two people who occupy desks next to him, "Hey, Bett, Mel— I need your suggestions. I'm having some trouble getting this drawing done today. I can't seem to get it started. Can we brainstorm some ideas?" But in other cases the personal goals are not revealed and constitute hidden agendas. Suppose that Frank wants Bett's job. Then he may engage in efforts to downgrade her work, cause her to perform less effectively, and make her appear unreasonable. This kind of hidden agenda can interfere with the group functioning. One means of coping with hidden agendas is by having the group discuss and set agendas together.

How to Set Agendas

personal planning

As a student of communication aware of the importance of agendas, you can exert positive influence in groups. Take the initiative prior to the meeting to plan an outline for the group to follow. State a goal or goals for the group and outline a tentative procedure to follow during the discussion. In cases where you haven't had the time to do that degree of preparation, you can at least take the initiative to say, "Let's start by clarifying what exactly is our goal and how we plan to go about making this decision. Perhaps we should establish an agenda."

secure group agreement

When you have introduced a tentative agenda to follow, you'll probably increase the speed with which the group clarifies its goal and
261   decides on a plan to follow during the discussion. Be careful, how-

ever, that you aren't defensive or possessive about your plan. Remember, the agenda should be a *group* plan, not one imposed on it by an individual. Don't be defensive about suggestions for changing it before the group adopts it. You should, of course, be able to explain the value of following the plan you outline, but don't let the agenda-setting portion of the meeting degenerate into needless argument.

> Even when the experts all agree, they may well be mistaken.
>
> BERTRAND RUSSELL

reassess agenda periodically

Even when agreed to, agendas should never be cast in concrete. Any adopted agenda should be periodically reassessed as a group moves toward its goal. The group may occasionally need to stop its work and examine the agenda to see if it should be changed. When an adopted agenda is no longer helpful, it should be changed. Agendas can be compared to planning before taking a trip. You read a road map and plan a route to follow. But along the way you may decide the plan wasn't appropriate. Perhaps you discover the road has too much slow traffic, or is under construction. You may choose an alternate route. Similarly, groups plan agendas and then at times change their plan. But having the plan at the outset is still useful.

Suggested Agendas

Depending on circumstances, several alternative, standard agendas can be used. At times when the group is to solve a clearly defined problem, a *problem-solving agenda* can usefully be followed. At other times the major task of a group is to come to a sound decision to present to another group for action. In these cases, a *decision-making agenda* is useful. Sometimes groups must make decisions that involve implementation of procedures, gathering or analyzing information. In these cases a group might find a *task agenda* appropriate. When none of these three agendas apply, a group should set its own agenda using a kind of *topical* outline covering all areas necessary for the particular task or purpose.

For task accomplishment, it's not necessary that any particular, prescribed agenda be followed; but it is important, at the outset of each session when decisions are required, to identify the purpose of that particular session and agree on a process for getting there. That means adopting an agenda. The standard agendas mentioned above are as follows:[1]

A PROBLEM-SOLVING AGENDA

I. *Awareness–Ventilation* (Group clarifies its goal and establishes agenda and climate.)

> What is the specific goal? of this session? overall?
>
> What research will be necessary?
>
> Are there specific barriers faced in the group or the process?
>
> —Strong individual member attitudes toward problem?
>
> —Important points of view not represented among members?
>
> What will be the best procedure to insure participation?
>
> —Time, place? room arrangement?
>
> —Leadership: shared, single, or designated?

II. *Description* (Group determines the current status of the problem.)

> What terms within the problem area need to be defined and/or clarified?
>
> What is the present situation related to the problem area?
>
> —What is the current policy (policies)?
>
> —Who is involved or affected?
>
> —What has happened to date? Has any previous action been taken to solve the problem?
>
> How serious is the situation?

III. *Analysis* (Group attempts to discover causes of the problem and to set criteria for evaluating solutions.)

> What are the basic causes of the problem?
>
> —Why did the problem develop?
>
> —What specific factors have prevented solution?
>
> What criteria must any solution meet?
>
> —What standards must any solution meet to be acceptable?

IV. *Proposals* (Group suggests many possible solutions.)

> What are *all possible* solutions? (Brainstorm)

V. *Selection of Best Proposal* (Group chooses the "best" solution.)

> What proposal is "best"? "Best" should answer all the following:
>
> —Which solves the problem?
>
> —Which eliminates the basic causes?
>
> —Which meets the criteria?
>
> —Which does not create other problems?

---

[1] Adapted from outline in Linda and Richard Heun, *Developing Skills for Human Interaction* (Columbus, Ohio: Charles E. Merrill Co., 1975), pp. 255–56.

VI. *Implementation* (Group decides how to implement the chosen proposal.)

How can the proposal be put into effect?

— Who must be involved?

— What is cost of implementing?

— When is the best time?

— What should be done first?

What obstacles may block implementation?

— What approaches are most likely to overcome the obstacles?

A DECISION-MAKING AGENDA

I. *Awareness–Ventilation* (Here group members attempt to clarify the goals and establish a climate and agenda.)

What is the specific goal? of this session? overall?

What research will be necessary?

Are there specific barriers faced in the group or the process?

— Strong individual member attitudes toward problem?

— Important points of view not represented among members?

What will be the best procedure to insure participation?

— Time, place? room arrangement?

— Leadership: shared, single, or designated?

II. *Statement of Objectives*

Group lists all possible objectives. (Brainstorm)

III. *Ranking Objectives*

Divide objectives into two classifications:

— Those that are MUSTS (i.e., that MUST be accomplished if goals are to be met).

— Those that are WANTS (i.e., that would be nice to accomplish but are not essential).

IV. *Identifying Any Obstacles to Reaching Objectives*

What, if any, obstacles prevent reaching objectives?

What, if anything, prevents removing obstacles?

V. *State Alternative Means for Reaching Objectives*

List all possible alternatives. (Brainstorm)

VI. *Analysis*

Will the various alternatives work? Can they be implemented?

Will the various alternatives achieve the objectives?

–Which alternatives will achieve the musts?

–Which alternatives will achieve the musts and wants?

VII. *Tentative Selection of Decision*

Choose the alternative that achieves the "must" objectives and the most "want" objectives.

VIII. *Test Tentative Alternative*

Are there possible unexpected or undesirable results?

What is the cost?

Are there obstacles to implementation?

Can the obstacles be removed?

IX. *Choose the "Best" Alternative and Implement*

Select another alternative and repeat step VIII if chosen alternative cannot pass test of VIII.

Decide on steps for implementation.

— How can the proposal be put into effect?

Who must be involved?

What is the cost of implementation?

When is the best time?

What should be done first?

— What obstacles may hinder the implementation?

What approaches are most likely to overcome the obstacles?

A TASK AGENDA

I. *Gathering and Evaluation of Information by Individuals*

II. *Awareness–Ventilation* (Here the group members attempt to clarify and establish climate and agenda.)

What is the specific goal? of this session? overall?

What research will be necessary?

Are there specific barriers faced in the group or the process?

— Strong individual member attitudes toward problem?

— Important points of view not represented among members?

What will be the best procedure to insure participation?

— Time, place? room arrangement?

— Leadership: shared, single, or designated?

III. *Comparison of Individual Conclusions of Members*

IV. *Establish Areas of Agreement Between Members*

V. *Examine Areas of Difference Between Members to Search for Means of Resolving Disagreements*

VI. *Reach Conclusions, Resolving Differences by Consensus If Possible*

Use of Brainstorming

Brainstorming is a useful technique in group decision making or problem solving. It's especially valuable when people are searching for possible solutions or trying to determine the objectives of a group. Brainstorming involves setting aside a period of time during which members agree to offer ideas without criticism or evaluation of them. The aim of brainstorming is to enhance creativity to secure all possible ideas relevant to the issue. The goal of this particular segment of the agenda is *quantity* of ideas, not quality. The advantage of brainstorming is that people will suggest ideas they'd hesitate to mention if they expected evaluation at the time of the suggestion. This way the group gets many possible ideas. What often seems a ridiculous suggestion may trigger the thinking of someone to combine previous ideas and come up with a completely new idea that isn't so far afield. So in addition to getting many different suggestions, the group often finds one idea generating another, leading to fresh and untried answers.

Brainstorming can be started by declaring: "For the next _____ minutes (amount of time depends on group, problem, and situation) we will list all possible solutions (or objectives) that we can think of. No criticism or evaluation of ideas is allowed, either by the person who makes the suggestion or anyone else. The aim of this time is to get as many ideas as possible." The group should appoint someone to act as recorder. All ideas suggested should be listed, no matter how absurd they may sound. Members of the group should enforce the "no criticism" rule on themselves and on anyone who forgets and begins to evaluate. Brainstorming is a time for creative thinking. Evaluation will take place later, when the specified time is up, or when people run out of ideas.

Exercise: Brainstorming

Objective: To practice brainstorming in a creative situation, and to secure as many answers as possible to each problem presented.

Directions:
1. The class will be divided into groups of six or more.
2. One person will be recorder, and one will be process observer.
3. Taking each of the questions below, the group members are to brainstorm responses. The recorder is to list everything suggested,

and the process observer is to stop any person who starts to evaluate any suggestion.
4. At the end of the class period, groups may be asked to share their lists of answers to compile a total class list of possible answers.

Brainstorm Problem #1:
1. Suggest solutions (practical, imaginative, or scientific) to the problem of getting students registered in school each semester.

Brainstorm Problem #2:
2. Suggest uses (actual, potential, imaginative) for an out-of-date auto license tag.

Brainstorm Problem #3:
3. Suggest possible consequences (whether immediate, long-range, probable, improbable) that might occur if your instructor decided not to teach, but just to attend class.

Brainstorm Problem #4:
4. Suggest possible causes of the energy shortages in the world today.

METHODS OF DECISION MAKING

Whether a group wants to solve a problem, make a recommendation, implement someone else's recommendation, or come to some conclusion and test it, groups must make many different decisions. Many methods of deciding are used. Sometimes groups use "follow-the-leader" type of decision making. An influential person, an opinion leader, or a person who for some other reason exerts strong influence on the group says, "This is the way it ought to be," and the others follow. This behavior may not really deserve the label of group decision making, except that group members decide to follow the decision of the leader. More commonly, one of the following methods are used.

Majority Rule

A familiar kind of decision making is *majority* rule. When two or more opposing points of view are presented, people frequently vote. The side with the majority or most votes wins the decision. Even though this may be a common procedure, there are serious disadvantages to majority vote decision making. The losing members may not feel involvement in or responsibility for the decision. They usually have no commitment to carry out the decision and indeed may have personal agendas, hidden or open, to see that the decision doesn't work. Then they can say, "We told you so." Moreover, majorities often consist of people on the same side of an issue for different reasons, which can also interfere with implementation. *Majority rule leads to polarization,* and if polarization can be avoided the group will usually be more productive.

Compromise

When two or more differing points of view exist, another common mode of decision making is *compromise*. When politicians do this, it's often called porkbarreling. The compromisers say, "I'll give you a little of what you want if you will give me a little of what I want, and we'll both come out with something." Politicians aren't the only ones who use compromise, although they may be the only people accused of selling out when they do so. This mode of deciding may be most common in situations in which members of the group making the decision are responsible to constituencies, and have to have something to show them. When group members represent others outside the group, they need to make it appear that no portion of the group emerges as a clear loser. Collective bargaining is an example of a group that uses compromise by necessity.

Compromise decision making also has disadvantages. Short-range benefits sometimes justify or require the compromise, but often long-range goals or benefits are sacrificed. From the long-range viewpoint, compromise often results in poor decisions. The conclusion may not have been based on logical procedure or on ideas that members thought "best," but on reasons extraneous to the problem, such as political influence or power of the groups represented. Moreover, because everyone gave up something they wanted and accepted some things that weren't desirable to them, lack of commitment to implement the decisions often results.

Consensus

Most groups find it most effective, when time and circumstance permit, to employ *consensus* as a mode of decision making. Consensus occurs when *all members of a group agree on the decision.* Consensus is probably the most difficult decision-making process to employ, but in the long run, is usually the most productive. When a decision is accomplished by consensus, all members feel committed and responsible for it, and are more likely to work to see that it is effectively implemented. Moreover, because consensus eliminates a losing side, it contributes to cohesiveness and increases productivity.

The disadvantages to deciding by consensus include the difficulty of achieving it and the great amount of time it requires. If time is available, and some members of the group are skilled at leadership, consensus can usually be achieved. The dividends are usually worth the effort. At times, however, groups are so polarized that consensus can't be achieved. In these cases, either compromise or majority rule may be needed. But in many situations increased productivity, high commitment to implement the decision, and

268

Constructive conflict in groups can be helpful.
Source: Sybil Shelton.

member satisfaction are important enough to make decision making by consensus worth the time and effort.

CONFLICT AND COMPETITION

> Where all think alike, no one thinks very much.
>
> WALTER LIPPMANN

People often think of group discussions as situations in which competition should be avoided and cooperation is the ultimate goal. Certainly consensus requires a cooperative spirit, but it's misleading to believe that all competition or conflict is harmful. In the first place, it's an unrealistic idea. In addition, it would be unwise. Valuable effects can result from competition and conflict.[2]

Effects of Competition and Conflict

Competition and conflict within a group are often healthy. If no competition exists, ideas will probably not be examined thoroughly, different points of view won't be considered, and untested decisions will emerge. Groups without conflict may reach consensus quickly, but in doing so may fail to consider all the alternatives. They need the valuable person who plays the "devil's advocate."

---

[2]Some writers distinguish between conflict and competition. We don't think that is necessary in an introductory book. Both occur when people are seeking different goals. Both can either interfere with group decision making or benefit it, depending on how they affect the group. We suggest ways to cope with the effects of competition and conflict, not to eliminate them, and see no need at this point to be concerned with what are the differences between them.

This is one who says, "Wait a minute—there's another side to this issue. Let's look at it from that perspective."

A major advantage of group over individual decision making is that more different points of view are expressed. With each additional member, more informational resources are available to bring to bear on any issue. *Without competition, fewer information resources are introduced* and the major advantages of group decision making are missing.

Of course, conflict or competition within the group needs to be constructive. If it is not, it will interfere with group accomplishment. Two main types of conflict exist. The first relates to task. *Conflict regarding different points of view is needed for a thorough examination of all sides of issues.* If a group is to have confidence in its conclusions, they should be thoroughly tested. Task conflict is so valuable that a member should take a devil's advocate role when no disagreement exists. On the other hand, interpersonal conflict or competition can be damaging. Competition because of personal dislike or hidden agendas can interfere with task accomplishment and reduce both member satisfaction and productivity. *Interpersonal conflict leads to defensiveness*, which causes communication barriers that are almost always damaging in task groups.

adversary relationships

Many groups have members with adversary relationships. Adversaries are people who come to a group with either hidden or open agendas to reach goals inconsistent with those of others in the group. (See the discussion of antagonistic goals in Chapter 9, pp. 248–49.) The extreme case of this kind of group may be presented by collective bargaining situations.

We don't have time to discuss adversary relationships here. Groups with adversaries within them present a different situation from one in which members begin with similar goals. If you need to learn how to cope with these situations, you'll want to study group communication in depth. We have included some suggested readings that can provide more insight, and most colleges provide advanced study in the area. In this introductory book we limit our suggestions to those helpful in coping with conflicts in groups that begin as cooperative.

Avoiding Destructive Conflict or Competition

The differences between destructive and helpful competition in groups are largely differences in attitudes. That is, if members have certain attitudes, they'll communicate with each other in ways that either cause or prevent development of destructive conflict. The attitudes result in communication behaviors that are either helpful or harmful to group process.

destructive attitudes

Foremost among harmful attitudes are those related to *defensiveness*. Because defensiveness occurs when a person perceives a threat, it is a source of much conflict in groups. You'll recall from our discussion of climates in Chapter 7 that defensiveness in groups results partly from attitudes and partly from specific behaviors. *Evaluation* is an attitude, and it is communicated both verbally and nonverbally. While evaluation of ideas is necessary in task groups, evaluation of people is not. If you approach a group with evaluative attitudes toward the other members, you'll create defensiveness. *Control* is another example. If your attitude is that you should be able to control others in the group, you'll behave both verbally and nonverbally to cause conflict. Similar comments could be made regarding each of the other climates described by Gibb. *Superiority, strategy, certainty,* and *lack of empathy* are attitudes that reflect in your communication. If these attitudes are evident during group decision making, defensiveness is likely and a source of destructive competition is present.

helpful attitudes

In contrast, by *creating supportive climates*, you can help develop trust and reduce defensiveness. Climates of description, problem orientation, equality, honesty, provisionalism, and empathy can help you cope with excessive competition or interpersonal conflict.

Other attitudes are helpful in channeling task conflict and dealing with interpersonal conflict. Most important in dealing with task conflict is to *recognize the value of conflicting ideas.* If all group members believe that conflict of ideas is healthy, competition will usually be constructive. If they believe that people can disagree without being disagreeable, the group will probably have healthy conflict that contributes to improved decision making. If, on the other hand, members interpret disagreements over ideas as personal attacks, or react to evaluation of ideas as evaluations of the source, then the situation can quickly deteriorate into interpersonal conflict.

One technique that helps avoid the problem of disagreement being perceived as personal criticism is to have the group *focus on the situation.* A short discussion can lead members to recognize that ideas are no one's personal possession. Because very few ideas in the world are really new, and all people learn most of what they know from someone else, people can usually see that no one person has a monopoly on ideas. Open discussion of this philosophy, either at the awareness–ventilation stage or when the problem emerges, can head off the development of interpersonal conflict. Once the perspective is openly discussed, less idea possessiveness occurs, and task disagreements are less likely to develop into interpersonal conflict. When members realize that the processes of interaction generate most of the ideas in a group, they'll respond positively to task conflict and reduce their idea possessiveness.

A second way to cope with conflict is for members to *approach group decision making with an awareness of the influence of personal interpretive systems*. If members recall that each person has a view of the world based on very individual life experiences, they are more likely to recall that no one of them has all the facts, or all the relevant information, or all the truth. They are more likely to recall that no member can know everything there is to know about any subject. Members should remember that when disagreements exist, the conflicting ideas are all probably partly right and partly wrong. If they do, they're less likely to react with defensiveness when someone disagrees with them.

A third way to cope with conflicts is to *neutralize the effect of members who think of others as adversaries*. Many people regard decision situations in groups with the feeling that they are in a win-lose situation. They think, "If I don't achieve this result, I lose." To prevent this adversary attitude from interfering with group process, members have to realize that the group is not necessarily a win or lose situation. Everyone can gain something. That realization requires members to see the benefits of conflicting ideas and sharing different points of view. They need to see that the product of the group can be better than if each individual worked alone—a win-win situation. This "better" quality may be because a decision will be more readily accepted and implemented, or it may be a better decision. In either event, all can benefit from the group efforts.

Not everyone shares the everyone-win attitude. Some people cling to the win-lose perspective. They may have commitments outside the group that make the decision-making task for them an actual win-lose situation. Personal or vested interests, promises to constituencies, strong biases, are only a few reasons some people see group decision-making as win-lose in nature. Coping with these people is not simple. The next suggestion can help, but no solution is perfect.

A fourth way to deal with conflicts is to *focus openly on group processes*. During the awareness–ventilation step, members should emphasize the necessity to be as critical of their own suggestions as of others', and remind one another that ideas are no one's personal possession. If a general discussion of group process occurs early, reminders are probably all that will be necessary later.

Sometimes when conflict arises, the discussion must be stopped long enough to focus on group process. Bring the conflict or problem into the open. You can say, "Can we stop a minute and focus on what's going on here? A conflict that doesn't relate to the issues seems to be present. I think we might be better off to get it on the table and resolved. Then we can return to talking about the subject: What do you think?" Address the question to one of the parties involved. This kind of focusing on process isn't easy, or pleasant, but it usually clears the air. Members can then continue the discussion with better focus and less disruption.

The Cooperative Spirit

A cooperative spirit is how we describe the attitudes in a group when members believe that

1. No one "possesses" any ideas
2. Value is gained from expression of conflicting points of view
3. No one has a monopoly on the accurate perspective of the world
4. Everyone's perspective is needed to develop an accurate view of the world
5. Group processes can improve decisions

If a group displays this cooperative spirit, interpersonal conflict is less likely to develop from competition over ideas.

LEADERSHIP IN GROUPS

> As for the best leaders, the people do not notice their existence. The next best, the people honor and praise. The next, the people fear; and the next, the people hate . . .
>
> When the best leader's work is done the people say, "We did it ourselves!"
>
> LAO-TZU

Wide agreement exists that *leadership* is vital in achieving group purposes effectively. But how to provide that leadership is not widely agreed. Leadership is a much-studied group variable because the question, What makes good leaders? is not easily answered.

Group *leaders* are often described as fitting one of three basic styles. One is *authoritarian*. An authoritarian leader determines policies, parcels out the tasks necessary to carry out the group purposes, and overall seems to be the authority of the group. A second style of leadership is *democratic*. The democratic leader guides group members in making important decisions relating to establishing group goals, priorities, policies, and procedures. The third

273

type is *laissez faire,* which is more accurately a description of a group without a leader. This is an attractive three-part distinction; but it's too simple to be helpful in determining what behaviors are needed in what groups.

A Functional Analysis

We believe the most useful approach to group leadership begins with understanding what functions must be performed for a group to accomplish its purpose. To us, *leadership is any behavior that aids a group in accomplishing its goals.*

What functions are necessary will vary according to the group. And thus, what is leadership varies from one group to another. Generally, three kinds of functions can be distinguished. First are those relating to accomplishing the tasks that must be done—the "task" *leadership* functions. Second are functions relating to maintenance of the group. Obviously, a group must exist long enough to accomplish its purpose, and many interpersonal interactions are required to maintain the group. These are *"climate" leadership* functions. Third are functions that must be performed for individual members' needs to be satisfied, at least those needs that bring and keep the individuals in the group. These are *"personal" leadership* functions.

The functions of leadership are usually distributed throughout the group. Rarely does one person perform all the leadership functions. Though the concept of a single leader is popular in most groups, that's not what actually happens. Even though groups usually select a person they consider the leader, this person seldom performs all the leadership needed by a group. A person may be selected to chair a meeting or head a department or speak for a committee. But these particular functions aren't synonymous with being the leader of the group. This designated head is more likely only one of several group leaders.

We think of a leader as one who performs more leadership functions than others in the group. Thus, leaders can be identified by observing groups. Asking members, "Who contributes most to accomplishment of the task?" or "Who contributes most to an effective working climate?" or "Who contributes most to keeping members satisfied?" is one good way to spot group leaders.

A few groups have only one leader, but most have several. We describe this as shared leadership. Many groups have one person who is the task leader, and one who is the climate leader. Also commonly, groups have separate *opinion leaders.* By opinion leaders we mean people whose ideas are listened to with respect and often accepted by others in the group without much examination. Occasionally, the task or climate leaders are also opinion leaders, but not always. Nor is it uncommon for a group to have two or three leaders in each category. Often in a group, two or three people contribute heavily to task accomplishment, and two or three others do more to establish a good working climate.

Sometimes, especially in mature groups that are fairly homogeneous, no leaders exist. By this we do not refer to the laissez-faire situation. A laissez-faire group is one without leader*ship*. By lead-er*less,* we mean a group in which all members contribute equally to accomplishing the purposes. A leaderless group is one in which no person stands out as recognizably more valuable than anyone else. A leaderless group is not necessarily without leader*ship*. That is an important distinction. To be without leadership means that the important task or climate functions aren't performed. To be without leaders means that no one performs more leadership functions than anyone else. A leaderless group may be without leadership, but not necessarily.

> The difficulty in defining what the leader does or in constructing a value theory of what he[she] should do is certainly due in part to the fact that the leader is usually required to do different things at different times, according to the condition of the group and its common culture system.
>
> A. PAUL HARE, EDGAR BORGATTA, ROBERT BALES

what are the leadership functions?

Now let's be more specific about leadership functions. Let's describe what leaders do. We list these functions in three categories.

Task Leadership Functions

1. *Goal Setting* — proposing goals, seeking clarification and agreement on goals, determining significance and priorities of different objectives
2. *Planning* — assessing needs, setting agendas, preparation for sessions, physical arrangements, providing for special resources, publicity when necessary
3. *Guiding* — attending to procedural considerations, keeping group attention on agenda, summarizing when necessary, keeping or seeing that necessary records are kept
4. *Information Giving* — giving needed data, opinions, experiences
5. *Information Seeking* — seeking needed data, opinions, experiences
6. *Analysis* — clarifying ideas, testing information, assessing inferences and judgments, examining implications, seeking standards for assessment, relating procedures, information and conclusions to goals, being devil's advocate, reality testing
7. *Synthesis* — summarizing, bringing related ideas together, testing for consensus, seeking compromises when necessary

Climate and Personal Leadership Functions

1. *Encouraging* — supporting others, building status and confidence of members, building status and confidence in group

2. *Mediating*—suggesting middle or common grounds when differences among members arise, harmonizing, maintaining emphasis on issues, not personalities
3. *Opening Communication*—maintaining permissive atmosphere, encouraging reticent participants, preventing dominance by one or two, counteracting private or subcommunication patterns
4. *Tension Reducing*—resolving conflicts, diverting attention at points of tension, seeking catharsis when helpful, improving interpersonal relations
5. *Following*—listening to others, accepting group decisions
6. *Directing Self-Oriented Behaviors toward Group Goals*

The sixth climate function reflects our recognition that satisfaction of individual members' personal needs may have negative effects. This is especially true when individuals' goals are antagonistic, not complementary. Listed below are some functions that satisfy personal needs and usually cause antagonistic goal situations. One important task of personal and climate leadership is to minimize these negative effects. Destructive personal behaviors include:

1. *Aggression*—lowering status of others, building personal status
2. *Obstruction*—blocking progress by irrelevant digressions or dwelling on points already covered, rejecting ideas without adequate consideration
3. *Recognition Seeking*—claiming credit for ideas, demanding to be heard on all points, dominance
4. *Withdrawing*—remaining silent and nonparticipative, engaging in side conversations, pursuing tangents
5. *Competition*—trying to outdo all others, needing to win
6. *Distracting*—clowning, diverting attention to tangents, disrupting
7. *Special-Interest Pleading*—supporting personal projects and interests, supporting vested interests, pressing others for support

How Does Leadership Relate to Other Variables?

Accomplishing the necessary task, climate, and personal functions often requires acquaintance with other elements of groups. In an earlier chapter we discussed several of these: type, size of group, members' interdependence and cohesiveness, roles, status, and norms. Let's look now at other group variables that relate directly to leadership.

Leadership Styles and Member Satisfaction

Member satisfaction is often important in group decision making. Though a one-to-one relationship between leadership style and members' satisfaction doesn't exist, they are interrelated. Both in turn relate to the nature of the group task. In situations with high demand for productivity, in which a high priority is on efficiency and group members have high task orientation, members would probably be dissatisfied with diffused leadership. Groups with little time to achieve goals and whose members perceive great rewards for efficiency are usually more satisfied with centralized leadership.

Many successful executives have noted that member satisfaction is highest in situations in which members believe that (1) they are contributing to establishment and accomplishment of group goals, and (2) they can have some control over their own behavior in accomplishing those goals. A thorough analysis of group member satisfaction in many different kinds of businesses and industrial organizations is reported by Rensis Likert in *The Human Organization*.[3] Likert's research demonstrates that participative management, or leadership, results not only in increased worker satisfaction but also in increased productivity. Perhaps the increased productivity results from increased satisfaction.

Likert's research describes leadership in organizations according to seven variables: personnel motivation, communication, interaction, decision making, goal setting, control, and performance. Depending on how each variable is handled within the organization, leadership style is categorized along a continuum. The styles range from authoritarian to participative. Labels given each style are loaded, but descriptive. One style of leadership is described as *exploitative authoritative;* another as *benevolent authoritative.* A third type is called *consultative,* while the recommended style of leadership is called *participative.* The following table illustrates some of the differences among the four styles.

This table reflects a continuum for some of the aspects of each of the seven leadership characteristics. It illustrates some of the differences among authoritative, consultative, and participative leadership styles. You can find the complete table in *The Human Organization* by Rensis Likert, pp. 14–24.

The vertical line in the table shows where executives indicated they would like their own organization to be. This information is significant here for four main reasons. First, the survey was of successful managers employed in various kinds of institutions. Second, participative leadership is what executives would *like* their organization to reflect, even if they don't think it now does. Third, most of the items involved relate directly to communication. Fourth, the participative leadership system relies on clear (and high) performance goals and group decision making. Likert's research shows that leading groups in decision making is an important ability requiring successful application of communication skills. Comparing results of various styles of leadership, Likert concludes

---

[3] Rensis Likert, *The Human Organization: Its Management and Value* (New York: McGraw-Hill, Inc. 1967).

ORGANIZATIONAL AND PERFORMANCE CHARACTERISTICS OF DIFFERENT MANAGEMENT SYSTEMS BASED ON A COMPARATIVE ANALYSIS*

	SYSTEM OF ORGANIZATION			
Operating Characteristics	Authoritative		Consultative	Participative
	EXPLOITIVE AUTHORITATIVE	BENEVOLENT AUTHORITATIVE	CONSULTATIVE	PARTICIPATIVE GROUP
1. Character of motivational forces				
a. Underlying motives tapped	Physical security, economic security, and some use of the desire for status	Economic and occasionally ego motives, e.g., the desire for status	Economic, ego, and other major motives, e.g., desire for new experience	Full use of economic, ego, and other major motives, as, for example, motivational forces arising from group processes
b. Manner in which motives are used	Fear, threats, punishment, and occasional rewards	Rewards and some actual or potential punishment	Rewards, occasional punishment, and some involvement	Economic rewards based on compensation system developed through participation. Group participation and involvement in setting goals, improving methods, appraising progress toward goals, etc.
2. Character of communication process				
a. Amount of interaction and communication aimed at achieving organization's objectives	Very little	Little	Quite a bit	Much with both individuals and groups
b. Direction of information flow	Downward	Mostly downward	Down and up	Down, up, and with peers
c. Psychological closeness of superiors to subordinates (i.e., how well does superior know and understand problems faced by subordinates?)	Far apart	Can be moderately close if proper roles are kept	Fairly close	Usually very close
3. Character of interaction-influence process				
a. Amount and character of interaction	Little interaction and always with fear and distrust	Little interaction and usually with some condescension by superiors; fear and caution by subordinates	Moderate interaction, often with fair amount of confidence and trust	Extensive, friendly interaction with high degree of confidence and trust
b. Extent to which subordinates can influence the goals, methods, and activity of their units and departments				
(1) As seen by superiors	None	Virtually none	Moderate amount	A great deal

Organizational variable	System 1	System 2	System 3	System 4
(2) As seen by subordinates	None except through "informal organization" or via unionization	Little except through "informal organization" or via unionization	Moderate amount both directly and via unionization	Substantial amount both directly and via unionization
4. Character of decision-making process				
a. At what level in organization are decisions formally made?	Bulk of decisions at top of organization	Policy at top, many decisions within prescribed framework made at lower levels	Broad policy and general decisions at top, more specific decisions at lower levels	Decision making widely done throughout organization, although well integrated through linking process provided by overlapping groups
b. How adequate and accurate is the information available for decision making at the place where the decisions are made?	Partial and often inaccurate information only is available	Moderately adequate and accurate information available	Reasonably adequate and accurate information available	Relatively complete and accurate information available based both on measurements and efficient flow of information in organization
5. Character of goal-setting or ordering				
a. Manner in which usually done	Orders issued	Orders issued, opportunity to comment may or may not exist	Goals are set or orders issued after discussion with subordinate(s) of problems and planned action	Except in emergencies, goals are usually established by means of group participation
b. To what extent do the different hierarchical levels tend to strive for high performance goals?	High goals pressed by top, resisted by subordinates	High goals sought by top and partially resisted by subordinates	High goals sought by higher levels but with some resistance by lower levels	High goals sought by all levels, with lower levels sometimes pressing for higher goals than top levels
6. Character of control processes				
a. At what hierarchical levels in organization does major or primary concern exist with regard to the performance of the control function?	At the very top only	Primarily or largely at the top	Primarily at the top but some shared feeling of responsibility felt at middle and to a lesser extent at lower levels	Concern for performance of control function likely to be felt throughout organization
b. Extent to which there is an informal organization present and supporting or opposing goals of formal organization	Informal organization present and opposing goals of formal organization	Informal organization usually present and partially resisting goals	Informal organization may be present and may either support or partially resist goals of formal organization	Informal and formal organization are one and the same; hence all social forces support efforts to achieve organization's goals
7. Performance characteristics				
a. Productivity	Mediocre productivity	Fair to good productivity	Good productivity	Excellent productivity
b. Excessive absence and turnover	Tends to be high when people are free to move	Moderately high when people are free to move	Moderate	Low

*Subentries have been renumbered. From *The Human Organization* by Rensis Likert. Copyright © 1967 by McGraw-Hill, Inc. Used with permission of McGraw-Hill Book Co.

that a manager with a well-organized plan of operation, high performance goals, and high technical competence who uses the participative style of leadership will have: greater group loyalty, higher performance goals, greater cooperation, less feeling of unreasonable pressure, and more favorable attitudes toward managers. In business organizations Likert found higher motivation to produce, higher sales volume, lower sales costs, higher quality of goods sold, and higher earnings by salesmen.

Questions for Discussion of Likert's Table

1. Which of these items apply to all kinds of decision-making groups?
2. Where would various groups to which you belong fit along these scales?
3. Are any of these items totally unrelated to communication?
4. How do these scales relate to leadership in task groups?
5. Can task and climate functions both be found in these scales?

Any discussion of leadership style related to member satisfaction must include mention of the research of Fred Fiedler,[4] who analyzes leadership as situational. He suggests that effective leadership depends on the circumstances of the situation. Effective leadership depends primarily on the *proper match between the leader's style of interacting with other group members and the degree to which the situation gives control and influence to the leader.* Fiedler distinguishes between leaders who are primarily task-oriented, and those who devote more time and concern to relationships between the leader and the members. He also distinguishes groups along a continuum of high to low power by leaders, defining as powerful those who can fire, hire, discipline, and reprimand members. His research showed that task-motivated leaders perform better in situations that are either very favorable or thoroughly unfavorable to them. Relationship-oriented leaders tend to perform better in only moderately favorable situations in which leaders have only moderate control or influence. Fiedler concludes, "It makes no sense to speak of a good leader or a poor leader. There are only leaders who perform well in one situation but not well in another."[5]

---

[4] Fred Fiedler, "The Trouble with Leadership Training Is That It Doesn't Train Leaders," *Psychology Today* (February 1973), p. 26.

[5] Ibid.

This research is important to the study of group leadership because it shows that answers to the question of how to lead groups are never easy. More importantly, Fiedler shows that the situation always influences the answers. You will find the principles presented in this chapter a useful foundation for developing leadership skills only as long as you remember to consider the situation when you choose leadership behaviors. No one behavior will work in every case. The skills are many and the situations widely different. Probably the only constant in leadership is the necessity to communicate accurately and effectively.

LOOKING BACK

Decision making in groups is a skill most people need. Most groups benefit from agendas to guide their decision-making processes because agendas assure that all members of the group know its goal; provide a means for focusing members' attention and a way to organize the discussion; and help groups avoid overlooking important considerations. A problem-solving format, a decision-making format, or a task agenda can be used depending on the purpose of the group. In cases when none of the three is appropriate, a topic process agenda should be adopted by the group. Groups should adopt agendas at the start of their work and pause regularly to reassess the agenda, being prepared to change when it appears that the agenda is no longer appropriate.

Several modes of decision making are possible, each with some advantages and some disadvantages. Majority rule, though common and efficient, has the disadvantage of polarizing a group and making some members feel they have lost. This losing minority thus has no commitment to making the decision work; indeed, they sometimes have hidden personal agendas to make it fail. Moreover, majorities are often composed of people who support a position for different reasons and lack real unity in their commitment to implement the decision. Compromise is a form of decision making in which supporters of every side give a little to create a result in which everyone gains a little. The disadvantage of compromise decision making is that it often results in poor decisions and all parties often lack commitment to make it work. It has the advantage, especially in groups responsible to other constituencies, of having no losing side. Compromise also tends to reduce polarization. Consensus decision making is recommended. Though often requiring a great deal of time and leadership skill from group members, it is superior in securing commitment to the implementation of the decision, membership satisfaction, cohesiveness, and ultimately, as a result, increased productivity.

Competition is useful in groups as long as task conflict doesn't become interpersonal. Conflict helps insure that all viewpoints are examined and hasty, ill-considered decisions aren't made. To prevent conflict over ideas and tasks from evolving into interpersonal conflict, the cooperative spirit is recommended. The following elements in a group lead to a cooperative spirit: belief that no one has sole possession of any idea; that no one has a monopoly on the accurate perspective of reality; and that widely varied perspectives are needed in order to acquire an accurate view of reality.

Leadership in groups results from behavior of individuals that helps the group accomplish its purposes. Three kinds of functions can be distinguished: task leadership, climate leadership, and personal leadership. Leaders are defined as people who perform recognizably more leadership functions than others in the group. Most groups have more than one leader, often one a climate leader and the other a task leader. Opinion leaders also exist in some groups.

Task functions are goal setting, planning, guiding, information giving, information seeking, analysis, and synthesis. Climate and personal leadership functions include encouraging, mediating, opening communication, tension reducing, following and directing self-oriented roles toward group goals. Leaders need to prevent the personal need satisfaction behaviors of members from disrupting group progress. Among the destructive personal-oriented behaviors are aggression, obstruction, recognition seeking, withdrawing, competition, distracting, and special-interest pleading.

Leadership style does not have a direct relationship to member satisfaction. Though the variables are interrelated, the situation and member and group goals are also influential factors. Research demonstrates that member satisfaction and productivity in business and industrial groups are highest in organizations in which management uses participative leadership, but this is not always true. In situations that are very favorable or unfavorable to the leaders, task-oriented leaders seem to perform more effectively. In situations that are only moderately favorable to leaders, the relationship-oriented leader seems to perform better.

Exercise: Roles I Take in a Group

Objective: To become aware of the roles you perform in decision-making groups.

Procedures:

1. You will perform this analysis in combination with the assigned group decision-making or problem-solving tasks of the following exercise.
2. The instructor will create groups of six to eight for three (or more) discussions in class.
3. Before the first discussion, fill in Roles Analysis Form 1. All forms are in Activity Guide.
4. After each discussion, complete Roles Analysis Form 2.
5. After the third discussion, complete Roles Analysis Form 3, making the decisions based on the people who performed the role most consistently and recognizably during all three discussions.
6. After all group members have completed Roles Analysis Form 3, they should compile all responses, so there is a composite description of the two or three people who performed each of the roles most often. If you cannot as a group decide that only two or three did any or all of the roles, you probably are experiencing shared leadership in those functions.
7. Compare the group composite with your analysis when you have completed both forms 2 and 3.
8. As a group, discuss the following:
   a. What were the differences in reporting perceptions?

b. Which roles were the most different in perceptions by members?

c. Why were there differences in these roles?

d. Upon which roles were the group perceptions the most alike?

Questions for Discussion

1. What value have agendas in group decision making?

2. Outline two major types of agendas. How are appropriate agendas chosen?

3. What are the advantages and disadvantages of the different modes of decision making in groups?

4. How can competition be useful to groups?

5. How can you become a task leader? a climate leader? an opinion leader?

6. What are the relationships between leadership style and member satisfaction?

Suggestions for Further Reading

BRILHART, JOHN K., *Effective Group Discussion.* Dubuque, Iowa: William C. Brown, Pub., 1974.

BURGOON, MICHAEL, JUDEE K. HESTON, AND JAMES MCCROSKEY, *Small Group Communication: A Functional Approach.* New York: Holt, Rinehart & Winston, Inc., 1974.

COLLINS, BARRY E., AND HAROLD GUETZKOW, *A Social Psychology of Group Processes for Decision Making.* New York: John Wiley & Sons, 1964.

DAVIS, JAMES, *Group Performance.* Reading, Mass.: Addison-Wesley Publishing Co., 1969.

FIEDLER, FRED E., *A Theory of Leadership Effectiveness.* New York: McGraw-Hill, Inc., 1967.

———, "The Trouble with Leadership Training Is That It Doesn't Train Leaders," *Psychology Today* (February 1973), pp. 23–29.

FISHER, B. AUBREY, *Small Group Decision Making: Communication and the Group Process.* New York: McGraw-Hill, Inc., 1974.

HARNACK, R. VICTOR, AND THORREL FEST, *Group Dynamics* (3rd ed.). New York: Harper & Row, 1968.

KORDA, MICHAEL, *Power, How to Get It, How to Use It.* New York: Random House, 1975.

LIKERT, RENSIS, *The Human Organization: Its Management and Value.* New York: McGraw-Hill, Inc., 1967.

11

Communicating in the Family

goal:

To learn how to improve communication within the family group.

probes:

The material in this chapter should help you to:

1. Describe how the following can cause communication breakdowns in families:

   Unshared goals, p. 297
   Antagonistic goals, pp. 298–301
   Roles and norms not agreed upon, pp. 286–93
   Failure to clarify expectations, pp. 286–91
   Double standards for children, pp. 291–93
   Intimate living conditions, pp. 294–96

2. Use communication principles that help avoid communication breakdowns in families. pp. 301–4

3. Use language in a way that can assist children to learn right from wrong without behaving possessively. p. 304

4. Explain why communicating with the aged in the United States presents special communication problems. pp. 305–8

5. Suggest two means by which you can improve communication with aged members of your family. pp. 308–10

The most familiar group communication situation for most of us is our family. Moreover, for most of us, family was the primary social group. It was the group in which we learned to function within a social unit. We learned the basic patterns by which we relate to all people from our family—whatever its composition might have been.

Families remain important to us long after we leave childhood. They are usually the source of our most intimate and lasting interpersonal relationships. Therefore, communicating effectively in families is important to us. Even those of us with pleasant family relationships sometimes communicate in ways that hurt each other. Even happy families occasionally have painful communication breakdowns. In this chapter, we suggest principles useful for coping with the communication problems that interfere with happy family relationships.

One suggestion for improving family communication would be simply to say, "Use the principles of supportive interpersonal communication." But it isn't that easy. Intimate living creates special communication situations, and imposed on those situations are problems arising from the special relationships of a family. For that reason, we want to note several sources of communication breakdowns that are inherent in families and suggest some ways you can try to avoid those breakdowns.

POTENTIAL CAUSES OF COMMUNICATION BREAKDOWNS

A family represents more than biological or social bonds. In a very real sense, a family is a miniature society, and is subject to many of the same stresses. Causes of communication breakdown in families are similar to those in other groups, with some special problems

caused by the existence of family relationships.

> But what on earth is half so dear—
> So longed for—as the hearth of home?
>
> EMILY BRONTE

Roles and Norms Not Agreed On

As in any society, roles, rituals, status, and norms develop and affect communication in families. But because of the relative stability of a family compared to other groups, members are often unaware that roles, status, norms, and rituals exist within the family. *The rules and roles of the family mini-society are based on expectations that are supposedly shared but often are not.*

unstated expectations

In families problems often arise simply because the roles and norms of the family are not stated. Agreement on unstated expectations is assumed, but it often does not exist. These differences in expectations can be between wife and husband, or between parents and children. Sometimes the differences aren't noticed. Often they are noticed but not discussed. When differences exist, however, they will emerge eventually, usually at a time of strong emotion. Potential for communication breakdown always exists whenever unstated expectations disguise disagreement as assumed agreement.

> Love is an ideal thing, marriage a real thing; a confusion of the real with the ideal never goes unpunished.
>
> GOETHE

A good example of problems caused by assumed agreement on unstated expectations is provided by newlyweds. Partners approaching marriage usually do not clarify the agreements related to the role choices that will have to be made. They don't answer specifically, "What will it mean for us to be married? What behaviors do I expect from my partner?" Men and women bring different perspectives into the marriage relationship as to what their respective roles are. They have probably gained their perspectives largely from their parents, and in today's mobile society those parents may be from quite different social cultures. Even between families from similar social groups, differences in wife-husband roles will exist. If

286

The traditional family has given way to the nuclear.
Source: (left) Fujihara—Monkmeyer.
(right) The Bettmann Archive.

newlyweds do not clarify how they expect marriage to affect one another's behavior, the unstated expectations result in hurt feelings when they are not fulfilled. Communication can quickly become burdened with bad feelings. With each succeeding failure to meet unstated expectations, the emotional load piles up and contributes to growing misunderstandings. An excellent example of how this happens is provided in the following excerpt.

THE TIES THAT BIND: EIGHT DAYS IN THE MAKING OF THE CLOSED CONTRACT
Nena and George O'Neill

John and Sue, very much in love, have been married two weeks. Most of that time was spent on a honeymoon vacation in the Caribbean. Before their marriage, John kept house for himself in the same apartment in which they are now living as husband and wife. He works for an architectural firm, and Sue is going to continue with her secretarial job. Over the threshold they carry not only their vacation suitcases, but also the cumbersome (even though invisible) baggage of their respective pasts, weighted down by their personal experiences, their cultural conditioning and their idealistic expectations. Unconsciously, with only the desire to please one another and to express their

From *Open Marriage, A New Life Style for Couples* by Nena O'Neill and George O'Neil. © 1972 by Nena O'Neill and George O'Neill. Reprinted by permission of the publisher M. Evans & Co., Inc., New York.

love, this young couple begins to bind themselves to a closed marriage contract. They are happy, smiling and in love, for their pleasure in each other is new and fresh, but they are unknowingly painting themselves into corners and guaranteeing themselves future frustration and unhappiness. Let us see how it happens.

DAY 1: It is Sunday morning. Sue wanders sleepily into the kitchen and begins to make breakfast. John follows after bringing in the paper from the hallway. While Sue fries bacon and scrambles eggs, John sits at the kitchen table reading the paper. ... It is, in one sense, a charming scene. But under the surface, binding assumptions are being made. (CLAUSE: The woman is the cook.) ...

Later in the day the telephone rings.

"Darling," Sue whispers, "it's my mother. They want to come over and say hello. You know how much they want to hear about the trip. Is it all right?"

"Sure, honey," he answers obligingly. (CLAUSE: When you marry, you marry not only a husband or wife but an entire network of relationships and responsibilities.) John suddenly remembers that they had promised to get together with Linda and Bill, who first introduced them and are their closest friends. . . . Clearly on their first day back it is only to be expected that John will go along with the idea of inviting Sue's parents over. But having agreed this time, he will find it more difficult to say no next time. . . . Sue makes a further assumption, too. "Don't worry," she says, "I'll give Linda a call. We can see them during the week but Mom and Dad can only get free on weekends." (CLAUSE: It is the wife's role to make decisions concerning the couple's social activities. And this presumes the wife's right to decide how the husband's time is going to be spent.) . . .

DAY 2: Sue cooks breakfast, leaving the dishes in the sink, and they both rush off to work. At his office, John is confronted with a new project, as well as some leftover problems from an old one. The old problems involve personality differences and the blueprints for the new project are inaccurate; it's all very depressing. That evening, John arrives home before Sue and makes himself a drink. Sue comes staggering in with two huge bags of groceries. (CLAUSE: Shopping is the wife's job.) He helps her unpack them and then mixes a drink for her while she does the breakfast dishes and prepares dinner. (CLAUSE: Mixing drinks is the husband's job, but the dishes, as well as meal preparation, are the wife's responsibility.) John is preoccupied with his problems at work, but he tries to pretend that everything is just fine. (CLAUSE: The husband must always be strong; if he has problems, he must never communicate them to his wife, because to do so might make him vulnerable.) They eat dinner, making small talk, mostly about Sue's job and when to see Linda and Bill. John, however, continues to be upset about his problem at work. Still, he refrains from saying anything. (CLAUSE: You must always live up to the ideal conception of your role as husband—or wife.) Anyway, he tells himself, Sue probably wouldn't understand what in hell he was talking about—she doesn't know anything about blueprints. (CLAUSE: Women's minds are *different* from men's—the male's is abstract, the female's is intuitive.)

Even if it were true that Sue would not understand the nature of John's problem (although the assumption that she won't understand is a throwback to the Victorian view of women) that is not to say that she couldn't, one way or another, make John feel better. Just to talk about it might relieve some of his tension. By not talking about it, John instead is guaranteeing himself future tension; the underlying, hidden clauses in the psychological contract are binding him to a position of non-communication with his wife. . . . Misunderstanding between a husband and wife becomes inevitable in this kind of situation. And it is all based upon an attempt to live up to the clauses of an unspoken, crippling psychological contract.

DAY 3: Sue calls John at his office to suggest dinner out with Linda and Bill that night. Although John had hoped for some time alone at home that evening to wrestle with some of his professional problems, he says, "Sure, darling," and they eat dinner out. (CLAUSE: Husband and wife must always see friends as a couple.) . . .

DAY 4: When John arrives home from work, Sue isn't there yet. She can't be shopping since the refrigerator is still stuffed with food from her Monday marketing. John likes to eat around 7:00, but by 6:15 Sue still isn't home. He's tired and hungry and he begins to get irritated. (CLAUSE: Cooking is the wife's job.) In spite of the fact that John made perfectly creditable meals as a bachelor, it never even occurs to him to start preparing the dinner himself. Now that he is married he thinks of the kitchen as Sue's territory and responsibility; he is completely bound by an antiquated concept of proper roles for husband and wife. Not only does he fail to bend with the situation, doing the sensible, practical thing and getting dinner started, he is sufficiently disturbed by Sue not being around to do what he sees as her job that he is unable even to sit down and concentrate on *his* job now that he finally has a few free minutes to give full attention to his blueprints. (CLAUSE: Husband and wife must surrender their selfhood, or identity, to the couple unit.) John is already so caught up in the myth of couplehood that he is losing his power to act independently.

A few minutes later, Sue breezes in happily. She's late because she ran into an old friend from college just as she left the office. "Harry Bigelow, I've told you about him. Anyway, we had a drink and I told *him* all about my marvelous husband." John smiles and gives Sue a hug, but at the back of his mind he is still a bit piqued. (CLAUSE: Each partner in the marriage belongs only to the other and not anybody else.) This kind of possessiveness, since it is based on an unrealistic ideal (CLAUSE: I will be everything to you and you will be everything to me), leads to a basic lack of trust and to a sense of insecurity. Every couple knows, deep down, that they cannot be everything to each other, but since this admission is not made on a conscious level, it finds its way to the surface in terms of mistrust. John, for instance, cannot resist asking, "Did you have to have a *drink* with him?" Sue answers, "Oh, well, the bar was right next door, and he probably won't be in town again for ages."

This is fertile ground for further misunderstanding, though. John, preoccupied with his job problem, is more silent than usual during dinner. His quietness leads Sue to mistakenly assume that he is brooding about her drink with Harry. "You're not mad at me, are you?" she asks. And John who had been about to ask if she'd mind if he did some work by himself for a while after supper, now feels he has to spend the evening watching television with her. If he said he wanted to be alone, she'd be hurt, and be convinced that he *was* mad at her. (CLAUSE: Togetherness is one of the most important things in marriage. You must always be willing to sacrifice your own needs on the altar of togetherness.)

DAY 5: Morning dawns. John is bleary-eyed from lack of sleep. He lay awake until 3 A.M., too tense to fall asleep. ... He doesn't mention his insomnia, though, nor does he tell Sue that he really isn't hungry. He manages to get down the hot breakfast she cooks him, but it gives him heartburn all morning long. In fact, if he had only known it, the last thing Sue felt like doing was cooking breakfast. Each, in the name of love and at the expense of self, has done something he didn't want to do, and that it was unnecessary to do, simply because they both were being controlled by the unwritten clauses of the closed marriage contract. Each is responding according to what he *thinks* the other expects of him, instead of trying to find out what is actually expected.

During the day, Lenny, an old friend of John's, calls him to suggest a drink after work some evening, or maybe dinner on Saturday when Sue could join them. Much as he would like a little change of pace, and though he's very fond of Lenny, John refuses the drink for that evening, anyway, and says he'll see what Sue has planned for Saturday. (CLAUSE: The husband's time belongs to the wife, except when he is actually at work.) He has misgivings about Saturday because Sue has always been put off by Lenny's forthrightness and brash sense of humor. And, as he suspected, Sue turns the idea down. "I really don't enjoy Lenny much," she says, and reminds him that the Millers, a couple down the hall, have invited them to drop in at their open house Saturday night. (CLAUSE: All friends of the married couple must be *mutual* friends.)

DAY 6: Friday, at last. Sue reminds John that she will be late getting home because she is having her hair done. And when John calls Lenny to say they won't be able to make Saturday night, Lenny suggests instead that John join him and his new girl for a drink after work. Since Sue will be late anyway, John agrees, but he feels guilty about it from the start. If Sue really doesn't want to see Lenny, then it's likely to seem kind of pushy of John to have a drink with him the next day—as though he were telling Sue off in a subtle way, which he doesn't want to do at all. If Sue really can't stand Lenny, then he'll just have to give up the friendship.

John has such a good time with Lenny and his girl, though, that it gets to be even later than he realized. He calls Sue to tell her why he's behind schedule. She's just been home a few minutes herself but was beginning to worry about him, she says. He stops at the florist to pick up a dozen roses, beginning the pattern of appeasement that develops inevitably in the closed marriage. It is not, of course, *only* to appease her that he buys the roses. He is newly married and very much in love. Nevertheless, there is an element of guilt involved—for not being at home when she got there and for seeing Lenny at all. . . .

DAY 7: In the morning, while Sue cleans house, John takes the laundry to the laundromat. Laundry is something he would usually consider one of the wife's jobs, but he is not actually going to sit there and watch it spin around in the machine—he will leave it with the attendant and pick it up later in the day, paying extra for the service of having it done for him. Besides, the laundry bag is heavy and awkward, and Sue would have a hard time carrying it. (CLAUSE: The husband must never do anything out of line with his image of himself as a "man.") . . .

That evening, as they get ready for the Miller's party, Sue asks John what she should wear. "You look good in anything," he says. But when she appears in a slinky, spangled gown, looking very 1920s, he says, "My God, Sue, where are you going, to a costume ball?" (CLAUSE: Husband and wife are reflections of one another; neither is allowed, therefore, to wear clothes that don't suit the other's taste.) Although Sue actually looks terrific, and right in keeping with the tone of the party, John's words are enough—off comes the dress. Both John and Sue are demonstrating their lack of personal identity, or selfhood, here. Sue had the right instinct as to what she should wear, but showed her lack of confidence in herself by asking John's approval in the first place and changing when he disapproved. . . . And John, in making her change, is simply illustrating his lack of confidence in himself: if what his wife is wearing can so easily embarrass him, then his sense of himself as an individual is sadly deficient.

At the Millers' party, John and Sue

290

spend most of the evening moving around as though they were chained to one another. (CLAUSE: Husband and wife exist primarily as a couple, and must always maintain the couple-front. Otherwise someone might think they were not married, or worse still, that they weren't getting along.) Nevertheless, they eventually get separated when Judy Miller asks Sue to give her a hand in the kitchen for a moment. When Sue gets back to the living room she sees John sitting on the sofa talking intently to a woman she doesn't know, who apparently has only just dropped by. Sue rushes over to join them. (CLAUSE: Neither husband nor wife is even allowed to show interest in a member of the opposite sex unless the mate is right there too.) When John introduces her, Sue is perfectly polite. But her physical action in charging over to join them has clearly indicated to the other woman that she is regarded as an intruder. Sue might just as well have said, "He's mine. Get away from him." And, indeed, the woman takes the hint and excuses herself after a moment or two. In fact it turns out that she is also an architect, and had worked before with the client who's been creating John's problems. She was giving John some helpful hints on how to handle the man, but Sue's instant jealousy has brought the conversation to an end. Sue's actions said to the other woman, "He's mine," and to John they say, just as clearly, "I don't trust you." Of course she doesn't trust John—how could she? She has been taught to believe fidelity consists of a rigid, mechanical rule: Never take an interest in any member of the opposite sex. Deep down, Sue knows, as all of us do, that this is a standard impossible for John to live up to. In respect to such a rigid view of fidelity, what mate *could* trust another? Sue would do better to question the rigidity of the rule.

DAY 8: It is Sunday again. And just as last Sunday, Sue's parents call and suggest coming over. "You don't mind, darling, do you?" Sue asks. John had been hoping they might go to a movie, but if he were to refuse to see her parents, she'd be hurt. "Fine," he says. And the pattern becomes more deeply implanted.

The hidden contract has been accepted by both.

The problem of unstated role expectations is particularly severe precisely because they are unstated. Often young married partners aren't even aware of their expectations or the effects, as the tale of John and Sue illustrates. They tend to assume that because mom and dad did it this way, everyone does. Because the expectations often apply to small things (who makes the morning coffee, who washes the dishes, carries out the trash, gets into the bathroom first), they aren't discussed. It's not worth the hassle. But little things build up when people live together, and often explosions occur over small events.

Compounding the problems of unstated role expectations is the arrival of children. Even when children are planned and wanted, partners often fail to prepare for them by clarifying their individual ideas of parental roles and responsibilities in advance. What is a mother to do in this family? How is a father to behave? These are matters of choice. And the choices can usually be discussed rationally with good likelihood of reaching consensus when the partners start with love, trust, and the expectation of pleasing each other, IF that discussion occurs before the choice is made. Once a child is on the way or has arrived, alternatives available to one or both partners are severely limited. When differences of opinion occur then, it's more difficult to keep the discussion unemotional and to resolve differences without resentments. It's more likely then that the emotional load from disappointed expectations will distort the communication and lead to defensiveness, resentment, and hostility.

changing roles of children

Unstated expectations create problems in parent-child relationships also. *Too often children don't know why particular behaviors are expected of them.* Even when they know why, they frequently don't share the expectations. This is especially true of status relationships in the family. Though family membership is largely involuntary for children, roles and status relationships are not. Any parent can testify how quickly children begin to show their individuality in handling the role of child. As children grow from infancy through the teenage years, the roles and relative status of children and parents continually change. All roles and status relations—especially those of parents and growing children—should be considered as processes and not as static concepts. The role of mother, for example, shifts in responsibilities as children grow. Other changes in the family situation also result. The role responsibilities of both parents as well as each child must be adapted constantly to the changing situation.

The role of parent might more accurately be described as *parenting*. Parenting, as distinguished from parent, suggests that *the parental role is ongoing, developing, and changing.* The behaviors of people who engage in parenting are continually adjusting, or should be. A continual negotiation process occurs as children mature. They quickly begin to work toward becoming full citizens of the family society. With citizen status, they see, come rights that as children they don't have. Very young children are frequently assigned second- or even third- or fourth-class status within the household. They can recognize this lowly status very early. One 5-year-old put it this way: "I'm five, that's too little; I have to go to bed at 8:00 o'clock; and everyone else gets to boss me." As children mature they expect to increase their status.

Continued refusal by parents to accept changes in a growing child's status creates communication breakdowns. Adolescents often demand full status in families and are denied it, partly because parents have not accepted the changes as children grew toward that critical age. Complete breakdowns between adolescents and parents can result from this one factor alone. When parental behavior assumes static roles and status, real troubles for the family's communication are ahead.

This analysis of status relationships also relates to rules established to govern family behavior, especially that of the children. These rules often become rituals: for example, waiting your turn in line, not telling lies, sharing with others, being polite to your elders, not stealing. Children are expected to accept family rituals without challenge even if they did not share in creating them.

double standards

Worse than simply expecting children to accept unchanging status, *parents often fail to see that a double standard exists in family rules and roles.* Children quickly notice that many of the rituals they are expected to follow do not always apply to their parents. They find this a hard norm system to adopt. Parents tell them, in behavior if not in words, "Do what I say, not what I do." Parents say to children, "Don't lie, it's wrong"—then they tell the tax assessor that they donated $300 during the year to a church. The children, listening, know the parents rarely go to church. They say to children, "Don't steal," then keep the $10 extra change a sales clerk has returned by mistake. A child may be punished for taking a candy bar off a store shelf by a parent who mails personal letters with company stamps.

Parents are often less aware of the double standard than are the children. Children are told, "Don't interrupt adults" by parents who freely interrupt children. A parent and child conversation may be marked by many interruptions of the child: "Don't talk with your mouth full"; "Say *aren't*, not *ain't*"; "Stand up straight";

"Look at me when you talk to me." Parents often aren't even aware their behavior expresses a double standard. But a child who interrupts conversation of adults is likely to hear, "Don't interrupt when other people are talking." And if a child is talking to one parent, the other frequently feels free to interrupt that conversation. This rule says to the child, "Your rights of conversation are different from those of parents and other adults."

The double standard causes special difficulties as children grow and begin asking questions. A 13-year-old whose chain-smoking parents forbid her to smoke finds it hard to reconcile the behaviors. Parents who admonish a 15-year-old to stay away from drugs while they are having two or three martinis before dinner present that youngster with a very difficult status position to accept without resentment.

Once a child is considered able to recognize verbal commands, a host of rules are imposed by parents to govern the child's behavior. As a second-class citizen the child usually neither participates in adoption of the rules nor shares agreement regarding how important they are. Still, parents often assume that children have only one choice with respect to those rules: compliance. In reality, even very young children have other alternatives. By early adolescence, compliance for many is no longer an acceptable response. Adolescents, and sometimes much younger children, resort to other choices: they try to argue the parents into acceptance of different norms; or they remain deviant and deal with the resulting frustrated parents; or they even leave. That thousands of youngsters run away from home monthly is evidence that many make choices other than compliance. Much communication breakdown results from double standards.

ETIQUETTE LESSON
Erma Bombeck

On TV, a child psychologist said parents should treat their children as they would treat their best friend—with courtesy, dignity and diplomacy. "I have never treated my children any other way," I told myself. But later that night, I thought about it. Suppose our good friends, Fred and Eleanor came to dinner and . . .

"Well, it's about time you two got here! What have you been doing? Dawdling? Shut the door, Fred. Were you born in a barn? So, Eleanor, how have you

been? I've been meaning to have you over for ages. Fred! Take it easy on the chip dip or you'll ruin your dinner.

"Heard from any of the gang lately? Got a card from the Martins—they're in Lauderdale again. What's the matter, Fred? You're fidgeting. It's down the hall, first door on the left. And I don't want to see a towel in the middle of the floor when you're finished. So, how're your children? If everybody's hungry, we'll go in to dinner. You all wash up, and I'll dish up the food. Don't tell me your hands are clean, Eleanor. I saw you playing with the dog.

"Fred, you sit there, and Eleanor you

At Wit's End by Erma Bombeck, courtesy of Field Newspaper Syndicate.

sit with the half glass of milk. You know you're all elbows when it comes to milk. Fred, I don't see any cauliflower on your plate. You don't like cauliflower? Have you ever tried it? Well, try a spoonful. If you don't like it, I won't make you finish it, but if you don't try it, you can forget dessert. Now, what were we talking about. Oh, yes, the Grubers. They sold their house, and took a beating, but—Eleanor, don't talk with food in your mouth. And use your napkin . . ."

At that moment in my fantasy, my son walked into the room, "How nice of you to come," I said pleasantly.

"Now what did I do?" he sighed.

Exercise: Family Roles

Objective: To become aware of role expectations as they operate in your family.

Procedures:

1. Circle the roles you play in your family in a typical day:
   father, mother, son, daughter, sister, brother, husband, wife, aunt, uncle, niece, grandmother, grandfather, granddaughter, grandson, stepson, stepdaughter, stepmother, stepbrother, stepsister, stepfather, other _____ .
2. Choose from the ones circled and list the role positions you interact with in a typical day.
3. For each person (role) interacted with, list the expectations that person has for your behavior in your role. List what you expect from them.
4. Show your list as compiled in #3 to the person. Ask her/him to confirm your perceptions of her/his expectations or to explain why your perceptions are inaccurate.

Pressures from Intimate Living Conditions

Any intimate, long-term relationship, whether the people involved are a family or not, can provide satisfying communication experiences. The intimacy inherent in living with others can add richness to lives that might otherwise be very lonely. At the same time, *the demands and pressures of living together create tremendous stresses on interpersonal relationships.*

restricted freedom

Even as it prevents loneliness, living with someone restricts your freedom to behave at every moment just as you please. The time you choose to eat, bathe, sleep, or dress may be determined by others. Restrictions of dozens of small freedoms often become the source of interpersonal stress. For instance, a breadwinner, just home from a hard day at work and a nerve-wracking bout with commuter traffic, may want nothing more than to collapse into an easy

294

chair for a few quiet moments. But that may not be possible—responsibilities and demands from others in the household face that person immediately upon opening the door.

To show how restricted freedom can create pressures that cause communication breakdowns, consider the following. Our breadwinner, entering the door, is immediately confronted:

Question: Do you know what Jackie did today?

Answer #1:   No, what? (in a resigned, unenthusiastic tone of voice) [Verbally expresses the internal expectations that this is how a good parent/spouse behaves, but nonverbally says, "No . . . and I don't want to know." Communicates lack of concern in spite of verbal expression of interest.]

Answer #2:   "I really couldn't care less at the moment." (irritated voice) [An honest response, if not tactful. Fails to report the reason for lack of interest, while nonverbally communicating anger. It's not clear whether the anger is with the question, the questioner, Jackie, or the answer.]

Answer #3:   "Of course not—I just got here." (sarcastic voice) [Responds to the verbal message, not the real question. Expresses anxiety and emotion—perhaps caused by the hard day and traffic, not the question—but does not make clear the source of the anger.]

Answer #4:   "No, but let's talk about it later, O.K.? I'm really bushed." (voice contains traces of irritation) [Is an honest expression of feelings that shows concern for the other person, though still leaving open the possibility for misunderstanding. Receiver can infer many other reasons for not wanting to talk about Jackie's behavior.]

In any of these responses, the person speaking may assume that the other receiver should understand all the messages not verbalized. As we all know, that doesn't always happen.

faulty assumptions

Family communication problems that arise from intimate living conditions often come from the assumption that shared experience equals understanding. Family members may believe their shared memories create shared referents when they communicate with each other. This is often true—family members usually do know what others in the family mean better than do strangers. But not always. Intended and perceived messages differ between family members just as between other communicators. In talking with strangers, however, people usually use feedback to check understandings, and try to make sure they share referents for words used. It's not so common to do this with members of the family. We tend to assume members of our family should *know* what we mean, and often become angry if they don't. How often have you heard, "Oh you know what I mean!" and been rewarded with irritation if you say, "Well, no, I really *don't*." *In families, the assumption of shared meanings leads to much apparent agreement that is not real.*

Intimates in families, particularly married partners, often believe in the romantic fallacy, "If you love me you'll know what I mean." The folklore of romance leads lovers to believe that some sort of intuitive click or sensitivity links all intimates. They don't realize how much work it takes to communicate well within families.

Intimate communication requires that partners make understandings clear just as in other settings. Yet often information is withheld from a family member in the name of tact, or because of role expectations, or game playing to avoid real intimacy and to avoid revealing "I'm Not O.K." feelings. Men or parents may not want to burden the "little woman" or children with problems, or a wife may want to keep domestic problems from bothering the husband. Information about sexual preferences, for instance, is often not shared. People assume their partners will know what they think or feel, and then are hurt when behavior shows they don't. Once this information is exposed, as it usually is eventually, the shielded partner may then feel he/she wasn't trusted or that the other didn't care enough to share. Sometimes partners actually cause one another to withhold information without knowing it by a habit of reacting evaluatively. Whatever the cause, assumptions that partners understand one another merely because they've lived together for a long time are a common source of communication breakdowns in families.

emotional loads

For people in intimate relationships, words, phrases, and communication situations gradually build up emotional loads. The human memory system then attaches this emotional luggage to succeeding communication situations that are similar or that use the same words and phrases. This can cause complete breakdowns between intended and perceived messages in situations that would be simple between people with less intimate relationships.

For example, consider a question intended as a simple request for information, "What time will dinner be ready?" The emotional load of shared past experiences includes times when dinner was late and the cook felt guilty; other times when dinner was ready on time but the questioner was late and the meal was ruined; times when the questioner grew enraged and yelled at the cook when it was late; times when the meal was late because the cook had burned the biscuits or charred the steak beyond recognition. If any of these shared experiences occurred, chances are the question is not perceived as a simple request for information. The emotional luggage affects both intended and perceived messages.

What emotional luggage might be developing in that situation involving the tired breadwinner? To almost any of the answers, the questioner could have negative responses:

"She/he doesn't care about the kids and me,"
"He/she is still angry from yesterday,"
"She/he is never interested in anything except that job,"
"What a grouch!"
"He/she doesn't understand how hard it is to stay here all day and cope with these kids. What an insensitive lout!"

These, of course, do not exhaust the list of possible responses. The problem for intimates is that emotional loads usually continue to grow, giving each succeeding situation more emotional luggage to separate intended and received messages.

Unshared Goals

Another cause of communication breakdown in nuclear families is the absence of shared goals. In the traditional, agrarian family, all worked together for survival and shared their social lives. Members of nuclear families seldom share work goals. Even though work is a major part of their lives, married partners do not usually share work tasks, and this causes natural barriers to communication. The commercial phrase, "The family that plays together stays together" is a recognition of this problem. Families no longer work together, and so logically they feel they should share their leisure activities. But people do not automatically share interests just because they are a family: many wives consider themselves widows to their husbands' interests while many husbands don't really enjoy the social activities that their wives do.

Often the only shared goals in nuclear families are to establish effective interpersonal relationships to satisfy personal needs for love and belonging. When a member of any group seeks primarily to satisfy personal needs, monumental stresses on the group result. This is as true in families as in any other group. When parents see children as their reason for living, or when husbands and wives believe marriage will solve personal insecurity, breakdowns are inevitable. Self-centered interpersonal relationships cause major communication problems in families.

More serious than absence of shared goals in families is the presence of *antagonistic goals.* The circumstances of society can create antagonistic goals among many families, but the most significant cause of antagonistic goals is an attitude family members have toward each other that they bring to few other relationships. This is the attitude of *possessiveness.*

possessiveness

> For how do I hold thee but by thy granting?
>
> SHAKESPEARE
>
> It is better to bind your children to you by respect and gentleness than by fear.
>
> TERENCE

For many reasons, family relationships can result in an attitude of possessiveness and a consequent belief that members have a right to control or influence the behaviors of each other. Many people interpret family as a situation in which they "possess" another person or persons within a family. Think what it means to say, "That's mine." If something is mine, it belongs to me. Now think how commonly we hear (or say) "my" husband, "my" wife, "my" children. How many parents have said, "No child of *mine* is going to . . ."? These common phrases imply ownership or possession. This attitude of "you are mine," implies covertly, if not openly, an *expectation of control* over the other person.

In communicating with one another, family members often forget that their relationships are matters of choice. At the beginning, married partners recognize that they are choosing each other. But once the choice is made, they frequently behave as if they have a right to control the other's behavior and to limit the other's freedom. Commonly we say, "My wife shouldn't dress that way"; "My husband shouldn't behave that way"; "My husband/wife shouldn't _____". You can fill in the blank easily with many phrases whether you're married or not. The expression is familiar.

Of course, the attitude is usually stated differently. Partners say, "If she/he loved me, he/she wouldn't behave that way." Parents say, "If you cared about us, you would do that." The implication is that what the speaker *expects* from another person will be done because of concern for the feelings of the speaker. To a limited extent, it is. People who love each other want to please each

ON MARRIAGE[1]

Then Almitra spoke again and said, And what of Marriage, master
And he answered saying: You were born together, and together you
shall be forevermore . . .
But let there be spaces in your togetherness,
And let the winds of the heavens dance between you.
Love one another, but make not a bond of love . . .
Give your hearts, but not into each other's keeping.
For only the hand of Life can contain your hearts.
And stand together yet not too near together:
For the pillars of the temple stand apart, And the oak tree and
the cypress grow not in each other's shadow.

other. But when such expectations are carried to the extent of expecting changes of behavior and personality, they reflect controlling, possessive attitudes.

results in defensiveness

Married partners usually, at least at the beginning, want to please each other. They often try to change to please the other. But when either partner wants the other one to change, it is controlling, evaluative behavior. Wanting change implies current inadequacy. With that suggestion, defensive reactions are virtually inevitable. Even people who respond to evaluation by trying to change may resent the implication that they are inadequate. When any family member feels something must be changed (or hidden) to please another, the conditions for trust in the family are damaged. The absence of acceptance has been recognized, and honesty often begins to diminish as a result. Control and evaluation destroy trust and create defensiveness.

Possessiveness causes defensiveness in parent-child relationships, too. Children can't choose their parents, but they do have choices regarding how they perform the role of daughter or son. Parents, however, too often forget that. They often feel, or act as if they feel, that their children are *theirs* to be controlled, molded, and developed as the parents desire. Parents set rules, issue ultimatums, and feel they should control the smallest behaviors of their children. They don't realize this behavior shows a lack of acceptance of the children as separate, individual human beings. Too few parents recognize their possessiveness as the cause of defensiveness in growing children.

[1] Reprinted from *The Prophet* by Kahlil Gibran, with permission of the publisher, Alfred A. Knopf, Inc. Copyright 1923 by Kahlil Gibran; renewal copyright 1951 by Administrators C.T.A. of Kahlil Gibran Estate and Mary G. Gibran.

Right now, we can hear many of our readers who are parents protesting, "But it's our responsibility to protect our children. We have a duty to raise them to know right from wrong." Of course, that parental protest is accurate. Parents have the responsibility to protect their children from an environment with which they are not prepared to cope. But very early in a child's development, parents can begin to teach them that life consists of a series of choices and that each choice has inevitable consequences. As soon as a child can accept the consequences, the choices about living it should be made by the child, not the parent. Children can learn to guide their own behavior at a very early age.

A basic element of maturity is learning that in any situation you have at least one and usually many alternatives, and that the consequences depend on the choices you make. Even not to choose is to choose. It's a choice to let someone else decide. As long as children are not required to make the choices or to understand the consequences of their behavior, the maturing process is delayed, sometimes forever. It's seldom too early to begin applying this principle to interpersonal relationships between parents and children. Certainly by adolescence the learning process should long since have begun.

We're trying very hard to be clear here. You may still believe parents have a "right" to control their children's behavior. That is, of course, your choice. Your parental philosophy is not an issue here. What is important is for you to recognize the consequences of such behavior. Family members who act as if they have a right to control one another's behaviors and to limit one another's freedom are be-

ON CHILDREN[2]

And a woman who held a babe against her bosom said, Speak to us of Children.
And he said:
Your children are not your children.
They are the sons and daughters of Life's longing for itself.
They come through you but not from you.
And though they are with you yet they belong not to you.

You may give them your love but not your thoughts,
For they have their own thoughts.
You may house their bodies but not their souls . . .
You may strive to be like them, but seek not to make them like you.
For life goes not backward nor tarries with yesterday. . . .

having possessively. And when you think about it, you know that possessiveness expressed toward any person, whether that person is a member of your family or not, an adult or a child, will almost always create defensiveness and all the distortions of communication that accompany it. If you cannot allow individual freedom within your family relationships, expect the defensiveness and accompanying communication problems that result.

Exercise: Causes of Communication Breakdowns

Objective: To assess my family group as it is affected by potentials for communication breakdowns.

Directions:

1. Assess the potential causes of communication breakdown discussed in the chapter as they affect your family group.
   a. roles and norms agreed on
      unstated expectations of members
      changing roles of children
      double standards
   b. pressures from intimate living conditions
      restricted freedom
      assumptions of shared understandings
      emotional loads in situations
   c. unshared goals
   d. existence of antagonistic goals
      possessiveness
      other causes of defensiveness

AVOIDING COMMUNICATION BREAKDOWNS

In the first part of this chapter we discussed how the familiarity inherent in family life creates strains on communication. Roles and norms are often not clarified, faulty assumptions exist, parents have trouble accepting changing roles of children, and children resist double standards. Other pressures result because of the restricted freedom inherent in intimate living, and unshared or antagonistic goals of family members. To deal with these problems, many positive steps can be taken to prevent communication breakdowns in families.

Supportive Communication

Earlier, we cited one suggestion for coping with the problems of family communication: "use the principles of supportive communication." We indicated that is oversimplification. Now, however, having looked specifically at some of the stresses on communication in the mini-society that is the family, we can refer you to some specific applications of that principle.

> A truly personal relationship between two people involves disclosure of self, one to the other, in full and spontaneous honesty.
>
> SIDNEY JOURARD

What families need most are the behaviors that allow trust to develop. Family members need to be open and honest with each other, to accept each other, and to display empathy toward each other. We don't intend to repeat here everything said in Chapter 7. But most of it is relevant. You may want to review the chapter at this point, thinking specifically about your family relationships. How much honesty exists in your family communication? How much acceptance? How much empathy? How effectively is feedback used to insure that intended and received messages are similar? How often is directive feedback used when nondirective would be more appropriate?

recognize purposes motivating communication

Family members need also to understand why each of them sends the messages they do. Again, we can't repeat all of Chapter 6. But much of it is relevant here. If you consider the purposes related to self, subject, and other that motivate the interactions among family members, you'll be in a better position to respond in a supportive rather than destructive manner.

work at empathic listening

Once more we refer you to an earlier chapter, Chapter 8. Specifically we repeat the injunction to listen so that you can hear the message as the sender intends it. Don't forget, as we so often do, that people in your family are different from you. They are individuals with perspectives that aren't the same as yours. Differences of age, sex, values, even of socialization and culture exist. The wider the differences, the more difficult it is to "get inside the head" of people you're listening to. In families it's even more difficult because we maintain the attitude that such differences don't (or shouldn't) exist—just because it's a family. Empathic listening is never easy, but it's often most difficult when talking with family members. Still, it will help avoid communication breakdowns if we do it.

302

Families need to listen
empathically.
Source: Sybil Shelton.

Benefits of Supportive Communication

Supportive communication can do more than allow family members to recognize and avoid the potential causes of communication breakdowns.

avoids defensiveness

Accepting, supportive relationships aid people to change and grow better than do evaluative, controlling behaviors. Evaluation and control lead to defensiveness. Defensive people feel threatened. They concentrate their attention and energy on defending themselves against the threats they perceive. They are less honest, less open, and more likely to justify their behavior. They spend their energy thinking of reasons why they act as they do; they think about rationalizations for their behavior and feelings instead of reasons to change. People tend to reject communicators who are evaluative and seek those who accept them. Ironically, the possessiveness common to families often results in members having less influence over each other than if they were accepting and maintained openness in family communications.

promotes growth

When a person feels accepted by significant others, it contributes to increased self-esteem. We've noted earlier that a person with positive self-concept is the one most likely to be able to share feelings honestly with others, to learn from others, and most importantly, to feel that he/she can change in positive ways. People with high self-esteem feel able to cope with themselves and the world, and thus are most able to risk changing themselves.

In contrast, people with low self-esteem often seek to confirm their belief in personal inadequacy. They'll continue the criticized

303

behavior, eliciting over and over the criticism that justifies their negative self-concept. They do not feel able to cope with changes in self without warm, accepting communication. Evaluation and control, especially if sustained and repeated, as they often are in family communications, reinforce lowered self-esteem, and reduce the probability of changing the criticized behavior.

unrestricted codes promote self-discipline

A communication pattern established early between parents and children appears to have long-range implications. This pattern involves the use of restricted codes when talking to children. *A restricted code refers to the general use of command statements without complete explanations.* "Tom, don't light that match," is such a statement. An unrestricted code *provides an explanation:* "Tom, if you light that match, you can easily burn yourself and the furniture. Don't light it." To influence children without controlling their lives, parents can learn to use unrestricted code phrasing. Then a child's compliance will be based on understanding of predicted consequences, not on expected blind obedience to authority.

Children respond well to unrestricted models of interaction. Two 4-year-olds arguing over the use of a wagon quickly settled their conflict when the present user explained, "I just started to play with this. I want my turn, then you can have a turn." A child who had learned this pattern of interaction would be able to see that the explanation was reasonable. Using unrestricted code gives the reasons for behavior. Very young children are able to use and respond to unrestricted codes. They learn to base behaviors on understanding of the consequences of various acts, not on fear of punishment, or desire for reward. They can learn *self*-discipline by learning to rely on themselves, not external forces, to guide their behavior.

To sum up, using supportive communication in families is not easy, but is usually worth the effort. Applying the principles of effective interpersonal communications can make intimacy a rewarding situation.

Exercise: Possessiveness in My Family

Objective: To become aware of possessiveness behaviors in your family, whether by yourself or others.

Directions:
1. Keep a journal for one week, recording situations in your family when you observed possessiveness attitudes and resulting control behaviors, and what your perception of the result was.
2. Be sure to watch your own as well as others' behavior.

> We do not count a man's years until he has nothing else to count.
>
> RALPH WALDO EMERSON

Any analysis of family communication must include a discussion of communicating with the aged. Most of us now have, have had, or will have members of our family who have reached the so-called "golden" years. At best, these are people who add richness and experience to our family group. At worst, they are rejected isolates who contribute little but friction. For most families, communicating with elderly members falls somewhere between the two extremes. The experience is not totally unpleasant, but neither is it as pleasant as it could be. In this section we discuss some of the problems of the aged that affect their communication and suggest some approaches for improving your interactions with them.

Problems of Aging

More than 22 million United States citizens are over 65 and the number increases every year. Watch their faces and the story unfolds—too many feel tired, sick, unneeded and unwanted. They have so many unmet needs, and yet have so much they can still give. For too many, the years of old age are not golden at all, but instead years of poverty, loneliness, and boredom.

forced retirement results in unmet needs

The situation of many aged in our country is not of their own making. Retirement is forced on all but a few with often inadequate pensions. Present social insurance, though very expensive to government, does not accommodate the needs of the elderly at a comfortable level. Millions live on social security or welfare, barely at survival level. Others' income is from retirement programs that do not keep up with the continually rising cost of living. Thus, at an age when many are forced out of their jobs, fixed incomes are inadequate, survival needs only partly satisfied.

Low income also leaves safety needs unmet. Housing and transportation present problems. Homes that required a lifetime to pay for deteriorate. It becomes impossible to meet rising taxes and maintenance bills. Many houses cannot accommodate walkers or wheelchairs, and getting assistance with strenuous physical tasks without becoming entirely dependent is difficult. Adequate, safe, low-cost and convenient mass transit is absent from many (if not most) communities.

For most of the elderly, however, the problems of unmet survival and safety needs are less severe than the impact of retirement on the satisfaction of higher-level social and personal needs. Retiring can cause a great loss in satisfaction of the needs for love and belonging, esteem, and self-actualization. Reduced incomes, coupled with an inability to work productively in a work-oriented society, may cause social isolation. The mobility of this society has widely separated many old people from their families. Work companions no longer exist. Old friends may die. People in the community have no time or interest in "old fogey" neighbors. "Everybody needs somebody" is a truism. The need to love and be loved does not diminish with age.

The media in the U.S. celebrate youth and beauty, and society responds by spending millions on cosmetics and youthful fashions. Aged parents, grandparents, or neighbors are a painful reminder that "this, too, shall pass." In a society in which youth and physical beauty are very important, and the prevailing philosophy is to "live for today," the presence of old people is ignored, or worse, resented. When work is no longer a means for the elderly to belong to society, the social attitudes isolate them even further.

Above belonging in the hierarchy of needs are esteem and self-actualization needs. People need to feel that they are of value, that others consider them essential, or with high regard. For too many of the elderly, these needs for esteem and sense of self-worth are unmet. People who are forced to retire from a job often feel no longer useful. For many, retirement brings questions like "Now what? What is left?" Children are grown up, have moved away, and

Planning for retirement often is the difference between happiness and unmet needs. *Source: (left)* A. DeVaney, Inc., N.Y., *(right)* Al Kaplan—Design Photographers International.

no longer seek the advice of parents. Many of the aged lose a sense of worth, feel that they are no longer useful, needed, or wanted. Without the work that gave them a sense of contributing to society, the absent family connections are even more noticeable, and more painful.

poorly planned retirement

The problems cited above were those of people who didn't want retirement. But what of those who dreamed about retiring, waiting eagerly for the days when they didn't have to get up and go to work? Too few of them have planned for active retirement, and the reality of it is a shock. *Active retirement is how we describe the planning and execution of a lifestyle that enables a person to continue to grow after the working years are over.* This preparation is beyond financial considerations. Adequate money, is, of course, needed. But too many people think of retirement as an escape from the 8 to 5 drag—time to fish, hunt, play golf, or just rest and relax. Sadly, they soon become bored, and begin to long for those days they had so eagerly hoped to leave behind. They wish for the usefulness they had when employed; they miss the job that made weekends worth looking forward to. When all of life is a weekend, it may be a lost weekend.

People who work with the aged stress the need to plan for active retirement. An avocation, part-time or volunteer work, political campaigning, supervising investments, learning new skills, returning to school, all or any could fill the need for esteem and self-actualization. The necessity to fulfill these higher-level needs does not end at age 65; indeed, the trauma of a drastically changing lifestyle often strengthens and heightens this need. Unless they can feel productive and useful, it's difficult for the aged to maintain a sense of self-esteem. In a work-oriented society, in particular, people who have nothing to do find self-esteem hard to maintain.

Being productive is only part of active retirement. An important aspect of it is that it should include activities that make a person feel needed. Older people feel, often accurately, that their families no longer need them. When they fail to plan for active retirement, they find it difficult to meet people, to continue to develop relationships with others, to *grow.* Thus they reduce the chances of fulfilling esteem, belonging and love needs. When these are unmet, the sense of self-worth is weakened. Active retirement involves continuing activities to which a person feels committed, activities that offer interpersonal relationships and a sense of continued growth.

These factors are related. Everybody requires a sense of worth, which in part comes from being loved and needed, and in part comes from self-actualization. When these needs aren't met, damage to self-concept results in increasingly difficult communication. The lowering of self-esteem begins a vicious cycle that is no less destructive to older people than to youngsters. The self-fulfilling prophecy takes over. Persons often *become* inactive and useless because they believe they must be. The result confirms the lowered self-esteem. The spiral continues—downward. An elderly person who feels unwanted may not call the children or grandchildren— "They're busy and not interested anyway." He or she may not seek to make new friends—"Who wants to know *me*, I'm old and ugly"; may not volunteer for community services—"They don't *want* me." As a result, many elderly isolate themselves from community and family. They *become* more and more difficult to communicate with.

Improving Communication with the Aged

Communicating with elderly people who have some of these problems becomes very difficult. Those whose survival and safety needs are unmet are frightened and insecure; those who have increasingly lowered self-esteem perceive interactions as threats. They are closed and guarded and suspicious. Thinking badly of self leads to thinking badly of others—another vicious circle. It is common to evaluate others negatively in order to try to feel one isn't alone in being "Not O.K." Communicating with people who desperately need to love and be loved is difficult; they can be totally negative and rejecting, or they can cling and grasp and often stifle others in the relationship. Freedom, acceptance, and empathy are difficult to extend to people whose personal problems cause them to be demanding, suspicious, and self-pitying or closed, "turned off," and uncommunicative.

recognize the problems

The catalogue of problems we have listed here is rather depressing. Communicating with elderly persons is often difficult and demanding. Moreover, communication cannot solve many of the problems. They have societal causes and require societal cures, especially those related to survival and security. But some suggestions can be helpful. First, *be aware of the range of unmet interpersonal needs that may exist.* Listen to your old relatives actively and empathically. Empathy can enable you to realize the importance of communicating regularly with elderly family members. Many of us live long distances from aging parents and grandparents, and don't realize how important a visit or phone call can be to an old person. Even more of us who live close enough to visit often, do so with dread. We expect complaints, evaluations, distrust, and self-pity. But we forget the Pygmalion effect of our expectations. If we keep in mind that we tend to receive the kinds of messages we expect, we'll see how much we may cause the very behaviors we dread. Moreover, understanding all the causes of defensiveness in the elderly can help us prepare to deal with it. A basic understanding of the problems of the aged can in itself lead to empathy, acceptance, and other aspects of supportive communication.

reject the myths

One important problem facing many people as they age is that they and the society share largely inaccurate stereotypes about older people. Books, plays, television, movies, magazines all reflect these stereotypes. We are constantly confronted with the image of the senile, dirty old man and the crabby, meddlesome old woman. How long has it been since you've seen a *non*comic hero or heroine in a movie or TV show who was over 65?

But the media only reflect popular attitudes. Our interpersonal interactions reflect the same stereotypes. For example, what happens when sex over 60 is mentioned? It's the subject of snickers and jokes. Yet most recent research demonstrates that it should be no funnier than sex at any age. The predominant mood of the 1960s, "Don't trust anyone over 30," suggested that those over 60 are virtually out of commission. Unfortunately, while we have begun to accept that youth have important contributions to make toward social understanding, many have yet to accept that the old do too. Old age does not mean automatic senility, but our expectations of old age might *cause* it. History still has some things to teach us. If we reject the myths about the aged, we can begin to *communicate* with them—we can listen to them and personally benefit from their experiences. This can be a two-way street, increasing their sense of worth and, indeed, their *real* worth; we, too, can benefit from the exchange.

One result of prevailing societal myths about aged uselessness has been the coalescing of the elderly into retirement communities. Because human beings are endlessly adaptable, the results of these communities are not entirely negative. One analysis found that residents of a "senior citizen" housing project became increasingly involved with one another as a source of friendship, largely because of their segregation from families and places of work.

If we reject the stereotype of the sexless, useless aged, we can help make the community a place in which the elderly can participate without withdrawing from the larger society. We can provide the aid and/or encouragement needed to create interactions that allow older people to satisfy needs for love, belonging, esteem, and self-actualization. We can assist them in finding ways to meet and develop relationships with others, both of their age and younger. We can assist them in developing interests and activities outside their living rooms. We can help them find transportation to and from volunteer work, or political, or church activities. And from all of this we, too, can be richer.

Exercise: Family Group Characteristics

Objectives: To become aware of the characteristics of your family group.

Directions:

1. Analyze your family according to the following group characteristics:
   a. Purpose
   b. Length of existence and maturity
   c. Public or private
   d. Goals: agreement between member and group goals: goals shared or not shared
   e. Size
   f. Communication patterns
   g. Cohesiveness, satisfaction, attractiveness
   h. Interdependence and control
   i. Roles, norms, status: external and internal
   j. Decision-making processes
   k. Type of leadership; style of leadership
   l. Influence of power and authority

Communicating within families is at once the most rewarding and most difficult communication that many people have. Many sources of communication problems within families exist. They include: the absence of agreement on the family rules and rituals, and on the status and roles of family members; the failure to clarify or state the expectations that members have for themselves and others within the family relationship; the failure to remember that roles and status relationships in families require constant adjustments as members grow and develop and as the outside society changes; the imposing of parental double standards on children regarding adherence to rules and rituals; the absence of shared goals; the existence of divergent goals of family members.

Many problems of family communication arise solely out of the pressures of intimate living conditions. Living with someone else restricts the freedom of each individual. Many breakdowns are caused in family groups when, despite apparent agreement, there is really disagreement because of the assumption that meanings are shared by communicators. Also, because of closely shared experiences and faulty assumptions, there is a buildup of emotional loads on words and situations.

Perhaps the greatest source of communication breakdowns in families, however, stems from the existence of possessive attitudes the members of families have toward one another. Husbands and wives toward each other and parents toward children often display attitudes of ownership and the right to control the behaviors of the others. Parents behave in a controlling manner toward children because they believe in a responsibility to protect the children and teach them right from wrong. In doing this, however, parents fail to recognize that an individual learns from making choices freely, recognizing the consequences of those choices, and accepting the responsibility of having made the choice instead of blaming someone or something else for the consequences. Parents who behave possessively toward children, and husbands and wives who act that way toward each other, must learn to recognize the consequences of their behavior in defensive attitudes in the communication. It is possible to teach right and wrong by the use of unrestricted code phrasing. Acceptance between partners or parents and children provides more opportunity for the person to change than do evaluation and control.

Means of avoiding these potential breakdowns are sincere efforts to employ the principles of supportive communication: use of feedback to clarify messages, use of empathy to understand different viewpoints, acceptance and honesty, and employing noncontrolling attitudes.

A special problem of family communication is the necessity to deal with aging members. In the U.S., as people age, they are forced to retire. They are subject to decreased self-esteem because they no longer feel useful and because the society degrades age and venerates youth. Too few Americans have planned for active retirement and they find retirement a negative experience. The resulting decreases in need satisfaction produce people who are lonely, hostile, and defensive, with the obvious resultant communication problems. Communicating with the elderly is often quite difficult because of their defensive attitudes. By understanding the problems, family members can more easily respond with supportiveness, with acceptance, and empathy. They can also seek means of providing active retirement for the aged in their families.

1. How does contemporary society affect communication in families?
2. Why is communicating within the family one of your most difficult communication situations?
3. How do goals, roles, and expectations affect communication within your family?
4. How does possessiveness affect your family communication?
5. How can supportive communication be used to improve family relationships?
6. How can you cope with the special problem of communication with aged members of your family?

Suggestions for Further Reading

ADAMS, BERT N., *Kinships in an Urban Setting*. Chicago: Markham Press, 1969.

BLISTEN, DOROTHY R., *The World of the Family: A Corporate Study of Family Organizations in Their Social and Cultural Settings*. New York: Random House, 1963.

BLOOD, ROBERT O., AND DONALD M. WOLFE, *Husbands and Wives: The Dynamics of Married Living*. New York: The Free Press, 1960.

DOUGLAS, JACK D., *Understanding Everyday Life*. Chicago: Aldine Publishing Co., 1970.

ELKIN, FREDERICK, AND GERALD HANDEL, *The Child and Society*. New York: Random House, 1972.

ERICKSON, ERIK H., *Childhood and Society*. New York: W. W. Norton & Co., Inc., 1959.

GINOTT, HAIM, *Between Parent and Child*. New York: Avon Books, 1960.

———, *Teacher and Child. A Book for Parents and Teachers*. New York: Avon Books, 1972.

GOODE, WILLIAM, *The Family*. Englewood Cliffs, N.J.: Prentice-Hall, Inc., 1972.

GORDON, THOMAS, *P.E.T.: Parent Effectiveness Training*. New York: Peter H. Wyden, Inc., 1970.

LAVETELLI, CELIA A., AND FAITH STENDLER, *Readings in Child Behavior and Development*. New York: Harcourt Brace Jovanovich, 1972.

MATZA, DAVID, *Becoming Deviant*. Englewood Cliffs, N.J.: Prentice-Hall, Inc., 1969.

MCCALL, GEORGE T., et al., *Social Relationships*. Chicago: Aldine Publishing Co., 1970.

NISBET, ROBERT A., *The Social Bond*. New York: Random House, 1969.

O'NEILL, NENA, AND GEORGE O'NEILL, *Open Marriage*. New York: Avon Books, 1972.

ROGERS, CARL, *Becoming Partners: Marriage and Its Alternatives*. New York: Delacorte Press, 1972.

RUDDOCK, RALPH, *Roles and Relationships*. London: Routledge and Kegan Paul, Ltd., 1969.

SKOLNICK, ARLENE, AND JEROME H. SKOLNICK, eds., *Intimacy Family and Society*. Boston: Little, Brown and Co., 1974.

WINCH, ROBERT F., *The Modern Family*. New York: Holt, Rinehart & Winston, Inc., 1971.

12

Communicating at Work

goal:

To learn how to communicate more effectively in work situations.

probes:

The material in this chapter should help you:

1. Demonstrate the most effective method of gaining an interview for employment. pp. 316–18
2. Prepare for employment interviews. pp. 318–23
3. Explain how to use interviewee power. pp. 322–23
4. Use nonverbal communication effectively during interviews. pp. 323–25
5. Identify the different types of interviews and explain how to use each most effectively. pp. 326–329
6. Describe the differences between open and closed-end questions, showing how to use and respond to each appropriately. pp. 329–32
7. Define the term "organization," and distinguish between the formal and informal organizational structure. pp. 332–35
8. Give examples illustrating the difference between vertical and horizontal communication in organizations. pp. 335–39
9. Describe some of the problems of organizational communication and indicate some steps to cope with the problems. pp. 336–46
10. Indicate ways to cope with the problem of unclear role definitions in organizations. pp. 340–42
11. Describe some of the problems of secretaries in organizations and indicate how they might be solved. pp. 342–44
12. Use assertive communication effectively in work situations. pp. 350–54

Work is an important part of daily life. For most people, being at work, getting ready for it, getting there, and getting home consume most of their waking hours at least five days a week. So communicating within the work setting is critically important for most of us. And for most of us, communicating at work means communicating within an organization, whether large or small.

In this chapter we attend to two important aspects of communicating within organizations. First, we analyze the role of communication in interviews, concentrating on the entrance-employment interview. Then we discuss the organization itself, and several uses of communication that help us accomplish our tasks within the work situation.

INTERVIEWING

Interviewing is a form of oral communication involving two parties, at least one of whom has a preconceived and serious purpose and both of whom speak and listen from time to time.

ROBERT S. GOYER, W. CHARLES REDDING, JOHN T. RICKEY

Securing employment is something most of us don't do very often, but it's terribly important when we do. And getting jobs requires use of communication principles. In all interviews, whether you are the interviewer or interviewee, you need to know and apply principles of effective interpersonal communication. *Interviewing skills include accurate interpretation of information received, avoiding breakdowns, building trust, avoiding defensiveness, using feedback and listening skills,* and *sending clear messages.* Additional specific suggestions are also useful for the entrance-employment interview.

315

We intend to be quite specific here, and if you have already secured a few jobs in your life, you've used some of these suggestions. Even if you are already aware of the importance of the following ideas, you can benefit from a periodic review of them.

> It has been estimated that at least 150 million employment in-
> terviews occur in the United States each year.
>
> L. ULRICK, D. TRUMBO

Securing an Interview

The first step in preparing for interviews is securing one, and this
can be done in at least three ways. You can get an interview for a
job by calling, writing for an application, or by going to the organization and asking for one. Your application may be in response to
an advertisement, but shouldn't be limited to that. Many times you
can get into a reserve employment pool by seeking entrance to an
organization even if no job is available at the time.

apply in person

When you can, apply for jobs in person. Not only will this enable
you to gain information about positions available and the job requirements, but you can also learn a little about the organization.
By seeing it, the setting and layout, perhaps even by talking to
people who work there, you can infer much about the organization
that will help you in the interview itself. If you can't go in to arrange for the interview, the next best alternative is to telephone.
This way you can learn who might do the interviewing, and you can
ask questions about the job opening, requirements, and options regarding interviews. If you must telephone, remember to check all
inferences and information, since the chance for misunderstandings
is greater Often a letter confirming a phone conversation is useful
to be sure you have understood everything accurately.

letters of application

Sometimes you can neither phone nor go to the company or institution. Then you must write to secure a job interview. Because a
letter applying for a job or seeking information may be only one of
dozens an employer receives, you must do what you can to increase
the probability that it will be read and responded to favorably. Be
sure your letter is not recognizable as a form letter, even if it is.
Form letters tend to end up in wastebaskets. You can send a dupli-
cated résumé, but the letter accompanying it should be adapted so
that it applies individually to the particular organization.

If possible, direct the letter to a specific individual and use the proper title. Sending a letter to "Dear Sir" is much less desirable; besides, a "Dear Sir" salutation might create an unfavorable impression on a female department head or supervisor. If you can't find the name of the particular individual or the exact title, use "Dear Sir or Madam," or some non-sex-tied form of address, such as "Personnel Director."

This letter will be your first contact with the people in the organization who might hire you. It often is the first item in a file created to be studied by all who will participate in the hiring decision. Thus, this first letter is very important. Keep it brief, seldom more than one page. Put detailed information on a separate sheet in a résumé. Direct the letter specifically to items that make your application attractive to this particular employer. You may want to refer to items in your résumé, but don't try to put your entire history into the letter itself.

RÉSUMÉ FORM

Personal Data	Name, address, telephone number
Education	List from most recent to earliest Include all relevant education, not just in formal schools
Work Experience	List from most recent to earliest
Other Relevant Experience	Include anything relevant to *this* position
Honors and Awards	Include this only if the items to be listed are relevant to *this* position
References	Include names, positions, and relation to your work experience of at least three persons. Most important is to include your present employer or supervisor if you can

This form doesn't fit every case, but is a standard form that can be helpful. Such a summary statement like this is usually included with any application you make, whether the initial contact is by letter, telephone, or in person. When the résumé accompanies a letter, you should also indicate a willingness to send any additional information desired by this particular organization.

Above all, make sure both your letter and résumé, and anything you put on the application form itself, are neat and accurate. These documents create the first impression about *you* to a prospective employer. The nonverbal elements in them are often as important as the words themselves in creating good impressions.

Should your résumé include a picture? That is a judgment you will have to make for yourself, depending on many factors. You need to know your potential employer and your own assets and liabilities before you can decide whether a picture will be to your advantage or not. There is some evidence that those at the extremes of an "appearance continuum" should not include pictures. As you know, stereotyping and labeling affect first impressions, and your physical appearance in a photograph may not send the messages you want. This is a decision only you can make.

One problem in writing for jobs is that you have no way of knowing what will happen to your letter. You can improve your chances of getting a response by enclosing a self-addressed, stamped postcard. The person who receives your letter then can respond easily. The card might look something like this:

Date _____

Dear _____ : (insert your name with appropriate title)

We have received your letter.

_____ Your qualifications appear to meet minimum job requirements. Your application is being examined and you will hear from us later.

_____ At present we have no openings for which you would be qualified.

_____ An application form is being sent to you.

_____
(name)

_____
(title)

Using this technique will improve your chances of learning what has happened to your letter.

Preparing for the Interview

Once you have secured an interview, the next step is to *prepare* for it. You can do several things to be ready for your interview.

Find out how long the interview is expected to last. This will give you some idea of the depth and breadth of information that will be sought. Determine whether this is a screening interview, or if you will be hired on the basis of this one meeting. How many people or to whom will you talk?

Find out as much as possible about the organization itself. Learn about such things as products and services; employment policies; potential layoffs or transfers; competitive situation; union relations.

Learn what physical appearance will be the most appropriate. Generally, the guideline of being neat, clean, and natural will apply, but other limitations must often be considered. You might want to know organization or interviewer attitudes toward long hair, beards, length of skirts, amount and kind of makeup, formality and style of clothing. Either being too casual or too overdressed for a situation can destroy the impression you want to make. As always, the more you know about both the organization and the interviewers in advance, the better for you.

Find out how to get there. If you didn't visit the organization to apply, find out how to get there and how long it takes. Allow yourself plenty of time. Leave early enough to allow for error, traffic jams, mass transit delays, or parking problems. Your goal should be to arrive a few minutes (like 15) early so you can catch your breath, get acquainted with the place and situation, and appear at the interview slightly ahead of the appointed time. This will help convey an impression of punctuality and trustworthiness. Arriving late or hassled is almost guaranteed to get the interview off to a bad start.

Learn about the job. Only then can you decide how you fit it, if you want to fit it, what you might need to do to adapt yourself to fit, or how it might be adapted to fit you. Is the job long- or short-range, permanent or temporary? What potential does it have? Is it a starting point from which you can climb some kind of ladder? Will it provide upward mobility? What are the benefits, salary, and responsibilities?

You probably won't be able to find out all these things in advance. But you can learn some of them. And having made an attempt, you'll be more knowledgeable during the interview. This information will also help you know what questions you want to ask in the interview.

Think carefully about the questions you'll be asked. The résumé and application will have presented basic information about you, so interviewers will probably be seeking more interpretive information. They'll want to learn how you feel about your career and the potential job. They'll probe for your attitude toward the organization, its product or services. They'll be trying to assess how your personality and character might fit into the job or situation. If you consider these things in advance, you'll be better prepared to answer more completely and confidently.

Questions You May Be Asked in an Interview

1. Why do you believe you are qualified for this position?
2. How have your previous jobs or experiences prepared you for this situation?
3. What are your attitudes toward this organization? its product? its policies?
4. How do job security and job mobility compare in your value system?
5. Do you see this position as long-term?
6. What are your attitudes toward unions, their importance? What problems do you perceive from the presence or absence of unions in this organization?
7. How would you handle a conflict between yourself and a subordinate? between you and a supervisor? between two people of equal status in your department?
8. What are your occupational goals? (Commonly asked as, What do you see yourself doing in ten years?)
9. How do you feel about punctuality? Absenteeism?
10. Are there any home or personal problems that might interfere with your job performance?

We will have more to say later about the *types* of questions you may have to respond to.

Be ready to ask some of your own questions. Having given some thought to the interview and the position in advance will prepare you to get information you need. After all, employment-entrance interviews are not all one-sided. You, as the interviewee, also have an element of choice. Do you really want this job? Salary is not the only factor that will influence your decision. Consider the following questions and decide which ones you need answered before you make a decision.

Questions You May Ask During an Interview

1. What are wages (salaries), improvements, methods and intervals of performance reviews? means of advancement?
2. How does the organization support employee advancement? Are there educational grants or opportunities? training programs?

3. What kinds of unions are affiliated with the organization? What types of relations exist? Are any contract difficulties present? Are there no-strike clauses?
4. What are the layoff policies?
5. What is the organizational climate and morale?
6. What is the identifiable leadership? Do employees work in groups or individually?
7. What are the grievance procedures?
8. What are the channels for vertical communication?
9. What are organization relations with the community? consumers? related organizations?
10. What are the long- and short-term future plans of the organization?
11. What are the research and development facilities? means of long-range planning?
12. What are perceived potentials for advancement in this position?

Questions of this kind will show the interviewers that you've thought about the position and organization, and that you are interested enough to want to know more than wages, hours and pension plan. The questions you ask employers show what you're interested in; the intentions you have; the seriousness with which you've approached the interview.

Several factors in the interview situation will influence its success or failure. We isolate them for discussion under separate headings because they relate partly to your preparation before the interview and partly to things you may want to do during the interview itself.

determine expectations

One important aspect of the job interview involves the goals and expectations of both participants. *Goals should be clear* to you, if not before the interview, at least by the time you finish. Presumably, you know your own goals in the situation. Do you want to find out information about the organization and position? To get the job? To decide if you want it? To convince the interviewers you are qualified for it? To find out if you're qualified? To find out if you would fit into the organization? You should decide what your goals are before the interview. You can then direct your efforts toward accomplishing these goals.

What about the interviewers? Do they want information about your education and experience? Or information relative to personality and character? It's also useful to learn who sets the expectations of the interviewers. Are the expectations regarding preparation, experience, and personality based on organization policy or personal attitudes? What are the standards? Are the interviewers in a position to interpret and innovate within guidelines? Do they view their role as strictly that of deciding whether or not you fit predetermined qualifications? Is the policy of the organization rigid or flexible? Are interviewers rigid or flexible?

Finding the answers to these questions will sometimes involve talking to others besides the interviewers. It may be important to find out some things before the interview. Sometimes that isn't possible, so you'll need to ask questions during the interview. What you do or ask depends largely on the situation, the kind of job you are seeking, and the organization itself.

interviewee power

Another factor you should be aware of is your relative power as a participant. Power is defined as *the ability to influence someone else's behavior.* The degree of power varies, and generally in interview situations, interviewers are considered to have the most power. They usually set the time, place, and type of interview, and control the conversation and line of questioning.

Interviewers don't have all the power, however. You usually don't have to agree to an interview time that is inappropriate for you. You don't have to submit to a physical setting that is totally inappropriate. Though your ability to modify the setting may be somewhat limited, you have some control over the environment, perhaps to the extent of asking for a different location.

This factor is one you should assess carefully, but don't enter a situation thinking your only alternative is to follow the dictates of interviewers. In some situations and for some jobs, interviewers would be favorably impressed with the character, competence, and confidence of an interviewee who expressed dissatisfaction with a setting or situation, as long as specific, realistic suggestions for changing it were made. For example, if the interview was scheduled to be held in a cubicle that is crowded and not private, you have the option of suggesting a move to a coffee shop or another more pleasant surrounding. If the furniture places you in an awkward relationship to interviewers, you have the option of rearranging or suggesting a rearrangement of chairs, or at least moving your own chair to a better location.

Sometimes you are prevented from doing anything about an unpleasant or uncomfortable situation. In such cases, you still have the option of mentioning it. Acknowledging a difficult situation can have the effect of making it less difficult. At other times such an acknowledgment can call a difficulty to the attention of an interviewer who simply did not notice it before. At the very least, the interviewer is made aware that some negative impressions are due to the situation and not the interviewee.

It's also commonly thought that interviewers will ask the questions and control the conversation. We've already suggested you should have questions of your own. And you can and should decide which questions to answer briefly and which to answer with greater detail. In response to some questions, you can ask to have a question elaborated or clarified. "I'm not sure I understand . . ." or "Are you asking if . . .?" are acceptable responses to some questions. Never be rushed into replying hastily. Explaining a misstatement in response to a misunderstood question creates more difficulty than making sure the question is clear before replying. Usually interviewers consider it a sign of good judgment if you refuse to answer questions until you're sure what is being asked.

You can and should refuse to answer some questions. For example, it has been common in the past for interviewers to ask women seeking any job above the lowest clerical or maintenance positions about their family responsibilities and intentions. Now, these questions are not only prohibited by law, they are recognized as inappropriate and discriminatory. If you are a woman and faced with such questions, you can refuse to answer. You should not, of course, be hostile or sarcastic in your refusal. But a calm, confident refusal and redirection of the interview toward relevant professional or personal qualifications can be an asset to you. It can display your confidence and ability to deal with difficult situations.

You should also feel free to question the expectations laid down for the job. If you find that some of the requirements are too restrictive for your qualifications, you can take the initiative in showing why the expectations are unreasonable, or not necessary for the job. You can show why you have special qualifications or abilities that make up for not meeting some of the predetermined expectations.

Behavior during the Interview

Much of what we're about to add here goes without saying for most people. Much of what makes a good impression in an interview is simply applying common sense. But in the stress of an interview situation, people sometimes forget their common sense, so permit us for a bit to state the obvious. You should attempt to control four major elements during the interview: eye contact, personal space, body action, and voice.

eye contact

Eye contact is probably the single most important variable in an interview. Good eye contact, in our culture, suggests confidence, honesty, interest. You will convey a better impression if you look directly at your interviewer both when listening to questions and when answering them. In addition, as you know, good eye contact improves communication. You can do more than hear what interviewers ask. You can assess how they feel about what they're asking, and decide how important the question is to them. You can assess how they react to your answers. Eye contact will help you judge to a large extent the impression you are creating.

personal space

The element of personal space is also one you should be alert to, as noted in our discussion of interviewee power. Appropriate personal space depends partly on the particular job or position. Review the information from Chapter 3 regarding personal distances for different degrees of formality. Assess both the interviewer and the organization to determine what personal space would be comfortable in this situation. If your aim is to dominate, you may want to invade an interviewer's personal space, but such a tactic should be used with care. It can create negative impressions and could backfire. Certainly you don't want to establish so much distance between you and the interviewer that you appear cold and overly formal. If you can choose seating, take a seat that will foster the impression you want. If you have a choice of side-by-side or face-to-face seating, choose the latter. If physical barriers separate you, eliminate or work to minimize them. Establish a distance that is close enough to convey the degree of formality and warmth you judge appropriate.

body action

Body action is another element of the interview that you should control. Slouched, too-casual *posture* is as bad as being excessively stiff and formal. Sit comfortably, where you can face the interviewer, and lean toward him/her slightly. This will convey an impression of poise and interest. Nervous *mannerisms* should be controlled. Don't fiddle with a pencil, your hair, a mustache, your purse. Chewing gum or fingernails is out. Restless drumming of fingers, tapping or swinging of feet won't suggest confidence or competence. Sometimes you'll fall into one or more personal mannerisms as you think about a difficult question. That's probably not harmful. It will help convey the part of you that's real. What you don't want to show is excessive nervousness, insecurity, lack of confidence. One behavior should be considered carefully: *smoking*. Avoid it if you believe it could have a negative impact; and when you do smoke, be sure to ask if it's O.K. Many people have negative reactions to smoking, and that attitude could be transferred to you.

Facial expressions are important. You should be as honest in conveying yourself, your feelings, and attitudes as is possible within the constraints of the situation. If not, your face will probably betray you anyway. But interviews demand control. It's critical to avoid all mannerisms and nervous habits that in any way suggest you don't feel equal to the situation.

Among the most important elements of body actions is the first entrance. The *handshake,* while not always appropriate, is usually a good way to establish that you feel confident and competent. "Pressing the flesh," as President Lyndon Johnson used to describe it, is a source of important information in the work world in the U.S. But remember, stereotypes accompany handshakes. You'd best have a firm, confident grasp or avoid the handshake. This is especially true for the women among our readers. One of the pervasive stereotypes facing women who attempt to move up in the working world is that they are passive, weak, and not up to the stress of organizations. Guard against a weak, wobbly, handshake that reinforces the stereotype. Reaching out to shake the hands of interviewers, whether you're male or female, is a good way to suggest confidence. But make sure the handshake equals the expectation.

voice

Finally, your voice is an important element in conveying a good impression in an interview. Talking too loudly or with a high-pitched voice can display nervousness. Women particularly need to guard against letting their voices rise under the stress of the interview. Again, stereotypes must be combated. Aggressiveness is needed and sought for in many jobs, especially management positions. But conveying the proper impression of aggressiveness is difficult for women because of the stereotype that aggressive women are bitchy and hard to get along with. One of the strongest conveyors of this unpleasant impression is the voice. A tense, high-pitched voice is often the difference between a woman who is a nag and one who is appropriately assertive. Because voices tend to rise under stress, attention should be given to keeping the *pitch* low and the voice pleasantly modulated.

All interviewees need to make sure their voice *volume* is appropriate for the setting. Talking too loudly is interpreted as nervous or boorish. Talking too softly signals lack of confidence and insufficient aggressiveness to get the job done. Note the acoustics of the setting and regulate your voice volume accordingly.

If your voice is tight or strained or your mouth becomes dry while you talk, don't hesitate to ask for a drink of water. It will often relax your vocal cords just to swallow the water, and being thirsty is normal enough if the interview is at all lengthy. Even if you don't drink coffee, it's not a bad idea to accept a cup at the outset of the interview when it's offered, because often water won't be available. Then if your voice gets dry, you can sip on the coffee.

Finally the interview should be closed with skill. The interviewer will usually signal when it's over, but you should never leave without finding out what further information that person may want, what follow-up steps will be appropriate, and how and when you may learn the outcome. Be sure to establish what comes next and who will be responsible for doing it.

Exercise: Employment Interviews

Objective: **To become aware of the differences in roles, power, and use of communication in various interviewing situations.**

Directions:

1. Construct interview questions that you would plan to use both as interviewer and interviewee in the following situations.
2. In class, you will be assigned in groups of two to role play the various situations.
3. For a few minutes before each role-playing session, discuss with your classmate to agree upon the missing data in each situation: e.g., what company, specific job, sex, or ethnic background of both parties, etc.
4. After each role-playing situation discuss
   a. What preconceptions regarding each role did each person bring to the situation?
   b. What communication skills could you use to improve the outcome?

Situation I:

A white male personnel director is interviewing a prospective female fork-lift truck driver for a position in a plant that presently has all men employees.

Situation II:

An owner of a small business is discussing possible employment with a black college student. The business is a retailing establishment with several outlets in a metropolitan area.

Situation III:

A sales manager is conducting an interview for a sales position with a high school dropout.

Situation IV:

A young mother is interviewing a 20-year-old male college student for employment as a babysitter for her 4- and 5-year-old children for five hours every morning during the summer.

Situation V:

A female advertising supervisor is interviewing a newly graduated male advertising major for a job in the office.

Other Types of Interviews

Up till now we have been talking about you as an interview*ee*. Now let's consider some common situations in which you might be the interview*er*. Most commonly the interviews used at work are for information gathering, performance appraisal, giving reprimands, or persuasion. We'll introduce each type briefly.

information gathering

You often need to interview people at work to secure specific information. One way to get it is to go to the person or people who have the information and ask for it. Of course, informational interviewing as done by journalists, poll takers, and researchers is beyond the scope of this book. Those certainly require skillful use of speech communication, and to prepare to do that kind of interviewing you need more in-depth study. Still, many of us with less sophisticated needs use the information gathering interview.

The basic guidelines for this kind of interview are simple. Plan in advance. Decide exactly what you need to know. Plan questions to elicit specific responses. Make clear at the outset of the interview precisely what you need to know. Ask your questions as concisely and concretely as possible. Don't waste time, but be sure to give the person time to give you all useful information. Use the techniques of active listening to be sure you understand what you hear.

performance appraisal

Another common interview in work settings is performance appraisal. These interviews are often very distasteful for both parties. Too often it's simply when the boss, usually much belatedly, sits down and tells you what you aren't doing right. When carried out effectively, a performance appraisal interview is far more. It gives the employee an opportunity to see how the supervisor perceives job performance, including strengths, weaknesses, and what the future in the job is. At the same time, it gives the supervisor an opportunity to learn how the employee sees the same things. The performance appraisal is often the employee's best opportunity to ask what the supervisor expects.

Effective performance appraisal usually involves a written assessment by the supervisor of the employee's work and a similar self-appraisal by the employee. Each then reviews the assessment of the other and they discuss the two sets of perceptions. Discussion is focused on job-related factors. Performance, not personality, is the topic for effective performance appraisal interviews.

One effective way for this discussion to be directed is for supervisor and employee to mutually establish a set of goals or objectives for the employee to accomplish in a specified period of time. Then the two can meet again periodically (and regularly) to assess progress toward these goals. This is called *management by objec-*

tives, and it provides an ideal way to combine performance appraisal with goal setting by the person being evaluated.

A major problem in performance appraisal is that it tends to be conducted in a defensive climate. If the total climate of the organization or the relationship between the two individuals involved is open, permissive, and supportive, defensiveness can be reduced. This is why focus on anything other than task-related factors is inappropriate. Discussing non–job-related issues, such as personality, increases ambiguity of the items discussed and reduces the objectivity of both parties.

reprimands

Another type of interview sometimes needed at work is the reprimand. This happens when a supervisor finds that an employee has violated some organizational policy, principle, or procedure. In this situation, the supervisor should first determine why the violation occurred. Was it due to lack of information? Did the employee not know the policy? Or was the problem a motivational one? Did the employee willfully behave contrary to organizational policy? In this stage of the interview, the techniques of information gathering are needed. The supervisor needs to avoid prejudging, and to give employees the opportunity to be heard.

When the supervisor decides why the violation occurred, the rest of the interview follows naturally. If the violation was due to lack of information or failure to understand, the supervisor needs to give the necessary information. If it is determined, on the other hand, that the problem for which the interview is required is a willful or motivational problem, then the procedure differs. The supervisor should be totally clear in indicating what is the perceived violation, how serious the organization considers it, and what will be done if the violation is repeated. Then the matter of how to respond is up to the employee.

Effective communication within reprimand interviews can reduce the amount they are needed. First, a supervisor should be sure that preplanning is adequate. Any penalty planned as a consequence of repeated violation must be appropriate. This means several things. It should fit the violation, not being too severe so that higher management will uphold it in case of an appeal. At the same time, it should not be too minor so that it fails to deter behavior. Moreover, the penalty should be possible to implement. Planning is necessary to insure that the penalty is within organizational policy and the contractual arrangements that govern employees. This kind of forethought has another advantage. Having given careful consideration to the penalty in advance, the supervisor will be less likely to respond with either anger or defensiveness if an employee responds emotionally to the reprimand.

Once the supervisor has determined what is an appropriate penalty if the behavior that created the need for the reprimand continues, clear communication is essential. The supervisor needs to use feedback, asking questions and being sensitive to nonverbal as well as verbal responses. Only in this way can the supervisor be certain that the employee understands what the problem was, and what the penalty for continued violation will be. Indeed, without such accuracy, ambiguous reprimands can actually increase the number required.

The need for this kind of interview can be greatly reduced by effective performance appraisal conducted on a regular basis and by an open, supportive climate within the organization. Open communication channels within the organization, and effective job orientation (also a communication activity) help to give the employees the information they need in an atmosphere that will encourage them to do their work in accordance with company policies.[1]

persuasive interviews

Another type of work-related interview is the persuasive interview. In this situation one person has a goal in terms of selling something or convincing another person of an idea or a course of action. In the general sense that persuasion involves influencing someone else's behavior, all the previously mentioned types of interviews are persuasive. But in this case persuasion refers to a goal of selling another person a product, an idea, or a course of action. While many of the techniques of interviewing still apply, the principles of persuasion are more useful. The information included in Chapters 13 and 14 will help you learn how to conduct persuasive interviews.

Using Questions

Questions are what interviews are primarily about. We all know that answers we get in any situation depend on the kinds of questions asked. This is as true of interviewing as of other situations. Basically, questions used in interviews can be divided into two categories: *open-end* and *closed. An open-end question has no restrictions on the answer*. It seeks a response, but the answerer must provide the structure for the response. "What do you feel about the new policy?" "How do you react to the president's statement?" are examples of open-end questions. *Closed questions are*

---

[1] Grievance interviews are related to reprimands, but we don't spend time discussing them because procedures are usually carefully prescribed within each organization.

restrictive. They indicate specifically what answer is desired. The most closed question asks for a yes or no, as in "Will you do it?" Others ask for a less restricted, but still limited response. For example, "How often did you report under the old policy: daily, weekly or semi-annually?" or, "Is the president's statement acceptable to you, or do you think it should be modified?"

Often the two types of questions are combined. If, for instance, you replied to the question above, "Yes, it needs modification," the questioner might ask, "How?" This represents a combination of primary and follow-up questions. A questioner may begin with a general, opening question, then use several follow-up questions to investigate an entire area. Follow-up questions may also be used when the primary question doesn't elicit the information sought. Follow-up questions can vary from the open-ended "Yes, go on" to a slightly more restricted "For example?" or "Then what happened?" A questioner who isn't sure of understanding a response might say, "I'm not sure I understand—could you clarify?" Often follow-up questions seek clarification or definition of concepts referred to, or words used: "How much is a significant increase to you?"

More valuable than simply knowing the types of questions that can be used is to know which to use for what purposes and how to respond to them. *Open-end questions require you to assess the intent of the questioner.* You have to decide, "What is that person getting at?" Then you must decide how to respond.

In responding to open-end questions it's often appropriate to probe before answering, to learn the sense of the question. When asked for opinions regarding George's plan, you might respond, "Do you want to know if I think it's workable? Or if I like the idea? Or did you want me to estimate its cost?" It's not at all unreasonable to use feedback before you answer a question to try to insure you know what is sought. Nor is it inappropriate to seek to learn the general intent of the questioner. One of the worst things you can do in most interviews is to waste time. And it's easy to waste time if you answer in a totally different manner from a questioner's intent. Finally, once you've decided what an open-end question seeks, remember to provide some structure in your response. Decide what the question means and organize your response accordingly.

From a questioner's point of view, *open-end questions are useful because they tell more about the mind frame of the person answering.* A closed question suggests the alternative responses. When you don't want to structure the answer, use an open-end question, which will reveal the perspective of the respondent. Open questions seek to probe feelings, discover points of view and attitudes. For those purposes they are often useful.

The major *disadvantages of open-end questions are that they result in subjective responses and are time-consuming.* Answers often go in directions you aren't interested in, and people often ramble in response. Many people cannot structure answers to respond to open-end questions meaningfully. If that limitation is what you're attempting to discover, however, the time may be well used.

Preplanning can help you decide which type of questions to use and how to combine questions to achieve your purposes in the interview. In all kinds of interviews preplanning is important. The person who initiates the interview should know what the goal of the session is and have a plan for achieving it. Interviews should be conducted with a definite structure in mind. At the beginning the interviewer makes clear to all participants what the purpose of the session is, and in a general way, what the procedure will be. This is an agenda, in essence, and as in any discussion, it should be followed as long and as closely as it's useful. As with all agendas, it should be changed if need arises, but having a plan changed for good reasons is much better than not having a plan at all. Finally, interviews should have closure. Once the goal is achieved it should be made clear, as well as clarifying who has follow-up responsibilities and what they are.

In short, interviewing is similar to other forms of discussion, and has the elements of roles, norm, and status relationships, the elements of organization, nonverbal communication, and the elements of interpersonal relationships. Thus, much of the information throughout this book is relevant toward the accomplishment of particular goals in a two-person setting.

Exercise: Interviews

Objective: To practice communication skills required for interviews in work settings other than entrance-employment interviews.

Directions:
1. Construct interview questions and plans for the following situations. Plan as both the interviewer and interviewee in each situation.
2. In class, you will be assigned to groups to role play the various situations.
3. For a few minutes before each role-playing situation, decide with your classmate(s) about the missing specific data needed to complete the role play—e.g., age and sex of participants, location, other necessary details.

Situation I:
A plant manager conducting a problem-solving interview with a good engineer who is chronically late for work.

Situation II:
A school teacher discussing a motivation problem with an eighth-grade student and his/her parents.

Situation III:
A concerned citizen arguing for stricter controls over public relations

advertising by oil companies. The citizen is talking with a local television station manager.

Situation IV:

A welfare caseworker discussing a housing problem with an elderly couple.

Exercise: Types of Questions

Objectives: To practice phrasing closed and open-end questions.

Directions:

1. Choose two of the situations specified in the preceding exercise, "Interviews."
2. For each situation, phrase three open-end questions and three closed questions.
3. For each question, specify the purpose. What do you hope to learn by the question and why did you choose for it to be an open, or a closed question?
4. In class, in groups, you will be asked to compare your questions and discuss the following questions:
   a. How could each question be improved?
   b. Considering the purpose for which it was intended, was it appropriately phrased as either open or closed?

THE ORGANIZATION

> Community is orchestrated individuality.
>
> REUEL HOWE

In this section, we discuss strategies for coping with the communication problems that are peculiar to *organizations. We think of organizations as complex systems that intentionally coordinate the actions of their members for accomplishing specific purposes.* What does calling an organization a complex system suggest? In a system, individual parts interrelate to form a whole. In organizations, many parts exist, each with particular functions related to the systemwide goals.

Structure

Organizations usually seek to accomplish their goals through a division of tasks and functions, supervised through a structure of authority and responsibility. The structure aims to coordinate members' behaviors toward organization goals. Because system and individual members' goals are not always the same, these differences are common sources of communication problems within organizations. For the continued existence of any organization, however. at least minimum coordination of members' behaviors toward system goals is essential. This coordination is the function of the formal organization.

the formal organization

The formal organization structure is created to accomplish organizational goals. In most organizations the formal structure of authority and responsibility is *hierarchical.* It reflects the levels of management created to supervise the various parts of the system. The structure often has a president or board chairperson who has ultimate responsibility for managing the organization. Subordinate levels of authority often include several vice-presidents, more division and department heads, and many supervisors (foremen). At the bottom are workers with no authority over any other employees and responsibility only for the specific tasks they are to do.

Whatever titles may be used, they reflect the levels of authority and responsibility. This formal structure is often represented in organizational charts such as this:

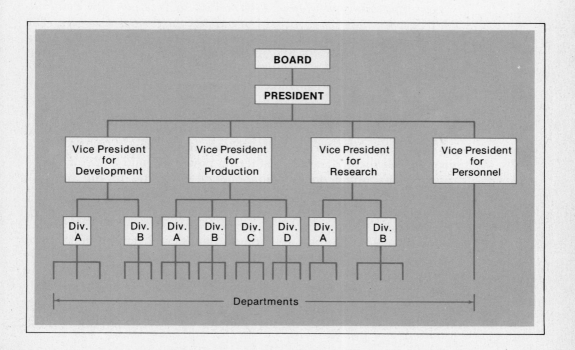

Organizations consist of many subgroups. A department, unit, division, or company is often a subsystem within a larger system, as Pontiac is a company within the General Motors system. Subsystems also contain subgroups, as when departments exist within divisions. All subgroups, whatever the level, develop their own roles and norm systems even while they are influenced by the expectations of the larger organization. A department, for instance, must work within company policies, but often interprets them in its own way. For example, "on time" according to policy may be 8:00 A.M., but if no one in the department gets upset when you regularly arrive at 8:15, then the norm for "on time" in that department is 8:15. Thus, the department norm differs from the formal organization policy. Because most of us work within an organization subgroup, we need to be aware of subsystem roles and norms as well as those of the larger system.

Groups within organizations are interrelated and interdependent. The Production Department cannot accomplish a task without the aid of Engineering, and both are dependent on Purchasing. *The need for coordination among the subsystems creates a need for effective communication to accomplish organization goals.* The interrelationships create complex networks of communication even within the formal organization structure.

the informal organization

The term *informal organization* refers to *interpersonal relationships within the organization, but outside the formal structure.* The informal organization is not determined by the formal structure, but sometimes parallels it. It reflects contacts from social and interpersonal interactions among individuals in the organization.

The informal organization often constitutes formidable power. While authority results from position in the formal structure, power does not rely on the formal organization. Power springs from broader bases: recognized competence, perceived potential upward mobility, special interpersonal relationships, access to critical information. All these means of gathering power beyond a specific position in the formal organization operate primarily in the informal structure. For example, suppose that in a company with two vice-presidents, the president and vice-presidents have a regular Wednesday afternoon golf game that includes department head Jones. Jones, one of six department heads, will have higher status in the informal organization than other department heads primarily because of access to information and interpersonal relationships not available to the others. Similarly, if four department heads regularly lunch together, but two others do not, this both reflects and creates informal structure as well as power and influence. Many businesswomen find themselves without the power of their male colleagues because they are excluded, or exclude themselves, from groups that lunch together daily. By not participating in the informal structure, they do not acquire the power it often provides.

The informal structure cannot be described as readily as the formal structure. Being aware of it, however, can help you understand how an organization operates. The informal structure fills many gaps in the formal; individuals' influence and power often make more sense in terms of the informal organization than the formal. Anyone trying to get ahead in an organization needs to understand the informal structure. Violating it can cost you your job; using it can gain advancement for you.

Communication Channels

> One conclusion is eminently clear: Today's organization requires communication performance at an unprecedented level of excellence.
>
> WILLIAM HANEY

Communication occurs along both the formal and informal organization structures. Formal structure determines the channels of most official communication in work settings. The formal channels are the legitimate interoffice, interdepartment, intraoffice, intradepartment, level-to-level communication systems. Sending and receiving messages within formal channels is regulated by prescribed means and methods. For instance, in most organizations, not everyone can pick up the phone and call the president directly. Instead, assistants and secretaries act as *gatekeepers* to communication lines to the president, screening messages that get to and from the top. Members who aren't aware of the formal channels of communication, or for some other reason fail to follow them, can encounter real trouble. Official communications usually must follow the chain of command. A complaint lodged elsewhere will be considered "going over the head" of the person in the proper position, and can create hard feelings or even worse repercussions for the complainant. Many communications will not even be recognized until they are processed through proper channels. A grievance that lands first in the wrong office will often be sent directly to the proper place without any consideration *and* with a reprimand to the source of the communication, unless the informal organization is at work.

vertical channels

The vertical channel has great importance in the formal structure. Communication along this channel is both upward and downward.

Downward Communication. Downward communication channels messages originating higher in the organization to lower levels. Examples of downward communication are messages from board to president, president to vice-presidents, vice-presidents to department head, supervisors to laborers, or spanning the structure, from president to workers. Downward communication usually serves specific functions for the organization:

1. To give instructions or orders
2. To give rationale for jobs or relationships within the organization
3. To give information about procedures and practices
4. To give feedback on job performance
5. To provide explanations of organizational goals.

Downward communication is usually not direct from the top to the bottom of an organization unless it's in writing. Oral messages usually pass down the chain of command before reaching their final destination. This is called *serial communication.* (See Chapter 9.)

Upward Communication. Upward communication starts in the lower levels of the formal structure and moves up, following the chain of command. Laborers' messages to foremen, department heads to vice-presidents, vice-presidents to president, president to board are examples of upward communication. Upward communication is also serial communication. And in the formal channels, upward communication, whether written or oral, doesn't usually cross more than one level. Only rarely does a laborer initiate a message directly to a president or vice-president. Upward communication is usually directed through department and division heads in formal channels.

problems of vertical communication

Because most vertical communication is serial communication, it suffers from all the problems of serial communication. Studies of serial communication show that as much as 70 percent of information is lost or changed between its original source and the ultimate receiver.[2] Upward communication is especially subject to distortion, often more so than downward. Upward communication usually requires an employee to report to a supervisor, or to someone with power over her/his job. Thus many people are closed and guarded

---

[2] Gordon Allport and Leo Postman, *The Psychology of Rumor* (New York: Holt, Rinehart & Winston, 1947).

in these interactions. Employees tend to tell the boss only what they think he/she wants to hear, or only what they want that person to hear.

Because vertical communications in organizations are between people who are unequal in status, defensiveness frequently causes more distortion of the messages than is due simply to its serial nature. Employees often don't hear their supervisors' intended messages because defensiveness causes suspicion and mistrust. Very different perceived messages between unequals in communication are common. Studies within organizations have shown that personnel at the top often have widely different perceptions of company policies, aims, functions, and climate from those at the bottom.

Free use of vertical communication channels is the best way to improve accuracy of communicating within organizations. Employees should feel free to speak openly to their supervisors and other higher company officers without fear of reprisal. Then communication throughout the organization will be better not only because it's more accurate but also because there is more of it. The people at the top will know their organization, its capabilities and limitations much better; the people in lower levels will understand company policies, plans, and goals much better.

Achieving this communication climate is not easy. Differences in positions, status, roles, and perspectives interfere with communication in organizations. Individual supervisors can try to reduce defensiveness when they talk with employees, but their efforts are often hampered by the total organization climate. Moreover, the supervisory-evaluative role, and other influences beyond individuals' control, can interfere with open communication. In most organizations, the hierarchy and the evaluative structure cause defensiveness in workers even when individual supervisors behave supportively. If you refer to Likert's scale for participative management (pp. 278–79) you can see many behaviors that can be employed to help keep open communication channels in organizations.

What can employees lower in the organization do to increase the accuracy of communication? For one thing, they can check with more than one source to verify information. Obviously, this isn't possible or even desirable in all situations. If you were given a task to do by your supervisor, it wouldn't be considered kindly if you checked with someone else regarding the accuracy of the assignment. A safer method to check accuracy of communications received from above is to *use feedback to clarify messages* when they are received.

Awareness of supportive communication climates is important for all members of an organization, but the primary burden of keeping vertical channels open lies with the people at the top. In communications between unequals, only those at higher levels can create the organization climate that counters defensiveness. Only they can prevent status, roles, and job insecurity from closing channels and preventing the transmission of important information. In communications between boss and secretary, laborer and supervisor, department head and president, the subordinate can do little to create a climate of openness. It is really up to those in mid-management and higher positions to create and maintain the all-important supportive communication climate.

horizontal and diagonal channels

Horizontal communication channels are direct communications among peers, or between members of departments of equal stature in the organization. Horizontal communication occurs among the laborers, among the supervisors, among equal departments, among the vice-presidents, among the members of the board. *Horizontal channels provide interrelations required for the total system to function.* They enable the right hand to know what the left hand is doing, and thus must be kept open to insure the achievement of organizational goals.

In diagonal channels, communication crosses departments and levels. For example, a clerk in Engineering may call the head of Purchasing to find out what is holding up a late order, instead of first going to the Engineering department head. Diagonal channels that cross more than one level tend to be informal. The official chain of command usually doesn't provide for diagonal communication to cross more than one level. Informal structure often reflects diagonal channels that follow networks from top to bottom.

Improving Organizational Communication

Accurate communication along all channels is vitally important to organizational survival. Accomplishment of organization goals re-

Too much paper can result in less communication.
Source: Sybil Shelton.

quires it. Members at all levels must exert constant concern for accuracy in communication. Several approaches can help limit distortion, especially in serial communication. *Written messages* can help, though all the nonverbally transmitted information is lost when spoken messages are changed to written. The memo pads labeled "Write it, don't say it" in many companies illustrate that this method is often used. But people often find themselves buried in an avalanche of paper and fail to read carefully the many memos and reports they receive. Thus, writing messages is no panacea. People who expect memos and newsletters to solve communication problems within an organization are naive.

Usually, once decisions are made, it's best to record them in writing. Memos confirming important telephone decisions and minutes of conclusions drawn at meetings are examples. *Learning what to write down and what to transmit orally is one of the most important lessons in learning to work effectively in any organization.* Part of the answer to the question of when to use oral and written messages depends on the particular organization and its climate. Your behavior must fit the system, at least to a degree. Part of the answer depends on whom you are dealing with. Some people respond better to messages in writing; some to speech; others require both. No simple answer to the question, "When should I write it down?" exists. Your best guideline is *use feedback* to be aware if accuracy is achieved. In addition, create written records when they are valuable or required in the system.

Informal communication channels function both for the individuals and for the total system. *The informal channels reflect and create opinion leadership that doesn't appear on the organizational chart.* In some departments, the most influential person is not the department head; in some work units, the real supervisor is not the one with the title at all, but a worker of special strength, expertise, or influence. The climate of some groups is controlled by a leader who has low formal status, but without whose approval and cooperation the unit's success will not be secured either. Knowing these informal influences within an organization can help you be more effective in the organization, whether in accomplishing personal or systemwide goals.

Communication Problems at Work

Dozens of communication situations arise in work settings that require special application of communication skills. At one time or another during a work week you probably need to understand fellow workers; deal with those who are at different levels; work to develop or maintain trust relationships; cope with conflict and/or defensiveness; listen actively and critically; listen empathically;

make decisions in groups; persuade someone to do something. The list could continue to include virtually every topic covered in this book. We don't intend to repeat everything here, but we will recognize some special problems within the work setting, and suggest ways of solving them. It's not possible to suggest all the answers to the problems. Not all can be solved. But, use of the appropriate communication skill or principles can help you seek solutions.

You'll notice we approach most of these situations from the employee's perspective. That's not because supervisors need not be interested. They certainly are, for in truth, management is primarily communication. People training to become managers need much study of communication — more than they can get in this book. The principles included here provide a foundation for managers to build upon. Important as any other supervisory skill is ability to understand the employee's point of view. Thus, the material below can be helpful to supervisors and employees alike.

unclear role definitions

The problem of unclear roles confronts many people who work in an organization in which a clear or strong contractual arrangement doesn't govern them. Usually, but not entirely, this occurs in non-union situations. But even union contracts do not always clarify every job in an organization.

The major difficulty in dealing with unclear role definitions occurs because job limits are not clear. In these situations, employees may be expected to perform far beyond what they believe they have been hired for. Many of us cause this problem for ourselves. We are often so anxious to have a job that we don't ask to find out exactly what the limits of the job are. We accept a kind of open-ended contract, with the supervisor or employer holding all the cards.

No simple solution to this problem exists. One thing that can help is to ask the employer or the supervisor to specify the tasks you agreed to when you took the job. Ask for a *written job description*. This will clarify the job. But if your particular problem is caused by a supervisor's excessive expectations, simply writing them down won't solve anything. Still, most people are reasonable, and if expectations are unreasonable, writing them all in a single list can illustrate the problem.

Written job descriptions can solve a slightly different problem, *inconsistent expectations.* In such cases you may be expected to do one thing one time and at other times are reprimanded for doing exactly that same thing. Inconsistency may be more frustrating than excessive demands that at least are always the same. With specified job limits, inconsistent expectations can usually be identified and eliminated.

You also need to recognize that advantages to unclear job limits also exist. More freedom exists in places where work roles are ambiguous. Written job descriptions can be limiting of individual effort and initiative. Perhaps you choose to go beyond what is expected of you so you can demonstrate you are capable of doing another job, are worthy of promotion, or are really invaluable to the company. Writing a job description won't tell you when to exceed the limits and when not to. These are matters of personal judgment, depending on particular situations. Still, having clear job limits can make it more obvious to both you and your supervisor when you are exceeding them, whether to your own or the company's benefit.

In many situations it's difficult to secure a written job description, especially after having established the work contract orally. Some supervisors resist specifying job descriptions precisely because they do limit that person's freedom to make demands. You might accomplish the result by seeking not just a single job description, but a clarification of roles throughout the organization, as in an employee's manual. Creating an employee's manual is usually management's responsibility, but in its absence, employees can informally accept responsibility for developing their own job descriptions. Employees can form groups to achieve specific goals.[3] You can sometimes increase your likelihood of getting more favorable responses from an employer or supervisor when a group rather than an individual is involved. Assess your situation carefully, however, before attempting any type of group action. You might stand a better chance of securing your goals working alone. Think carefully about the goals you seek before choosing channels and means of communication to achieve them.

need for assertive behavior

A problem many people encounter at work is the need for assertive behavior. While it is suggested by some, perhaps accurately, that the difference between being assertive and being aggressive is in the perceiver and not in the behavior, it's still worthwhile to recognize the need for assertive behavior. Many of us occasionally (or even frequently) allow someone to take advantage of us. One popular book illustrates the problem in its title, *When I Say No, I Feel Guilty.*[4] Another recent publication even tells people how to get ahead in the business world by intimidating other people.[5] Assertiveness is useful in all aspects of our lives, but it is essential in

---

[3] This is not to suggest that employees in all organizations should form unions. Indeed, unions and written contracts are not appropriate in many work situations.

[4] Manuel J. Smith, *When I Say No, I Feel Guilty* (New York: Dial Press, 1975).

[5] Michael Korda, *Power, How to Get It, How to Use It* (New York: Random House, 1976).

work situations. This is particularly true where you have unequal status relationships, whether they are unequal in the formal hierarchy or in the informal organization. Whatever your level in the organization, you can use assertive communication to cope effectively with people around you.

To be assertive means that, regardless of the difference in status levels between you and others, you are *aware of the basic rights that parallel your responsibilities and are willing and able to assert these rights.* You will be listened to, and probably respected, if you assert yourself. If you believe yourself in need of learning how to communicate assertively, you'll find the appendix at the end of this chapter helpful.

the secretary's role

The communication problems confronting people in the secretarial role are complex and numerous. We can't possibly cover all of them here, but we want to note some of the difficulties that arise from this unique service role.

The Gatekeeper Position. Secretaries are often gatekeepers who occupy a critical position within the institution's grapevine system. Secretaries must recognize their gatekeeper position. For their own benefit and that of the organization, they should realize they have some information they should not pass on—at least to the wrong persons. Secretaries also have the power—as mentioned above, to select who sees the boss, and when.

They can use their powers as gatekeepers to benefit themselves, their supervisors, and the institution, though doubtless that's more easily said than done. It's also true that the three sets of goals don't always coincide. Coping with all three isn't simple. To be effective as a secretary, a person must have a thorough acquaintance with both the formal and informal organization, as well as a great deal of good judgment of people.

Secretaries represent their organization and their supervisor to clients, visitors, and to other parts of the system. Thus, their gatekeeper role is very important to the organization in accomplishing its goals. To a large extent, they are public relations officers, not only in the neatness of their typed communications but also in their interpersonal communication with people who must use them to contact others in the organization. All the interpersonal skills discussed earlier in this book are needed to perform this role effectively.

Divided Loyalties. The secretary's gatekeeper role is complicated by a second problem area: *divided loyalties.* A degree of loyalty to the supervisor by her/his secretary is expected. However, some supervisors believe that all other personal and organizational interests should be subordinated to this role. In these cases assertive communication is critically important. In many situations, preventing the service role from becoming a servant role is a delicate task.

Divided loyalties can cause severe problems when a secretary believes that a supervisor's behavior is not beneficial to the organization. Necessity for loyalty still exists, but so does a responsibility to the institution. No simple solution to this dilemma exists. Knowing the informal organization well so that messages can reach the people who need them is partially an answer. So, too, is behaving assertively enough to report feelings honestly, first to the supervisor, and then to other appropriate authorities in the formal organization. But neither is easy, nor guaranteed to be completely effective. Either can get you into trouble depending on the persons and the situation. The task of dealing with divided loyalties is indeed difficult.

Prejudice. A third area of difficulty for secretaries is the prevailing *prejudice* toward the position. Because secretarial roles are largely identified as female roles, they are subject to many prejudices. The role is low in organizational hierarchy, and often equally low in status. Many people, men and women alike, believe that secretarial skills aren't difficult to achieve, and aren't worth much. Even people who do not share the prejudice toward secretarial positions take advantage of the fact that many women must work, and thus will continue to work in low paid positions.

As a result of these conditions, the job continues to be low status even though, in most organizations, secretarial skills are indispensable. People who do them well are not easily replaced. Many can type, but not as many have the interpersonal skills that can and have made many secretaries the unofficial office manager. These interpersonal skills are valuable and not widely recognized as part of the secretary's role.

> Remember, no one can make you feel inferior without your consent.
>
> ELEANOR ROOSEVELT

Coping with Problems of the Secretarial Role. How does a secretary cope with the problems? The first step is recognition, and then achieving awareness by others in the organization. Certainly the difficulties described are not news to people working in secretarial positions. Others may not be aware of the problems, though. If possible, learn the attitudes of other persons in the organization toward secretarial work before you take a job. But if you must work where people have negative attitudes, and sometimes you must, the necessity to behave assertively becomes crucial for you. Insist on proper recognition for your important role, socially and interpersonally. You might eventually begin to gain economic recognition for it.

Second, and perhaps most important, don't let the prevailing attitude work a Pygmalion effect upon you. Many secretaries share prejudices against secretarial positions. They believe their skills have low value and thus deserve low status. If you hold this kind of attitude, try to imagine the organization of which you are a part completing one week without secretarial services. What would happen to it? It doesn't take great vision to realize that most work organizations would collapse without their secretarial services. Recognizing the importance of the role can help you avoid sharing others' prejudices toward it. It can also help you maintain sufficient self-esteem to assertively seek appropriate recognition for your services.

Finally, remember that in many situations you can achieve in groups what cannot be achieved by a single individual acting alone. If nothing more, social reinforcement to counteract the Pygmalion effect of low pay can be achieved in formal and informal associations. And at best, you can use group support, group decision making and group problem-solving techniques to discover ways to eliminate the peculiar working problems that face you.

using the telephone

One vital area of communication within the organization that is almost always taken for granted involves using the telephone. Telephones provide a major contact within and among organizations and the clients they serve. Yet telephone conversations are subject to more barriers to understanding than most other forms of communication. Telephone communication is subject to all the limitations of speaking, especially the necessity for instant understanding and for immediate recall. But it has the additional limitation resulting from the loss of most nonverbal communication. A person communicating on the telephone has voice and words, and that is all.

Voice becomes very important in telephone communication. Qualities that may not even be noticed in face-to-face communication, such as abruptness or harshness, are highlighted and emphasized. And because the speaker is not facing the people he/she is talking with, it's easier to say tactless, unkind, or unpleasant things. Indeed, often a telephone is used for just that purpose. This impersonal aspect of telephone communication creates special problems for secretaries, receptionists, and assistants. People may say things they would really like to say to the boss, but are afraid, unwilling or unable to say. Those who answer telephones in an organization receive a lot of abuse, and must learn to respond calmly and positively.

Another problem of telephone communication is that sounds are easily misunderstood, especially names and numbers. Ninety sounds like 19 on the telephone, and nine like mine! Constant use of feedback in telephone communication is necessary because all nonverbal communication besides voice is absent. Use of feedback, checking spelling, pronunciation, and numbers are very important. Learn to repeat what you hear, and to summarize important parts of a conversation.

Here we also need to remind you of comments made earlier about voice. Vocal pitch and quality are nonverbal elements that lead to many negative impressions. At the same time, these are precisely the factors highlighted in telephone communication. Thus, it is important for both men and women to be sure their voice is pleasant and well-modulated when talking on the telephone, though the problem is greater for women because of their naturally higher pitch. A tense, high-pitched voice can be perceived as strident (harshly aggressive) or whining (weak and sniveling). In either case, it's not the impression you want people to have of you as a person or as a representative of your organization.

A related area in which telephone communication magnifies voice problems is articulation and enunciation. Articulation refers to the way in which sounds are formed, and enunciation describes the clarity of individual sounds. Because the word "articulation" popularly describes both functions, we'll use that meaning. Most people could benefit from improved articulation. We do not speak as

Herman By Jim Unger

"Oh elephants! . . . I thought you said we're gonna cross the Alps with 'elegance'."

Source: Copyright 1975 Universal Press Syndicate.

clearly as we could. Our words are often slurred or mumbled (I wanna go; you gonna go?); or syllables dropped (pa-tic-ly, for par-tic-u-lar-ly; ja get? for did you get?). We also distort sounds (dese for these; dose for those; tomorra, for tomorrow). In face-to-face situations, these habits aren't so noticeable because of all the other nonverbal communication. But on the telephone competing nonverbal stimuli are eliminated, and sloppy articulation becomes a major hindrance.

Applying Communication Principles

Many areas exist where effective communication is needed at work. Many work situations require that you attend to the communication skills and principles discussed earlier in this book. For instance, critical for both supervisors and supervisees is *giving and receiving clear, accurate directions*. To do that it's necessary to *use feedback* to prevent or correct misunderstanding. Remember, words do not mean the same thing to different people, and denotations as well as connotations vary. Quite likely, source and receiver will have totally different meanings for the words and no one is to "blame" for those differences. Words that are perfectly clear to a source may be decoded differently by a receiver because of the ambiguity inherent in language.

A warning about the use of feedback to check the accuracy of decoding is called for. Some people resent being asked to clarify what they said, or are insulted by the implications if you use restatement to check your understanding. They feel you are suggesting their message is inadequate. They don't realize the inherent ambiguity in use of words. You may need to be very skillful in order to seek accuracy without offending. (You may need to teach others what you learned in Chapter 3!)

Recall that connotative reactions to words can cause as much difficulty in communicating as denotative reactions. A word loaded with *negative connotations* for one person may be neutral to another. Thus, you can cause emotional distortions in communication even without knowing it. You need to be sensitive and able in reading nonverbal feedback.

Also worth pointing out is that in many work situations *ritualized relationships* exist and many ritual communications are required. If you're going to operate effectively at work, you need to be aware of these rituals. You may need to participate in some that are very important. You'll need to learn which can be ignored with no penalty, which with some penalty, and which you cannot ignore if you want to stay and advance in the organization.

Also remember the numerous ways that *nonverbals* affect communication: arrangement of furniture; coping with noise; establishing appropriate personal spaces between you and others; use of objects; manipulating appearance through dress and physical characteristics. You could go on with the list. All aspects of nonverbal communication become especially important at work because of the sustained nature of work relationships. Because feelings aren't usually considered appropriate subjects of communication at work, you may need to learn to understand the feelings of co-workers from nonverbals. You can often learn through nonverbal cues what is appropriate to do and to say, and when.

We also need to restate the necessity to listen well. *Listening skills,* whether active, empathic or critical, are necessary to communicate effectively at work. Often it's said that "the worst problem here is that people don't pay attention!" This is, of course, just another way to say that people don't listen, or at least don't listen well. If you want to communicate well on the job, learn to use listening skills effectively.

LOOKING BACK

Communication is important in the work situation, which for most people is within an organization. This chapter analyzes the use of communication to gain entry to organizations and then treats some factors that can enable a person to communicate more effectively within organizations.

Most often entrance to an organization is through an interview, but first it is necessary to get one. Securing an interview can be done by applying for a position in person, calling, or writing. The first is the best if it is possible. Personal letters of application and a response card for the employer to return can improve your chances of getting a response to a written application. Suggestions for résumés are also given.

Preparing for the interview is perhaps the most important step. If possible, learn whether it is to be a screening or hiring interview, how long it will last, and what is the role of the person doing the interviewing. Preparing for the interview also involves learning about the organization, learning what appropriate dress will be, determining what questions you will want to ask during the interview, and giving thought to questions that you may expect to be asked so your answers will not be totally off the cuff.

Examine the setting of the interview both before and during the session. Be sure you know or are prepared to find out the expectations the interviewer has of you, and assess your own expectations of the interview and the job. Don't think of yourself as powerless in the interview. You can ask questions, influence the physical arrangements, and determine which questions you will answer, which you'll ask for more clarification before answering, and which you will refuse to answer.

During the interview, attention should be paid to nonverbal and interpersonal communicating. Use feedback, eye contact, personal space, body action, and voice to present the best impression. A proper balance between confidence and respectfulness will be helpful in achieving your goals.

Once you are part of the organization, an understanding of the system can help you function more effectively within it. Organization is defined as a complex system that intentionally coordinates the behaviors of its members for completion of specific purposes. Most organizations are systems of groups that interrelate to accomplish the organization goals. These interrelations result from the division of labor necessary to accomplish the tasks. Coordination is accomplished through a hierarchy of authority and responsibility.

The hierarchy reflects the formal organization. The informal organization results from the complex of interpersonal relationships among the members of the organization that sometimes parallel the formal organization but often do not. Communication channels follow both the formal and informal organization structure. The effective person in an organization is aware of both and knows when each should be used.

Communication along the formal channels is vertical—often called serial—horizontal, and diagonal. Much distortion occurs in vertical communication, both in upward and downward flow of information, partly owing to information losses that naturally derive from numerous transactions. Other losses are due to defensiveness caused by the organizational climate, the different levels of status among those communicating, and the supervisory-evaluative role of those in higher levels. Vertical communication is so important to survival and effectiveness of the organization that all organization employees at all levels need to work for its accuracy, though the primary burden for effective vertical communication lies with those in the higher levels of each transaction.

Several steps to improve organizational communication can be taken. Some messages should be written down, but a careful assessment of which ones is needed to prevent information overload. Also, the identification and use of informal channels can help, as will encouraging an open, supportive climate to achieve free use of vertical channels in the formal organization. Use of many of the principles of communication outlined in earlier chapters is necessary in organizations.

Several special problems within the organizational situation require attention. Unclear role definitions are a major problem for many employees. The solutions are not simple, but can be aided by seeking written job descriptions and displaying assertive behavior. The secretarial role is a source of communication difficulties, partly because many people do not recognize the need for communication skills in that position and because of its low status in the organization. The secretary needs to recognize his/her gatekeeper role and to perform it with care, even when coping with the difficult problem of divided loyalties. Using the telephone is particularly important, requiring attention to pleasant well-modulated vocal pitch, as well as clear articulation and constant use of verbal and nonverbal feedback.

Questions for Discussion

1. What steps can be taken to prepare for an interview?
2. What behaviors can aid the interviewee during an interview?
3. What types of interviews are used in organizations besides the employment-entrance interview?
4. What communication channels exist within an organization, and how can you use this knowledge to your advantage?

5. How can you cope with problems of unclear job limits?

6. What can secretaries do to improve their communication within organizations?

7. What are some of the sources of distortion of messages in an interview? Within an organization's structure?

Exercise: Relationships in the Organization

Objective: To become aware of the factors involved in interpersonal relations within the work setting.

Directions:

1. Consider yourself a supervisor in the following situation. You are informing an employee that her/his work is to be reviewed in the annual performance review. The content of your memo to this person is to explain the importance of the annual review, what it is to accomplish, and what the person can expect.

2. Write different versions of the letter for each of the following perspectives, but remember that the denotative content of each should be the same. Each should be *no more* than 150 words.

3. The different perspectives from which you should write are:
   a. A supervisor hostile toward the employee
   b. A supervisor who is also a friend of the employee
   c. A supervisor who tries to use participatory decision making in the organization (Likert's System 4)
   d. A supervisor who is new on the job
   e. An authoritarian supervisor

4. After writing the different memos, share them with a group of your classmates. Compare your perceptions of the task with theirs, and discuss the differences and/or similarities in your finished products. What accounts for the differences? Are different connotations suggested by the different situation memos?

Suggestions for Further Reading

BABBITT, H. RANDOLPH, et al., *Organizational Behavior.* Englewood Cliffs, N.J.: Prentice-Hall, Inc., 1974.

BARNARD, CHESTER I., *The Functions of the Executive.* Cambridge, Mass.: Harvard University Press, 1968.

COFFEY, ROBERT E., AND ANTHONY ATHOS, *Behavior in Organizations: A Multi-Dimensional View.* Englewood Cliffs, N J.: Prentice-Hall, Inc., 1975.

DAVIS, KEITH, *Human Behavior at Work, Human Relations and Organizational Behavior.* New York: McGraw-Hill, Inc., 1972.

GOLDHABER, GERALD, *Organizational Communication.* Dubuque, Iowa: William C. Brown Publishing Co., 1974.

HANEY, WILLIAM, *Communication and Organizational Behavior: Text and Cases.* Homewood, Ill.: Richard D. Irwin, Inc., 1967.

LIKERT, RENSIS, *The Human Organization: Its Management and Value.* New York: McGraw-Hill, Inc., 1967.

LUND, HERBERT F., *The Real Official Executive Survival Handbook.* New York: The Dial Press, 1973.

————, *Effective Communication on the Job: A Guide for Supervisors and Executives.* New York: American Management Association, 1963.

MCGREGOR, DOUGLAS, *The Human Side of Enterprise.* New York: McGraw-Hill, Inc., 1960.

———— , *The Professional Manager,* ed. Caroline McGregor and Warren G. Bennis. New York: McGraw-Hill, Inc., 1967.

PETER, LAURENCE, J., *The Peter Prescription.* New York: William Morrow and Co., Inc., 1972.

REDDING, CHARLES, *Communication Within the Organization: An Interpretive Review of Theory and Research.* New York: Industrial Communication Council, 1972.

RUSSELL, G. HUGH, AND KENNETH BLACK, JR., *Human Behavior in Business.* Englewood Cliffs, N.J.: Prentice Hall, Inc., 1972.

SCOTT, WILLIAM E., AND LARRY L. CUMMINGS, *Readings in Organizational Behavior and Human Performance.* Homewood, Ill.: Richard D. Irwin, Inc., 1973.

STEWART, CHARLES AND WILLIAM CASH, *Interviewing Principles and Practices.* Dubuque, Iowa: William C. Brown Co., 1974.

TOWNSEND, ROBERT, *Up the Organization.* New York: The Fawcett World Library, 1971.

APPENDIX TO CHAPTER 12

ASSERTIVE COMMUNICATION

Communicating assertively involves two factors: attitudes and behavior. The two interact. If one holds certain attitudes assertive communication is simple. But if you are one who needs to *learn* to communicate assertively, you must first gain cognitive awareness of new attitudes. Your previous attitudes have led you to behave nonassertively. So we begin by discussing attitudes, seeking that awareness. Then we introduce communication patterns that can change your behavior. Eventually changed behavior can help you internalize the needed attitudes.

The material in this appendix is drawn from *When I Say No I Feel Guilty,* by Dr. Manuel Smith.[1] Dr. Smith states a "Bill of Assertive Rights," from which we draw five central attitudes needed by an assertive communicator.

Right #1 *You have the right to judge your own behavior, thoughts, and emotions and to take the responsibility for their initiation and consequences upon yourself.* This right is based on a point of view expressed throughout this book: each individual should make the choices that govern his or her own life. Corollary to this is taking responsibility for the consequences of the choices. Sometimes it's a subconscious or even conscious

---

[1] Manuel J. Smith, *When I Say No I Feel Guilty* (New York: The Dial Press, 1975). This excellent guide to assertive communication contains many illustrations and examples of how to apply these skills. Adapted by permission.

effort to avoid the consequences of our behavior that leads us not to communicate assertively. Sometimes we don't want to be responsible for our own behaviors. We find it easier to allow someone else to judge or decide, and thus we avoid bearing responsibility for the consequences of our behavior. But to learn to communicate assertively, we must accept this first right—to be the ultimate arbiter of our own behavior.

Right #2 *You have the right to stay out of other people's affairs.* Other people will often attempt to manipulate you into feeling responsible for them or their problems. Because many people prefer not to bear the responsibility for their own behavior, they will attempt to find someone else to solve their problems or tell them what to do. The other person then bears responsibility for the wrong choices. Right #2 means that you have the right to let others be responsible for their own behavior, without guilt. You have no responsibility to solve problems or make choices for other people.

Right #3 *You have a right to offer no excuses to justify your behavior.* You can behave as you wish because you want to, and that is sufficient reason. You don't have to justify your behavior to anybody unless *you choose* to do so. Again, this right emphasizes the element of choice. We are all free to choose the components of our own lives.

Right #4 *You have the right to change your mind.* When you make a choice, you may later decide it was the wrong one. Therefore, you have the right to decide you want to do something different, again with no apologies or guilt. We are all human; we aren't perfect. We all make mistakes. We don't have to make excuses for being human. You are free to take back what you said; undo what you did before. You have the right to change your mind.

Right #5 *You have the right to say, "I don't know."* No guilt need accompany an admission of not knowing something. No one has answers for everything. So you don't have to feel guilty if you have no solutions. You neither have to understand or be able to explain everything.

All the assertive rights grow from the fundamental conclusion that a person is not responsible *to* other people. You are responsible to yourself. This is the foundation of assertive communication. Because attitudes are only predispositions to behavior, communicating assertively involves more. If you need to learn to be assertive, you haven't internalized these attitudes even if you intellectually agree with the rights. By that we mean you may believe the rights but you still feel guilt about behaving that way. So what you need to do is to begin communicating assertively. From your behavior you will eventually internalize the attitude; it will become a predisposition because you will feel good about your beliefs.

Persistence. The first assertive communication skill is persistence. Once you have decided your rights have been violated, you must be persistent in seeking redress. When you resist attempts to manipulate you, the person trying to control you will not give up easily, particularly if your relationship has any history. In the past you have probably done as the person wanted and resented it, or not done it and felt guilty. Even if you refused, your guilt may have been used against you the next time manipulation was tried. So you must learn to resist the manipulation without feeling guilty. That requires persistence. You need to learn to say "no," to say it quietly, calmly, and to continue saying "no," if necessary, over and over and over again. The repetition must not become angry, irritated, or loud. Dr. Smith describes this as the *Broken Record.* Learn to speak as if you were a broken record. Stick to the point.

When, on the other hand, you are the one requesting something of another, it's a matter of learning to say, "I want so and so." You must learn to say, "I must have so and so. This situation must be corrected," consistently, calmly and firmly. Broken Record repetition does not increase emotional intensity. This is a very difficult communication skill. Learn it and you're well on the way to being an effective assertive communicator.

Compromise. Dr. Smith describes the second important verbal skill of assertive communication as the *Workable Compromise.* In a situation in which you've been using the Broken Record skill, you will reach a point at which the other person recognizes you will not be manipulated. At the same time, you may learn that achievement of your goal is not possible or reasonable. Then you and the other person must reach a compromise. The Workable Compromise is a middle ground that will make the situation respectable for both of you. You must realize, in beginning to apply your skills, that situations will occur in which no amount of persistence will achieve your goal. These call for the ability to work out, calmly and without emotion, a reasonable middle ground, a Workable Compromise.

Feedback. The third skill of communicating assertively involves using feedback. From one point of view, communicating assertively is simply a matter of communicating to another person who you are, what you want, and what you expect. A concomitant skill is securing that kind of information from the other person. If it's not freely given, you'll need to use feedback to seek it and to get it. You need skills of empathic listening to understand the other person and what is being said. You need to listen totally, to recognize volunteered verbal and nonverbal messages: then you need to use feedback to seek information not volunteered.

Disclosing information about yourself. When you are seeking information from others, the best way to get it is to be willing to disclose information about yourself. Thus, assertive communication involves the skill of disclosing information about yourself. It requires telling people how you feel, how you react, what things are happening to you as you communicate with them. What you are really saying to someone when you communicate assertively is, "No, you cannot manipulate me. I will not do that, and I will not feel guilty." To do that you must share with them your feelings about the situation and your perspective. You need the skill of talking about your feelings and being able to describe the world as you see it. You need to be able to avoid evaluative communication. In seeking information from others you shouldn't communicate judgment of their behavior. You simply focus descriptively on the external situation and internally on your feelings, applying the principles we introduced in Chapters 6, 7, and 8.

Acceptance. Being able to communicate assertively means that you recognize that your feelings, whatever they are, are respectable. And similarly, that applies to the other person. This communicates acceptance, both of yourself and others. To behave assertively you should never feel guilty about the way you feel. You need to accept yourself and your own behavior as legitimate, just as you need to accept the behavior of others. You need to say, "At the moment, this is the way I feel; I may change my mind tomorrow; I may not feel that way tomorrow, but right now at this moment, I feel this way and I accept it as legitimate." When we are able to accept ourselves and our behavior as legitimate, then we can relate our feelings to other people without guilt.

So far, we've dealt only with the attitudinal aspect of responding to criticism. In addition, specific communication behaviors can help respond to the evaluation used by those who try to manipulate us. Dr. Smith calls these *fogging, negative assertion,* and *negative inquiry.* As we learn these three skills, we can turn manipulative criticism to our benefit. Usually when we are criticized, we defend our behavior and deny we should be criticized. Both behaviors tend to increase the criticism and not reduce it. This amplifies the evaluation and manipulative behavior of others. Therefore, it makes a spiral of the problems.

Fogging. A more effective response than denying, even if you feel you have a good reason for your behavior, is simply to agree in principle. Don't deny the criticism, just agree with whatever truth there is in the statement. This is fogging. You don't have to agree with the whole criticism, but refusing to deny it can deflect the criticism. Dr. Smith gives an example: a parent criticizing a teenager: "You stayed out late again. I tried to call you until after midnight." The teenager could respond, "Yes, I was out late last night." Thus, the youngster accepted no guilt, nor did she bother to dignify any implication of guilt with a denial. She simply agreed with the truth there was in the accusation. If you can find no truth to agree with, you can agree with the principle. For instance, the parent might say to the daughter, "Well if you stay out so late, you'll get sick again." The daughter doesn't have to deny or agree. She can agree only in principle, "Yes, that could happen—that is possible." Of course, anything is possible. So the criticism is blunted.

Dr. Smith describes this technique as fogging because the response is similar to a fog. A fog bank is very assertive. It is very persistent. You can't get rid of it. You can't do anything about it. At the same time, it's not defensive or aggressive. It offers no resistance. It gets out of the way but doesn't go away. That's the same as the technique of agreeing with whatever truth is in a statement or with the principle. You don't argue, but you don't give in, either.

This won't always end the criticism. It can continue. But if you respond without being defensive, without fighting back, at least the situation won't intensify and your emotions won't be wrought up. Eventually the critic will learn that nothing is to be gained by criticism because you refuse to feel guilt or behave defensively. Possibly, the critic might get angry because you do not respond. But if you maintain your calm, persistent refusal to react, that anger need not manipulate you either. You are not creating the argument. *The main value of fogging is that you cope with criticism and respond to it without becoming emotionally involved and anxious.*

Negative assertion. The skill of negative assertion relates to Right #4, that all of us have the right to make mistakes. Negative assertion is saying, "Yes, I made a mistake," without loading the mistake with great guilt. The skill is to be able to recognize whatever truth exists in the evaluation and to accept your own behaviors that may have been mistakes. If you believe in Right #4, negative assertion is easy. Having recognized that we erred, we can say, "Yes, that was a mistake," "Yes, I did a dumb thing," "Yes, it does appear to have been poor judgment." Without anxiety, without guilt, simply recognize the fact. This is a most effective way to blunt evaluative manipulation. When you say, "Yes, I made an error," it's very difficult for criticism to continue.

Negative inquiry. The skill of negative inquiry requires skill in the use of feedback. This is the ability to turn the question around when you are criticized. Seek to find out what, from the critic's point of view, is the problem. With this skill of assertive communication you learn to improve your personal relationships. If you care about those criticizing you, you care that they do not like something you have done. Instead of just feeling guilty and being manipulated, find out more about it. Use the skill of inquiry to discover what is *causing* the criticism. In the case of the parent criticizing the teenage daughter for staying out late, the teenager could respond, "Yes, I was late last night. What is it about my being late that bothers you?" The question to seek more information is the negative inquiry. This uses feedback to find out what is bothering the manipulator. It makes the evaluator focus on his or her own feelings. If the parent responds, "Well, I'm afraid you might be doing things you shouldn't be doing," then the teenager can answer, "What things are you afraid I might be doing? And why in being late am I any more likely to do them?"

If questions in negative inquiry are calm, without emotion, this approach can gain information for you that you couldn't get with a defensive response. Negative inquiry has two values. First, you find out more about how the critic feels. Second, by asking questions about the evaluations, you force the person to evaluate his or her own judgment structure. Perhaps the judgment employed really isn't rational or sensible. In being forced to examine feelings, a critic might decide, "I was wrong," or "That really wasn't important to me." The skill of using feedback to find out *why* people are criticizing you not only provides you with more information about them but also provides them with an opportunity to examine their feelings.

In conclusion, learning to behave assertively involves both rights and responsibilities. When you begin to communicate assertively, you accept responsibility for your own life, and do not feel guilty about refusing to let others manipulate you. Similarly, assertive communicators recognize others have the same rights. We don't have responsibilities for others' lives or the right to control them. If we behave assertively and not manipulatively, we can gain our own rights, allow others theirs, and develop closer personal relationships with others.

This key attitude is how assertiveness differs from aggressiveness. If you are aggressive, you are not simply trying to protect yourself and your right to make your own decisions about your life. Aggressive behavior is manipulative behavior in the sense that it goes beyond what I want for me to what I want for someone else. When you behave assertively, you're likely to be described by someone else as aggressive—but don't let that threaten you, either. It is not a simple distinction, but ultimately it is a fairly clear distinction. When you attempt to control or manipulate somebody else or when you attempt to suggest what choices other people should make, then you are not communicating assertively. You are behaving manipulatively, and the strength with which you attempt to control others might mean you are being aggressive. The difference is that the person who behaves assertively says, "I am responsible for me and you are responsible for you. If the two of us choose to be close to each other, we may choose to modify our behavior in ways that are acceptable to each other. But we emphasize the choice, and we de-emphasize the manipulative aspect." Whenever you are in contact with others, you affect each other.

When human beings communicate, they cannot avoid an interactive influence. The difference between being *affected* by people around you and being *controlled* by them is the important difference made by communicating assertively.

Key to Words and Phrases

Agenda: a plan or step-by-step procedure that a group agrees to follow

Authority: holding a position that conveys a "right" to make decisions or engage in actions that affect and/or control others

Cohesiveness: refers to the forces that influence members to remain in the group

Decisions, compromise: group members accept a decision that is somewhere between various competing proposals

Decisions, consensus: all members of a group accept a decision

Decisions, majority: more than half of a group votes in favor of a decision

Gatekeeper: a person who has the power to control and regulate the flow of information through communication channels

Goals, antagonistic: a situation with a group when one member can reach his/her goals only when others do *not* reach theirs

Goals, complementary: a situation within a group when each member can achieve her/his individual goals only when other members achieve theirs

Group: a communication system in which a series of interactions among members determines structure and identity

Group, casual: a collection of people that is accidental and transient

Group, permanent: a group that continues to exist indefinitely, even when individual membership changes

Group, private: a group in which members' interpersonal interactions are not observed by outsiders; not to be confused with closed membership groups

Group, public: a group in which the interactions among the members may be observed by others outside the group

Group, reference: a group that an individual uses to help define attitudes, beliefs, and values and to guide behavior; the person has a sense of identity with a reference group but need not actually be a member

Group, social: a group that exists to provide social satisfactions to individual members

Group, task: a group that exists to accomplish a specific task or set of tasks

Group, temporary: a group that exists for limited durations of time, usually just long enough to accomplish specific purposes

Group, therapeutic: a group that exists to provide physical or psychological therapy for individual members

Interdependence: a variable that exists within groups, referring to the extent members need each other to achieve group and individual goals

Leader: a person who performs recognizably more leadership behaviors than others in the group

Leadership: behavior that aids a group in accomplishing its goals

Leadership, climate: involves behaviors that assist in maintaining the group; includes encouragement, mediation, expediting communication, reduction of tension, helping individuals meet personal needs

Leadership, task: involves behaviors that assist a group in achieving the task; includes goal setting, planning, guiding, information giving and seeking, analysis, and synthesis

Norm: refers to a standard of expected behavior for which a social penalty is paid if the standard is violated

Norm, external: a norm that is imposed on a group by a larger system of which the group is a part

Norm, internal: a norm that develops *within* a group

Organization: a complex system that intentionally coordinates the action of its members for accomplishment of specific purposes

Organization, informal: the structure of interpersonal relationships among people in an organization but outside the formal channels

Possessiveness: an attitude that indicates a person has a "right" to control or influence the behavior of another person; an implication of ownership

Role: a word used in many different ways; used here to refer to the behaviors expected of persons perceived to occupy particular social positions; sometimes this is referred to as role expectations

Role, performances: the behaviors of a person perceived to occupy a specific role position

Serial communication: describes communication that must follow a chain, a channel in which messages pass from one person to another to reach their final destination

Status: describes the rights, privileges, or esteem accorded to the occupants of social positions

part 4

Public Communication

Public communication is a major influence in all our lives. True, most of us do little public speaking, at least in the sense of appearing before a large group of persons with a prepared message to deliver. When we do that, however, success is very important to us. Beyond that, we all frequently find ourselves in an audience, receiving public communication. Moreover, most of us hear commercials, news, entertainment, and political and religious messages every day as we watch television or listen to the radio.

Whether as receiver or source of public communication, we use it regularly, for important purposes. Thus, we need to study the processes of public speaking, persuasion, and mass communication so we can understand and use them better. Whether our purpose is to protect ourselves against attempts to manipulate us or to attempt to influence the beliefs, behaviors, and attitudes of others, knowing the principles and techniques of public communication will be useful.

13

Public Speaking

goal:

To learn how to speak in public more effectively.

probes:

The material in this chapter should help you to:

1. Distinguish the three major purposes for public speaking. pp. 359–60
2. Choose and phrase central ideas and purpose statements for speeches. pp. 360–61; 368
3. Choose appropriate introductions and conclusions for speeches. pp. 361–64
4. Structure speeches in at least four different ways. pp. 364–68
5. Choose supporting materials for different types of speeches. pp. 368–76
6. Suggest a method of adapting a speech to a particular audience. pp. 376–79
7. Given a particular speech thesis and purpose, give five examples of factors that will help maintain the attention of a particular audience. pp. 379–82
8. Name and explain five principles that are guidelines for effective presentation of speeches. pp. 382–88

> If all my talents and powers were to be taken from me by some inscrutable Providence, and I had my choice of keeping but one, I would unhesitatingly ask to be allowed to keep the Power of Speaking, for through it, I would quickly recover all the rest.
>
> DANIEL WEBSTER

We've called all communication purposive. Speaking in public most clearly fits into this category. You won't give a speech in public unless you have a reason for doing so, a purpose. Often public speeches are classified according to purpose: thus there are *speeches to give information, to persuade, or to entertain.* From one point of view, all public speaking is persuasive, because it all is intended to produce a response. But from the point of view of a speaker, one of three different kinds of responses may be desired. This chapter discusses the techniques helpful to a public speaker in any of the three situations, emphasizing those related to informative speaking. The next chapter covers persuasion more thoroughly.

We'd like to make one observation at the outset. Because everything about communication is situational, accomplishing your purpose either as a speaker or a listener depends on complex interactions. In the final analysis, whenever you ask, "Will this work?" we must respond with the truism, "It depends." In the next few pages we're going to make suggestions for coping with many public speaking situations. But that the suggestions will always be relevant to your particular case, or will work for you in your situation, we can't promise. "It depends." It depends on you, on the others involved, and on the situation. You can learn the principles discussed here and adapt them to fit each different communication situation. Then you can analyze your own speaking to understand both your successes and failures.

STRUCTURE

Good speeches are structured. They don't all have to be structured the same way; no magic structure exists, but good speakers will have in mind a thought structure. *Good speeches have a unity that begins with clear purpose.* They have somewhere to go and are specific. Generally a speech will also need a beginning, called an introduction, and an end, called a conclusion.

Purpose and Thesis

Good speakers know more about what they hope to accomplish than whether they want listeners to be informed, persuaded, or entertained. They know *precisely* what they want from listeners: to secure votes in Tuesday's election; to sell the endowment life insurance policy; to explain how a catalytic converter works; to teach the listeners how to work a slide rule; to dramatize the personality of a Shakespearean character.

In almost every case, you will have one predominant purpose as a speaker. In telling an audience about the Perkins Plastic Potato Peeler you may *inform* your listeners that it peels vegetables 1.6 times faster, and that it is made from highly durable material; you may *entertain* them by donning a chef's hat, a moustache, and an apron to demonstrate the use of the product; but, your main purpose is to *convince* people to buy your P.P.P. Peeler. You may also give information to entertain, and sometimes you entertain to hold attention while you inform. You may have had a teacher who was a real entertainer as he or she lectured, but unlike a paid comedian, the professor was entertaining for the purpose of informing you. The paid comedian, on the other hand, is entertaining primarily for the purpose of making you laugh. At the same time, good teachers are also good persuaders. They make you want to learn. The teacher who motivates, who inspires you to be interested in and excited about the subject, does so not for the purpose of convincing you of anything, but to improve your learning. Thus, you can see that a speaker may use the techniques of giving information, being persuasive, or entertaining to accomplish a purpose of informing, or persuading. Remember, though, *the best speakers usually have only one predominant purpose:* they don't try to go two or three directions at once; and they decide specifically what their purpose is before they speak.

Good speeches develop a *thesis. The thesis is the main point or main idea of the speech.* Sometimes a thesis is called the central idea. A thesis is the idea *central* to everything you say in the speech. As with purpose, good speeches revolve around one *central idea* —they don't try to cover several different main ideas. Thesis is not the same as subject. From one subject many theses could be de-

To accomplish your purpose either as a public speaker or a listener depends on complex interactions.
Source: Paul S. Conklin—Monkmeyer.

veloped. Using the subject of basketball, for instance, any of the following could be a thesis:

1. Basketball is an exciting sport
2. The rules of basketball are intricate
3. Club basketball is a good way for adults to stay in shape
4. The number of scholarships to the college basketball team should be increased

Many others could be listed. Any topic can provide many possible central ideas.

A thesis and purpose statement can be combined. The central idea is a subject-centered statement and the purpose describes what you intend to do with it. For instance, to add the purpose to the above, you'd merely clarify your intent:

1. To convince the students that basketball is an exciting sport
2. To inform the class about the intricacy of basketball rules
3. To convince the members of the local YMCA that club basketball is a good way for adults to stay in shape
4. To convince the college administration that the number of scholarships to the college basketball team should be increased

Using the three parts of the overall speech structure effectively can help you accomplish your purpose for speaking. Let's look at each in more detail.

The Introduction

Introductions to speeches have two basic functions: (1) *to get the favorable attention of listeners* and (2) *to start receivers thinking in the desired direction.* You've probably been in circumstances in which a speaker starts a speech with four or five jokes, then says,

361

"Okay, enough story telling—now let's get to the point." Usually you were sorry the speaker stopped telling jokes. You may have been entertained, and may have liked the speaker, but this still wasn't the most effective way to begin. Jokes can be effective introductions if they relate to the topic. If you can make a point from a humorous story related to the thesis you're going to discuss, the jokes will aid you in accomplishing one or both of the purposes of introduction. They assist in gaining favorable attention, and in leading the audience to think about your thesis. But if the jokes don't do the latter, there is probably a better way to start.

An introduction can vary in length, depending on how much time is needed to accomplish its purpose. The complexity of the subject, audience interest in either the speaker or subject, and their relationship with the speaker also influence length of the introduction. Securing the favorable attention of your audience may be very difficult. Perhaps your listeners have their minds on something else, or perhaps they're hostile toward you or your topic. In those cases it takes far longer to get people to listen favorably than when they're informed and friendly.

introduction techniques

Several techniques can be used to introduce speeches. We have already suggested a common and useful way to begin: the use of *jokes or humorous stories* relevant to the thesis. Another frequently used introduction is nonhumorous *illustrations or anecdotes*. You might begin with a story, one that relates to the point you want to make, and that illustrates something about that point.

Quotations are often effective ways of beginning. For example, you can quote the words of a well-known or a well-respected writer, speaker, political leader, or philosopher. Use familiar phrases or quotations or *state familiar ideas in a new way*. A student in one of our classes recently started a speech by saying, "Four score and seven days ago, I came of age." Or you might employ a *startling statement*. Cite a statistic that has impact and relates to your listeners. In a speech on smoking, for instance, you might start by saying, "One out of three of you sitting in this room will have cancer or heart disease in your life." Thus, you use a statement that's relevant and striking. It gains attention and relates to your topic.

Another often-used method to begin speeches is the *rhetorical question*. This is a question whose answer is implied in the question. It doesn't call for a direct answer, but does evoke a thoughtful response. You might say, for instance, "What would you do if a tornado alarm sounded while I was speaking?" Questions are good devices to secure audience involvement. Occasionally in an introduction you'll ask a *direct question*, to seek overt responses. At times you'll need information from the listeners, or want to learn what they want to hear you emphasize. Sometimes direct questions are used to make listeners aware of information about each other. Asking direct questions and getting answers from at least some of your audience is a good technique to establish a sense of directness between speaker and receivers. You may ask for verbal responses or a show of hands from all listeners or from a part of the group.

Often a useful way to begin is with a *specific reference to the audience or occasion.* Note the reason you're speaking, or why you were invited, or make a personal reference to your relationship with the situation or this particular audience. Political speeches are often started this way. People who are invited to speak at graduations, or at service or social clubs, also often refer to the occasion or the reason they were invited. One certain thing speaker and audience have in common is the occasion. Reference to the occasion helps establish common ground, common understanding, and shared liking between them.

A final suggestion for introducing speeches is to use a *direct reference to the subject* or problem being discussed. If your audience is highly interested and knows something about your topic, it's often useful to begin with immediate attention to it. Listeners may have come specifically because of the subject. Sometimes you're invited to speak because a group wants to hear something on which they know you are expert. In those cases they came because they wanted to hear you, and your introduction should probably not be long—they are already interested in the topic and you need do nothing more than get started.

Even though it is the beginning of a speech, you should *plan the introduction only after you have planned the rest of the speech.* After all, you must know what is to be introduced before you can introduce it, right? So in preparation stages, don't start with the introduction. Plan the introduction after you know what the body of the speech will consist of, so you'll know what you're introducing.

The Conclusion

Conclusions to speeches, like introductions, vary according to the situation. After a persuasive speech, for instance, you may actually want the audience to exhibit the behavior you're after. The conclusion for speeches to sell is often getting the listeners to sign on the dotted line. A speech seeking contributions may end by a call for the audience to put the money in a collection plate, or to sign the pledge card you've placed in front of them. In speeches to inform, your conclusions may require that you assess listeners' understanding and retention of your message.

The content of conclusions varies, but all have similar functions. In ending a speech, *you want to leave your listeners in an appropriate mood with their minds refocused on the thesis.* They should know that you're closing so that their mental set will reinforce your idea. If you say "And in conclusion," you'll have provided a reason for the listeners whose attention has wandered to come back and refocus. Let them know that you're finishing.

Though conclusions vary in length, take no longer than you need. We've all heard speeches that had five endings. And the audience probably got bored and restless by the end of the second and perhaps quit listening before the fourth stopping place. In those cases, the speaker would have been much better off stopping at the first conclusion point. An effective speaker doesn't continue past the closing point; he or she quits in time to *leave the listeners with a feeling of closure.*

Conclusions are often the most difficult part of a speech to prepare because achieving the proper balance of mood and ideas is tough. Informative speeches are less difficult to conclude than are persuasive speeches. All informative speeches should include a *summary of the points made,* and it's usually effective to combine that with some other device. A summary restates to emphasize for memory; adding a story or quotation helps maintain interest until the very end. Other techniques for concluding speeches are similar to those used for introductions. You might use quotations, a striking epigram or statement, an illustration or anecdote. Plan with care so the emotional impact of whatever device you choose will match the appeal or request you intend to leave the audience with.

Body: Thought Structure

How do you develop the thesis? First, you determine a *thought structure* for your speech. We think of the thought structure as the skeleton of the speech. In your body, the skeleton is what holds you up. The flesh, the organs, the skin are all attached to the skeleton. People wouldn't look like human beings without skeletons; they'd just be masses of living matter. Similarly, a speech needs its skeleton, its thought structure. This skeleton is the framework onto which all the material used to develop the thesis is attached.

We usually refer to the thought structure as the main point structure. An important question as you plan your speech is, "How many main points should I use?" As always, this depends on the situation and the subject. One important consideration is that you want your listeners to recall your thought structure. So in developing the main point structure, don't have too many main points. We suggest two to four. Obviously, that's only a guideline, because the number of main points must vary according to content. Sometimes many main points are required to fully develop your thesis. If you're going to have more than four, however, it will be hard for listeners to keep the total thought structure clear. If you have many main points, you should use a handout or a flipchart or a blackboard to keep the ideas visually in front of your audience. Something your listeners can look at will help them keep the overall thought structure in mind.

Usually one of two patterns is displayed in a speech—inductive or deductive thought structure. With *deductive thought structure* the thesis is stated early in the speech and then is developed. The *inductive thought structure* pattern withholds the thesis statement until later in the speech. In the inductive approach, the thesis emerges as the evidence develops. Usually informative speeches follow the deductive pattern. Retention and clarity are aided when the thesis is stated first because you can show how each point relates to the thesis as you introduce it. Speeches to persuade usually follow an inductive pattern. This is because such speeches are often made to an audience that disagrees, or is hostile or skeptical. If listeners know you're going to try to sell them something or influence their behavior in some way, they have their natural defenses up. In such situations it's effective to let the thesis emerge as you develop your credibility and give the reasons and the evidence to support your purpose. You may thus disarm the listeners' defenses before boldly asserting your central idea.

You can arrange the main points of a speech several ways. Let's look at some now.

main points arranged by time

You can arrange the thought structure of your speech in a time or chronological structure. Using a chronological order, you speak of what happens first, then what happens second, then third, etc. This kind of arrangement is particularly effective for "how to" speeches. When you are explaining how to do something, it helps to start with what you do first! The time arrangement uses time to structure the thinking but doesn't follow strict chronological order. You might start with the way the situation is now, then go back and examine how it developed, point by point, to this stage; or you can use a flashback technique somewhere during the development.

Main Points Arranged by Time

Thesis: *Swinging a golf club properly involves four parts.*

   I. First, grip the club properly.
  II. Second, the backswing is important.
 III. Next, the weight shifts to start the downswing.
 IV. Finally, the proper follow-through is needed.

main points arranged by space

Sometimes a topic will naturally break down into a spatial arrangement. Discussing air-pollution control, for example, you might talk about what happened in New York City, what happened in Chicago, and what happened in Los Angeles. Travelogs often employ a spatial thought structure. What you want to tell about in a travelog, for instance, is not a daily routine. Usually your audience isn't interested in what you had when you got up for breakfast and where you went the second day, and so forth. What people want to know is what you saw in Venice, what you saw in Paris, what you saw in Rome, etc.

Main Points Arranged by Space

Thesis: *Endangered species of wildlife must be protected.*

I. Whales in the oceans need protection.

II. Bird nesting and wintering areas must be preserved.

III. Wildlife management in the eastern U.S. is especially needed.

main points arranged by topics

Topical main point structure is very common. Some subjects break naturally into topics. This chapter, for instance, uses a topical outline. In developing the thesis that certain techniques improve public speaking, we first discussed speech purposes, then speech structures, and soon we'll go on to discuss the topics of supporting materials, audience analysis, attention devices, and speaker behaviors. For much public speaking, topical outlining is the most appropriate form. Some specific topical outlines are useful in specific cases. Especially in persuasive speaking you may find topical structures useful, but they are also common in informative speaking. One specific method is the *cause-effect* topical outline. In cause-effect thought structure, you talk first about a cause and then discuss its consequences or effects. Or you can reverse the order. For example, in discussing "the energy crisis, a problem caused by over-consumption," you might talk about the effect, the energy crisis, and describe the crisis and how it affects your audience. Then you can go back and talk about what you perceive as the causes.

Main Points Arranged by Cause-Effect

Thesis: The energy crisis affects our society because we consume at too high a level.

I. The U.S. has used its resources too rapidly in the past.

II. Limited resources cannot support U.S. society at the present high standard of living.

III. Our overconsumption has resulted in shortages of 90 percent of our basic resources.

Using *problem-solution thought structure* is also a common way to organize a speech. You might first analyze a problem, then propose and/or explain its solution. This arrangement is common for persuasive speaking; it is also useful when you must give information or analyze possible solutions to a particular problem.

Main Points Arranged by Problem-Solution

Thesis: There is a need for basketball scholarships.

I. Lack of scholarships has caused several problems.
   A. Some good players from the local area go to other colleges because the team only offers eight scholarships.
   B. Some good players can't practice or play because they need to work to support themselves.
   C. Basketball is a second-class sport here because many fewer scholarships are given than to football, track, and baseball players.

II. Increasing scholarships would solve many problems.
   A. Recruitment would be improved.
   B. Poor students could play as well as the more affluent.
   C. Status of the team would be increased by equality with other sports.

The *advantages-disadvantages topical outline* also can be helpful in presenting a balanced analysis of a controversial thesis.

Main Points Arranged by Advantages-Disadvantages

Thesis: Club basketball is a good way for adults to stay in shape.

I. Club basketball has only a few disadvantages.
   A. Members must commit time to a schedule.
   B. Meeting practice sessions may be difficult.

II. Club basketball has many advantages.
   A. Regular workouts will be required.
   B. Running and stretching are the best kinds of exercise.
   C. Exercising with a group is more fun than alone.
   D. Games are more fun than just jogging or exercising on machines.
   E. Club basketball can help people make many new friends.

Exercise: Organizing (Outlining)

Objective: To practice organizing ideas.
Directions:
   1. The class will be divided into groups of four or five.
   2. In a first meeting, each group should
      a. Choose a subject for a speech
      b. Establish a specific purpose for giving the speech to the class
      c. Phrase a tentative thesis
   3. Next, each group member should prepare an outline for a speech on the tentative thesis, using one of the five suggested standard main point outlines.
   4. Members should then compare and discuss their individual outlines, working out a "best" organization.
   5. The instructor may ask each group to share their "best" outline with the class, explaining how they decided it was best.

SUPPORTING MATERIALS

In planning, preparing for, or analyzing a speech, what do you do after determining your purpose, thesis, and thought structure? You *develop the ideas.* In this step you put flesh on the skeleton; you develop the main point structure. You select supporting materials.

Supporting materials are used for several reasons. You may need to amplify or clarify, to illustrate or explain to aid understanding. You may need to emphasize so that listeners will remember what you say. Supporting materials also aid development of speaker

368

credibility. You'll recall from Chapter 5 that information from credible sources is perceived more favorably and remembered longer.
Use of supporting materials helps create credibility.

In discussing the use of supporting materials, we return to that
one truism of communication. What supporting materials you use
"depends" on your purpose and on your audience. Perhaps to understand your purpose, your audience won't need amplification.
Sometimes, if they are well-informed, all you have to do is to give
listeners a bare minimum of information—but that's generally not
the case. Usually you need to give amplification or explanation or
you wouldn't be even giving the speech. And sometimes, after you
first explain your ideas, the receivers still don't understand. Then,
you need more amplification and illustration. Often you'll have to
use verbal feedback to find out why. What supporting materials you
need and how many varies according to the situation. It depends
on: (1) your goals, (2) your audience, and (3) where the audience is
with reference to your subject and purpose.

Many different kinds of supporting materials can be used.
Some are very common and you're very familiar with them; others
are less common. Let's discuss the ones that are most useful to most
speakers.

Visual and Nonverbal Supporting Materials

You may show pictures, or use charts, objects, or demonstrations.
"A picture is worth a thousand words," the saying goes; and in public speaking, it probably is. If you're trying to explain the proper
golf swing, words alone are terribly inadequate. Diagrams, pictures,
and actions are helpful. Best of all, if it is possible and appropriate,
use feedback. Have your listeners do what you are telling them to
do, and use their actions to show them how it best works.

We always recommend use of *the multisensory approach. It's
usually more impressive, almost always more memorable, and it
helps people understand better* what they didn't previously know.
Most of what we first learned was multisensory. We learned by
seeing, touching, tasting, and smelling, as well as hearing. All our
senses first helped us know what words meant. In public speaking,
as in interpersonal communication, use many senses to help your
receivers understand what your words mean, and to reinforce those
words and help your audience remember them.

guidelines for use of visuals

Under this heading, we include all visual aids—charts, diagrams,
cartoons, graphs, outlines, flipcharts, objects, models, slides, demonstrations. Keep several guidelines in mind as you use visual aids.

Visual aids should be appropriate. Gimmicks that aren't related to the idea you're discussing often detract from understanding instead of aiding it. Make sure your models, displays, or demonstrations don't take listeners' attention away from what you're saying, and that they are fitting. A speech to a local Kiwanis or Rotary Club appealing for aid to injured veterans might appropriately use pictures of them in combat and in hospitals. But such pictures probably wouldn't be appropriate if the speech were being given to a local group of parents and family.

Visual aids should be clear. Simplicity is usually a virtue. Because the purpose for using visuals is to clarify, omit anything that's unessential; eliminate all confusing details. Charts or diagrams should be designed to emphasize the most important points. Sometimes you can use contrast in color or size, or arrangement of figures to highlight major ideas. Visual aids should be visible! Make them large enough to be seen and put them where all of the audience can see them. If some listeners can't see the visual, it won't achieve its purpose.

Visual aids should not interfere. The way visual aids are used is important in their effect. Make sure you don't stand between the display and your listeners, so they can't see it. Avoid falling into the common trap of talking to your visual aid—it's awfully easy to do. It will help if you stand where it's easier to look at your audience than at the chart. Visual aids should *focus on the message and not on the visuals* themselves. Don't pass things out to your receivers while you're talking. They'll tune you out while they study what you've passed around. While looking at your visual, they won't be listening. Also, put visuals away when you're through with them. It's too easy for listeners to drift back to the visual when you want their attention on you, especially if you have used statistics, charts, or diagrams. On the other hand, if your visual consists of a keyword listing of main points, it will probably reinforce your ideas to keep it in front of the audience. Use of a flipchart or chalkboard is especially good in this situation because you can add one point at a time to help your listeners focus on the ideas as you discuss them.

Verbal Supporting Materials

Many kinds of verbal supporting materials exist. Let's examine a few.

statements of observation and explanation

Recall that we use the term "statement of observation" to refer to what people commonly label facts. Speakers often need to use statements of observation to clarify or prove points. You may describe what something looks like, or sounds like, or what it weighs. In a speech to explain how air pollution is destructive, for example, you might describe paint damage to cars and buildings and give the count of cars damaged in a particular city in a particular week. Statements of observation are among the most useful supporting materials, but you may need to combine them with explanations. Describing damaged paint probably won't connect the problem to air pollution. But explaining how acids in polluted air cause damage can clarify the relationship between air pollution and the destruction.

comparison and contrast

You can also develop points by showing differences or similarities with other things. Make sure these comparisons and contrasts are with things familiar to your audience. This isn't difficult to do in a speech—it's much like what you'd do in ordinary conversation. In describing a new teacher to someone, for example, you might say, "What's Professor Jenkins like? Well, do you remember Fran Reis and the way she used to scowl when she got excited? That's what Jenkins does—and they look sort of alike, too, only Jenkins has blue eyes and wears her hair shorter."

Comparisons point out similarities between what is new and what is known. Contrast shows how the new differs from the known. In using comparison and contrast you may note similarities or differences not apparent on the surface, as we did when we compared the thought structure of a speech to the skeleton of the body. Or we could say that a speech is like a meal—the introduction is the appetizer, the body is the main course, and the conclusion is the dessert. This is called *analogy*—the comparison of apparently unlike items.

Comparisons are especially useful in improving the accuracy of communication if you analyze carefully what your receivers already know and choose comparisons that are meaningful to them. Comparing the effect of psychosis to the state of mind of a person lost in a blizzard would not be very effective if your listeners had never been north of Florida—they wouldn't have the connotative reactions of terror and confusion that would make the comparison vivid and useful to a Northerner.

examples

Another very useful type of supporting material is the example. *An example is a "case of" whatever point is being made.* If you were amplifying the point, "air pollution can be controlled," and described the results of the cleanup efforts in London over the past twenty years, you'd be using London as an example.

Short examples are usually called *instances;* long ones *illustrations.* They differ in amounts of detail. Instances and illustrations are often combined. To do that with the point "air pollution can be controlled," you could explain the situation in London in detail, describing thoroughly the experiences of Londoners in cleaning up their air, then cite briefly several other cities that used similar techniques and got good results.

Examples are especially effective for either informative or persuasive purposes. "Real" cases and experiences that others have actually had add attention value and believability to your speeches. Sometimes speakers will use hypothetical cases as examples. Often that's a good technique, but it works only as long as the case approximates what listeners can imagine to be real.

statistics

Statistics are also useful supporting materials. *Statistics consist simply of a lot of observations added up, with the relationships between them analyzed.* To report that the American Medical Association attributed 250 deaths in New York City in 1973 to air pollution would be using arithmetic, but not statistics. To report the AMA conclusion that 55 percent of the deaths from respiratory illnesses were due to emphysema caused by air pollution would be making use of statistics. Statistics count observations, but they do more than count. They use inferences to show relations among observations. Speakers find statistics especially useful in persuasive speeches, but they're also useful in informative speaking for explaining how or why things happen. Statistics can help in drawing conclusions about large groups of people. Politicians and marketing analysts often use statistics to make decisions.

Two guidelines are helpful in the use of statistics: *don't overdo, and make them clear.* Use what you need, but no more. Listeners must understand your point and remember it if they are to be informed. Information overload can confuse and lose listeners. Throwing a mass of figures at people will often create distrust or disgust. If people cannot keep up, they often quit trying to understand. With statistics, clarity is especially important. You should expect your receivers to be skeptical. Most have heard and believe that "figures don't lie, but liars sure do figure." Adapt to this attitude. You can round off figures to help understanding and memory. Also helpful is the use of charts and diagrams, for many people cannot cope with numbers unless they see them. Charts and diagrams aid both attention and retention of information. Use them whenever possible when you're presenting statistics.

Two kinds of testimony are useful as supporting materials. First and most often used is *expert testimony.* Often you're talking about things on which you're not the only expert. In these cases, it's helpful to quote someone your audience respects as an authority. This expert may say basically the same thing you want to say in a clear, concise or impressive manner. Testimony can be helpful in emphasizing points as well as in clarifying ideas. Quoting experts can support your point and improve speaker credibility at the same time. Take care, however, to quote only people respected by your listeners.

Sometimes nonexpert testimony is useful. This is described as *lay testimony.* It consists of statements by people who aren't considered experts. Showing how ordinary people look at things may be of value in some informative speeches, but as a technique it is most often used in persuasive situations. Soap, restaurant and automobile commercials rely on it extensively. Occasionally, lay testimony is used to motivate people to learn. Some people need to see how information can be of value to them before they will pay attention. Thus, lay testimony can help hold attention. For example, suppose you're a principal explaining to the local PTA the reasons for a new program being added to the school curriculum. Quote a student who had taken the program in a school where it existed. Let the words of the student describe its benefits. This can arouse attention as well as motivate and inform.

One of the most useful kinds of testimony is described as *reluctant* testimony. This is provided when a person expected to believe one way speaks out against that position. This would occur when a conservative barber concedes that long hair looks good on men. When a person admits what he or she wishes weren't true, it's described as reluctant testimony. Ronald Reagan won many voters by claiming, "I used to be a liberal Democrat. I now see I was wrong." Reluctant testimony is especially helpful in establishing credibility.

For some people, all you have to do is say something enough times and they'll believe you. Repetition, therefore, can be a useful device for speakers. We don't mean to be totally negative about the use of repetition as a supporting device. Sometimes people don't understand a point the first time you say it. Restating it by explaining in slightly different words can help them. Sometimes even repeating it with the exact words again can give your audience an opportunity to decode meanings they didn't get the first time.

Repetition and restatement are especially effective in securing retention of what you say. If you repeat an idea four or five times in a speech, it is likely to be remembered, while an idea repeated less than three times is less than half as likely to be recalled after a speech.[1] *Restatement is expressing the same idea in slightly different words, while repetition is repeating the exact words.* Repetition is often effective for a thesis, for your main point structure, or for a particularly apt expression you want your audience to remember as a key to your whole speech.

Supporting materials are ways to flesh out the skeleton of your speech. The trick, of course, is not that you recognize what the *types* of supporting materials are, but that you *choose the right ones.* Supporting materials in informative speaking should amplify, clarify, and emphasize. In persuasion they prove, reinforce, motivate, or stimulate. But they do these things only if they fit points you are making, and your particular listeners. You need to analyze your listeners to decide what they already know, what they are interested in, and what will best help them understand, remember, believe, or act upon the information you are giving them. In choosing supporting materials, you use *audience analysis,* which we discuss in the following section. But first, let's sum up what we've talked about so far in this chapter by looking at a sample outline of a speech.[2]

SAMPLE OUTLINE

Introduction

I. The experience of the French racing car driver is a dramatic example of the importance of safety belts (give example).

Central Idea

All of us should use safety belts in our cars.

Body

I. Safety belts increase your chances of surviving an accident.

    A. In the event of an accident you are safer if you are not thrown from from the car.

        1. Cornell studies of crash injury show that 12.8 percent of car occupants ejected through open doors, contrasted with a 2.6 percent of those who remained in the car, are killed. (**statistics; comparison and contrast**)

---

[1] Arthur Jersild, "Modes of Emphasis in Public Speaking," *Journal of Applied Psychology,* 12 (1928), 611–29.

[2] Loren Reid, *First Principles of Public Speaking,* 2nd ed. (Columbia, Mo.: Artcraft Press, 1962), 263–65.

2. The American Medical Association estimates that 5,000 lives could be saved annually if the hazard of ejection from the car were better controlled. (**testimony**)

B. In the event of an accident your chances of injury are reduced if you are not thrown into the windshield.

1. The American Medical Association estimates that you may be as much as 60 percent safer if you are held in place by a safety belt. (**testimony; explanation** will be given)

2. Consumers Union says that there is some evidence to suggest that in this respect even a poor belt is better than no belt at all. (**testimony**)

3. Cornell studies of crash injury estimate that use of belts by everyone would reduce fatal and major injuries by 35 percent. (**statistics**)

II. Commonly heard objections to seat belts are not justified.

A. The fear of being trapped in a wreck is ill-founded.

1. Fires break out in only 2/10 of 1 percent of injury-producing auto accidents. (**statistics**)

2. Submersion is involved in only 3/10 of 1 percent. (**statistics**)

3. Because your belt will more than likely keep you from being knocked unconscious, you have a better chance to escape than if you had no belt and were unconscious. (**explanation**)

4. Seat belts can be unfastened in an instant.

   a. The new metal-to-metal fasteners are easy to operate. (**explanation**)

   b. Lt. Leslie Williams of the Connecticut State Police can release his belt and draw his automatic with one quick move of his right hand. (**example**)

B. The problem of requiring children to hook their belts may be solved in various ways.

1. Younger children can be told that the family car is a spaceship, requiring that belts be fastened before blast off. (**explanation**)

2. Older children can be taught that fastening belts is a safety procedure, like operating a direction-indicator signal. (**explanation**)

C. Cases of belt failure are rare.

Conclusion

Seat belts are not a substitute for careful driving, but they increase your chances of survival if you are involved in an accident. No one expects to have an accident; we always expect accidents to happen to someone else. But they may sometimes happen to you. Be prepared to survive. Fasten your safety belt.

Note: Visual aids should be used throughout to present the statistical evidence. Graphs, as well as cartoon-type pictures will be used.

Exercise: Evaluating Supporting Materials

Objective: To develop skills in recognizing and evaluating evidence offered by public speakers in support of their assertions.

Directions:
1. From a magazine, newspaper, or book find a copy of the printed text of a speech given by a public figure recently. See *New York Times, Vital Speeches,* and other major metropolitan newspapers for current speeches.
2. Find out who was in the audience during the speech.
3. Identify the main points made by the speaker.
4. Identify the supporting materials used to develop the ideas.
5. Conduct whatever research is necessary to determine the validity of the evidence.
6. Assess the supporting materials. Consider adequacy, relevance, clarity, accuracy, audience adaptation.
7. Your instructor may ask you to share your conclusions with classmates on assigned day.

AUDIENCE ANALYSIS AND ADAPTATION

No two people are exactly alike, and the more different they are, the less are the chances of accurate communication. Most people explain ideas in the way they themselves would find it easiest to understand. Thus, they usually talk as if they were addressing themselves in a full-length mirror. To avoid this, you need to *recognize your listeners as specific and unique individuals.* Listener adaptation is the foundation of most successful speeches.

Analysis

To adapt to your listeners, you need to know some things about them so you can anticipate how they will decode the messages you send. Essentially, you need answers to the following questions:

1. What do they already know about the subject?
2. What are they interested in?
3. What are their attitudes and feelings about my subject and purpose?
4. What are their attitudes and feelings about me in relation to this subject and purpose?
5. What are their attitudes and feelings about related subjects, issues, persons?

How can you find answers to these questions? We suggest four means, three of them relating to information you gather before the speech.

376 *Find out what the group leaders think.* If the communication

situation is a personal one, the receivers are often known to you. You can learn by asking. Seek out leaders in the group and get their answers to important questions.

Ask questions. If you don't have direct contact with the receivers, you might know someone who has. Following this suggestion may involve you in polling, sending questionnaires, or interviewing. These methods are often used to find out more about people before messages are sent to them. Most large corporations spend millions each year researching potential buyers before sending advertising messages. So do politicians. You may not have the resources to do the kind of research that businesses do, but you can often find much about your audience by asking questions of people who know them or who are like them.

Draw inferences based on data you can find out. Demographic data is usually not hard to discover. Demography is the science of gathering vital statistics for groups of people. General demographic information about listeners can help you empathize with people who are quite different from you. Useful demographic data include age, sex, occupation, income level, educational level, special areas of education or experience, whether listeners come from rural, urban, or suburban locations, and what part of the country they are from. This information is worth knowing if it influences how the receivers will decode your messages. For example, knowing a person's educational level or occupation might help you know what vocabulary to use. Knowing audience backgrounds, sex, or ages might give valuable clues about their interests and values. Knowing religion or political affiliation might help you determine appropriate choices of language, examples and arguments. This alternative is not as desirable as the first two suggestions for *audience analysis,* but it is often the only one you have.

Use feedback to assess the audience while you speak. Audience analysis should continue the entire time you're speaking. Watch and listen to your receivers both in the situation before your speech and while you are talking. Draw inferences from what you see and hear. Before you started, you drew some hypotheses in answer to the important audience analysis questions. Keep in mind, as you talk, what those questions were and how you answered them. This will help you judge what your receivers' responses mean. It will also help you adapt to any responses that suggest your pre-speech hypotheses might have been wrong.

Adaptation

Audience adaptation isn't just a matter of telling people what they want to hear. It's *preparing and sending messages in ways that re-*

ceivers will decode as you intend. Audience adaptation is a critical process in effective public speaking.

In planning your speech, draw conclusions about your audience in answer to the five questions given on page 376. Then use the answers to plan the way you will develop the speech. Adaptation involves answering the following four questions:

1. What thought structure would best adapt to their attitude and interest structure?
2. What supporting materials will best relate to their attitudes and interests?
3. How can I enhance my believability as a source?
4. How will I need to utilize the situation (setting) to best accomplish my purpose?

Exercise: Selecting Supporting Materials for Specific Audiences

Objective: To practice adaptation of supporting materials to specific audiences.

Directions:
1. Start with the speech outline developed in the exercise on page 368 of your text. (If you did not do that exercise, you will need to review it to develop outlines to use for this exercise.)
2. Identify three different audiences to which the speech could be given. Use this class as one audience, but try to find others that are quite different. Think of off-campus groups to which the speech might be given. Indicate whether or not the different audiences will require any adaptations of specific purpose.
3. Each member of the group should then try to find one of each of the several kinds of supporting materials to use in developing a speech using the thesis and outline.
4. Group members should then decide how to develop the speech for each of the different audiences, choosing supporting materials based on the group's assessment of how to best adapt to each audience.
5. The instructor may ask you to share with the rest of the class your three speech outlines as developed with appropriate supporting materials.

Exercise: Audience Analysis

Objective: To practice analyzing an audience by identifying audience needs.

Directions:
1. Each class member, on the assigned day, should bring an advertisement from a popular magazine that she/he believes clearly illustrates an effort to gain a response based upon the identifiable human needs (Maslow's hierarchy in Chapter 4).
2. Class will be divided into groups of four or five.

3. Using the advertisements and outlines for audience analysis given in the text, answer the following questions:
   a. Who are the intended receivers of the ad?
   b. What need(s) did the advertiser appeal to?
   c. What else does the advertisement show about how the advertiser analyzed and adapted to the needs of the audience?
4. The instructor may ask you to share your conclusions about the advertisers' audience analysis and adaptation.

MAINTAINING ATTENTION

Audience analysis helps you answer the questions: How can I keep my audience interested? How can I make people *pay attention?* Few answers are more valuable to a speaker.

You may have the best information in the world, but if nobody is listening, it won't do anyone any good. Earlier we defined attention as the *focus of the receiving senses.* An effective speaker must keep her/his ideas in the focus of listeners' receiving senses.

Speakers can also use marginal attention. Most nonverbal communication, except visual aids that give direct information, should receive only marginal attention from receivers. You don't want most of your nonverbal messages to call attention to themselves—it is your ideas—your main points—that you want to be the center of audience attention. Anything such as delivery, that *should* be marginal, will distract if listeners focus on it. Imagine someone saying after your speech, "Hey, wasn't that a great speech!" Someone else asks, "What did he/she say?" and the listener replies, "Well, I don't know; I was so taken with that beautiful voice and that fantastic diagram that—well, I guess I don't really remember." Clearly, that listener was impressed. If the purpose was to impress, fine, but if the purpose was to inform and listeners left uninformed, the purpose was not accomplished.

Ideas should be the focus of receivers' attention, and you want that focus to be involuntary. Your listeners shouldn't have to work at listening to you. And you don't want them to think about how hungry they are, or the date they have tonight, or the parking ticket they just got. You want them to listen to you and to think about the ideas you're presenting. You want your listeners to pay attention because they cannot help it—because they're riveted to what you say.

That's not easy to accomplish. Often, especially when listening to informative speakers, receivers have to *work* at paying attention. Because attention spans are short, and trying to pay attention requires considerable energy, the speaker soon loses the audience. The speaker who wants the undivided attention of the audience will have to work at maintaining attention.

A number of things naturally draw attention of people, at least in this society. Not all of these factors will work in every case, but most of them will work most of the time to create involuntary attention. Let's note some of the *factors of attention* — which you'll recognize are both verbal and nonverbal.

relevance, proximity, or importance

If something is relevant or important to your listeners, they are more likely to pay attention than if it is not. Those things that people are proud of, that are close to them, that are familiar, that they care about, capture the attention of your receivers. Show how your ideas have relevance for them, will benefit them, or will affect them; they will probably pay attention with ease. For example,

> As today's speaker for the sixth-grade assembly, I will not just discuss safety — I will demonstrate ways to handle a skateboard with skill and control.

familiarity combined with novelty

People pay attention to the familiar only until it becomes boring. Usually if you are presenting something your audience already knows, or at least some of which they already know, they will lose interest unless you present it in a new way. Give the information a novel approach, a new twist, a new phrasing, or provide a new way of looking at familiar ideas:

> My sermon on Stewardship today is entitled, "Many Are Cold, but Few Are Frozen."

variety, movement, and activity

A kind of "Newton's Law" might be applied here: a moving stimulus is always preferred to one at rest. If you're looking at two things and one of them moves, you'll notice the one that moves, not the one that stays still. Variety, activity, and movement are among the best attention devices. This principle applies equally to content and presentation. A varied, lively manner aids greatly in maintaining audience attention. A speaker who uses body movements purposefully will have less difficulty in maintaining attention than one who stands still. Moving around helps hold attention. But bear in mind that constant movement can be distracting — or it can be as monotonous as speaking without movement. It's not just movement you need, but variety of movement.

380   The principle of variety applies also to speech content. If all

you have is a collection of statements of observation, explanatory material, or a whole slate of statistics, you'll probably lose your audience's attention. One very important statistic, or a couple that are striking, can aid in maintaining audience attention, but an unrelieved diet of statistics will turn your listeners off. Testimony and explanations are needed in most speeches, but unless they are combined with examples, visual aids, analogies, the speech is likely to become boring. Among the best aids to maintaining attention are a variety of supporting materials and lively varied presentation.

curiosity

When people are curious, they pay attention—most people are curious about things they don't know. If you can show how an idea might be beneficial or relevant or important, listeners will be curious. People have a lot of natural curiosity. They want to find out about things affecting them. They enjoy learning about the world if they have a prospect of reward by satisfying their natural curiosity. Arouse your listeners' interest in the unknown, show them how they can gain from learning, and curiosity will keep them listening:

> What is it about that dark and mysterious cave that lures people again and again to its icy, forbidding interior?

conflict

A vital attention factor is conflict. People love to watch conflict and to hear about it. They'll go to a football game but not to a practice. The conflict is what attracts them; and the lure is competition. Fans are thrilled by highly skilled players and well-executed plays, but most won't attend events that display skill unless competition is involved. Knowing this can help you devise ways to hold an audience's attention. We caution you, however, not to use conflict between you, the speaker, and the audience. Although it would probably maintain attention, this would probably destroy any chances of accomplishing your purpose. People pay attention to someone they're arguing with, but they're usually neither informed nor persuaded in such a situation. Use conflict by siding with the audience against a cause or a common opponent:

> All of us here tonight are angered by the decision of the city to terminate the services of the school crossing guard.

humor

Humor can be an important attention factor. Though it's difficult to define, we know humor holds attention. What is funny to one person may not be to somebody else; what is humorous in one situation may not be in another. But whatever your listeners find humorous, they'll pay attention to. If you're listening to a speaker who says, "That reminds me of a story," you'll listen because you think something funny might be coming. You must be careful to use humor that is appropriate to you, the listeners, and the situation. But if it's appropriate, humor can be a superior attention device.

concreteness

Concrete images are preferred to abstract. People respond to things they can see, things they recognize, things that recall actual images or events. Abstractions are hard to visualize and pay attention to. For example, philosophy as an abstract concept isn't likely to hold the attention of many. But if you talk about philosophy as it affects the lives of people, specifically your listeners, it can hold listeners' interest.

> We are not going to discuss the effect of nuclear energy on people of the next century; what we are concerned about is its impact on your life and mine—today.

SOURCE BEVAVIORS IN PUBLIC SPEAKING[3]

How should I deliver my speech? Probably this is the most commonly asked question about public speaking. It's natural for people to be concerned about presentation because the way a speaker behaves while sending the message is so obvious and so apparently important in the outcome. We don't have a set of easy answers for effective delivery, but do have some guidelines to suggest.

The Most Important Principle

> Seldom or never will a man be eloquent but when he is in earnest and uttering his own sentiments.
>
> HUGH BLAIR

The basic rule for speaker behaviors relates to your purpose. *Any behavior that helps to achieve your purpose is recommended.* That's the only totally accurate generalization regarding public speaking

---

[3] In this chapter we are emphasizing the speaker in public communication. We've discussed the receiver role in Chapter 8, and will return to the topic of how receivers can cope with persuasion in Chapters 14 and 16.

Without eye contact it's difficult for a speaker to gauge audience reaction.
Source: Forum, newspaper of Florissant Valley Community College.

that we believe makes sense, because effective speaker behaviors vary with the speaker, the audience, and the message.

While recognizing the situational nature of communication, we can suggest one rule of thumb. *A speaker should sincerely want to communicate, should be prepared, and should be natural.* If you really want to communicate, if you have ideas or information you really want to share with your listeners, and they sense your desire to communicate, they will forgive many speaker errors. If you are well-prepared, you will usually convey an impression of credibility, and your audience will tend to have confidence in you. Perhaps the best aid to credibility, however, is to be yourself. Don't pretend to be someone you aren't. Public speaking is only an expanded conversation. Instead of conversing with one or a few persons, you talk with many people at once. Most speakers are most effective when they are relaxed and natural in a conversational setting, talking about something they know about and are interested in. Therefore, the most important principle of public speaking is to sincerely want to communicate, to be prepared, and to be yourself.

The Multisensory Approach

Another guideline for speakers we have already mentioned in our discussion of supporting materials. It applies to both content and presentation: *use the multisensory approach whenever possible.* A good example of this approach was provided by a speech instructor who was demonstrating that people tend to react not to the denotative meaning of words, but to their connotations. He told his students they were to test a new food for a large company, and they were asked to taste the food and report on it. They responded that the food wasn't terribly tasty, but said nothing very negative. After the instructor received the student responses, he told them that they had been sampling dog biscuits! Everyone, of course, groaned and complained, reacting to the words that described what they had just eaten and their feelings about those words, rather than the product itself. The instructor effectively used taste to illustrate his point.

As a speaker, you will almost always use both sight and sound. Most speakers have direct, face-to-face contact with audiences. And if listeners can see you, you will inevitably use nonverbal communication as well as verbal. Your nonverbal communication should support the verbal. This means you should be physically in control. It also means your verbal messages should be consistent with your nonverbal, because as you recall, when the two conflict, receivers tend to believe the nonverbal messages. You'll also recall that nonverbal messages are primary communicators of feelings. In the U.S., people have been socialized not to talk much about feelings, certainly not in public. But they're still expressed nonverbally, and because listeners respond to feelings, as much or more than to words, your nonverbal communication should support your words. Finally, to restate an important point made earlier, use visual aids and other nonverbal supporting materials whenever you can. These will improve delivery, increase receiver attention, improve the clarity of your verbal messages, and improve retention.

Vocal Variety

Your voice should reflect your personality as well as any special aspects of the situation. If you talk to a large group of people, you'll probably talk more slowly than usual. If you are talking about a serious subject or a subject that's hard to understand, you'll also slow down. However, don't talk too slowly for too long. Variety in voice requires variety of rate. You may want to slow down on important or serious materials and speed up at other times.

Other kinds of vocal variety should also be used. Both pitch and volume should vary. Your voice, in natural conversation, will rise and fall in both. Learn to use a lively voice in the public speaking situation also. Over the years you've surely had at least one instructor who talked in a monotone and put you to sleep during the first ten minutes of class. Reading aloud generally causes a monotonous tone—that's one reason we suggest you shouldn't read a speech. Most people don't need to. A president, or a secretary of state, or a person whose words are watched for every nuance can read speeches. Otherwise, it's not a good idea. Reading interferes with effective speaker behavior in almost every way. It interferes with vocal variety, with eye contact, with the ability to assess audience response, and damages credibility.

Another important element in vocal variety is *the use of pauses.* Sometimes a pause comes before an important point. Other times, a pause *after* an important point will be effective, giving your audience time to reflect. Pauses can be dramatic as well as informative, and you can use them to emphasize and highlight your important ideas and transitions. Effective speakers learn to use pauses for many effects.

Variety in Bodily Action

Variety of action, also important, will come from applying the enlarged conversation guideline. When you are speaking in public, try to do what's natural for you in conversational situations. Learn to duplicate yourself at your best.

be natural

When you are natural and animated, your body supports your ideas, and you use a variety of gestures. If you rehearse a gesture, it will probably look terrible. Moreover, you'll feel unnatural and your concentration on ideas and listeners will be broken as you worry about what movements you are going to make. But if you are concerned about the subject and can let yourself be natural, you'll gesture normally. You can observe this in many situations. Try the student center or a cafe sometime. Sit down and watch some people in a conversation whose voices you cannot hear. You'll notice that they, like you, talk with their hands and do not repeat the same gesture all the time. You'll see a lot of variety. If you apply the principle the same way in public speaking, you will use effective bodily action to express your ideas. Talk with your audience. Let your listeners feel they are in an enlarged conversation.

John Kennedy, for instance, often overused a single gesture. Some of you may have seen his famous chopping hand. But one of the reasons that he could speak effectively and still overuse a single gesture was that he used much variety in other aspects of speaking. He illustrated the one general principle regarding public speaking: he communicated a sincere desire to speak with his listeners and was forgiven many delivery faults. Of course, speakers should use appropriate posture, stand where they can be seen, and display an attitude of confidence. All these are among suggestions for effective public speaking. But above all, *varied delivery springs from natural, concerned, well-prepared presentation.*

be friendly

This guideline is important because much of the meaning in face-to-face situations is communicated through *facial expressions.* Face and eyes are the basic communicators of feeling, but they also help us interpret the speaker, the speaker's intentions, attributes, and attitudes. If you watch your audiences, you'll learn to recognize when they don't understand you by reading their faces. They, in turn, will be watching yours. If your face conveys messages inconsistent with your words, your face will be believed. You'd be surprised how difficult it is to get students to smile in public speaking situations. Not recognizing that their faces are important sources of communication, many speakers never change expression. Sometimes, as a speaker you'll be nervous, but a smile is the best way to change that. It can make a real difference. Some listeners will probably surprise you and smile back, and it will help establish rapport between you and your audience. If you stand in front of an audience with a stony face and say that you're a friend of theirs, concerned about communicating to them, they'll probably ignore your words and believe your face.

be direct

A special aspect of facial expression is *eye contact.* A public speaker needs eye-to-eye contact with listeners. If you aren't able to look directly at individuals in your audience, you have a serious disadvantage. In the U.S. whenever you're in a face-to-face situation and don't look directly at the people you're talking to, they'll draw negative conclusions about your credibility. They will doubt your confidence, competence, or honesty. People in our culture generally assume that failure to look directly at a person as you speak implies a lack of belief in your subject, embarrassment, shame, or fear.

This is another reason we believe that reading a speech is such a damaging mode of presentation. Unless you're a very skilled reader, naturalness and eye contact will be destroyed when you use a manuscript. It's very important for speakers to look at individual members of their audience, to see them and communicate directly with them. We think the worst mode of presentation is reading. Only the very best speakers can read a speech effectively. For others, reading interferes with eye contact and severely limits the use of feedback.

Some students have told us about devices they use when they feel unable to look listeners directly in the eye. Some look at the back wall or between the chairs. Don't do that. Learn to look at your listeners; learn to talk *with* your audience. How else can you read their feedback and adapt to it? Feedback is important enough to you as a speaker that you should actively seek it. As we have stressed in earlier pages, you may need to assess the receivers' knowledge, their understanding, their awareness. Don't hesitate to use direct questions when necessary, but only direct eye contact will let you know when those questions will be helpful.

Environment

When you *can* affect the environment in which you speak, make sure that the environment supports your communication. Several aspects of this are worth noting. Audience arrangement is one. How is your audience to be seated? Can you arrange your listeners in a way that supports effective communication? If your purpose is interaction among your listeners, then arrange the chairs in a circle or semicircle, or perhaps even around a table. If you want regimentation to display authority and to discourage interaction among the listeners, use a typical classroom or theater-type setting. If the auditorium or room is only half full, and everyone is seated at the back, get them to move; ask them to come up where you can talk to them. Or perhaps you may want to move closer to them. The principle is to *improve the setting in any way that supports your purpose.* Remove distracting objects, choose a room that is of suitable size, suitable color, and with suitable surroundings. Be sure you have microphone and easel or table for visuals if you need them. Plan in advance for all aspects of the environment that can be controlled. When you cannot change the environment in which you speak, recognize that you may need to compensate for it and be prepared to do so.

Physical Appearance

Recall from Chapter 5 how important personal appearance is in interpersonal perception. In your daily life it might not matter too much to you how you dress, but in the public speaking setting, it does. If you are speaking to people who care how you appear, then you'd better dress and groom yourself accordingly. You don't necessarily have to conform to the dress of your audience, but you should not offend. If you are speaking, for instance, to a group known to be conservative, and your hair is long, comb it neatly. Speaking to a local Lions club you don't have to dress as the Lions do, but your customary apparel may not be appropriate.

The way you dress and look is important to credibility. Appearance tells the listeners things about you, and how you feel about them and the occasion. You show respect or disrespect for them by the way you look. They draw many conclusions about your personality and authority from the way you look. Plan your appearance with care. Remember you don't have to look the same as your audience but you shouldn't offend them unless it's your purpose as a speaker to offend. And if you want to inform or to persuade, you usually can't afford to offend.

In concluding this section on speaker behavior in public speaking situations, we want to be honest with you. You can do many things as a speaker to improve your audience's attitude toward you, and we have suggested some of these to you. But if you follow our basic guideline, you can get away with many mistakes. To reiterate, *if you sincerely want to communicate, are well-prepared, and are being yourself, you can be an effective public speaker regardless of many other barriers* — you have the basis for effective public speaking.

Public speaking, like all communication, is goal-directed and situational. One major principle guides almost everything about public speaking. The principle is, "It depends." What works in public speaking "depends" on the speaker, the specific receivers, and the situation. Within this framework, however, several guidelines for effective speaking can be offered.

Good speeches are usually structured. The purpose of a speech relates to the behaviors desired from listeners, and the thesis is the central idea of the message. Good speeches usually have one major purpose and thesis. Structure usually involves an introduction, the purpose of which is to gain attention and to start listeners thinking about the subject; a body, in which the thesis is completely developed; and a conclusion, which sets the proper mood and leaves the listeners with a feeling of closure. Both introductions and conclusions may use the following devices: humor, serious or funny anecdotes and illustrations, quotations, rhetorical or direct questions. Introductions also sometimes use direct reference either to the subject or occasion. The body of the speech is usually most effective when it is structured so that the audience can follow the speaker's thought structure. Two general patterns of body structure may be used: the deductive, which presents the thesis and then develops it; and the inductive, which lets the thesis emerge as the ideas of the speech are developed. Several standard thought structures may be used for selection and organization of main points: the time or chronological structure, spatial, and topical. Common topical outlines are cause-effect, problem-solution, and advantages-disadvantages.

Supporting materials are needed to amplify, explain, prove, or emphasize the main ideas of the speech or to motivate receivers, maintain their attention, and help them remember. Appropriate supporting materials also create *source credibility*. Supporting materials are chosen on the basis of the specific receivers, the thesis, and the speaker. Different kinds of supporting materials may be used: nonverbals including visual aids; and statements of observation and explanation, comparison and contrast, examples, statistics, testimony, repetition, and restatement.

Audience analysis is needed to know what supporting materials will be effective and what thought structure will be useful. Speakers need to learn all they can about the receivers, especially those things that will influence how the messages will be decoded: knowledge, interest, and attitudes toward the subject, speaker, and other important related issues. Audience analysis can be done by asking questions when possible directly of receivers or of people who know them. This sometimes involves the speaker in questionnaires or polling. When this isn't possible the speaker may have to infer on the basis of demographic data that can be discovered. Audience analysis also involves the use of feedback to draw inferences while speaking. Using nonverbals to interpret listeners' reactions can help a speaker know how to adapt message and delivery to improve chances of accomplishing the purpose. Adaptation involves selecting thought structure, supporting materials, and manner of presentation as well as manipulating the environment in ways that improve speaker credibility and chances of purpose accomplishment.

Maintaining attention is important to a speaker. The speaker wants the speech ideas to be involuntarily in the focus of listener attention. The factors that can be used to help accomplish that goal are relevance, proximity, importance, familiar ideas presented with novelty, variety of content and movement, curiosity, conflict, humor, and concreteness.

An important factor in clarity, maintenance of attention, and credibility of the speaker is delivery. Most important in speech delivery is that the speaker communicate a genuine desire to talk to listeners, a sense of being well-prepared, and a sense of honest presentation of self and ideas. Beyond this basic principle several guidelines for speech delivery are: the multisensory approach; vocal variety; variety of body action; sincere, interested facial expression; direct eye contact. Speakers can also manipulate the environment in which the speech is given to their advantage. Finally, speakers should use feedback to assess the effectiveness of both the content and the delivery of the speech.

Exercise: One-Point Speech

Objective: To practice developing ideas for a speech.
Directions:
1. Each person should prepare a three- to four-minute one-point speech.
2. The thesis must be carefully selected and limited. It should be an inference statement you can support directly with supporting material, not one that must be divided into subpoints to be supported.
3. Use this pattern: illustrate, state, amplify, and restate.
   a. *Illustrate.* Begin with a detailed example, either factual or hypothetical, from which your main idea (thesis) can be drawn. Do not bother with preliminaries: "I was wondering what to talk about when an idea struck me. This morning I'd like to talk to you about one of my favorite subjects." Just open with the example.
   b. *State.* State your thesis as clearly, concisely, and strikingly as possible. Use a single declarative sentence to state the thesis, although you may include several sentences of transition relating the illustration to it.
   c. *Amplify.* Use at least two other kinds of supporting material to make your assertion clear, interesting, and compelling.
   d. *Restate.* Although you may wish to restate your thesis several times during your speech in relating supporting material to it, make a final restatement that will serve as a simple summation.

Questions for Discussion

1. What are the basic purposes of public speaking?
2. Why organize speeches?
3. What are some useful organizational plans for speeches?
4. What types of supporting material can a speaker use?
5. What guidelines should a speaker use to choose supporting materials?
6. How does a speaker analyze the audience?
7. What basic guidelines apply for effective speech presentation?

Suggestions for Further Reading

GIBSON, JAMES, *Speech Organization: A Programmed Approach.* San Francisco: Rinehart Press, 1971.

——, AND MICHAEL HANNA, *Audience Analysis: A Programmed Approach to Receiver Behavior.* Englewood Cliffs, N.J.: Prentice-Hall, Inc., 1975.

HART, RODERICK P., GUSTAV W. FRIEDRICH, AND WILLIAM D. BROOKS, *Public Communication.* New York: Harper & Row, Publishers, 1975.

JEFFREY, ROBERT, AND OWEN PETERSON, *Speech: A Text With Adapted Readings.* New York: Harper & Row, Publishers, 1975.

MARKLE, MARSHA, AND THOMAS R. KING, *A Program on Speech Preparation.* Columbus, Ohio: Charles E. Merrill Publishing Co., 1972.

McCABE, BERNARD P., JR., AND C. COLEMAN BENDER, *Speaking Is a Practical Matter.* Boston, Mass.: Holbrook Press, Inc., 1973.

MONROE, ALAN, AND DOUGLAS EHNINGER, *Principles and Types of Speech Communication.* Glenview, Ill.: Scott, Foresman and Co., 1974.

MUDD, CHARLES S., AND MALCOM SILLARS, *Speech: Content and Communication.* New York: Thomas Y. Crowell Co., 1975.

14
Persuasion

goal:

To learn how to accomplish specific persuasive goals.

probes:

The material in this chapter should help you to:

1. Establish specific persuasive goals and
   assess the attainability of the goals
   identify the goals as long- or short-range pp. 394–98

2. Given specific persuasive goals,
   assess receiver persuasibility based on factors of prior information, attitudes, and expectations. pp. 398–401; ch. 13, pp. 376–79
   assess your credibility as a persuader, indicating ways to increase it. pp. 402–3; ch. 5, pp. 151–55
   choose appropriate evidence. p. 403; ch. 13, pp. 368–74
   identify motive appeals that would be persuasive to receivers. pp. 413–16
   develop and organize a persuasive message. pp. 401–16; ch. 13, pp. 364–68
   plan and use language and nonverbal messages to achieve your goal. pp. 408–9; ch. 13, pp. 379–88
   evaluate your persuasive effort and assess how it could have been improved. pp. 360–422

3. Explain the major theories of attitude change and indicate how they can be used to achieve persuasive goals. pp. 416–22

Persuasion is a universal communication experience. Friends, family, salespersons, politicians, newspapers, magazines, radio, and television constantly confront you with messages designed to change your attitudes or induce specific behaviors. Similarly, you regularly attempt to induce behaviors or change attitudes in others: family members, friends, colleagues at work, members of clubs or churches, public officials. Persuasion is not limited to public speaking, though often the study of persuasion is combined with practice in public speaking. Persuasion is something you do and something you are the target of in many facets of your daily life. For these reasons, this chapter introduces principles that you can use to improve your persuasive efforts and to evaluate how to respond to those who try to persuade you.

WHAT IS PERSUASION?

Persuasion, as we use the term, describes any communication process in which a source attempts either to secure changes in beliefs or attitudes or to induce overt behavior in one or more receivers. The second type of goal mentioned is easiest to recognize. Persuaders may try to get receivers to stand up, sign petitions, buy products, quit smoking, vote for a particular candidate, go to church on Sunday, drive more safely, be good, make contributions, carry a sign, or devote time to a cause. The list could go on indefinitely. The other type of persuasion mentioned is less easily recognized because the goals (of changing beliefs or attitudes) do not deal with overt behaviors. Let's examine a few of the possible goals related to securing changes in beliefs or attitudes. A persuader may seek to *reinforce or intensify an existing belief* (make you feel more strongly about helping the needy, which you already support); to *add something new to existing attitude systems* (convince you that you need vitamin G, a product you never heard of before); to *create a dis-belief in an existing cognition* (convince you that Senator Blue, whom you like, is really a very bad Senator); or to *modify existing attitudes by weakening their stability or importance* (change your attitude about getting a new car from "I absolutely *must* have a sports car" to "It would be nice to have a sports car if I can").

The overt and the not-observable goals of persuaders interact. When trying to induce a behavior, for instance, you often must first modify existing attitudes. To sell a new product, you might have to convince a person it is better than one presently used. Some confusions arise regarding persuasion because the term involves three different referents. Persuasion refers to (1) the *intent* of the source (what the persuader wants to accomplish); (2) the *process* that occurs (the things a persuader does and says to accomplish the goal); and (3) the *effects* in receivers (the changes that actually occur). To understand persuasion, all three aspects should be considered.

ESTABLISHING GOALS

Your study of persuasion should begin where a persuader begins: with *analysis of desired goals.* Your first step in preparing for a persuasive effort is to answer the question, What do I want to accomplish? First *decide specifically what you want, and state your goal in terms of the desired receiver response.* To overemphasize the importance of goal setting is difficult. Failure to clarify goals is one major reason for failure of persuasive efforts. Be sure to identify the specific changes in attitude or belief systems you want, or the exact behavior you're after. Make sure your goal statement specifies *what* you want done, *who* should do it, and *when.*

Situation: Student talking to instructor about the grade received on a term paper.

Specific Goal: Student wants instructor *(who)* to change his/her attitude toward the paper and to give it a grade of C instead of D *(what)* before awarding final grades *(when).*

Assessing Attainability of Goals

Once your goal is identified, decide if it is *attainable,* given the time and other resources you have. Ask, "Can I achieve the goal?" Several factors influence the attainability of goals.

existing receiver attitudes

The difficulty of a persuasive task depends primarily on the initial position of the receiver. It's fairly easy to secure a behavior based on an existing attitude that is favorable. If your friend is a Barbra Streisand fan, persuading her to attend Barbra's latest movie won't be too difficult. To visualize this concept of initial position, consider a scale on which 1 represents "ready to act against" and 7 represents "ready to act for" your thesis.

Thesis: You should attend Barbra's new movie.

1	2	3	4	5	6	7
Ready to Act Against	Strongly Opposed	Mildly Opposed	Neutral	Mildly in Favor	Strongly in Favor	Ready to Act for

Imagine a potential receiver whose position on this scale regarding a particular goal is 6. To achieve favorable action from that receiver would be much easier than getting the same behavior from a person at a position of 1 or 2.

We'll discuss shortly how you decide where a receiver fits on the scale. For now, remember that the task of the persuader is generally easier when the receivers are anywhere above the neutral middle of the scale. To change from one extreme to another $(2 \rightarrow 6)$ is more difficult than to strengthen existing predispositions $(5 \rightarrow 6)$. It's also more difficult than inducing behaviors based on existing tendencies $(5 \rightarrow 7$ or $6 \rightarrow 7)$. With this scale you can visualize your desired end results. If you know where you think receivers can be placed along the scale before you attempt to persuade them, and then decide where you would like them to be when you finish, you have identified the dimensions of your persuasive task.

total attitude system

It's easier to change attitudes that are less important and stable than intense or long-held beliefs. If you have spent three years and more than $5,000 to acquire 96 of the 120 credits required for a B.A. degree, if you have enjoyed your experiences in college and have been successful, it would be very difficult for anyone to change your attitude about completing your senior year. Less stable attitudes, with little personal commitment or investment, are not so difficult to change. Using the above example, it would be easier to get you to attend another college or change your major than to quit altogether.

Changes in existing attitudes are more difficult to achieve than developing new attitudes that don't significantly affect the existing system. New information can develop or expand attitudes without influencing ones that already exist. For example, you may believe that Carl and Mary are your good friends. You may later have experiences that lead you to a new attitude, that Tony is also your good friend. This new attitude requires no change in the other. Persuading you that Carl is not a good friend would be more difficult.

Seek Attainable Goals (Usually)

Persuasive goals ordinarily should be within reasonable limits. Why waste your time seeking a goal you know you can't achieve? To have a goal of persuading those attending a suburban PTA meeting that they should abandon their homes and jobs and search for a naturalistic lifestyle in a farm commune would be a tall order. A more attainable goal would be to convince them to take their families camping in state parks to expose their children to nature more often. To be effective, *persuasive requests should be within a range of acceptability.* If you were a fund raiser and your audience strongly believed in the merit of your cause, you might request $1 from a person with an $8,000 income. You could request more from those in higher income brackets. The principle is that persuaders ought to choose persuasive goals that probably can be reached.

Exceptions to the principle exist, but they are usually cases in which the ostensible goal of the persuader is not the real goal, or in which the persuader is unrealistic. The leaders in the major social movements of the 1960s and early 1970s illustrate this point: militant civil rights activists, radical feminists, and student radicals.[1] These people sought and were serious about enlisting their receivers into their movements, but the goal of securing the extreme changes they advocated was not attainable with most receivers.

The demands for radical changes served another purpose, however. They created a climate in which *moderate* goals were attainable. The more limited goals wouldn't have been considered moderate without the radical demands. For example, one of the original leaders of the women's movement, Ti-Grace Atkinson, repeatedly demanded radical changes of behavior from the women to whom she spoke. She coined the "bra burning" phrase that became a catchword for the radical goals she and others advocated. Those goals were probably responsible for the phenomenon of vast numbers of women who later said "Yes, I believe in equal work for equal pay, and that women should be free to choose roles in life other than housewife if they want, but I don't believe in Women's Liberation."

---

[1] We want to clarify that our intended meanings for the word *radical* have no negative connotations. Radical is not used pejoratively. We use the term to refer to sweeping changes, indicating no approval or disapproval of the changes. To us, radical only means that the changes sought are large, not small.

Militant civil rights activists created a climate in which moderate goals
were attainable.
Source: Wide World Photos.

The radical demands made less sweeping ones seem moderate, but without the radical demands, the moderate goals would not
have been attainable. Whether Ti-Grace Atkinson was aware of performing that function or whether she really expected to achieve the
radical goals isn't clear. Nor does it really matter. It is the description of what happened that matters, because the principle works.
Sometimes a persuader knows that the stated goals are unattainable,
but will pursue them anyway to make less radical demands pal-
atable.

Long-Range vs. Short-Range Goals

You may decide that a goal is unattainable in the short term, but
that over a period of time, you can bring receivers to the desired
position. If you can't immediately achieve your long-range goal,
plan shorter steps along the way that are attainable. Plan for several
persuasive efforts that eventually will reach the ultimate goals.
Movements seeking extension of civil rights to Blacks in the U.S.
include a number of leaders whose efforts over many years illustrate this approach. Martin Luther King's initial attempts to desegre-
gate lunch counters were only first steps in attaining a long-range
goal of equality for Blacks. At the time Dr. King began his efforts,
that goal was far removed—nor has it yet been achieved. But he
and many others saw equality as the desired end result, and
planned and presented countless messages to achieve short-term
397 goals as steps along the way to the ultimate goal.

Exercise: Setting Persuasive Goals

**Objective: To practice setting goals for persuasive situations.
Directions:**

1. Choose three real-life situations in which you might try to persuade someone.
2. For each potential persuasive effort:
   a. State the situation
   b. Name the persons you are going to try to persuade
   c. State specifically the effect you desire as a result of your persuasive effort (i.e., what the receiver will do or say if you are successful).
3. Now, check your responses in #2. Have you, for each goal statement, specified
   a. Who?
   b. Is to do what?
   c. Under what circumstances?
   d. When?
   If not, rephrase the goal statements until you have.
4. Your instructor may ask you to share your goal statements in class.

ASSESSING RECEIVER PERSUASIBILITY

Deciding the attainability of a goal for specific receivers is usually not easy. The difficulty increases with the number of people you want to persuade. *Assessing goal attainability, or persuasibility, is determining the chances that your receivers will respond favorably to your goal.* But how do you decide what the chances *are* for achieving your persuasive goals?

One way to conceptualize the persuader is as a gambler. A gambler challenges the laws of probability, and tries to use all available information to draw inferences about the results of an event. The gambler assumes an ability to use the laws of probability to beat the "house." A persuader behaves similarly. Odds for the persuader increase with favorable, friendly receivers, and a subject that doesn't polarize or antagonize. If a persuader faces opposed, hostile, or disinterested receivers, initial odds favor the "house." The persuader must then plan carefully to decide what strategies and information can tip the balance.

To improve the odds, a persuader can do two things: (1) *gain all possible knowledge about the receivers,* and (2) *use the information to decide on strategies to shift the odds* in favor of goal accomplishment. The discussion of audience analysis in the last chapter gave suggestions about ways of finding out what you need to know about your receivers before and as you speak to them. These suggestions also apply to persuasion in all settings. A persuader needs to use the techniques of receiver analysis to assess the likelihood of desired response.

Drawing Inferences

You will seldom be able to find all the information you want about your receivers. Often you wind up with partial demographic data and some items that seem unrelated to your goal. But, like the gambler, you make inferences knowing the risk of inaccuracy. *The whole effort of seeking information about receivers is to reduce the risk and increase the probability of accurate inferences.* For instance, the information that a prospective buyer dislikes salespersons, has just bought a new car, and lives in New York City might be of little direct help in an attempt to sell that person a color television. However, the information could lead to useful inferences. A dislike of salespeople could imply distrust. Ownership of a new car might suggest a desire for status, affluence, or convenience. The New York City address might lead to an inference that the person is politically liberal, regardless of party affiliation, because this tends to be true of many New Yorkers. Each conclusion is an inference with varying degrees of probable accuracy. Some are probably inaccurate, but you can see that such inferences can help in a decision about what strategies to use in achieving a particular goal.

The information a persuader most needs leads to inferences that create favorable odds of desired receiver response. What kind of people are they? How much information do they possess? How likely are they to respond, and to what appeals? Answering these questions is assessing receiver persuasibility. *Persuasibility refers to the tendency of a person to change attitudes or adopt an advocated position.* Persuasibility depends on several factors.

prior information

One factor affecting persuasibility is how much information receivers have. Are you an engineer talking to fellow engineers, PTA members, or a social club? The differences in what receivers know will affect how they will respond. Sometimes you can assess information level by years of education, but not always. Everyday experiences are ample sources of information, very important in reference to some persuasive efforts.

The importance of prior information to a persuader depends on whether or not it has been assimilated into attitudes. Information that hasn't become part of the receiver's attitude system related to your goal isn't relevant to the situation. Therefore, the major importance of receivers' information relates to receiver attitudes.

Prior attitudes are critical factors in receiver persuasibility. If you could measure attitudes toward your goal among any group of potential receivers, you'd probably find some are already partisans, others are opponents, and some are neutral.

Ready to Act Against						Ready to Act for
1	2	3	4	5	6	7

Opponents	Neutrals	Partisans

To predict receivers' responses to persuasive efforts, you can classify them in these three categories. If possible, also find out how strong are the partisans' and opponents' attitudes. A partisan who strongly agrees with your goal should be approached differently from a mild partisan. Similarly, persuading a strong opponent differs greatly from persuading those who are only mildly opposed. And the neutral receiver represents a still different task.

If a persuader faces a homogenous group, whether of neutrals, partisans, or opponents, the task is different from facing a mixed or polarized group. If your audience is mixed, your job is to avoid alienating anyone, if possible. You'll improve your odds by concentrating on the most persuasible: strengthen the mild partisans or convince the neutrals and mildly opposed. You might bring strong opponents to admit that they may not be totally correct, but odds are high against succeeding with them in any short-term persuasive effort.

If the opponents have publicly stated their opposition, or have made others aware of their position, they'll be harder to persuade than if they feel equally strongly but haven't made it public. Also valuable is to know whether attitudes toward the issue are closely related to receivers' self-concept, if they are important, stable, and interrelated with other attitudes. If a belief is close to a person's self-concept, the difficulty of changing it escalates and odds against accomplishing your task will be quite high.

prior expectations

Receiver expectations are an important factor in persuasibility. *Most receivers approach a persuasive situation with expectations regarding either the source, the situation, or the subject.* If you as a persuader fail to meet someone's expectations of you, this can result in rejection of your proposal. For example, a person selling autos, insurance, houses, or appliances is expected to know a lot about the item being sold. Customers seldom buy from a salesperson who can't answer questions about the product, especially if it's a major purchase. Politicians are expected to answer questions about the important issues in an election. If they can't, they can lose the support of their constituencies.

Receivers' expectations aren't always realistic, but realistic or not, they have an important effect on your success or failure as a persuader. You must be careful not to create unrealistic images about yourself or your product or proposal. Once created, expectations must be met or changed. And if you need to change receiver expectations, the process of changing can reduce your credibility and delay goal attainment.

Receiver expectations can benefit a persuader if they're not unrealistic. You should know what receivers expect from you, your product, or your idea. It can help you do or say what pleases them. You should also know receivers' negative expectations, so you can come to the situation forearmed. If receivers are basically conservative, for example, and you have been depicted in advance as a wild-eyed radical, you can dress and talk in ways that counter those negative expectations.

environment

Environmental factors also influence receiver persuasibility. For example, hot, humid conditions predispose people to negative reactions; pleasant, comfortable surroundings encourage favorable exchanges. If you place objects or space between yourself and others, you might create an impression of being distant, separate, or superior. This can work to your advantage or disadvantage. It could contribute toward increasing your perceived authority and thus aid in accomplishing your persuasive goals; or it could damage the communication by separating you from your receivers psychologically as well as physically. A close feeling between source and receivers usually increases persuasibility. No physical barriers should separate you from receivers, unless you are quite sure this will increase your authority in their eyes.

STRATEGIES FOR SUCCESSFUL PERSUASION

> Its name is Public Opinion. It is held in reverence. It settles everything. Some think it is the voice of God.
>
> MARK TWAIN

A persuader can do more than study receivers to decide the likelihood of success. Knowing your receivers can help develop strategies to improve your odds of succeeding.

Source credibility is a basic element affecting receiver persuasibility. We discuss credibility as a strategy, however, because you don't just study receivers to find it. *Your credibility as a persuader is a receiver perception that you can affect positively.* By influencing the situation, saying the right things, and acting the right ways, you can directly improve your credibility.

Recall that our perceptions of people, including our ideas about their credibility, are largely a composite. We draw inferences about character, competence, dynamism, poise, and extroversion based largely on appearance, environment, behaviors, and verbal messages. The effect of each factor varies according to the situation, but all influence receiver perceptions of how believable you are.

appearance

How you look affects your credibility. Sometimes you may need to dress or look as you are expected to. At other times you may choose to emphasize differences from receivers by ignoring or flouting conventions. However, this technique must be used with care. Though in some cases being different from receivers will enhance your credibility, more often it can reduce or destroy it. Permissible dress, make-up, hair length vary according to current acceptable patterns and specific receivers' expectations. Because appearance can improve, decrease, or destroy credibility, consider its effect carefully as you plan for persuasive efforts.

mannerisms

Personal mannerisms are another source of receivers' inferences about credibility. People react to personal, idiosyncratic behaviors sometimes without even noticing them. Some mannerisms appear to be negative and should be corrected or controlled. A nervous person wrings hands, paces, taps, or drums fingers. If you behave that way people may conclude that you're unsure or unprepared, not trustworthy. Similar traits can be attributed to persuaders who fail to use eye contact, who look everywhere but at their receivers. Some persuaders display these behaviors, not because of lack of confidence or honesty, but because of habits. Nonetheless most receivers draw negative conclusions about authoritativeness from nervous mannerisms and they decrease your credibility.

environment

Environment can contribute to source credibility in both direct and indirect ways. Signs, flags, emblems proclaiming relationships with authoritative or respected organizations can surround you. You can select a setting that elevates you from the others, places you behind a bigger desk or in a more spacious and elegant surrounding. You can direct attention automatically to yourself by picking the focal seat. All these, and many other ways to manipulate the environment, can increase the chances that your listeners will see you as an authoritative person. In cases in which you are trying to develop credibility of character, you may need to establish an environment that emphasizes warmth and friendliness. You may still need to maintain elements that enhance authority. Recalling that credibility is a perception that varies according to situation and subject, you'll need to assess the elements to be emphasized in each case.

One aspect of environment that can raise your credibility is to associate with people who are respected by the receivers. If you are introduced or endorsed by someone your receivers like or respect, it can contribute to what is called "halo effect." If you are introduced by a well-respected person, some of that person's esteem can "rub off" on you. The association seems to vouch for your ability or character. Similarly, you can gain halo effects by citing acquaintances, describing interactions with them, and using subtle name dropping.

Evidence and Argumentation

One important element in establishing credibility comes from what you say, from message variables called *evidence* and *argument*. Use of evidence and argumentation are valuable strategies for increasing your odds of accomplishing persuasive goals.

evidence

We define evidence as *a statement believed by your listeners that forms the basis for believing another statement. Evidence,* from this point of view, is determined by the receiver. It's more than facts, statements of observation, or conclusions by authorities. It includes any statements accepted by receivers as reasons for believing other statements. This perspective on evidence recognizes the principles of stimulus processing, and it's critical for a persuader to understand. Something that is evidence to you may not be to someone else. *To increase the odds of accomplishing your persuasive goals, you need to view evidence from the receiver's perspective.* No matter how unimpeachable your observations, how obvious your facts, or how high your authority, if your receiver does not accept what you offer as evidence, it isn't evidence—not for that receiver. For example, the Biblical injunction that Jesus Christ is the Son of God is sufficient for most Christians. "The Bible says so" is sufficient evidence for them to believe the conclusion. But this is not evidence to millions who believe in other religions and consider Jesus' status similar to that of prophets or great teachers.

argument

Evidence becomes persuasive through argumentation. *We think of an argument as a unit of thought containing a conclusion and the evidence leading to the conclusion.* The evidence may be statements of observation or inferences by authority. Sometimes the evidence is only an accepted assertion and sometimes arguments serve as evidence for other conclusions. But whatever the evidence is, an argument without acceptable evidence will have little effect on a receiver.

In argumentation, the link between the evidence and the conclusion is as important as the information itself. For example, look at the following argument: Nine out of ten heroin addicts first smoked marijuana; therefore, marijuana use should be illegal because it leads to heroin addiction. Many people reject that conclusion for reasons that have nothing to do with the evidence statement. One might reject the causal reasoning that marijuana leads to heroin use. This person might observe that heroin addicts also drank milk before they used heroin, and conclude "Because one event precedes another doesn't mean one causes the other." This analysis rejects the link between evidence and conclusion. Another person might accept the causal link, agreeing that marijuana causes heroin addiction, but still reject the conclusion that it should be illegal. This person might say, "Accuracy of the conclusion that marijuana causes heroin use is irrelevant to whether or not it should be illegal. Heroin addiction is an illness, not a crime. If addiction isn't criminal, then what causes it wouldn't be criminal either."

a model for argument

Persuasive messages usually involve several arguments linked together. Chances of creating persuasive messages are improved by examining the links carefully. A model for analyzing arguments is offered by Stephen Toulmin.[2] You can use this model to examine your reasoning, and to assess whether or not your receivers will accept your conclusions.

Evidence ⎯⎯⎯⎯⎯⎯⎯⎯⎯⎯⎯⎯⎯⎯⎯⎯⎯⎯⎯⎯⎯→ *Conclusion*

↑

Warrant

---

[2] Stephen Toulmin, *Uses of Argument* (London: Cambridge University Press, 1958).

In the Toulmin model, all sound arguments contain three basic elements. These are *evidence, conclusion,* and a *warrant.* The warrant is the link between evidence and conclusion. It's the reason for believing the evidence is relevant. Many weak arguments omit the warrants. Assuming receivers will follow the reasoning can reduce the believability of an argument. Mental processes that seem obvious to you often aren't obvious to your listeners.

The following argument shows these three essential elements:

> Peter is Irish (**evidence**), therefore, Peter is a Roman Catholic (**conclusion**). Unstated **warrant:** most Irish are Catholic.

Three other elements are involved in some arguments. These are the *reservation,* which is an "unless" clause; the *qualifier,* which is a clause that limits or restricts the conclusion; and the *backing,* or support for the warrant. These three are needed when the receiver won't accept a conclusion after hearing the initial three elements of an argument.

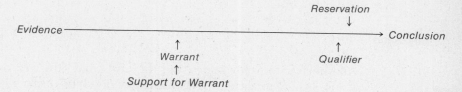

A qualifier comes between the claim and the other elements. It limits or specifies the conclusion to make it acceptable. Inserting words like "usually" or "probably" often makes a conclusion more believable. Backing or support for a warrant is often needed. Just as the connection between evidence and conclusion isn't always obvious, so the warrant is not always acceptable. Another element sometimes needed is the reservation. A reservation cites possible exceptions. It's usually introduced by words like "unless," "except," "other than."

To illustrate the qualifier, support for warrant, and reservation, let's add the following to the example.

> Peter is Irish, therefore, he is *probably* (**qualifier**) a Roman Catholic, *unless* (**reservation**) Peter is a member of the British Army.
> **Support for the warrant:** Ninety percent of Irish residents are Roman Catholic.

The Toulmin model of argument is useful because it exposes the essentials in an argument. You can use it to examine a reasoning process and decide where the weaknesses are. You can see needs for further evidence or for a warrant to link it to the conclusion. If neither the evidence nor the reason for connecting it to the conclusion is believed by the receivers, the argument will not be persuasive.

In the last chapter, different kinds of supporting materials that could be used as evidence were discussed. In persuasive arguments, you might use any of them: facts or other nonverbals, statements of observation, explanations, comparison and contrast, statistics, testimony, repetition, or restatement. In other cases you'll rely primarily on facts and statements of observation and statistics. Still other times, testimony of authority will be the major kind of evidence employed. As we've emphasized, to decide what evidence to use, you have to decide what will be persuasive to *your* listeners. What will *they* believe? That's the critical question the persuader needs to answer in using evidence. An argument can be perfect in its structure, but still not persuasive. It can't be developed in isolation from receiver analysis. Use of the Toulmin model can help you analyze your reasoning, but knowledge of the receiver is the most essential aid in choosing which items to use.

Organization

Another strategy for increasing the odds that you will achieve your goals is organization. *Organization involves ordering and categorizing the basic components of a message and is reflected in an outline.*

An organized outline is helpful for two reasons. First, it gives you *flexibility in presenting ideas and moving toward persuasive goals.* If you know where you're going, it's easier to get there. An outline helps a persuader as a road-map does a traveler. A map aids in deciding what routes to take to reach your destination. Similarly, an outline is not a rigid pattern from which you never stray, but suggests the steps that are planned for reaching your goals.

Most persuasive efforts require some strategy planned in advance. Whether the persuasive attempt will be a one-time shot or an extended process with several interactions, an overview plan is important. Organizing for persuasion involves planning for each individual message as well as for the overall effort. This outline should reflect your *planned* sequence to present ideas and get responses. It should be your guide as you send the messages, but as in traveling, changes may be made en route. Having outlined a plan, however, your decision to change is based on planning. The advance planning will also assist in evaluating feedback from receivers. It will help you assess whether or not you are getting the desired responses and decide what to do if you aren't.

The second reason organization aids persuasion is that it also *helps your receivers*. As we discussed in Chapter 13, when receivers understand structure in ideas, they find listening and remembering easier. Remember, though, organization must be apparent and meaningful to receivers or it won't help. Just because a thought structure seems logical to you doesn't mean it will be logical, meaningful, or clear to your listeners.

goals determine organization

Overall strategies of organization depend largely on your goals. Many patterns of organization that we suggested for public speaking are also helpful in persuasion. Especially useful for persuasion are outlines that arrange main points according to advantages and disadvantages or problem and solution. (See pp. 366–68, Chapter 13)

One-Sided and Two-Sided Messages. One important organizational decision is whether to use one- or two-sided messages. A one-sided message presents only one point of view; two-sided messages include arguments on both sides of the issue. A one-sided message is usually more appropriate when receivers basically agree with you, as well as when receivers are uninformed or undecided. You won't raise issues of opposition receivers may not have considered. But some listeners regard the one-sided approach as biased or unfair. In these cases, the alternative is to give both sides. Two-sided messages are generally more effective when receivers oppose or disagree with your position, or when they are well-informed on both sides of the issue. Some evidence suggests that well-educated listeners prefer to hear both sides of issues. Presenting both sides is also of value if receivers will later hear the other point of view. Then, two-sided arguments serve as a kind of "inoculation" against later counterarguments. When you speak in a format with other speakers who will oppose you, a two-sided message is generally superior. If you speak first, you should give a preview of the opponents' arguments. Receivers may then realize you've considered the opposing arguments. If you speak after your opponents, you should respond to their arguments.

When you use two-sided messages, you need to decide which argument goes first. Ordering the presentations may make a difference. When you give both points of view, it's probably better to present your argument last, although research is not conclusive on this matter. Basically, as long as receivers are aware of your point of view, and you present a stronger argument for it than do those who oppose it, the position of the other argument is less important. Some advantages might be gained by "slipping in" undesirable information about the opposite point of view after stating your position. Or you might name a "few" problems and then show how the advantages of your argument or proposal outweigh these difficulties.

In organizing for persuasion,

1. Include both sides of the argument if receivers have previously been exposed to both sides.
2. Include both sides of the argument if receivers are well-educated.
3. Include both sides of the argument if the receivers generally oppose your side.
4. Present one side if receivers basically agree with you or are relatively uneducated or uninformed.

If receivers will later hear opposing persuasion, you can

1. Present both sides.
2. Use attack methods to present the other side.
3. Mention, without elaborating on counterarguments the opposition could use against you.
4. Try to anticipate the opposition's arguments and bring them up on your own ground first.

Language

An important element in increasing your odds of being a successful persuader is your use of language. Language is a special tool of the persuader. It affects credibility as we discussed in Chapter 5; it also affects motivation. To persuade, some words and phrases may be required while others should be ruled out. Both denotative and connotative meanings affect receiver responses and require you to choose words and phrases with care.

In your everyday conversations, the "volleying" (back and forth) nature of interactions limits your ability to plan language use. But as a persuader, you need to use language with special care. When you can plan ahead, you can plan some off-court, pre-game strategy to use language to your advantage. Please note, we're not recommending that you write out any speech manuscripts. We're referring to the many persuasion efforts that employ combinations of writing or media advertising when the use of precisely the right words is important. We're also talking more generally about levels of diction and styles of talking. Diction or word choice involves decisions about vocabulary level, and which specific words, phrases, or word combinations will create the desired effects. Many different effects result from different word choices. We will discuss effects of intensity, clarity, and oral style and identification.

intensity

When you want to intensify receivers' feelings, language can be a useful tool. Intense language can attract attention, create a sense of immediacy, arouse emotional responses, and emphasize the importance or significance of statements. *Intensity* involves using words that create vivid images and have powerful negative or positive connotations. "Max did well," "Max did spectacularly," and "Max did O.K." are all positive statements, but their intensity varies greatly.

In conflict situations, name calling often is used to intensify the reactions of partisans. Calling an opponent, "my worthy opponent" will not get the same response as saying "that s.o.b." To say "that son of a bitch" is even stronger. There's no doubt which would arouse the most emotion! This illustrates that degree of intensity or language must be guided by the situation. Strong language is not always to a persuader's benefit.

The actual intensity in any word depends on the cultural backgrounds of the source and receivers, and the situation. Profane language sometimes attracts attention and conveys the persuader's sense of how important an idea is. In other cases, it's a natural identification of speaker with listeners. Profanity on the streets or a construction site probably conveys no special intensity. Change either the setting or the speaker and the same words could be very intense. A bricklayer whose language at work included constant profanity always blushed whenever he said "damn" in the presence of his boss's wife. "You crazy nigger," spoken by one Black to another among friends has quite a different intensity from the same words spoken by a white police officer to an apprehended Black speeder.

Knowing the effects of intensity upon receivers will help you choose words appropriately for each situation. Intensity can attract receivers' attention, convey speaker attitudes, reinforce significant aspects of the message, and convey a sense of urgency. These effects depend on your ability to assess the receivers' perceptual systems and adapt accordingly. Too much intensity for a situation can be as harmful as too little. Using profane language at church would probably interfere with accomplishing your goal, while talking with the same language to the same people in social situations may not.

A persuader needs to be alert to *receivers'* meanings for words. The intensity and acceptability of words change with time. For example, the negative connotations of many terms related to black and female went unnoticed for many years. But now, you'll find many people reacting negatively when out of habit you say, "the bad guys wear black hats," or constantly refer to the group leader as a "chairman," or use male pronouns to refer to all people.

Shifts in location can have the same effect. Speaking at a local political rally in Alabama requires word choices different from a speech at Harvard University. Addressing a Teamster's local would suggest a level of language different from that appropriate for the local Daughters of the American Revolution. The effects of word choice depend on the situation, the speaker, and the particular receivers. The better you can accurately predict the interactions among these three elements, the better are your chances of predicting receivers' responses accurately and of increasing the odds of reaching your goals.

clarity and ambiguity

One effect of word choice is message clarity. As a persuader, you usually want receivers to think of the same referents you do when you hear your words. The ability of two people to interact effectively requires some similarity in what they think of when the symbols are heard. For example, if a parent tells a teenager to be home at a "reasonable hour," and the youth appears at 1:00 A.M., the parent may be upset and the teenager confused. The confusion lies in their differing interpretations of the word "reasonable." The youth believed 1:00 A.M. was reasonable; the parent didn't. Had the parent said, "Be home by 11:30," ambiguity would not have been involved, even if the youngster had not heeded the admonition. Persuaders should remember how ambiguous symbols can be. When persuasive goals require clarity, special care is needed to clarify the denotations for words used. Goodrich Tire Company, for instance, spends millions trying to differentiate its product from Goodyear.

Sometimes ambiguity is intentional. When commercials say three of four doctors recommend the "ingredient" in Anacin for headaches, the ambiguity is intentional. If they said three of four doctors recommend aspirin for headaches, clarity wouldn't aid the sales of Anacin. The politician who says, "My opponent has a spendthrift voting record" intends to avoid specifying what the votes were for. If listeners knew, they might realize that they approved of some of the expensive legislation.

The persuader's task is to assess how words operate in the receivers' perspective. You should be aware of receivers' meanings for words and adapt your communication accordingly. A group of farmers who pay an expert to come discuss the advantages of some fertilizer expect the person to know more than they do. But they also expect the expert to choose words they understand or to define words that may be unusual. If a persuader misunderstands or fails to adapt language to receivers, the situation is usually confusing and not very successful.

Persuaders should consider several other effects of word choice. One comes from the use of oral or written style. Person-to-person persuasion usually requires an informal style. For that you shouldn't write a message and read it; you should use oral style. *Effective oral style means that speech should command attention and secure understanding as it happens.* Listeners, unlike readers, must understand at the moment of receiving. Most persuaders can't use the instant replay. Live receivers can't rerun a tape and relisten. A reader can reread difficult passages or put a book or magazine down and come back later. Listeners aren't as fortunate, so extra efforts to be clear and hold attention are needed by the persuader. Maintaining attention requires vividness, variety, and movement. Clarity requires concreteness and consistency with receivers' frames of reference. Concrete rather than abstract language should be used when possible. Repetition can help. Sentence fragments and contractions are common. Personal pronouns, such as "you," "me," "we," "us," are forms of direct address that help create conversational style.

When a persuader is preparing a written message that will be given orally (on radio, TV, or in a speech situation), it should be written in oral style. Oral style is not only more direct and personal, it also is wordier. It uses more repetition and restatement. Saying an idea once may be sufficient for written style. But a speaker needs to repeat for both clarity and understanding. Oral style also uses more examples, questions, and visual imagery. We have already discussed using pictures, objects, charts, and diagrams when you can to supplement verbal persuasion. When that is not possible, you can draw word pictures for listeners by selecting words carefully.

Other Variables

> You persuade a man only in so far as you can talk his language, by speech, gesture, tonality, order, image, attitude, idea, *identifying* your ways with him.
>
> KENNETH BURKE

Several other factors can assist in raising your odds of successful persuasion. One of these is *identification.* Your ability to cause receivers to identify with you is very helpful. *By identification, we refer to receivers' perceiving the source as similar to themselves, in*

411

characteristics considered important in the situation. We discussed the importance of this in Chapter 5 under the headings of *similarity* and *homophily.* Identification can result from role-oriented characteristics or dimensions, such as occupation or status, or from personality traits such as honesty or nervousness.

Role identification can be important if the persuader argues for changes that affect particular aspects of the receivers' occupations. Farm workers will be more likely to listen to fellow farm workers regarding joining a union than to a steelworker. The perception of common experiences and goals aids identification. If you're seeking action by a group, belonging to the group offers advantages in acceptability and believability. Trust is more easily created, and receivers will more easily perceive empathy in the persuader.

Sometimes, the wrong role identification can create undesirable results. If the persuader is supposed to be an expert or authority, it isn't usually helpful for that person to have the same role identification as the receivers. In some situations though, it is valuable to show that you "have been there." A dry alcoholic is more persuasive to active drinkers than someone who's never suffered from the disease. An ex-drug addict can have more impact telling teenagers to stay "off the stuff" than someone who has never experienced drugs.

When a role identification with receivers is unwise, *personality identification* may be used. Identifying with a personality requires receivers to draw inferences that the source is somehow like themselves. To identify with an expert persuader, receivers generally must perceive empathy, understanding, and trust. Although many of these qualifiers are partially inferred from roles, some are based on appearance and other nonverbals. Dressing appropriately, smiling, maintaining a comfortable personal distance, making direct eye contact, having friendly facial expressions can all help achieve identification. Other devices are to express preferences for similar things, believe in similar ideas, tell about like experiences, or show a similarity in desirable personality traits.

A related method to increase persuasibility through receiver-source interactions is the use of *common ground.* Common ground refers to attitudes, beliefs, and experiences that a source and receiver share. Common ground often relates directly to the persuasive goal, but that's not the only use of it. Finding out that a receiver has a hobby like yours or enjoys the same sports, can be useful. If you refer to shared interests, receivers may identify with you. A classic example of this is the introduction of Lincoln's Gettysburg Address: "Four score and seven years ago, our fathers brought forth on this continent a new nation, conceived in liberty, and dedicated to the proposition that all men are created equal.

Now we are engaged in a great civil war, testing whether that nation, or any nation so conceived and so dedicated can long endure."

If common ground exists in the area of your subject message or goal, an initial advantage is present. Agreement that small cars are stylish and safe would help a salesperson establish common ground with a customer. Insurance salespeople with families often use their shared beliefs, attitudes, and experiences related to caring for families to establish common ground with prospective buyers. Encyclopedia salespeople are even taught to "invent" children of their own to establish common ground with prospective buyers. These shared interests create likable images of you in receivers' perceptions.

Motive Appeals

> There is only one way under high Heaven to get anybody to do anything . . . and that is by making the other person *want* to do it.
>
> DALE CARNEGIE

> He that complies against his will,
> Is of his own opinion still, . . .
> SAMUEL BUTLER

Probably the most important strategy to improve the odds of accomplishing your persuasive goals is to *relate your arguments to receivers' relevant motivations.* We describe this as the use of *motive appeals.* The following argument is a motive appeal: "You should believe or behave as I suggest because it will satisfy your need for safety." Any of the needs could be substituted. Arguing that if receivers do as a persuader suggests, it will satisfy needs for survival, belonging and love, self-esteem or self-actualization is using a motive appeal.

The warrant in a motive appeal is the causal reasoning that connects the behavior and the need satisfaction. Let's take an example to illustrate. *Conclusion:* You should use Sparkle mouthwash in the morning. *Evidence:* Using Sparkle will prevent you from offending the people around you. *Warrant:* Sparkle will keep your breath from smelling bad. Several intermediate links, as well as reservations and qualifiers, would be involved to make the entire argument clear. But a motive appeal usually doesn't try to make the entire argument clear. It often intentionally shortcuts the reasoning required for a structurally sound argument.

Source: Funky Winkerbean by Tom Batiuk. Courtesy of Field Newspaper Syndicate.

which appeals to use

Motive appeals are most effective when they are directed at unsatisfied needs. Recall the hierarchy of needs. Appeals aimed at physical needs such as hunger or thirst are most effective if the receiver is presently hungry or thirsty. That's why you'll see MacDonald's or Burger Chef advertisements on television just before dinnertime. That's why you buy more when you grocery shop before eating than after. Similarly, a newly married couple is likely to respond to persuasion to buy things related to basic needs such as shelter. They're more likely to buy a house or furniture because of the security provided. Selling a new house or furniture to a couple married for several years, on the other hand, requires other appeals. They might respond to arguments that the new house or living room suite would improve status, esteem, or even self-actualization.

Motive appeals are usually most powerful when directed to unsatisfied needs at the base of the hierarchy. But any unsatisfied need, if it is related to the behavior you're urging, can increase likelihood of the desired response.

Some arguments are essentially motive appeals, but instead of using promised rewards as evidence, they use threat or fear. You need to use these with care. Threats or fear appeals aren't always effective. Some early persuasion research found that strong appeals seem to be less effective than milder ones. Numerous studies have been conducted either to confirm, contradict, or explain this puzzling conclusion.[3] Why, theorists wondered, is it seemingly more persuasive to arouse fears of minimum instead of maximum dis-

---

[3] Literally dozens of studies have been conducted, attempting to settle which appeals are most effective. A good summary and critique of the research is found in Gerald Miller, "Studies on the Use of Fear Appeals: A Summary and Analysis," *A Reader in Speech Communication*, ed. James Gibson (New York: McGraw-Hill, 1971),

comfort? The investigations have been inconclusive, and part of the difficulty lies in the definition of "strong appeal." Because the strength of any threat depends on receivers' perceptions, it's not certain that what researchers define as a strong appeal is defined by a receiver as strong.

Two factors seem related: a receiver's perceived ability to resolve the tensions, and self-esteem. If it appears to a receiver that the discomfort aroused by a persuader *can* be resolved, a strong fear appeal seems to be effective. This response is especially likely when a receiver's self-esteem is high enough that he/she feels capable of coping with the threat and resolving the problem. On the other hand, if a receiver sees no way to resolve the problem, the appeals tend to be disregarded. For example, early television ads linking fatal heart disease and cancer to cigarettes to discourage smoking were spectacular failures. The appeals were disregarded by millions of smokers. Part of the explanation is that many smokers couldn't be shown that stopping would prevent cancer; no real evidence existed that the damage wasn't already done—so why should they stop now? Later ads used indirect appeals that might also be called milder. Parents were shown that their behavior influenced their children, and that by smoking, parents could contribute to poor health in their children. For many, these were more effective appeals.

Receivers with strong self-esteem are more likely to respond to arguments with a feeling that they can cope with the problem; those with low esteem are not. Negative self-concept leads people to believe they are not able to resolve the problems they encounter. These people tend to reduce dissonance by disregarding or rationalizing the messages.

Because all human behavior is motivated to satisfy perceived needs, a persuader who ignores motive appeals runs a great risk. A basic argument in all persuasive messages is one that shows how the proposed action or belief will satisfy needs. Evidence, arguments, organization, and language should all lead receivers to think, "If I believe or behave as suggested, I'll have my need for _____ satisfied." In making a persuasive effort, choose needs that are most important to receivers and most related to the proposal; then show how those needs will be satisfied by doing or believing as you suggest. You may make the appeal directly or indirectly; you may use many facts or none; you may make your organization clear or ambiguous; but whatever other strategies you use, *motive appeals are the foundation for effective persuasion.*

pp. 307–15. Students who want to pursue this topic can find a thorough bibliography on the subject in Erwin Bettinghaus, *Persuasive Communication,* 2nd ed. (New York: Holt Rinehart & Winston, 1973), and Gary Cronkhite, *Persuasion Speech and Behavioral Change* (New York: Bobbs-Merrill, 1969).

Exercise: Selecting Motive Appeals

Objective: To practice identifying motive appeals that can be used to achieve specific persuasive goals.

Directions:

1. In groups of four or five, select a topic that could be used for a persuasive speech.
2. Phrase at least five different specific purpose (goal) statements that could be used if the topic were chosen for a speech to be given in this class.
3. Decide which of the human needs (in Maslow's hierarchy) could be the basis of motive appeals for each of the specific purposes. Try to choose one need from low in the hierarchy (survival or security) and one from the higher three levels for each of the speech purposes.
4. If the speeches were to be given at a local Lion's Club meeting, what changes in purpose and motive appeals might be required?

UNDERSTANDING WHY ATTITUDES CHANGE

In deciding what evidence, arguments, and motive appeals to use, you can use the principles that explain why and how attitudes change. The principles are explained in three major theories: reinforcement, equilibrium, and cognitive dissonance. In discussing these, we examine only the major elements of each that show why and how attitudes change. More thorough analyses of each theory can be found in the sources listed at the end of this chapter.

Reinforcement

The underlying process of *reinforcement* is learning. *Reinforcement refers to increasing the probability of a behavior by rewarding it.* What is reinforcement to one person, however, may not be to another. How important the perceived reward is to the person determines its strength as a reinforcer. A penny might not be a very strong inducement to you for studying hard for a test, but $10 would probably get your attention. On the other hand, to someone whose income is $50,000, the $10 probably wouldn't be a very strong reinforcer. Reinforcement is one of the processes that apparently makes the Pygmalion effect occur. When a significant person communicates approval of a behavior, this reinforces the behavior and increases the likelihood of its being repeated.

Reinforcement can occur in several ways. We'll consider two types: classical conditioning and secondary reinforcement mediated by rewards. Although both forms can be effective, the latter is probably a better explanation of changes in human behavior.

416

classical conditioning

Conditioning is accomplished by having behavior, caused by a primary stimulus, become associated with a secondary stimulus. The classic example of conditioning is the famous experiment by Pavlov. By ringing a bell every time dogs were presented with food, he conditioned them to eventually respond to the bell as if it were food. The food was the primary stimulus, the bell the secondary. Conditioning resulted in association of the secondary and primary stimuli. As a result, either caused the same behavior. The dogs salivated at the sound of the bell.

Association in classical conditioning represents a direct stimulus-response model of behavior. Though humans as well as animals can be conditioned, to describe human behavior in these terms is, in most cases, oversimplification. People usually perceive stimuli beyond pure associational levels and evaluate whether the reward is worth modifying or changing behavior. This involves secondary reinforcement.

secondary reinforcement

In secondary reinforcement, the reward is more significant than the secondary stimulus in the conditioning process. The reward is fulfillment of some perceived need. Behavior required to attain the desired reward is reinforced. A dog is taught to jump through a hoop for pieces of meat. The dog learns to relate the act of jumping with receiving the meat, which is the reward. The meat, the reward, becomes a reinforcer for the behavior. Eventually, with sufficient repetitions, the hoop itself or a verbal command can become the stimulus for the jump.

In using reinforcement to change attitudes or behavior, rewards are probably required every time the desired actions first occur. Teaching a child to share with others may at first require parental approval to reward the behavior every time it happens. Continual rewards build a degree of generalization. *After an association between behavior and reward has been made, the behavior itself can become rewarding.* The primary reinforcer will be required only intermittently to maintain the behavior. In humans, the use of reinforcement can create such strong rewards via the behavior itself that in some cases, even if the primary stimulus is never reintroduced, the behavior continues. A person who has learned to believe sharing is "good" will be rewarded by the act. Few new rewards may be required to maintain the behavior. An internal reward system (combined with reference group identification) reinforces many people who donate to charities to help people they never see. The act of giving is rewarding; responses from the grateful receivers aren't needed.

417

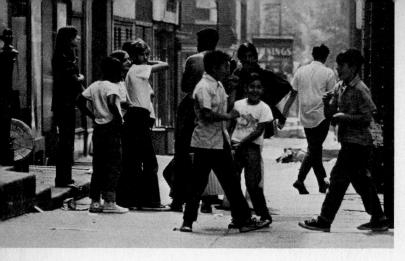

Social approval by a group often reinforces a belief or behavior.
Source: Hugh Rogers—Monkmeyer.

So far this discussion has cited only positive conditioning and reinforcers. *Negative conditioning* can also occur. Adverse consequences can become associated with a secondary stimulus. A child's play in a busy street can be associated with spanking and scolding. With repetition, the child learns to perceive the action of playing in the street as negative. If the association is strong enough, the result will be changed behavior, and the child will not play in the street.

Punishment is generally less effective than reinforcement as means of securing attitude changes, because punishment can have undesired effects. It can cause a person to leave the situation entirely, or stop all responses, instead of merely changing responses. One reason many educators argue for punishment-free classroom environments is the undesirability of some effects of negative conditioning. Failing or poor grades are often used to punish. But failure can instead result in students dropping out of school altogether. Punishment may not change the behavior, but merely cause a guilt response. Some youngsters don't work to avoid poor grades, but develop lowered self-esteem when they get them. Or, sometimes negative associations can be made with the source of punishment and not the punishment itself, creating unexpected and usually undesirable consequences for the persuader. Some students decide they don't like school and/or teachers. Poor grades don't cause better study habits for them. These students get more rewards making life difficult for teachers and school officials. Caution is necessary in using punishment to secure attitude changes.

A very important form of reinforcement is *social approval* or disapproval by a group that is valued highly. Acceptance or approval of an attitude or behavior by a group often reinforces the belief or behavior, while disapproval can help extinguish behaviors. Reference groups can reinforce attitudes or behavior. If you show people that a group they identify with approves the behavior you are attempting to secure, it can cause them to behave that way in order to secure the reward of identification, even if no one in the reference group ever knows about the person's behavior.

Equilibrium

The equilibrium theory suggests that people need to perceive a balance, a congruity or consistency, among related attitudes.[4] This theory suggests that imbalance is a difficult and uneasy state for people. Related attitudes perceived as inconsistent, or incongruent, will create imbalance. People will then try to act in a way that will restore the sense of balance among attitudes. Our purpose here is not to go into a detailed description of this theory, but to introduce you to the reasoning that can help you see how perceived disequilibrium among attitudes leads to changes.

Balance and imbalance can be illustrated as follows: suppose you respect your supervisor's ability very much and at the same time believe you are good at your job. These two beliefs are in balance as long as you perceive that the supervisor approves your work. The following diagram illustrates your sense of equilibrium.

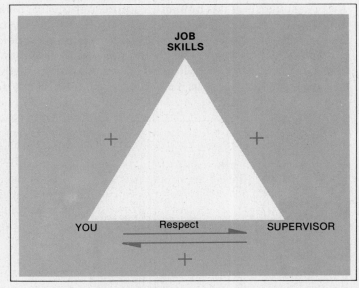

A state of equilibrium.

Now, suppose your supervisor becomes upset, says your work is poorly done, and that you must do it over. This creates imbalance. Your belief that you do good work, your respect for your supervisor, and the reprimand are incongruent.

---

[4] Fritz Heider ("Attitudes and Cognitive Organization," *Journal of Psychology*, 21 [1946], 107–12) is the first writer in balance theory. Many theorists have published research in the area since then. A later development of the theory is in Heider's *The Psychology of Interpersonal Relations* (New York: Wiley & Sons, 1958).

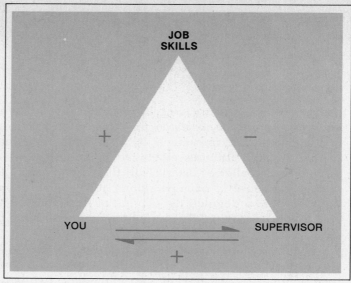

A state of disequilibrium.

Imbalance results in a state of disequilibrium. Equilibrium theory suggests that humans require return of balance. Several kinds of adjustments can restore equilibrium. Attitudes can be changed in degree of importance or intensity, or a belief can be reversed. In the case involving your supervisor, you may decrease the degree of respect you hold for him/her or the strength of your feeling that you are good at your job, as shown in the following diagram.

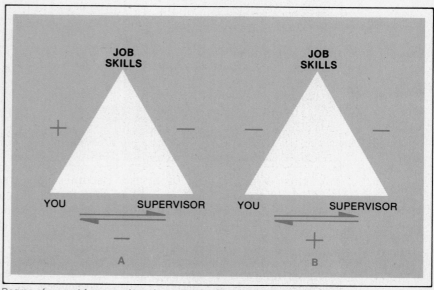

Degree of respect for supervisor changed.   Strength of feeling you are good at job changed.

In most cases, imbalance results in several attitudes being rearranged. For example, if you believe Joe Bloc is a good choice for Senator, and then learn he cheated on income taxes, you will feel an imbalance. You can restore balance by shifting both attitudes to reduce disequilibrium: "Joe Bloc is my choice because he is the best of many poor candidates, who all cheat a little on income taxes." Another possible shift would be to refuse to believe that Bloc had in fact cheated.

Sometimes the intensity of attitudes or their importance can't be changed. In these cases balance is achieved by other means. One way is to add *intermediate links*. For example, a person argues that the criminal penalties for use of heroin should be maintained because it is a harmful drug. Someone asks, "Should alcohol use also be treated as a criminal offense? It, too, is a harmful drug." The question shows that the speaker's attitudes toward heroin and alcohol are inconsistent. The speaker would then have a state of imbalance. If he or she is not inclined to modify either position, an intermediate link could be added to restore balance. The speaker might reply, "But heroin is more harmful than alcohol, thus the more severe penalty should be maintained."

Another means of achieving equilibrium is by disassociating the imbalanced attitudes. The speaker described above might refuse to see the two elements as similar, responding, "Yes, alcohol is harmful, but it isn't a drug. Therefore, it shouldn't be treated the same way as heroin."

Analysis of these arguments regarding drugs is provided here for several reasons. First, we want to show that *what might create imbalance for one person may not for another.* These beliefs will be seen as inconsistent to one, not to another. But, whenever imbalance does result from perceived inconsistency between beliefs, some process must restore balance or the inconsistent beliefs must be disassociated. Second, this shows how *equilibrium theory can be useful to persuaders.* Giving new information, creating new exposures, and different perspectives, can create imbalance among receivers' existing attitudes. This will cause pressure for change. Because most people have some attitudes that are inconsistent and have been isolated, showing how they are related can create pressure for change in attitudes by creating imbalance.

Cognitive Dissonance

Another theory concerned with the balance between attitudes is the theory of cognitive dissonance.[5] *Dissonance describes the state that*

---

[5] Leon Festinger's A *Theory of Cognitive Dissonance* (Stanford, Cal.: Stanford University Press, 1957) is the original publication of this theory.

occurs when inconsistency in relevant beliefs is recognized. The underlying principle of cognitive dissonance theory is similar to that of equilibrium theory. Both hold that people can't tolerate inconsistencies in relevant relationships. The cognitive dissonance theory suggests that *when inconsistencies are perceived and equilibrium can't be restored by changing or disassociating attitudes, the tensions produced require rationalization to reduce the dissonance.* For example, if a person wants a very expensive car but finds the expense dissonant with an attitude that people should be frugal, the dissonance can be reduced by rationalization. The person may say, "Well, the expensive car will last longer; it'll have more maintenance-free miles—and besides, it's necessary for my business." The rationalization doesn't reduce the perceived inconsistency—it provides a way to *explain* it. In the example cited earlier, involving your attitudes toward your job and your supervisor, several possible rationalizations could reduce the dissonance caused by the reprimand so that you wouldn't need to change any attitudes. You could say, "Well, the boss really got up in a bad mood today," or "I was daydreaming—I could have done better on that," or "The boss doesn't have the whole story. When I explain, the response will be different."

The cognitive dissonance theory suggests an active search for means to reduce dissonance. The rationalization process is active. The person who has dissonant feelings will search for reasons to justify the behavior. Have you ever purchased a car, and then noticed how many like it you now see, when you never noticed them before? That you are reducing dissonance is part of the reason you now see them. You are making an active effort to reduce any uneasy feelings you had about purchasing the car.

The persuader can use cognitive dissonance theory to aid the receiver in searching for reasons to justify behaviors. If you're urging behavior receivers might perceive as inconsistent with an existing belief, help them find ways to reduce the dissonance. Give them rationalizations or you probably won't get the desired results.

Exercise: Theories of Attitude Change

Objective: To practice identifying types of attitude change used in persuasive efforts.

Directions:

1. Refer back to the five specific purpose statements selected in the "Selecting Motive Appeals" exercise p. 416.
2. In groups, discuss and decide which of the theories of attitude change would be most useful in achieving the goals with your classmates.
3. What differences in means of securing attitude change might there be if you attempted to achieve the goals with members of the local Lions Club?

Exercise: Persuasion

Objective: To increase ability to use persuasion techniques to achieve a stated goal with a group of listeners.

Procedure:

1. Identify a realistic persuasive goal that you believe you can achieve with other members of your class. Confer with your instructor to insure that you have stated a clear, attainable goal.
2. Identify the major obstacles you will have to overcome to achieve your goal.
3. Assess your receivers to determine their persuasibility and what strategies will be most effective with them.
4. Plan a communication strategy to achieve your goal.
5. The instructor will specify a time limit for your effort, and schedule your time to present it.
6. To assess your effectiveness, survey the class both before and after talking to them.
   a. Prepare 3 × 5 cards for each listener on which you have written your central idea statement.
   b. Pass these out to students at least one class period before the day your persuasion is scheduled, and ask them to write how they feel about that statement by writing a number on the card according to the scale suggested (see p. 395).
   c. Compile an average of the score you got before your presentation.
   d. After sending your persuasive message, hand out blank 3 × 5 cards. Ask receivers to write what they perceive as the central idea of what you said. Ask them also to use the same scale to report how they feel about that central idea now that they have heard your message.
   e. Compile an average of the score you got after sending your message. Assess the amount of improvement you received.
7. Compare your statement of central idea with the statements as written by your receivers. How much similarity is there?
8. If time permits, pass out another set of cards with the central idea written on it about two weeks following the presentation of your message. Was there a loss from the time immediately following your presentation?
9. The instructor may choose to conduct a class discussion or to have you discuss this project in class after all have made their presentations. The discussion will cover the following questions:
   a. Which messages received the most shift of opinion? Why?
   b. Which messages received the least shift of opinion? Why?

LOOKING BACK

Persuasion, the attempt by one communicator to change the attitudes or behaviors of one or more others, occurs in both interpersonal and public communication settings. In a study of persuasion we must consider three elements: the intent of the persuader, the process that results, and the effects.

The first step in examining persuasion is analysis of the persuader's goals. A persuader should analyze receivers to determine if the intended effects in receivers are attainable, and modify the goals, or plan the effort to extend over considerable time, if the goals are not immediately attainable. In analysis of receivers, the persuader will use the techniques of audience analysis outlined in Chapter 13 and attempt to assess the probability of achieving the intended effects. In the assessment process, the persuader will make inferences about the receivers based on the amount of prior information they have, the attitudes they hold, the expectations they have both for the persuader and regarding the subject, and how susceptible they are as individuals to persuasion, and the degree of credibility the persuader will have with these receivers.

Source credibility is one of the important strategies in improving the probability of effectively persuading others. Credibility comes primarily from receiver perception of the source as being authoritative and having the personal characteristics of honesty, friendliness, and pleasantness. Receivers make judgments about source credibility primarily from persuader appearance, behaviors, environment, and message variables. Credibility is important to persuaders because highly credible sources receive preferential treatment in message reception and acceptance by receivers.

Message variabilities that increase likelihood of favorable responses by receivers include evidence and argumentation, organization, language, identification and common ground, and use of motive appeals that are relevant.

Evidence is defined as a statement accepted by receivers as a basis for believing a conclusion, and should be chosen by persuaders from the perspective of what will be believable to receivers, not what is considered reasonable to the persuader. Argument can be understood by using Toulmin's model, which analyzes the evidence, the conclusion, and the warrant connecting the two as the essential elements of an argument. The other three elements in the model, the qualifier, reservation, and support for warrant, are sometimes necessary for persuasive arguments.

Organization is most helpful to a persuader as a means of establishing a plan for the persuasion and should be viewed both from the overall perspective in long-range persuasive efforts and from the perspective of establishing a thought framework for each individual persuasive message. Some attention is necessary to whether one- or two-sided messages should be used, the decisions depending on several variables of audience and situation.

Language is a useful tool of the persuader in attaining emphasis through intensity and clarity when helpful. Sometimes a persuader will choose intense language for effect; sometimes it will be avoided because of its effect on receivers. Similarly, persuaders sometimes deliberately seek to remain ambiguous. Both uses of language depend on the persuader's ability to assess the reactions of receivers to the language used.

Persuaders can use identification with receivers as a strategy to increase probability of success. Sometimes they will seek role identification, and in other cases, when it's important to appear as an authority or otherwise different from receivers, they can still use common grounds of interests, personality characteristics, or experiences.

Perhaps the most important message variable in a persuader's success is the use of motive appeals to show that doing, believing, or feeling as the persuader suggests can fill a currently unmet need that the receiver has. Motive appeals are most effective when they are relevant to the persuader's goal and directed at currently unmet needs.

Use of persuasion is aided by understanding the theories of attitude change. Three theories were examined: reinforcement, the theory that concludes the likelihood of behavior is increased as it is rewarded; equilibrium, the theory that behavior and attitudes will change to reduce perceived inconsistencies (restore balance) among relevant attitudes; and cognitive dissonance, the theory that a person will actively seek new attitudes (rationalizations) to explain perceived inconsistencies that cannot be reduced by changing the attitudes.

Questions for Discussion

1. Why should you establish both long-term and short-term goals in persuasion?
2. How can you assess the likelihood of persuading your receivers?
3. What strategies will increase receiver persuasibility?
4. What is evidence, and how can a persuader use it to advantage?
6. How can motive appeals be used in persuasion?
7. How are attitudes changed?

Suggestions for Further Reading

BETTINGHAUS, ERWIN P., *Persuasive Communication*. New York: Holt, Rinehart and Winston, 1973.

BYRNE, DONN, *The Attraction Paradigm*. New York: Academic Press, 1971.

CRONKHITE, GARY, *Persuasion: Speech and Behavioral Change*. New York: The Bobbs Merrill Co., 1969.

HEIDER, FRITZ, *The Psychology of Interpersonal Relations*. New York: Wiley, 1958.

HOVLAND, CARL, et al., *The Order of Presentation in Persuasion*. New Haven: Yale University Press, 1957.

KIESLER, CHARLES A., et al., *Attitude Change: A Critical Analysis and Theoretical Approach*. New York: Wiley & Sons, 1969.

LARSON, CHARLES, *Persuasion: Reception and Responsibility*. Belmont, Cal.: Wadsworth Publishing Co., Inc., 1973.

LERBINGER, OTTO, *Designs for Persuasive Communication*. Englewood Cliffs, N.J.: Prentice-Hall, Inc., 1972.

MINNICK, WAYNE, *The Art of Persuasion*. Boston: Houghton Mifflin Co., 1968.

ROSNOW, RALPH, AND EDWARD ROBINSON, *Experiments in Persuasion*. New York: Academic Press, 1967.

ROSS, RAYMOND, *Persuasion: Communication and Interpersonal Relations*. Englewood Cliffs, N.J.: Prentice-Hall, Inc., 1974.

SWINGLE, PAUL G., *Experiments in Social Psychology*. New York: Academic Press, 1969.

TOULMIN, STEPHEN, *The Uses of Argument*. London: Cambridge University Press, 1969.

ZIMBARDO, PHILIP, AND EBBE EBBESEN, *Influencing Attitudes and Changing Behavior*. Reading, Mass.: Addison-Wesley Publishing Co., 1970.

15

Mass Communication

goal:

To understand how mass communication affects its receivers.

probes:

The material in this chapter should help you to:

1. Explain some of the theories regarding effects of mass communication in society. pp. 427–30

2. Indicate some of the gatekeepers in mass communication and describe how they affect the processing of information. pp. 430–35

3. Explain the role government plays in regulating mass communication. pp. 432–33

4. Describe the processes of diffusing ideas in a society, and indicate how mass communication affects the process. pp. 435–43

5. Distinguish opinion leaders from change agents, and indicate the role each plays in diffusion of ideas. pp. 439–41

Consider briefly the influence of *mass communication* in your life. How much time daily do you spend watching television, listening to radio, reading magazines and newspapers? How much of what you buy, do, and think is influenced by what you see, hear, and read in mass media? What of mass communication in society? Did you know that there are almost 100 million more radios in this country than there are people? That the average person watches seventeen hours of television a week, according to a Louis Harris poll? That A. C. Neilson reports the average television set is on 35 hours per week, and that television reaches 95 percent of the homes in the U.S.?

Clearly, mass communication is a major source of information and entertainment for us. But of what does it inform us? How does it affect our economy, our politics, our values? Much debate about these questions and others has occurred among philosophers, politicians, and scholars. But there is little agreement on the answers. These issues provide a fertile field for study and research. Meanwhile, we live surrounded by mass communication. Thus, understanding the mass media and how they affect communication is important to all of us. In this chapter we consider some aspects of the role of electronic media in our society.

EFFECTS OF MASS COMMUNICATION

We define mass communication as the use of technical media to send the same message to people who are widely dispersed. Thus, mass communication really began with invention of the printing press, and resulted in major changes in societies. But the communication explosion that occurred with the development of the electronic media was unprecedented. Though the shots fired by British

427

All languages are mass media. The new mass media—film, radio, TV— are new languages, their grammars as yet unknown. Each codifies reality differently; each conceals a unique metaphysics. . . .

EDMUND CARPENTER

troops and colonial rebels in Boston in 1770 may have been hear around the world, weeks were required for the news to reach Brit ain. In the 1970s, in contrast, word of a shot fired on a U.S. vessel anywhere in the world, or the slightest movement of a Russian missile, reaches Washington almost instantaneously. Revolutionary changes in human lives occurred as a result of the development of radio in the early 1900s and of television in the second half of the twentieth century.

For many of us, radio and television are such an integral part of our lives that it's hard to remember that they are really quite new. Few theories about their effects have been tested by experience. Thus, most of the theories we mention are largely speculative. Nonetheless, the thoughts of people who have studied the effects of electronic media can be instructive. By discussing these theories, each of us may be able to draw some useful conclusions about the impact of mass communication upon our own lives.

the medium is the message

"The medium is the message" because it is the medium that shapes and controls the scale and form of human association and action.

MARSHALL MCLUHAN

Marshall McLuhan, the philosopher-critic of television, believes that any medium will affect the society it becomes a part of. He reminds us of how radically railroads changed society, politically and socially as well as economically. What railroad cars actually carried mattered little. More importantly, the amount and pace of delivery were drastically altered. The entire fabric of society was changed. The changes caused by the electronic media may be even greater. Today we don't just read news reports. We see and hear news as it happens. Millions watched as Neil Armstrong stepped onto the moon, Vietnamese children were napalmed, Lee Harvey Oswald assassinated, two women shot at Gerald Ford. Television makes professional football a national pastime, creates heros as diverse as Archie Bunker, J. J. Evans, Joe Namath, Jackie Onassis, Matt Dillon, Billie Jean King, and Muhammud Ali. Television, says McLuhan, is creating a global village, an emerging total society.[1]

commercial control

That the electronic media have changed our lives is easy to see. More difficult to assess is the impact of the commercial control of the vehicle for entertainment and news programming. Doubtless the electronic delivery systems affect the economy. Our consumption-based economy relies heavily on mass communication. Some theorists argue that mass communication *creates* desires for improved living standards, that media make us want all the gadgets, beauty aids, appliances, cars, and other luxury goods that make up the contemporary scene. Others respond that media advertising merely informs people where they can get what they want. The argument is not settled. But we can easily see how important the question is. Whether mass communication creates desires or merely informs how to satisfy existing desires, media transmit information about products and services widely and vividly. Mass production wouldn't be possible without mass consumption. And without the mass media, the information upon which mass consumption is based wouldn't be as widely available. As long as radio and television are businesses, commercial influence will affect not only what is advertised but also what the programming is.

critics and speculations

Critics suggest that television causes us to expect quick and easy solutions to problems. Both TV advertisements and entertainment imply that problems can be quickly solved. Television characters solve their problems in a maximum of 90 minutes, usually no more than 60. Time is compressed in such programs—at most, two or three days are required to resolve any difficulties. And the problems are almost always solved, a situation not paralleled by reality. Some fear that a steady diet of such programming leads people to unrealistic expectations in their lives.

Many other charges about the effect of television in society have been made by respected thinkers. Some claim that television causes violence and delinquency, that entertainment programs and news both sanitize violence, if not glorify it. All forms of violent death occur with great regularity in television programs. Some say that death seems so common, so painless, that viewers may become

---

[1] Several of McLuhan's writings discuss these ideas. Perhaps the best is *Understanding Media: The Extensions of Man* (New York: McGraw-Hill Book Co., 1964).

immune or imitators. Others suggest that radio and television create poor readers, cause poor taste, lower public morality, and influence us to elect glamorous politicians with lovely families instead of deciding elections on issues.

At the same time, scholars and philosophers can be found who cogently refute each of the above charges. These people suggest that television has created a higher level of public awareness and understanding, a better standard of living, and wider audiences for cultural events (theater, art, music) than ever existed before. They point out that compared to pre-television times, more higher-quality entertainment is available to more people; more information is brought to wider audiences; we become acquainted with more of our fellows; and enrichment is provided to millions who otherwise may never have known a world larger than their own neighborhood.

Many claims are made regarding the electronic media. In truth, however, little is actually known. Research into the impact of mass communication, especially the electronic media, as Joseph Klapper has pointed out, has "not only failed to provide definitive answers . . . [but has] provided evidence in partial support of every hue of every view."[2]

We have outlined some theories for your consideration for more than one reason. We think you should be aware of the many possible effects of mass communication in your life. We think you should reject hasty generalizations about either its deficiencies or its benefits. More than that, we want you to contrast what is known about mass communication with what *isn't*. Having offered many of the guesses above, we now turn to introducing what is *known* about mass communication.

Sources of Information

The mass media are powerful. Even as they entertain, they play a major role in creating and influencing social change. Whether through advertising or entertainment or news, radio and television are sources of information for the social system. New information is given; existing attitudes and beliefs are confirmed; emotions are activated. Mass media reach a wider audience than other means of communication. The world is smaller as a result. Events around the world are beamed into living rooms daily. A closer acquaintance with people and events around the world make them seem familiar and close.

---

[2] Joseph T. Klapper, "What We Know about the Effects of Mass Communication: The Brink of Hope," in *Communication and Culture,* ed. Alfred G. Smith (New York: Holt, Rinehart and Winston, 1966), pp. 535–51.

Doubtless, mass media do more than bring people and societies information. They affect how that information is processed. By bringing more information, more rapidly, to more people, mass communication brings into conflict freedom of expression and freedom from enforced opinion molding. *Mass communication has created the need for an addition to the list of human rights, the right to be free from communication, as well as to be free to communicate.*

Gatekeepers Control Information

> Then shall we simply allow our children to listen to any stories that anyone happens to make up, and so receive into their minds ideas often the very opposite of those we shall think they ought to have when they are grown up?
>
> PLATO

Mass media use technical channels, and someone must control access to those channels. Those who control the access are called *gatekeepers.* Although gatekeepers exist in other forms of communication, as we have seen, their influence is stronger in mass communication. Take a news program, for example. The news reported on your television at noon, 6, and 10 is only a portion of what happened each day. Somebody must select what events to report. Somebody else selects what details about those events are going to be reported. These persons are the gatekeepers for news.

Gatekeepers control the information content of the media. Several gatekeepers control content of television news, for instance. The news director chooses where to send reporters and camera crews. Reporters covering stories decide what to say about events observed. Editors, directors, film editors, and sometimes even censors decide which stories will be included in the news show, which details from the reporters' stories will be aired. Even more gatekeepers are involved in selection of entertainment programming and advertising.

commercial gatekeepers

Some gatekeepers are individuals, some are institutions. Because U.S. television is primarily privately owned, many of its gatekeepers are commercial. Companies, for instance, choose to sponsor or advertise on a particular show or to drop it. A television station or network may decide not to air a show if there is no advertising

> What we have called low-taste content is the key element in the social system of the media. It keeps the entire complex together. By continuously catering to the tastes of those who constitute the largest segment of the market, the financial stability of the system can be maintained.
>
> MELVIN DEFLEUR

for it. The content of television and radio entertainment shows, the placement of stories in newspapers, and what and how products are advertised are all influenced by commercial sponsors or advertisers.

Gatekeepers also influence dissemination of information through indirect means. Not only do they control what information is received in a social system, they also control *when* it is received. In some cases, timing of information release can be as important as preventing its release. Delaying or early release (leaking) of partial information by gatekeepers affects how ideas are received. Examples are easy to find. The information released to U.S. citizens regarding the 1964 Vietnamese attack in the Tonkin Gulf was partial as well as inaccurate. This dissemination of partial information led to different reactions by citizens and Congress than if the entire story had been told at that time instead of several years later. Publication of the information contained in the Pentagon Papers when they were first written might have altered the entire course of U.S. involvement in the Vietnam War. Gatekeepers for mass communication are not limited to media employees.

government regulation

Commercial sponsors are not the only controllers of what may be put into the channels of the mass media. Public control also exists. Because the media are so powerful and access is limited, public control is required to regulate users. Less government concern is directed toward print than electronic media. In the United States, the only overt government control over the content of newspapers and magazines is through the libel laws. The theory is that all people have access to print media and that a free press guarantees that all ideas can be heard.

The electronic media at first were also not controlled. Government regulation became necessary because, unlike newspapers and other print media, airwaves are limited by the available frequencies. Before multiband cable broadcasting, relatively few broadcast channels were available. The enormous cost of radio and television broadcasting would also limit access, even if broadcast bands were unlimited. Abuse by early broadcasters, especially stations with massive power that drowned out others and wavered across the dial, led to the establishment of the Federal Communications Commission.

Television and radio are regulated by the FCC. This agency does not openly dictate what shall or shall not be aired. The manner of FCC regulation of broadcast content is indirect, but it is a definite influence nonetheless. The FCC awards and renews licenses and monitors stations to see that they transmit on the channels to which they are assigned and with the power permitted. The FCC also monitors to see that stations are broadcasting the kinds of things specified in their license applications. In the case of television, this agency determines to a large extent what kinds of programming will be provided in various time slots. The FCC monitors to see that the programs fall within the percentages of the various types promised in the application for the license. Radio and television station license renewals are regular, and stations are required to compete for renewal each time. A station must give public notice of the necessity for license renewal, and anyone who is dissatisfied or wants to challenge the renewal may do so. Renewals are by no means automatic. More applicants exist than frequencies are available, so competition is keen. Therefore, when the FCC makes pronouncements about content or schedules or programming, they are carefully listened to by broadcasters.

Limited controls also exist over the amounts and kinds of advertising permissible. Some self-regulation is conducted by the industry, other regulations are imposed by government. Government control over advertising is through the FCC and Federal Trade Commission regulations.

To avoid commercial control or private domination of public airwaves, alternatives have been provided. In both radio and television, certain channels are reserved for public use by educational or public non-profit institutions. In recent years, a national public network has been developed, using a high percentage of government funding, to provide programming that is an alternative to commercial programming.

Exercise: Effects of Gatekeepers

Objective: To assess the results of gatekeepers in reporting a news event.

Directions:

Class will be divided into groups of five or six.

1. Each group will choose a current national event on which to compare news coverage.

2. Members of the group will develop a schedule of news listening so that someone in each group hears the news reported on each television channel that can be received in the locality and also on the different local radio stations. If the area is a large metropolitan area, the group should not try to hear every radio station report the news, but should divide up so that someone listens to two or three leading stations of each type (rock, top 40, classical, general middle-of-the-

road, easy listening, educational, country, and an all-news channel if there is one in the area).

3. Groups should also collect all newspaper and national news-magazine coverage of the event.

4. After following the news coverage for a week (groups may decide the event needs to be followed a longer time), group members should compare the reports. They should attempt to answer at least the following and as much more as is necessary to cover the comparisons:

    a. Were there details reported by some stations that were not by others?

    b. What were the differences between print and electronic media reporting?

    c. Were the differences in reporting due to selection of what observations to report? or in the observations themselves?

    d. Were any of the differences contradictory?

5. The instructor may ask the groups to report their findings to each other in class.

Feedback Is Delayed

In mass communication, sources and receivers are not in direct contact. As a result, the source receives either delayed or no feedback. *Because feedback is delayed and indirect, the receiver has a different impact on the communication processes.* Many receivers feel they can't influence the communication at all. This feeling isn't really accurate, however, because delayed feedback is often received either by the gatekeepers or the originating sources. The producers, owners, advertisers, stations, and networks all attempt to discover how receivers react to information received from mass media.

The efforts to get feedback are sometimes simple and sometimes very complex. In the case of radio, stations often conduct contests to find out how many people are listening. They may ask listeners to send cards and letters or to call the station. They may have request shows. Often radio and television stations both engage in some very specific polling to determine the size and composition of their audiences and the effects of various kinds of broadcasting. Interviews in person or by telephone are both used.

In television, the rating systems are powerful. Samples are selected that are representative of the total population, and their viewing habits are studied. The Nielson ratings, which can determine the life and death of television programs, are based on this kind of selective sample. For these, a small box is attached to the television set in sample homes to record when the set is turned on and to what channel. Networks and advertisers thus receive information about how many homes watch particular shows. They can assess effects of both shows and advertisements.

Many critics of the rating systems charge inadequacy in measurement of the audiences. Just because a set is on, they argue, doesn't reveal who is watching. In response, both raters and advertisers often conduct follow-up studies to find out who watches what shows. When the ratings are published, statistical assessments of the accuracy of the results are also available. And sometimes studies to assess who are the *non*watchers are conducted. But the critics' arguments aren't totally answered. Assessing the role of mass media in society is still a very inexact science.

Diffusion of Ideas

> Some kinds of *communication* on some kinds of *issues*, brought to the attention of some kinds of *people* under some kinds of *conditions* have some kinds of *effects*.
>
> BERNARD BERELSON

As a major source of information within a society, *mass communication is a major influence in diffusing ideas throughout a society.* From the mass of conflicting research and theory, some basic generalizations about how this diffusion operates have emerged. These generalizations reject the simplistic notion that simply by injecting information into a system a direct, measurable effect can be assessed. Rather, it is recognized that *mass communication functions as part of a system, affects the system as a whole as well as individual parts, and is in turn affected by the system.* To examine these effects, we report a synthesis of writings by DeFleur, Rogers and Shoemaker, and Klapper.[3]

New information that enters a system can be described as an *innovation.* Innovations can be new ideas, objects, or procedures. Obviously, the "newness" of any information depends on the social system into which it is introduced. A car wouldn't be an innovation in the U.S. in the 1970s, but would be in some parts of the world. Diffusion describes the spread and adoption of innovations throughout a social system.

rates of adoption

Vast differences in rates of diffusion exist. The variations depend on the system, what the innovation is, and how it is introduced. Differing rates of diffusion can be illustrated by differences in time required for the various mass media to be adopted by people in the U.S.

---

[3] Melvin DeFleur, *Theories of Mass Communication* (New York: David McKay, Co., 1970); Joseph T. Klapper, "What We Know about the Effects of Mass Communication"; also Everett Rogers and F. Shoemaker, *Communication of Innovations* (New York: Free Press, 1971).

As each new medium arrived, it was adopted more rapidly than the ones before.

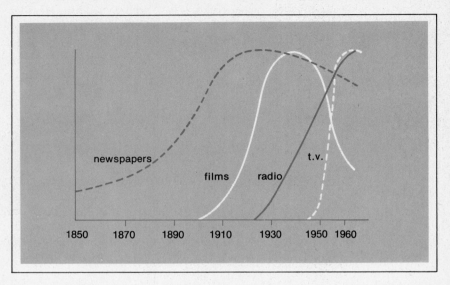

Standardized diffusion curves.* *Source:* *Theories of Mass Communication* by Melvin DeFleur. Copyright by Melvin DeFleur © 1975. Reprinted by permission of David McKay Company.
*Units on the vertical axis have been standardized, so all peak at the same point.

It required 60 years for newspapers to reach peak adoption; less than 10 years for television to be fully adopted.

means of introducing new ideas

Innovations are introduced in two ways. Members within a system may recognize the idea as needed or acceptable, and adopt it. This kind of adoption is described as *internally motivated* whether the innovation originated within the system or outside. An example of this kind of introduction and adoption is the way ice cream cones and hot dogs became U.S. trademarks after their introduction at the St. Louis World's Fair in 1904. No single individual decided to make hot dogs a national food; millions of individuals tried them and integrated them into daily use.

Innovations can also be introduced by individuals or by groups *outside* a system. The U.S. Department of Agriculture sent teams to less developed nations to introduce them to new means of production, fertilizers and machines. Introduction of these innovations was external, but adoption still remained internal. Individual members of the system were free to accept or reject the new ideas.

Occasionally a system exists in which control by one individual or group can influence the introduction and adoption of an innovation. Suppose a business manager of a company finds out about a new machine that would reduce the cost of production. The busi-

Adoption of innovations is influenced by both interpersonal and public communication.
Source: The Bettmann Archive.

ness manager takes the information about the new equipment to the president and supervisors in charge of the production; they decide to adopt the innovation. It is then instituted into company procedures and the system adopts the change. The change may or may not affect all individuals within the system, and it may affect people who had no idea about it before the company decision.

diffusion processes

New ideas, whether they are introduced internally or externally, are adopted only because people in positions to do so recognize the need for them. The processes of *diffusion* involve the spread of awareness throughout a social system. Mass communication is an important source of information about innovations and plays a role in creating or stimulating desires for them, but it is not the only influence in diffusion of ideas. Interpersonal, public, and mass communication interact in the diffusion processes because societies are systems and react to new information as systems. In introducing new information to any system, all three types of communication are involved.

In examining the impact of information within a system, we can see that several types of effects are involved. As we discuss these effects, we'll be emphasizing the role of mass communication, but keep in mind that all types of communication within a social system interact, affecting the diffusion process.

The Hypodermic Effect. The "hypodermic needle" effect is one way information is diffused. A direct, strong, and immediate influence on a large audience is achieved by a message transmitted by mass media. The idea of a hypodermic needle suggests the use of media to *inject* information into an audience. *In a hypodermic effect, masses of receivers get information at one time and are affected equally and directly.* Power of this effect is shown by the vast amounts spent for advertising on prime-time television or in **437** Sunday newspapers. For example, when advertisers spend $230,000 for 60 seconds during the 1976 Superbowl, they expect some direct, immediate responses. The hundreds who streamed into the streets in panic after Orson Welles' broadcast of the invasion from Mars in 1938 illustrate the hypodermic effect of mass media.

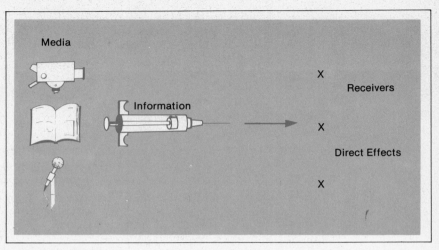

Hypodermic needle effect.

The One-Step Flow Effect. A one-step flow effect also shows a direct influence of information on receivers. *In a one-step flow all individuals in a social system are affected by information from the mass media, but not at the same time.* Though some receivers react and adopt more slowly than others, the one-step flow still describes a direct media-to-receiver effect.

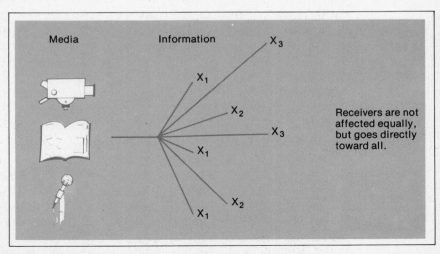

One-step flow effect.

These two kinds of information flow do not affect every element of a social system. But before discussing the more complete descriptions of how diffusion occurs, two nonmedia aspects of the process need attention.

Opinion Leaders and Change Agents. The processes of diffusion of ideas are affected by gatekeepers other than those who control access to or content of the media. One of these is the *opinion leader, a person, generally well-informed, who serves as an influence in the decision processes of others.* Opinion leaders are looked to by some people to *interpret and evaluate* information received, whether from the media or from other sources. You'll recall the discussion of homophily and credibility in Chapter 5, where the degree of similarity between communicators was described as an influence in perceived credibility and thus in acceptability of messages received.[4] *Homophily* (similarity) seems to be one reason why some receivers require opinion leaders to interpret and evaluate information received from the media. Many receivers of information via the media apparently do not perceive sufficient similarity between themselves and the source of the information. The source is too different to be credible, and they won't accept information from that source. Instead, they turn to people they perceive as more like themselves as interpreters.

Another person who influences the diffusion of innovations is the *change agent.* We use the term change agent to refer to a *person outside a social system who seeks to have those in the system adopt a particular innovation.* A change agent is an external source of social change. The change agent may be the originator of an innovation, as when the John Deere Corporation tries to sell tractors in Southeast Asia; or it may be some person or institution promoting innovations, such as occurs when the U.S. government supports birth control clinics in South America. Change agents are not limited to institutions. A salesperson who convinces the purchasing agent at city hall to add chloride to salt for use on icy streets is a change agent for that city. In one sense, television itself (or the advertisers and newscasters) is a change agent for families watching broadcasts. Change agents may be missionaries of their own ideas or can be persons hired or appointed to represent people or groups who desire changes. The distinguishing element about a change agent is that such a person or institution is a promoter from outside the system in which change is desired.

An effective change agent needs to do more than present new information clearly. Good relationships with opinion leaders and media gatekeepers in the social system are required. Again, perhaps the principle of homophily explains why change agents are less ef-

---

[4] That similarity between communicators will increase the effectiveness of communication is the principle as it was developed in Chapter 5.

fective than opinion leaders from within a system. Change agents often don't have much in common with receivers. They are from outside the system and may lack a similar cultural identification. As sources of ideas, their communications are usually less credible than those of opinion leaders perceived as more similar to receivers.

Change agents are usually most effective in influencing a system through opinion leaders. This contact may be through the mass media or through interpersonal influence or both. Opinion leaders not only influence adoption of innovations by others in the society, they are more likely to be early adopters of ideas from the outside. Their position within the society causes them to be more often exposed to new ideas from outside. They are often actively interested in changes they believe will improve the social system.

The Two-Step Flow Effect. A two-step flow of idea diffusion *results when opinion leaders must become adopters before other members of the society will respond.* The power of opinion leaders is measured by the number of people who turn to them for interpretation. Strong opinion leaders exert influence over a wide range of topics. Because many people are influenced not by information directly received from media, but by the attitudes of leaders toward the information, the two-step flow results. It shows that effects of media vary from person to person. Some are influenced strongly by information received through mass communication, while others reject it until sources perceived as credible approve it. The two-step flow reflects the choice people exercise over the amount that the mass media influence them.

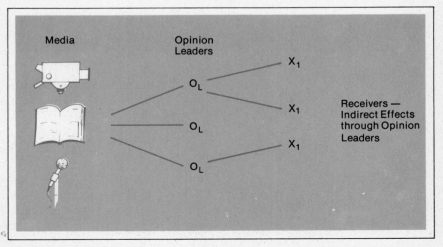

Two-step flow effect.

The Multi-Step Flow Effect. **The multi-step flow indicates that** *in a total system in which receivers make individual choices regarding adopting ideas the three effects previously described are combined.* In a multi-step flow a number of stages occur. Some receivers are immediately and directly affected (X_1). Others are directly affected but respond more slowly (X_2). Other people respond only after the innovation has been received and adopted by opinion leaders (O_L). These individuals (X_1) may then pass information onto and serve as influences in adoption by still others (X_2).

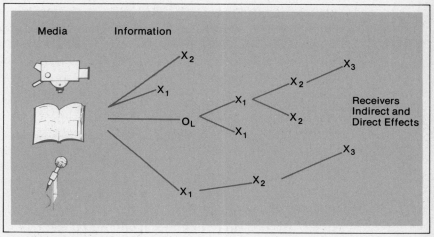

Multi-step flow effect.
*The exact number of stages is dependent on the particular message, the availability of channels, and when the messages are received.

The multi-step effect shows the broad range of possible responses to mass communication. With information of great importance, a hypodermic or a one-step effect often occurs. If television and radio stations in Los Angeles or New York City announced that a tidal wave would arrive in one hour, the effect would be immediate for most viewers. Some skeptics wouldn't respond without further confirmation, illustrating the one-step effect. Many people wouldn't hear the first media announcements and thus would respond only after some opinion source they respect informed them. With most innovations, the multi-step flow effect is the best description of how diffusion occurs.

Factors in Adoption

Adoption or rejection of innovations requires decisions by receivers either to accept or reject the changes in beliefs and behavior. Receivers, consciously or unconsciously, consider several aspects of the innovation before reaching the decision to change. Does the innovation have relative advantages over the present way of doing things? Is it compatible with the present system? How complex is the innovation? Can it be tried out before it is adopted? Can it be seen in action before use? Where else is the idea, object, or philosophy in effect, and how well has it worked there? These and other questions need to be answered to the satisfaction of receivers before they will become adopters.

Not all receivers are equally reached or affected by the information received. The individual differences result in differences in the rate at which ideas are adopted, as we saw earlier in this chapter. The rate of adoption refers to the length of time it takes a person to adopt an innovation. Usually this rate is measured in relative terms. Persons can be classified according to their rate of adoption of new ideas. The categories, ranging from fast to slow adopters, can be described as: innovators, early adopters, early majority, late majority, and laggards.[5]

To illustrate the categories of adopters, examine the spread of use of water fluoridation as a means to reduce tooth decay. Word was first spread by the mass media: print, television, and radio passed on the information as it was reported by scientists and doctors. A few cities and towns began the practice immediately. These were the *innovators*. Others had to hear the worth of the idea discussed further and required more influence by opinion leaders. These were the *early adopters*. Then, as the message was repeated by the media, and experiences of the towns and cities that had used the practice were shared, a large percentage of remaining towns and cities adopted the process. These were in the *early majority* group. Following wider and wider application through the society, a remaining large percentage, the *late majority*, began to fluoridate water. And still, twenty to thirty years after the introduction of the practice, some towns do not yet fluoridate their water, and probably never will.

Influences of opinion leaders, media, and the perceived impact are all factors in determining how rapidly an idea will be adopted, or if it will be adopted at all. Diffusion of innovations is not solely due to the effect of mass media. The model below shows the multistep flow from media and the influence roles of gatekeepers, opinion leaders and change agents.

---

[5] These are the terms used by Rogers and Shoemaker, *Communication of Innovations*. We emphasize that no positive or negative connotations are intended by the descriptive terms. No value is ascribed to being either an "early adopter" or a "laggard." Most people probably are in each of the categories at one time or another, depending on the particular innovation.

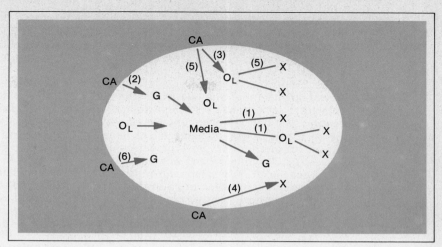

Social system.

(1) The mass media can carry messages directly to opinion leaders (O_L) and to ordinary members of the society (X). (2) Some information might be altered or filtered by gatekeepers (G). (3) Change agents may take information from the media or through it and use the opinion leaders. (4) Change agents may attempt to go directly to members. (5) An opinion leader may decide to transmit or ignore the message. (6) A gatekeeper might stop the information from entering the system via mass communication or might prevent the change agent access to the system.

Mass communication, which consists of the use of technical media to send information and to entertain large numbers of people who are widely dispersed, has become a strong influence in society. Mass communication differs from other types of public communication because it reaches a larger audience and thus has more influence. Also, the content of what is transmitted is more subject to influence of gatekeepers. Finally, the source receives only delayed or indirect feedback from receivers. Because of the influence and power of gatekeepers, mass communication is subject to both direct and indirect government control in the United States through the Federal Communications Commission and Federal Trade Commission.

Because of its widespread impact, mass communication is a powerful force in the diffusion of innovations throughout a society. Innovations are defined as new ideas or objects, and their adoption is subject to varying rates and processes in a society. Innovations may be introduced by agents either within or from the outside of a social system; and may be the kind that are adopted by some influential members of the system and forced on all others, or may be adopted only by individual members deciding to use the object or to believe an idea.

Innovations are diffused throughout social systems in varying ways. A hypodermic effect occurs when mass media inject information into a society that has a direct, immediate effect on masses of receivers. A one-step flow also describes a direct effect of media on receivers, but indicates that not all are affected at the same time. Some groups adopt innovations immediately upon receiving information, others respond more slowly. The two-step flow describes the kind of effect in which some receivers who are opinion leaders are immediate adopters and others in society adopt, following the influence of the opinion leaders. The multi-step flow is a combination of the three patterns of diffusion, and probably describes the manner in which most innovations are diffused throughout a social system. Often diffusion involves change agents, who are sources outside a social system who work either through media or through opinion leaders to insert ideas or information into the system.

Questions for Discussion

1. What effects does mass communication have in society?
2. What role do mass media play in your life?
3. What is the effect of gatekeepers in mass communication?
4. How does government regulate mass communication?
5. What is the role of mass communication in diffusing innovations through a society or system?
6. Distinguish change agents from opinion leaders.

Suggestions for Further Reading

BERELSON, BERNARD, AND MORRIS JANOWITZ, *Reader in Public Opinion and Communication*, 2nd edition. New York: The Free Press, 1966.

CIRINO, ROBERT, *Power to Persuade: Mass Media and the News*. New York: Bantam, 1974.

DEFLEUR, MELVIN, AND SANDRA BALL-KOKEACH, *Theories of Mass Communication*, 2nd edition. New York: David McKay Company, Inc., 1975.

GLESSING, ROBERT J., *Mass Media: The Invisible Environment*. Palo Alto, California: Science Research Associates, Inc., 1973.

KLAPPER, JOSEPH T., *The Effects of Mass Communication*. Glencoe, Illinois: Free Press, 1960.

MCLUHAN, MARSHALL, *The Gutenberg Galaxy*. Toronto: University of Toronto Press, 1969.

———, *Understanding Media: The Extensions of Man*. New York: McGraw-Hill, 1964.

PEMBER, DON, *Mass Media in America*. Palo Alto, California: Science Research Associates, Inc., 1974.

ROGERS, EVERETT, AND F. SHOEMAKER, *Communication of Innovations*, 2nd edition. London: Free Press, 1971.

SCHRAMM, WILBUR, AND DONALD ROBERTS (eds.), *The Process and Effects of Mass Communication*, rev. ed. Urbana, Illinois: University of Illinois Press, 1971.

SKORNIA, HARRY, *Television and Society*. New York: McGraw-Hill, 1965.

STEPHENSON, WILLIAM, *The Play Theory of Mass Communication*. Chicago: The University of Chicago Press, 1967.

16

Receiving Public Communication

goal:

To become more effective as a receiver of mass and public communication.

probes:

The material in this chapter should help you:

1. Identify the major purposes of advertisements. pp. 448–50

2. Recognize how motivations are used in selling and advertising. pp. 451–55

3. Recognize how packaging is used as a sales technique. pp. 452–54

4. Recognize the role of credit in selling strategies. pp. 455–56

5. Prepare intelligently for a discussion with a salesperson regarding a major purchase you are considering. pp. 450–57; ch. 8, pp. 224–30

6. Describe how mass communication is used to "sell" political candidates. pp. 457–58

How much do you listen to radio? Do you realize that some stations broadcast commercials at the rate of 20 minutes an hour? What about television? Have you ever wondered how many commercials you see or hear in a single day? Think about the countless other advertisements you see daily in billboards, magazines, and newspapers. Think for a minute how often someone uses mass communication to persuade you to do something: buy, vote, contribute, sign, help, etc.

How appropriate are your responses to these efforts at altering your behavior? Your responses play a major role in your daily life. What you wear, what kind of car you drive, what you eat, drink, with whom you identify, for whom you vote, and numberless other decisions are influenced by persuasion you receive via public and mass communication. *The purpose of this chapter is to point out how you can exercise greater control over your responses to that persuasion.*

YOUR ROLE AS RESPONDER

Before addressing the question of responses to mass and public communication specifically, let's re-emphasize the need to use the techniques of effective listening. Whether you listen to speeches or to radio and television advertising, you should apply all the principles of critical listening. Applying what you've studied about persuasion will also help. You'll be better equipped to respond appropriately when you decide what a persuader is trying to accomplish and how.

You should also see that many of the ideas discussed in this chapter will also apply in interpersonal persuasion situations. As the discussion of the diffusion of ideas in the last chapter illustrated, few persuasive effects have a single cause. When you buy a

447

car, for instance, the communications that lead to the purchase include far more than any advertisements you see or hear. They include what you know about the attitudes of your parents, friends, and reference groups toward cars. They include what the salesperson says, and your personal needs at the time. Other factors will also influence your thinking about the purchase. Responding to persuasive communication is never so simple as stimulus–response. Therefore, although the major focus of this chapter is persuasion received in public communication, it's not limited to that. Much of the information can be applied to responding effectively whenever anyone tries to persuade you to do something, believe something, or feel a particular way.

Understand the Purposes of Advertising

> If we think of ads as designed solely to sell products, we miss their main effect: to increase pleasure in the consumption of the product.
>
> EDMUND CARPENTER

If you know the purposes of advertising, you can use the knowledge to analyze and evaluate the persuasion you receive. Advertisements, whether for goods, politicians, or causes, usually attempt to accomplish one or more of the following purposes:

Consumer awareness and product differentiation
Consumer good will
Reinforcement of existing behavior
Making sales

Let's examine each purpose more closely.

consumer awareness and product differentiation

Some ads simply seek customer awareness of a product's existence—of its features, its quality, its purposes, or its uses. They give information to people who may not have known about it. Other advertisements seek to differentiate products, services, or persons. This kind of advertising is common in the mass-consumption society of the 1970s because so many products are basically alike. How different are brands of aspirin, really? Regulations of the Food and Drug Administration limit the differences in quantity and size of each pill. Some differences exist in compression, or how quickly the tablets crumble, but the brand that costs $1 and the one that sells for 35¢ are really pretty much alike. This is also true of countless other products you see advertised on television—soap, deodorant, beer, razor blades, etc. Therefore, massive amounts of advertising are required to make you see these products as different from one another, and to believe one is better than the others.

consumer good will

You constantly encounter good-will advertising. This is often done by utility companies—telephone, electric, and gas companies; and even by the postal service. Usually, you don't have any choice regarding who sells you gas or electricity, or who installs and services your telephone lines. And most ads placed by such institutions are not to sell products or to establish awareness of the institution. Knowing that you don't really have a choice regarding their services, they want to make you feel good about the company, to believe it is really trying to satisfy your needs. This is good-will advertising. Major oil companies used good-will advertising extensively during the fuel shortage scare and when the anti-pollution movement was strong in the early 1970s.

reinforcement of existing behavior

Reinforcement advertising is also common. Such ads are for products or services you're probably already aware of and using. The advertiser wants to keep them in front of you, to reinforce the habits

Good will advertising attempts to make you feel good about the company or product.
Source: Phillips Petroleum Company.

of use that you have. Examples of this advertising are the Pepsi and Coca-Cola advertisements you see. Millions of people in the U.S. and throughout the world are consumers of soft drinks. Generally it's not by advertisement that young children first become aware of soft drinks. Most people learned to use them through early socialization, from parents or friends. Advertising for these products merely reinforces existing habits. This type of advertising generally doesn't attempt to sell new customers; it reinforces the behavior that already exists.

making sales

Some ads are actually placed to make sales as well as to attract attention. Weekly in your local newspaper you find full-page ads by supermarkets featuring their "best buys" for the week. The ads are to attract your attention and your presence in the store. You go for the purpose of buying the meat on sale this week, or to take advantage of the specials on fresh fruit, or to save $2 by using those coupons. Television ads call your attention to these coupons and specials. Stores advertise this way because they know if they attract your attention to particular items and get you there to buy those items, you'll also probably do other buying in that store. Another example of advertising designed actually to sell is the late-night record special that urges you to send $5.98 "right now, tonight, to 'Record Hits' in care of this station." To receive a free bonus record along with the one advertised, you're urged to order *tonight*. These ads intend to activate a direct, immediate response.

Most mass-communication advertising, however, isn't intended to activate immediate results. Its goal is long-range: for you to remember something, become aware of it, feel good about it, or continue doing what you're doing. When advertising is actually to sell, it usually is for less expensive items: food, clothing, minor appliances, drugs, personal supplies. The direct approach of salespeople is involved in most sales of major purchases: houses, cars, large appliances, expensive clothes, recreational equipment, vehicles, and expensive services such as insurance. Ads for these things are to attract your attention, to reinforce your behavior, or to reinforce and activate your needs or wants.

APPROPRIATE RESPONSES

Subliminal and docile acceptance of media impact has made them prisons without walls for their human users.

Marshall McLuhan

From the general classification of the reasons people advertise, let's observe a couple of things. First, advertising is probably useful to most people. It makes us aware of new products and services, of many qualities about the products and services, of politicians and their ideas, and of causes needing support. But it is not to provide information that companies, institutions, and politicians spend millions for advertising each year. They spend that money because *they want a response.* They want dollars, votes, or behavior. And because these people are attempting to influence our behavior and to control us in some respect, it's important to realize how they try to do it. After all, in a capitalistic economy the basic philosophy of commercial communication is "Let the buyer beware." Thus, it's appropriate to examine the techniques for being wary.

Examine Motivations Appealed To

As we noted above, most advertising in the mass media is not directly intended to sell. Actual responses sought are more subtle. Ads attempt to arouse a feeling that you "need" the product or service. Vance Packard's popular book, *The Hidden Persuaders,* proposed the idea that advertising in the mass media may actually *create* motivations.[1] His thesis was that *many people are motivated by mass communication to think they need items* they wouldn't have wanted or needed without the advertising. Packard's thesis should be considered. Possibly we do buy products to satisfy desires that we didn't have before repeated exposure to media advertisements.

images

Whatever you may believe about Packard's thesis, one thing is clear about receiving commercial communication. You should carefully assess the motivations appealed to by the persuasion. You will find that *many ads are selling images, not products.* To illustrate, look at a few auto advertisements. Durability and economy are advertised by many auto makers. But how many more advertise the comfort and luxury offered by the interior? Or the fun people have who drive the car? Or the status and recognition offered you by the styling, or by the make itself? To be specific, how much does Cadillac sell quality compared to the impression you will make by driving the car? Even in cases in which ads mention both the quality of the car and its image, the image is what is emphasized.

---

[1] Vance Packard, *The Hidden Persuaders* (New York: David McKay Co., Inc., 1957).

Brut for Men.

If you have any doubts about yourself, try something else.

FABERGÉ

BRUT
FOR MEN

After shave, after shower, after anything.
Brut® lotion by Fabergé.

Many ads are selling images.
Source: Faberge, Inc.

> A television commercial is by definition an attempt at hypnosis, an attempt to use the power of suggestion. . . . What you want to do in a TV commercial is to implant an idea in the subconscious.
>
> ALVIN EICOFF

marginal appeals

Most commercials have an apparent or ostensible point, but their real base is *an unstated thesis: use of this product (or service) will satisfy a basic human need or desire.* The ad will show by implication how the product can satisfy human needs. Think about television car ads again for a moment. The narrator may say something about the economy or quality or durability of the car. But the picture emphasizes fun, or status, or luxury. Beer advertising illustrates the same principle. A narrator may talk of quality and good taste. But the pictures and music show good friends having a good time, and the pictures are of people the beer drinker would like to identify with. The real thesis of the ad isn't "Buy this beer because it tastes good"—it is "Buy this beer and you will have fun with many beautiful friends."

Identification. Identification is one marginal appeal commonly used in advertising. The person selling the product, or the one shown using it, looks and sounds as the potential buyer does or would *like* to look and sound. The housewife with laundry problems, the hard-working man having a beer with friends, the young father who worries about children getting their education if he dies, the teenager who fears offending a date with bad breath, all are people a viewer can look at and say, "Hey, that's me!"

Another way to use identification is to show people the receiver would *like* to be like—beautiful people driving big, shiny cars or having good friends in for a party; a very attractive woman getting attention from a man because she wears a certain perfume; the rugged individualist who smokes a particular cigarette. Perhaps the ultimate use of the process of identification is having popular heroes plug a product. By using Hank Aaron, Joe Namath, Billie Jean King, Bob Hope, and dozens of other well-known people to tell how good a product is, the advertiser uses the persons we most want to be like. We vicariously experience fame and success through such people. So we respond favorably to the product or service they are associated with.

packaging

Part of the process of image building is packaging. Above we've discussed the total package of the advertisement. But the product itself is often packaged in a way that contributes to the desired image. Good examples are sales of clothing and cars. Styles are regularly changed. Often you'll find yourself with clothing purchased last year that is still good, in terms of its quality. But now, styles have changed, and if you wear the item, you're made to feel you are out of date. If women wear short skirts for two or three years, manufacturers and designers try to sell longer skirts as the "in" style. If men wear button-down shirts, long collars become fashionable. Narrow ties are replaced by wide ones that give way to scarves that are replaced by turtlenecks. Most U.S. auto manufacturers annually change body style, though recent changes are not as drastic as they were in the 1950s and '60s. Still, a three-year-old car usually has an obsolete body style. Autos are given a new package every few years so that buyers who feel it's important to stay up to date will be more inclined to change cars frequently.

Implications of quality through packaging may be given by the store where the products are sold or in the total impression of the advertisements. The total atmosphere is designed to give an impression or image to the product. Compare, for instance, a Mercedes-Benz agency to a used-car lot. In a "mod" boutique, the total decorating effect is a far-out atmosphere, with flashing lights, music, and clothes out where you can touch them. In contrast, a store that sells only very expensive clothing will be plushly decorated with ornate furnishings—clothes won't be placed where you can handle them. A salesperson will look you over and bring out "appropriate" clothes for you. The surroundings are used to package the concept that this is an elegant product.

Sometimes packaging is used to suggest things that are only partly true. For example, boxes may be designed to appear larger than they really are—or sometimes, in fact, will be larger than they need to be. Cereal boxes, for instance, are often tall and wide and stacked so you can't see how narrow they are. Products are often labeled so they will appear larger. For some products, "giant size" is the smallest box sold. The common practice of automobile manufacturers of applying the name of their luxury model to smaller and smaller sizes reflects this pattern. Fairlane and Galaxie were once the luxury Ford, while BelAir and Impala topped the Chevrolet line. As new top line names were introduced, the smaller cars were given the name of the once larger model. This renaming associated the image of the larger car with the smaller ones.

attention

Packaging is often used to attract attention, as are many other devices. Color, music, changes in sound, use of humor, are all devices used by advertisers to gain attention. Attention may be the only purpose for an advertisement because it aids, often subconsciously, your differentiation of products. If you become aware of a product's name, your recognition of that name will contribute to a likelihood that you'll buy the product. This is especially true when you are dealing with products that are very much alike: soap, aspirin, appliances, cosmetics, etc. Humorous ads are often placed on television just for attention to the product name.

Another way that packaging affects attention is in the design of the product or the package. On grocery shelves, you see bright oranges, yellows, reds, or combinations of bright colors. That's because these colors are known to be attention-getters and you respond to them more than to dark ones. Packages are designed to catch your attention and in some cases that alone is enough to make the sale.

Exercise: Comparison of Advertisements in Different Media

**Objective: To increase understanding of methods of advertising;
              To increase awareness of differences in advertising in different media.**

Directions:
1. Select three advertisements from three different media.
2. Attempt to find advertisements for the same product. If that is not possible, at least select ads for similar kinds of products.
3. For each advertisement, identify the overall purpose of the advertisement, the appeals and strategies used to achieve the purpose of the ad.
4. Compare the ads and see if you can determine whether any of the differences in the ads were due to the different medium used or the different audience each might have.
5. Your instructor may ask you to present your comparison orally to the class.

Know Why You Respond

From all this the conclusion is fairly simple, though the receiver's responses are not. *Advertisers spend billions so that receivers will (1) notice the product or service; and (2) want the product because they believe it can satisfy basic human needs.* Image building, identification, and packaging are used to lead receivers to believe the product or service can satisfy the need.

understand your motivations

The effective receiver of this kind of communication does not reject all advertising. That person has wants and needs just as everyone else. The difference is that the effective receiver sees the advertising for what it actually is: he or she recognizes the attention devices and the role of attention in product identification; recognizes the real thesis of the advertising; assesses whether or not the product can in fact satisfy that need; and finally, decides whether or not having that particular need satisfied is worth the price of the product or service. If an automobile ad implies, "Buy this car because people will be impressed," you should see that as the basic argument. Then, if the car will do that and that is what you want, buy the car. But if what you really want is economy and durability, don't be misled by all the marginal appeals and attention devices into believing you want a Mercedes because of its quality.

examine the role of credit

Finally, the effective receiver of commercial communication recognizes that *credit is an effective persuasive technique.* "Buy now, pay later." A familiar line, right? First your wants or needs are activated, then you find yourself without the means to satisfy the wants. Most of us can't walk into a store and pay cash for a new frost-free refrigerator, self-cleaning oven, fur coat, outboard motor, or new car.

455

If we had to save the money for the purchases, fewer of us would buy them. Many of us are persuaded to buy items through credit.

Banks and large companies, such as oil companies and department stores, are very aware of this aspect of persuasion. Banks freely issue credit cards and strongly advertise the benefits of using them. Department stores urge you to apply for their charge cards. Thousands of stores accept Master Charge or BankAmericard or other shopper's cards. Major oil companies *ask* to send credit cards to large groups of consumers. They know you'll buy their gas more often if you carry their credit card. You may even drive more if you use credit cards. All these sellers know it's easier to get people to hand a credit card across a counter and sign a slip of paper than to write a check or hand over the cash.

We're not taking a position against the use of credit. Our point is that you, the buyer, should be aware if it is the credit that is persuading you. Examine your use of credit just as you do the product or the service you buy with it. Ask yourself, How much is this credit costing me? Is the service worth the price? Would I buy this item if I had the cash? That's the critical question; not whether you want the item or not, not whether credit is good or bad. But, if you had in your hands sufficient cash to cover the price of the purchase plus the interest, would you spend it on that purchase? Realizing the role of credit in persuasion is a good way to assure appropriate responses to it.

Listen Critically

Responding to persuasion received through public and mass communication involves the techniques of critical listening. Virtually every procedure in the section on listening (Chapter 8) will be useful to you. We'll restate the important ones briefly. *Prepare to seek more information than is provided by the sellers.* Recognize they have something to gain by the sale, and probably won't willingly give any unfavorable information about the product or service being sold. Prepare to ask questions. Arm yourself in advance with information with which to ask intelligent questions. Sometimes it's even helpful to be armed with the attitude that you won't purchase at your first exposure. Major purchases should seldom be made on a first exposure. Take time to check out the information given you, because you know the person selling is presenting the best possible view of the product. A number of ways exist by which you can do this. Listen carefully to the information given; get it as accurately as possible; take notes if necessary. Be prepared to compare. Then do so.

Numerous sources exist where you can *find out if information given by the seller is accurate,* or to learn if additional information is available. One good source is *Consumer Reports,* found in most college and city libraries. The Consumer's Union publishes this report monthly. It includes test results and information about literally hundreds of items. Reports cover services and small purchases like drugs and food as well as major items. You can also go to your local Better Business Bureau to find out if the store or the agency or business with which you are dealing is reputable or has had many complaints. If you discover that several complaints have been lodged against the seller, look at the sale with great caution. Regarding the purchase of cars, reports in auto magazines usually give more information and test results than any other source. Many major consumer items are evaluated in government tests and reports. More consumer information is now required by law than ever before. But usually the seller doesn't have to give it all to you. You have to seek much of it yourself.

Sometimes you'll seek information from previous buyers, other people like yourself. Advertisers know this is a persuasive source of information. They show many ads indicating that someone just like you has purchased this car, or used this service, or bought that insurance and was happy about the purchase. But that testimonial, just like the salesperson, is paid for. Random phone calls may have been made to get the response you hear or are shown, but choice of which phone call to televise or broadcast was not random. You'll want to seek out people who are informed and whose opinion you respect.

Other techniques of critical listening can be applied also: *assess the main ideas of the source; identify any errors of reasoning; compare the values on which the message is based to your own; evaluate important inferences with appropriate criteria.* All these can help you assess the value of persuasion received through the media just as much as in face-to-face listening situations.

POLITICAL COMMUNICATION

Political communication is similar in many respects to commercial communication. Political communication also intends to motivate you to believe something or behave in a certain way. Like advertising, political communication emphasizes only those features of the politician's or party's ideas that are likely to result in the desired voter behavior. Emphasis is not on total disclosure of information available about issues or candidates. During campaign years political advertisements are common. Advertising agencies and public relations firms are hired to package and sell politicians just as Procter & Gamble sells soap.

Frequently, the personality of the politician is sold rather than the issue or the record. For example, many observers believe that Nixon's 5 o'clock shadow and aggressive manner, revealed in the Kennedy-Nixon debates of 1960, lost that election for Richard Nixon. As a result, the public relations men in the 1968 campaign provided plenty of makeup and changed the format and style of Nixon's television appearances.

After 1954, image builders entered the political arena as commercial entrepreneurs. They used all media, but especially television because of its mass appeal. One public relations firm in California stated that for a certain amount of money, it could guarantee the election of a selected candidate to the House of Representatives. The basic concept underlying this approach to political communication is that regardless of the actual characteristics of a candidate, careful manipulation of appearance and projection of specific personality characteristics can result in adequate support from the public to elect. When this occurs, the persuaders have successfully motivated the public to take the intended course of action on the basis of an image rather than on the substance of the issues.

What protection do you have as a receiver of political communication? Again we suggest that your first line of defense is awareness. *Recognize the application of advertising and media manipulation* to politics. Second, *use techniques of critical listening and information seeking and testing.* Don't be misled by superficial means and devices. Don't buy images; rather, examine issues. *Assess credibility* of the politician with as critical an eye and ear as you would use on any salesperson. *Assess the motivating values* of the politician's messages. *Distinguish observations from inferences,* and *apply the criteria for evaluating inferences.* Possibly, more sophisticated political consumers could eventually change the character of political persuasion. But until they do, remember to apply the consumer's axiom, "Let the buyer beware."

Exercise: Receiving Public Communication

Objective: To apply skills of active and critical listening in a public communication situation.
Directions:
1. First, pick out a public communication situation in which the source is attempting persuasion and in which you can be a receiver.
   a. State a goal for listening in this situation.
   b. Specify which listening procedures you will attempt to use while a receiver in this situation.
   c. Identify the attitudes and/or expectations that you bring to the situation that might aid or interfere with your listening effectively.

2. Attend the speech—or otherwise listen to your chosen public communication attempting to apply your skills of active and critical listening.
3. After receiving the message, answer the following:
   a. Understanding the message:
      1. What was the central idea (thesis) and specific purpose of the speaker (source)?
      2. What was the thought structure (main points) used by the speaker?
      3. What nonverbal information did you use to assess the speaker, the message and the intent?
      4. What primary motivations did the speaker appeal to?
   b. Assessment of speaker's values:
      1. What were the values on which the speaker seemed to be basing the persuasion?
      2. Are these values compatible with your value system?
      3. What other unstated or implied inferences or assumptions do you need to accept in order to be persuaded as the speaker wishes?
   c. Use of criteria:
      1. What criteria are appropriate to use in evaluating this message?
      2. Applying the criteria, is the message acceptable?
   d. What techniques of identification, image-building, or "packaging" were used?

LOOKING BACK

In this society, receivers of public and mass communication need to learn how to listen so they can defend themselves, since the philosophy is "Let the buyer beware." The first step in this learning process is to identify the purposes of advertising: consumer awareness, product differentiation, consumer good will, reinforcement of behavior, and activation of behaviors.

Most advertising does not actually attempt to close the sale; that is usually left to the salesperson. In both cases, awareness of the techniques can assist you in avoiding spending money or buying ideas you don't really want or need. Sales techniques include using marginal and motive appeals to sell products, identification, use of credit, packaging, capturing attention with color and irrelevant appeals. Receivers should use the critical listening techniques, especially the application of criteria to messages, and should seek additional information to that given by the salesperson.

Political communication is very similar to commercial. Often politicians are "packaged" and sold as products. Political ads are often prepared and distributed by commercial advertising agencies, selling the politician's image and personality rather than focusing on the issues. In these cases also, the listener should apply the criteria of critical listening and demand to be informed regarding relevant questions. This process requires looking beyond the image to the issues in the particular campaign.

1. How can receivers of public and mass communication employ the principle of "Let the buyer beware"?
2. What does advertising try to do?
3. What role do credit and packaging play in selling?
4. Do we buy "images" or products?
5. How are the techniques of advertising used in political communication?
6. How are the techniques of identification used by both commercial and political persuaders?

Suggestions for Further Reading

BAKER, SAMM, *The Permissible Lie: The Inside Truth About Advertising.* Boston: Beacon Press, 1968.

CIRINO, ROBERT, *Power to Persuade Mass Media and the News.* New York: Bantam Pathfinder Publications, 1974.

ENGEL, JAMES F., DAVID T. KOLLAT, AND ROGER D. BLACKWELL, *Consumer Behavior.* New York: Holt, Rinehart and Winston, Inc., 1973.

HAAS, KENNETH B., AND JOHN W. ERNEST, *Creative Salesmanship.* Beverly Hills, Cal.: Glencoe Press, 1974.

KEY, WILSON BRYAN, *Subliminal Seduction.* New York: The New American Library, 1974.

McGINNISS, JOE, *The Selling of the President.* New York: Trident Press, 1969.

PACKARD, VANCE, *The Hidden Persuaders.* New York: David McKay, Inc., 1957.

TURNER, HOWARD M., JR., *The People Motivators, Consumer and Sales Incentives in Modern Marketing.* New York: McGraw-Hill, Inc., 1973.

Key to Words and Phrases

Argument: a unit of thought containing a conclusion and the evidence leading to the conclusion

Attainable goals: a persuasive purpose that can be achieved in the time available

Attention factors: factors which usually create involuntary attention; include relevance, proximity, importance, combination of the familiar with the novel, variety, curiosity, conflict, humor, and concreteness

Audience adaptation: preparing and sending messages that receivers will decode as intended

Audience analysis: a study of the receivers or potential receivers of a message to determine what their initial attitudes toward source and subject are; and to determine how the purpose can best be achieved

Central idea: *see* Thesis

Change agent: a person outside a social system who seeks to have those in the system adopt a particular innovation

Diffusion of innovations: the spread and adoption of new ideas or products throughout a society

Dissonance: describes the state of mind when a person recognizes that two or more of her/his relevant beliefs are inconsistent

Equilibrium: a state in which a person perceives attitudes held to be consistent and congruent; i.e., to be in balance

Evidence: statement accepted by receivers as reason for believing another statement

Identification: a process whereby a speaker or persuader tries to increase the degree to which a receiver sees source and receiver as alike; also used in advertising to show how a product can help a consumer be "like" someone he or she *wants* to be like

Intensity in language use: language that involves vivid images with powerful connotations

Mass communication: use of technical media to send the same message to people who are widely dispersed

Motive appeal: an argument used by a persuader which suggests that a receiver will satisfy a need or want by doing or believing as suggested

Opinion leader: a person who influences others to believe as she/he does

Persuasibility: the likelihood that a receiver will respond as a persuader desires

Persuasion: communication in which a source attempts either to secure changes in belief and attitude or to induce overt behavior in one or more receivers

Reinforcement: increasing the probability of a response by rewarding it when it does occur; uses conditioning

Reinforcement, negative: decreasing the probability of a response by not rewarding it when it occurs

Source credibility: believability of persuader in receiver's perception

Speech to entertain: a speech in which the primary purpose of the source is for receivers to enjoy the time during which the speech is given

Speech to inform: a speech in which the primary purpose of the source is for receivers to have new information or a new understanding regarding information they already have

Speech to persuade: speech in which the primary purpose of the source is for receivers to have a change of attitude, belief, intensified feelings, or to actually behave in specific ways

Supporting materials: materials used to develop (prove, amplify, clarify, emphasize) the main points; include visual aids and nonverbal behaviors, statements of observation and explanation, comparison and contrast, examples, statistics, testimony, repetition and restatement

Thesis (central idea): the major point or main idea of a speech; the one idea central to everything in the speech

Thought structure: the idea structure of the speech; the main points used to develop the thesis

Thought structure, advantages-disadvantages: a topical organization that gives both advantages and disadvantages of an approach

Thought structure, cause-effect: a method of organization in which the cause is discussed first, then its consequences or effects (this can be done in reverse as well)

Thought structure, deductive: an organization in which the thesis is given at the outset of a speech, with main points developed by referring back to the thesis

Thought structure, inductive: an organization that allows the thesis of a speech to emerge as the ideas are developed

Thought structure, problem-solution: a method of organization in which the problem is stated, and then solutions are given

Index

De Fleur, Melvin, 432, 435
Demographic data, defined, 377
Denotation, defined, 41–42
Denotative language, 408
Departments, in organizations, 334
Description, climate of, 233, 271
Devil's advocate role, 269–70
Diagonal communication, in
    organizations, 338, 348
Dialect, 139–40, 234
Dickinson, Emily, 89
Diffusion, of innovations, 460
Directive feedback, 234
Dissonance, defined, 460
Downward communication, 336, 348
Dynamism, and credibility, 153

Eicoff, Alvin, 452
Eliot, T. S., 60, 109
Emblems, defined, 89
Emerson, Ralph Waldo, 77, 118, 305
Emotion, and perception, 31
Emotional loads, in families, 296
Empathic listening, 213, 222–24,
    230–31, 234, 302
Empathy: climate of, 233, 271; and
    trust, 193–94, 207
Emphasis, and nonverbal symbols,
    88
Employee's manual, 341
Encoding, 46, 78, 125
Entrance-employment interview,
    315
Environment, and persuasion, 402–3
Equality, climate of, 233, 271
Equilibrium, 416, 419–21, 424–25,
    461
Ethnicity, and reference groups,
    241–42
Evaluation, 271; danger of, 220; in
    interpersonal relationships, 173;
    and memory function, 51–54; and
    trust, 196–97, 207
Evidence, 403–6, 424, 461
Expectations, and perception, 29–31
Experience, and perception, 28–29
Exploitative leadership, 277–80
Expressive speech, defined, 169
External group norms, defined, 254
Extrasensory perception, 7n
Eye-contact, 323–24, 347, 386–87,
    389

Face making, 109–10, 125, 194
Facial expressions: in interviews,
    324–25, 347; as nonverbal
    symbols, 80; in speeches, 386
Fact, defined, 73–74, 126
False alternatives, in thinking, 93
Families, 284–311; and the aged,
    305–10; goals of individual
    members, 297–300; pressures due
    to intimate living conditions,
    294–97; role and norm
    expectations, 286–94; supportive
    communication techniques, 301–5
Fantasy, 60
Federal Communications

Commission, 432–33, 444
Feedback: and communication
    process, 8–10, 22, 24, 126;
    directive, 204–7, 208; intentional,
    203–4, 208, 234; internal, 9; in
    interviews, 315, 347; in media,
    434; nondirective, 205–7, 208, 234;
    in organizations, 337, 346; to
    speeches, 377, 386, 387, 389–90;
    types of, 203–6, 208; use of, 202–3,
    208, 220
Feeling, and self, 99
Feminists, 396–97
Fiedler, Fred, 280–81
Fitzgerald, Ella, 43
Flipchart, use of, 365, 369–70
Focal attention, defined, 34, 124
Follow-the-leader decision making,
    267
Formal organization structure,
    333–34, 348
Fromm, Erich, 171

Games: catalog of, 178–84; defined,
    167; in families, 296; as structured
    time, 167–68
Games People Play (Berne), 178
Gatekeepers: defined, 245n4, 348,
    355; in media, 431–33, 434, 444;
    secretaries as, 335, 342, 348
Generalization, form of inference, 57
Generalized others, defined, 126
Gestures, in speeches, 385–86
Gibb, Jack, 196, 200
Gibran, Kahlil, 299, 300
Glittering generality, in propaganda,
    232
Goals: defined, 355; in families,
    297–300; group agreement on,
    248; of persuasion, 394, 396–98,
    424–25
Goethe, Johann Wolfgang van, 286
Good-will advertising, 449, 459
Goyer, Robert, 315
Group decision making, 259–82;
    agendas for, 259–66;
    brainstorming technique, 266–67;
    and leadership, 273–81; methods
    of, 267–69; role of conflict and
    competition in, 269–73
Groups: communications patterns in,
    242–56; as communications
    systems, 237; conflict and
    competition in, 269–73;
    discussions in, 269;
    interdependence and
    cohesiveness of, 247–50;
    leadership of, 273–81, 376–77; and
    personal satisfaction, 250; purpose
    and goals of, 240, 248–49, 260;
    roles and norms in, 251–56; size of,
    240–41, 242–43; types of, 238, 256.
    See also Families

Habits, in group communication, 246
Half-truths, in propaganda, 232
Hall, Edward T., 83
Halo effect, 403

Handshakes, in interviews, 325
Haney, William, 335
Hare, A. Paul, 259, 275
Harris poll, 427
Hasty generalization, 91
Hearing, 212. See also Listening
Hedgepeth, William, 31
Heroin, 404, 421
Hidden agendas, 260–61
Hidden Persuaders, The (Packard),
    451
Hierarchical structure, in
    organizations, 333, 348
Homophily: in communication,
    150–51, 156; defined, 150, 234; in
    media, 439; and similarity, 411–12
Honesty: and group decision
    making, 271; and trust, 194–95,
    207
Horizontal communication, 338, 348
Howe, Reuel, 332
Human Organization, The (Likert),
    277–80

Identification: in advertising, 453;
    defined, 461
If it weren't for you game, 183
Illustrations, in speeches, 362,
    389–90
Imagination, 60
Inductive thought: defined, 461;
    form of inference, 57; in speeches,
    365, 389
Inference: defined, 127; evaluation
    of, 227–28; and persuasion,
    399–401; from statistics, 372, 389;
    and thinking, 55–61; as verbal
    response, 75, 76
Informal organization, 334, 348, 356
Information-gathering interviews,
    327
Instrumental purposes, 171
Intensity, in language use, 461
Intent, in persuasion, 394
Intentional feedback, 234
Interdependence, and group
    communication, 247–48, 355
Internal norms, 254, 356
Interoffice communication, 335
Interpersonal attraction, 145–48,
    156, 234, 249–50
Interpersonal communication, 11,
    125
Interpersonal perception, 131,
    149–56, 234
Interpretation: in communication
    process, 7, 20, 22; defined, 126; of
    people, 137; storage in memory, 47
Interviewee power, 322–23, 324, 347
Interviewing skills, 315
Interviews: applying for, 316–18,
    347; behavior during, 323–26, 347;
    as communication, 315;
    expectations of, 321–22;
    preparations for, 318–23, 347;
    questions in, 320–21, 329–31;
    reprimands, 328–29; use by public
    speakers, 377

Intimacy, in families, 175–76, 285, 294–301, 311. *See also* Families
Intraoffice communication, 335
Intrapersonal communication, 10, 125

Job description, written, 340
Johari window, 114–18
Johnson, Wendell, 112
Jokes, in speeches, 361–62, 389
Jourard, Sidney, 302
Judgment, 75, 76, 127

Kennedy, John F., 385
Kick me game, 180
Kinesic behavior, as nonverbal symbols, 79–81. *See also* Body action
King, Martin Luther, 397
Klapper, Joseph T., 435

Labeling: in propaganda, 232; and stereotyping, 143–44, 156, 234
Ladder of abstraction, 49–51
Laing, R. D., 136
Lair, Jess, 189, 193
Language: as a code, 45–46; creative use of, 60; defined, 126; influence on perception, 31–32; and interpretation of persons, 139–42, 156; use in persuasion, 408–11
Lao-Tzu, 273
Laurence, Peter, 248
Leadership, 273–81; and audience response, 376–77; defined, 274, 355; functional analysis, 274–76; styles of, 276–81
Lee, A. R., 136
Letters of application, 316–18, 347
Level-to-level communication, 335
Likert, Rensis, 277–80
Likert's scale, 337
Lincoln, Abraham, 412–13
Lippmann, Walter, 269
Listening, 210–32; active, 218–20, 230; and advertising, 456–57, 459; to analyze and evaluate, 214, 224–30; distractions to, 219; empathic, 213, 222–24, 230–31, 234, 302; vs. hearing, 212; in interviews, 315; for pleasure, 212–13; preparation for, 218; setting goals for, 212–17; speed of, 218–19; to understand and remember, 213, 214, 217–24
Loaded words, in propaganda, 232
Long-term memory, defined, 47
Love, 163, 177
"Love Song of J. Alfred Prufrock" (Eliot), 60
Lunch bag game, 183

McKuen, Rod, 46, 54
McLuhan, Marshall, 428, 450
Majority rule, and decision making, 267
Management by objective, defined,

327–28
Mannerisms, in persuasion, 402
Marginal appeal, in advertising, 452–53, 459
Marginal attention: defined, 34, 125; in speeches, 379
Marijuana, 404
Masking, 109–10, 194
Maslow, Abraham, 161–65, 177
Mass communication, 11–12, 24, 125, 427, 444, 461. *See also* Media
Maturity, and group communication, 250
Meaning, 126; encoding and decoding, 46; meaning of, 41–43, 63
Media: and adoption of message, 435–36, 441–43; advertising in, 437–38; and the aged, 309; change agents in, 439–43, 444; commercial control of, 429; diffusion in, 437–43; and feedback, 434; gatekeeper functions, 431–33, 434, 444; government regulation, 432–33; homophily in, 439; as information source, 430; and opinion leaders, 439–43; responder role, 447, 455–57. *See also* Advertising
Memory, 46–54, 63
Mencken, H. L., 260
Messages: defined, 126; and emotional appeals, 230; evidence for, 229; identifying main ideas of, 221–22; in interviews, 315; invalid, 229–30
Miller, Roger, 43
Modeling, 104–5, 126
Motive appeals, 413–22, 461
Moulton, William, 40
Multi-step flow effect, in media, 441, 444
Music, 212

Name-calling, in propaganda, 232
Nationality, and reference group, 241–42
Networks, in group communication, 246
Neutrality, climate of, 233
Newcomb, Theodore, 239
Nichols, Ralph, 211
Noise: in background, 212; and communication process, 7, 24
Noncommunication, 77–78
Nondirective feedback, 234
Nonverbal communication, 9, 24; in organizations, 346–47; in speeches, 379
Nonverbal symbols: ambiguity of, 78, 94; defined, 43–45; functions of, 87–90; interpretation of, 77–90, 94
Norms, in group communication, 251, 254–56, 355

Objective interpersonal relationships, 172–73

Objects, as nonverbal symbols, 84–86
Observation, 75, 76, 127
Ogden, C. K., 68–69
One-step flow effect, in media, 438, 444
Open-end questions, in interviews, 329–31
Opinion leaders, defined, 274, 461; in media, 439–43
Organization, in persuasion, 406–8, 424–25
Organizations: assertive behavior in, 341–42; communications, problems of, 332, 339–47; defensiveness in, 337, 348; defined, 332, 356; feedback in, 337; improving communication in, 338–39; status in, 337; structure of, 332–35, 348
Others: awareness of, 104–5; generalized, 107–9, 126; perspective of, 223; purposes of communication with, 170–76; and reflection of self, 106, 108–10; significant, 106–7, 127
Outlines, in persuasion, 406–7
Overt actions, 80

Packaging, and advertising, 453–54, 459
Packard, Vance, 451
Paley, William, 80
Parenting, defined, 291–92
Participative leadership, 277–80
Pastimes, and structured time, 167
Patterns of information, 246
Payoffs, and self-concept, 168
Perception: defined, 126; influences on, 27–33, 63; interpersonal, 234; and selection process, 33–37
Performance appraisal interview, 327
Permanent groups, 240, 355
Persecutor, role of, 180–82
Personal goals, and hidden agendas, 260–61
Personality, 136
Personality identification, in persuasion, 412–13
Personal leadership, 274
Personal needs, and communication, 161–70, 177
Personal space: in interviews, 324; as nonverbal symbol, 83–84
Perspective: effect on perception, 35–36; of others, 223
Persuasibility, defined, 398, 461
Persuasion, 447; in arguments, 406; defined, 393, 461; effects of, 394; in interviews, 329; process of, 394, 424; threat of, 414–15; Toulmin's model, 404–6, 424
Phillipson, H., 136
Physical appearance; and interpersonal attraction, 145–46, 156; in interpretation, 137–39, 156; and persuasion, 402; for speakers, 387–88

Status (*Cont.*)
251, 253–54; in organizations, 334, 337, 341–42; of secretaries, 343
Steinem, Gloria, 86
Stereotypes: and the aged, 309; and appearance continuum, 318; and culture biases, 149–50; defined, 234; effect in communication, 149–50, 156; handshaking and, 325
Stewart, John, 137
Stimuli, in communication process, 6, 24, 127
Stimulus processing, 127
Stimulus-response, in media, 448
Strategy, climate of, 234
Subliminal attention, defined, 34, 125
Substitution, and nonverbal symbols, 88
Superiority, climate of, 234
Supporting materials, 368–74, 389–90, 461
Supportive communication: in families, 301, 303–4; in organizations, 337–38
Symbolization, defined, 40–46, 63, 127
Symbols: defined, 127; kinds of, 43–45, 63; languages as systems of, 45–46

Task agenda, 265–66, 281
Task groups, 239, 355
Task leadership, 274, 275, 355
Telephone, use of, 344–46, 348
Telephone game, 245
Television, 427, 428–30, 433, 434–35, 438. *See also* Media
Temporary groups, 240, 355

Tension, role in communication, 169
Terence, 298
Testimonial, in propaganda, 232
Testimony: in persuasion, 406; in speeches, 373, 375, 389–90
Therapeutic groups, 239, 355
Thesis: in advertisements, 452–53; defined, 461; of messages, 221; in speeches, 360–61, 364–68, 389
Thinking, 55–61, 63, 98; careless, 91–93
Threat, use in persuasion, 414–15
Time: influence on groups, 240; as nonverbal symbol, 87; structuring of, 165–68
Touch, as nonverbal symbol, 81–83
Toulmin's model, 404–6, 424
Tournier, Paul, 132
Transactional Analysis, 167, 184
Transfer, in propaganda, 232
Travelogs, 366
Trumbo, D., 316
Trust: benefits of, 188–91, 207; defined, 234; in families, 302; in interpersonal relationships, 187; qualities of, 197–99
Twain, Mark, 161, 401
Two-step flow effect, in media, 440, 444

Ulrick, L., 316
Unintentional feedback, 234
United States Department of Agriculture, 436
Unrestricted codes, in childrearing, 304
Unshared goals, 297–99, 301
Unstated role expectations, 286–91, 301

Uproar, game of, 183–84
Upward communication, 336, 348

Values: assessing in messages, 225–26; defined, 127; influence on communication, 51–53
Verbal response, kinds of, 74–75
Verbal symbols: defined, 43–44; interpretation of, 68–77, 94
Verne, Jules, 60
Vertical channels of communication, 336–38, 348
Visual aids, in speeches, 369–70, 379, 389
Vocal symbols, defined, 43–44
Voice: in interviews, 325; as nonverbal symbol, 78–79; in speeches, 384; and telephone, 344–46, 348; women's, 325
Voiceprints, 101

Webster, Daniel, 359
Wheel pattern, of group communication, 244–45
When I Say No I Feel Guilty (Smith), 341
Whorf, Benjamin, 56
Why Am I Afraid to Tell You Who I Am (Powell), 188
Wilkinson, Charles, 237
Women: power of, in organizations, 334–35; secretarial role, 343; telephone voice, 345
Words, creation of, 60

Y pattern, in group communication, 244–45